Lecture Notes
in Business Information Processing 201

Series Editors

Wil van der Aalst
Eindhoven Technical University, Eindhoven, The Netherlands

John Mylopoulos
University of Trento, Povo, Italy

Michael Rosemann
Queensland University of Technology, Brisbane, QLD, Australia

Michael J. Shaw
University of Illinois, Urbana-Champaign, IL, USA

Clemens Szyperski
Microsoft Research, Redmond, WA, USA

More information about this series at http://www.springer.com/series/7911

Henriqueta Nóvoa · Monica Drăgoicea (Eds.)

Exploring Services Science

6th International Conference, IESS 2015
Porto, Portugal, February 4–6, 2015
Proceedings

 Springer

Editors
Henriqueta Nóvoa
University of Porto
Porto
Portugal

Monica Drăgoicea
Politehnica University of Bucharest
Bucharest
Romania

ISSN 1865-1348   ISSN 1865-1356 (electronic)
Lecture Notes in Business Information Processing
ISBN 978-3-319-14979-0   ISBN 978-3-319-14980-6 (eBook)
DOI 10.1007/978-3-319-14980-6

Library of Congress Control Number: 2014960081

Springer Cham Heidelberg New York Dordrecht London
© Springer International Publishing Switzerland 2015
This work is subject to copyright. All rights are reserved by the Publisher, whether the whole or part of the material is concerned, specifically the rights of translation, reprinting, reuse of illustrations, recitation, broadcasting, reproduction on microfilms or in any other physical way, and transmission or information storage and retrieval, electronic adaptation, computer software, or by similar or dissimilar methodology now known or hereafter developed.
The use of general descriptive names, registered names, trademarks, service marks, etc. in this publication does not imply, even in the absence of a specific statement, that such names are exempt from the relevant protective laws and regulations and therefore free for general use.
The publisher, the authors and the editors are safe to assume that the advice and information in this book are believed to be true and accurate at the date of publication. Neither the publisher nor the authors or the editors give a warranty, express or implied, with respect to the material contained herein or for any errors or omissions that may have been made.

Printed on acid-free paper

Springer International Publishing AG Switzerland is part of Springer Science+Business Media
(www.springer.com)

Preface

Service Science enables people, enterprises, and societies to build knowledge – concepts, methods, properties, platforms, environments – by means of multidisciplinary, multiinstitutional, and multinational approaches. Nowadays, Service Science has become more and more relevant for making clear these complex situations, which individuals, companies, and corporations are facing.

Knowledge in Service Science plays a pivotal role in such developments. In this context, the series of International Conferences on Exploring Service Science (IESS) offers researchers and practitioners the possibility to present, discuss, and publish their exploratory research results.

The International Conferences on Exploring Service Science 1.5 was the sixth in the IESS series. It was hosted by FEUP, Faculty of Engineering of the University of Porto, Portugal, during February 4–6, 2015. It included three special motivating sessions on hot topics: SME education, Exploration in Service Science, Education as a Service.

The challenging proposal of IESS 1.5 attracted scientists and practitioners from all over the world to submit their contributions. Up to 69 submissions were received from 16 countries, out of which the Program Committee selected 27 top-quality full papers and 8 abstracts, which were published in an internal research series. All the submissions were reviewed by at least three members of the IESS 1.5 Program Committee, composed by well-known and relevant scientists related to the different topics.

The papers of IESS 1.5 consider one or several topics of the IESS conference: service innovation – service exploration – service design – IT-based service engineering – service sustainability.

Some papers explore complex situations by means of Service Science and explain how they obtain perspectives or platforms in various fields as: academia, education on service science management and engineering, social research collaboration, electronic medical record, emergency medical service, sport, tourism, customer relationship strategies, impacts on repurchase, branding, redesign of organizational activities, total manufacturing enterprise integration, inter-generational cooperation, to encourage the use of public transport.

Other papers propose to (re-)invent important approaches for the purpose of Service Science like: a new framework for urban data visualization, a service framework of e-mobility services, corporate social responsibility, alignment, software-based services, Business Process Management systems, trust dynamics, influence factors for value co-creation, product-service systems, image dominant logic, contributory development, multi-channel service research, connecting requirements – architectures and business – technology.

All these papers, with different research approaches, bring new light to Service Science. They are motivating for new explorations in Service Science.

We would especially like to devote special thanks to the members of the Program Committee and referees for doing excellent work in reviewing the submitted papers.

We also thank the keynote speakers for their contribution to the high relevance of this conference.

We wish to give special thanks to the local organizers at the Faculty of Engineering of the University of Porto (FEUP) for their commitment. Thank you very much!

Finally, we thank very much the Faculty of Engineering from University of Porto (FEUP) and its Dean Prof. João Falcão e Cunha. FEUP organized and hosted the IESS 1.5 conference with extraordinary involvement.

We wish you a very pleasant reading and a fruitful integration of these results in your research exploration in the wonderful and crucial domain of Service Science.

December 2014   Henriqueta Nóvoa
                                                                       Monica Drăgoicea
                                                                       Michel Léonard

Organization

General Chair

Michel Léonard — University of Geneva, Switzerland

Program Chairs

Henriqueta Nóvoa — University of Porto, Portugal
Monica Drăgoicea — Politehnica University of Bucharest, Romania

Program Committee

Adi Wolfson — Sami Shamoon College of Engineering, Israel
Ana Šaša — University of Ljubljana, Slovenia
Anelize Van Biljon — University of the Free State, South Africa
Antoine Harfouche — Université Paris Ouest Nanterre La Défense, France
António Brito — University of Porto, Portugal
Arash Golnam — Swiss Federal Institute of Technology Lausanne, Switzerland
Bernardo Almada-Lobo — University of Porto, Portugal
Bettina Campedelli — University of Verona, Italy
Camille Salinesi — Université de Paris 1, Sorbonne, France
Claudia Lucia Roncancio — University of Grenoble, France
Claudio Pinhanez — IBM, Brazil
Davor Meersman — Curtin University, Australia
Dominique Rieu — University of Grenoble, France
Eric Dubois — Centre de Recherche Public Henri Tudor, Luxembourg
Geert Poels — Ghent University, Belgium
Gerhard Satzger — Karlsruhe Service Research Institute, Germany
Gil Regev — Swiss Federal Institute of Technology Lausanne, Switzerland
Henriqueta Nóvoa — University of Porto, Portugal
Isabel Horta — University of Porto, Portugal
Jaap Gordijn — University of Amsterdam, The Netherlands
Jean-Henry Morin — University of Geneva, Switzerland
Jelena Zdravkovic — Stockholm University, Sweden
Joan Pastor — Universitat Oberta de Catalunya, Spain
João Falcão e Cunha — University of Porto, Portugal
Jolita Ralyte — University of Geneva, Switzerland

Jonas Manamela	University of Limpopo, South Africa
Jorge Cardoso	University of Coimbra, Portugal
José Faria	University of Porto, Portugal
José Palazzo	Universidade Federal do Rio Grande do Sul, Brazil
Lia Patricio	University of Porto, Portugal
Maddalena Sorrentino	Università degli Studi di Milano, Italy
Malgorzata Spychala	Poznań University of Technology, Poland
Marco de Marco	Università Cattolica del Sacro Cuore, Italy
Mara Valeria de Castro	Universidad Rey Juan Carlos, Spain
Marion Lepmets	Centre de Recherche Public Henri Tudor, Luxembourg
Marite Kirikova	Riga Technical University, Latvia
Marlene Amorim	Universidade de Aveiro, Portugal
Mehdi Snene	University of Geneva, Switzerland
Michel Léonard	University of Geneva, Switzerland
Miguel Mira da Silva	Technical University of Lisbon, Portugal
Monica Drăgoicea	Politehnica University of Bucharest, Romania
Natalia Kryvinska	University of Vienna, Austria
Paul Lillrank Aalto	University, Finland
Paul Maglio	UC Merced and IBM, USA
Pere Botella	Universitat Politècnica de Catalunya, Spain
Riichiro Mizoguchi	Osaka University, Japan
Selmin Nurcan	Université de Paris 1, Sorbonne, France
Sergio Cavalieri	University of Bergamo, Italy
Shai Rozenes	Afeka Tel Aviv Academic College of Engineering, Israel
Shlomo Mark	Sami Shamoon College of Engineering, Israel
Slim Turki	Centre de Recherche Public Henri Tudor, Luxembourg
Soe-Tsyr (Daphne) Yuan	National Chengchi University, Taiwan
Taro Kanno	University of Tokyo, Japan
Theodor Borangiu	Politehnica University of Bucharest, Romania
Tomáš Pitner	Masaryk University, Czech Republic
Vera Miguéis	University of Porto, Portugal
Vicente Pelechano	Universitat Politècnica de Catalunya, Spain

Contents

Towards a Framework of Influence Factors for Value Co-creation
in Service Systems 1
    Peter Hottum, Axel Kieninger, and Peter Brinkhoff

Towards Contributory Development by the Means of Services as Common
Goods 12
    Anastasiya Yurchyshyna

Knowledge Sharing and Value Co-creation: Designing a Service System
for Fostering Inter-generational Cooperation 25
    Sabrina Bonomi, Stefano Za, Marco De Marco, and Cecilia Rossignoli

Towards a Cyberinfrastructure for Social Science Research Collaboration:
The Service Science Approach 36
    Thang Le Dinh, Van Thai Ho, Theophile Serge Nomo, and Ayi Ayayi

Evolution and Overview of Linked USDL 50
    Jorge Cardoso and Carlos Pedrinaci

An Agile BPM System for Knowledge-Based Service Organizations 65
    José António Faria and Henriqueta Nóvoa

A SoaML Approach for Derivation of a Process-Oriented Logical
Architecture from Use Cases 80
    *Carlos E. Salgado, Juliana Teixeira, Nuno Santos, Ricardo J. Machado,
    and Rita S.P. Maciel*

A Service Oriented Architecture for Total Manufacturing Enterprise
Integration 95
    *Theodor Borangiu, Cristina Morariu, Octavian Morariu,
    Monica Drăgoicea, Silviu Raileanu, Iulia Voinescu, Gheorghe Militaru,
    and Anca-Alexandra Purcărea*

On the Necessity and Nature of E-Mobility Services – Towards a Service
Description Framework 109
    *Carola Stryja, Hansjörg Fromm, Sabrina Ried, Patrick Jochem,
    and Wolf Fichtner*

Towards the Alignment of a Detailed Service-Oriented Design
and Development Methodology with ITIL v.3 123
    Bertrand Verlaine, Ivan Jureta, and Stéphane Faulkner

How Social Responsibility Influences Innovation of Service Firms:
An Investigation of Mediating Factors.................................. 139
  Gheorghe Militaru, Anca-Alexandra Purcărea, Theodor Borangiu,
  Monica Drăgoicea, and Olivia Doina Negoiță

Verifying the Image-Dominant (ID) Logic Through Value Cross-Creation
Between Social and Imagined Communities............................. 152
  Mari Juntunen and Jouni Juntunen

E-Health and Value Co-creation: The Case of Electronic Medical Record
in an Italian Academic Integrated Hospital............................ 166
  Sabrina Bonomi, Alessandro Zardini, Cecilia Rossignoli,
  and Paola Renata Dameri

Service Convenience on Call Centers: Impacts on Repurchase........... 176
  João F. Proença and Marisa Fernandes

Tourism as a Life Experience: A Service Science Approach............. 190
  Jesús Alcoba, Susan Mostajo, Ricardo Clores, Rowell Paras,
  Grace Cella Mejia, and Romano Angelico Ebron

Technological Trends in the Sport Field: Which Application Areas
and Challenges?.. 204
  Luisa Varriale and Domenico Tafuri

Shared Services: Exploring the New Frontier.......................... 215
  Maddalena Sorrentino, Luca Giustiniano, Paolo Depaoli,
  and Marco De Marco

Towards a Conceptual Framework for Classifying Visualisations of Data
from Urban Mobility Services... 228
  Thiago Sobral, Teresa Galvão Dias, and José Luís Borges

Agent Based Simulation of Trust Dynamics in Dependence Networks...... 243
  Stefano Za, Francesca Marzo, Marco De Marco, and Maurizio Cavallari

Towards an IT-Based Coordination Platform for the German Emergency
Medical Service System... 253
  Melanie Reuter-Oppermann, Johannes Kunze von Bischhoffshausen,
  and Peter Hottum

Education on Service Science Management and Engineering:
A Comparative Analysis... 264
  Esperanza Marcos, Valeria de Castro, María Luz Martín Peña,
  Eloísa Díaz Garrido, Marcos Lopez-Sanz, and Juan Manuel Vara

Business School Innovation Through a Service Science Approach:
Organizational and Performance Measurement Issues.   278
   *Valter Cantino, Alain Devalle, Silvia Gandini, Francesca Ricciardi,
   and Alessandro Zerbetto*

Disclosing Paths for Multi-channel Service Research: A Contemporaneous
Phenomenon and Guidelines for Future Investigations   289
   João Reis, Marlene Amorim, and Nuno Melão

Interrelations of Success Factors for Selling Product-Service Systems
from a Solution Sales Perspective   301
   Heiko Felber and Johannes Kunze von Bischhoffshausen

How to Encourage the Use of Public Transport? A Multiservice Approach
Based on Mobile Technologies.   314
   Marta Campos Ferreira and Teresa Galvão Dias

Relationship Bonds and Customer Loyalty: A Study Across Different Service
Contexts   326
   Mafalda Lima and Teresa Fernandes

Exploring Opportunities to Improve Retail Store Quality Using RSQS.   340
   Marlene Amorim and Fatemeh Bashashi Saghezchi

Author Index   351

Towards a Framework of Influence Factors for Value Co-creation in Service Systems

Peter Hottum[✉], Axel Kieninger, and Peter Brinkhoff

Karlsruhe Service Research Institute (KSRI),
Karlsruhe Institute of Technology (KIT), Englerstr. 11, Building 11.40,
76131 Karlsruhe, Germany
{peter.hottum,axel.kieninger}@kit.edu,
science@peterbrinkhoff.de

Abstract. According to modern service science theory, value is jointly generated by several partners forming a service system. In this work, we focus on a simple two-party system consisting of a service provider and its customer. The value created by this service system hinges on the contribution of both parties. That is, it also depends on the collaboration of the customer, which is a key characteristic of services in traditional definitions. Providers, however, lack knowledge on how to identify and measure the influence factors for value co-creation, such as customer contribution. Being aware of customer contribution, providers could design and manage value propositions purposefully. In this work, we provide a first version of a framework of influence factors for value co-creation in service systems, which may serve providers as a guideline for identifying different types of customer contribution.

Keywords: Service system · Value co-creation · Service science · Influence factors · Customer contribution

1 Introduction

In service science, the concepts of 'service systems' (e.g., [1]) and 'value co-creation' (e.g., [2]) are widely accepted. Service systems are seen as "value co-creation configuration[s]" [3] in which providers and customers are supposed to interact as partners and to jointly create value (e.g., [4]). Stating that provider and customer both contribute to service by integrating resources [5] emphasize the influence of collaboration between provider and customer on value creation. This collaboration is embedded into a service episode that "can be defined as an event of interaction which […] represents a complete service exchange" [6].

Nevertheless, a formal description of value co-creating interactions between these parties is difficult and so far rarely realized in practice. In service contracts as they are typically defined today (e.g. in the fields of insurance, outsourcing or consulting), service providers and customers do describe policies and safeguards for future service interactions, though. These contracts focus on the provider's value proposition towards the customer(s) [7] at best. Usually, providers define service quality objectives from a technical or provider process point of view [8]. In those contracts certain service quality objectives and general conditions (e.g. processes and workload) are stipulated within each contract party's realm of responsibility.

Comparing the theoretical perspective on value co-creation with daily routine in service practice, it gets obvious that service companies hardly consider customer contribution. They do not apply knowledge on how to identify and measure factors to describe, control and predict value co-creation. Instead, they initially handle each customer-related process equally and therefore potentially inefficient. Today, there is no established framework in service science and service practice considering the influence of provider and customer contribution as well as exogenous effects on the value which is co-created.

Providing a service without the understanding of co-creation in a partnership tends to shift the risk of value co-creation to mainly one of the partners. We illustrate this based on two established contract types - *time-and-material* and *fixed-price* contracts. In time-and-material contracts the risk of realization is "completely borne by the customer, while the provider gets his effort paid regardless of his success" [9]. In contrast, in fixed-price contracts the risk of realization is completely shifted to the provider who is responsible for delivering "a specified result regardless of his effort put in" (ibid.). This shows the need for a new approach, which is applicable to service providers and customers and describes how the change in co-created value hinges on provider and customer contribution. The application of advanced contract types, such as risk-reward sharing, would be beneficial to providers and customers. It would reflect the mutual responsibility to contribute to a value co-creation.

Thus, in the paper at hand, we address the question: How can a framework of influence factors for value co-creation in service systems be derived? We analyze fundamental definitions of service systems and value co-creation and validate the result with studies on 'service quality', 'value co-creation', and 'customer satisfaction'. We cluster these factors in different classes, which we assign to three 'influence categories', namely 'provider', 'customer', and 'service environment'.

In the following sections, a framework of influence factors for value co-creation in service systems is derived from initial service science definitions and discussed. To allow practical applicability of the resulting framework, we perform an extensive literature review with empirical studies and theoretical papers with a high influence on service science and locate them into the framework. Additionally, we could prove the novelty of the framework by comparing its holistic approach with the foci of the studies examined. After reflecting the proposed framework in the light of service science, we outline next steps towards a research agenda for the assessment of value co-creation in service systems.

2 Towards a Framework of Influence Factors

In this section, we first give an overview about related work on value co-creation and its definitions in service science and focus on studies, which depict the provider's and the customer's influence on the co-creation of value. Based on that, we identify essential influences on value co-creation through an extensive literature analysis and provide a first version of a framework of influence factors, which may serve providers as a guideline for identifying different types of customer contribution.

2.1 Fundamentals of the Framework

In this paper we examine the concept of value co-creation based on the work of [5], who take the view that "service, the application of competences (such as knowledge and skills) by one party for the benefit of another, is the underlying basis of exchange". They also emphasize, "the proper unit of analysis for service-for-service exchange is the service system, which is a configuration of resources (including people, information, and technology) connected to other systems by value propositions" (ibid.). The value that could be co-created through service systems hinges from the people that are involved as well as information that is exchanged and transformed. Furthermore it hinges from the technology, which is used to exchange that information and also technology that is applied to support the service processes.

The aspects of investigating value co-creation are twofold. On the one hand side there is the aspect of value, for the customer as well as for the provider. "In order to construct value propositions that are appealing to the customer the service provider must understand the customer's value system as well as his own" [10]. This requires deeper knowledge of the provider's and the customer's willingness to contribute, their value functions as well as their perceptions – as it is discussed in current research (e.g., [2, 11]). On the other hand, there is the aspect of co-creation, where both partners have to be involved and which addresses the customer's ability to contribute within a certain setting. "Resources [of the customer] should be deliberately chosen when possible. Selection should be based on an ability to add value" [12].

The aim of our framework is to capture the measurable value co-creation influencing factors. We identify two main *influence categories* for value co-creation, namely "service provider" and "service customer", in the definition of service systems by [1]. The definition states that "one organization (service provider) beneficially performs for and with another (service client)". We use these categories to classify influencing factors.

According to [13] a service system has a "systems exchanging matter with environment, as every 'living' system does". Consequently, a service system cannot provide a service regardless from its environment. Therefore we add a third influence category, which we denote as the "service environment", to our framework. This category of influence factors captures exogenous and therefore environmental aspects, such as the sphere in which a service is provided [14]. Following this, the generic level of our resulting framework consists of three influence categories on value co-creation (Fig. 1).

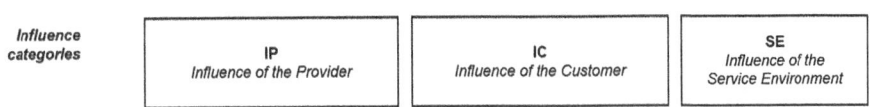

Fig. 1. Three main influence categories have been derived from defining papers on service systems: Influence of the provider, influence of the customer, and influence of the service environment.

In the next chapter influence factors for each category will be derived out of literature and located in a second level of the framework.

2.2 Literature Analysis

In the following section, we conduct a literature analysis to give a comprehensive overview about influences on value co-creation, which should be integrated into the framework as influence factors and therefore focused more intensively.

The concept of value co-creation was mentioned in the Service Science sphere for the first time in the 2000s (e.g. [1, 2, 15]). By focusing on the terms "value co-creation" and "cocreation" in our literature analysis, only a small cutout of papers about value creation between providers and customers would have been identified. To address even more relevant studies, written earlier than 2000, which do not contain that term, but are focusing on co-creation and result-related aspects, such as environment, satisfaction or quality, we extended our search terms with "service quality" and "customer satisfaction", and "service setting".

We followed the review approach proposed by Webster and Watson [16]: Analysis of the fundamental studies of the leading journals, backward-looking research based on citations in references, and forward-looking research on the basis of citations from the first step.

To allow practical applicability of the resulting influence factors, we focused on empirical studies and in case of theoretical papers, we assumed a high influence on service science or appropriately quoted underlying studies. The results have not been limited on temporal restrictions. The main part of studies has been published in the 1990s and the 2000s. In the next paragraphs each of the 18 studies is described very condensed, by pointing out the main aspects that are discussed concerning a framework of influence on value co-creation in service systems. Those identified aspects will be aggregated in the next chapter into influence factors.

Grönroos [17] developed a first model on how customers perceive service quality and out of which components it is composed. Besides traditional provider-induced information-based marketing activities (advertising, field selling, PR) and external factors (traditions, ideology, word-of-mouth communication), the technical and functional quality have been designated as impact factors on a service setting.

The SERVQUAL instrument as a basic framework for measuring customer perceptions of service quality in service and trading companies has been developed by Parasuraman et al. [18]. Values as infrastructure and technology, such as physical facilities and equipment, as well as personnel and their reliability, responsibility trust (knowledge to provide the required service) and empathy (attention to the customer) have been pointed out as important.

A model for the representation of the impact of service quality on behavior has been proposed by Woodside et al. [19]. Of importance are provider-related information, such as waiting and processing times, personnel (helpfulness, information), offering (selection, properties) and customer self-assess for re-use the service, which have been identified in a hospital environment.

Bolton and Drew [20] did an evaluation of the impact of service changes across time on the attitude of customer service quality. The technical shaped service setting of their considered telephone service has been characterized by billing, repair, directory, toll assistance, service order and quality of calls.

Danaher and Mattsson [21] modeled a "Hotel Delivery Process" for the analysis of customer satisfaction during contact at the service encounters. Performance (accuracy, facilities, and atmosphere), staff (handling) and time have been considered as impact factors.

A framework for explaining the relationship between perceived quality / customer satisfaction and the customer's valued relationship with the supplier has been developed by Liljander and Strandvik [6]. They stated the connection between provider and customer as relevant for the customer satisfaction and exceeding the importance of a customer perspective. Different bonds, such as legal, economic, technological, geographical, time and with a lower effect the knowledge, social, cultural, ideological or psychological have been pointed out as important.

Dabholkar et al. [22] designed a hierarchical factor structure of the dimensions of service quality for retail. They designate physical aspects (appearance, convenience), reliability (commitments, reliability), staff interaction (trust, attentiveness, and friendliness), troubleshooting and policies as impacts on a service setting.

De Ruyter et al. [23] focused on different stages of a "service delivery process" and how they can be split on axiological dimensions and investigated how these stages influence overall satisfaction. From a study of museum visitors they found emotional aspects (feelings of visitors), physical and functional properties of encounters, logical aspects ("rational and abstract characteristics of the stage", i.e. accuracy and correctness relevant).

A model of influencing factors of internal and external exchanges of market participants has been formulated by Lusch et al. [24]. Describing a service setting they set prefactors as nature of goods/services, entity apart from main factors as expertise capacity, resource capacity, time capacity, economic rewards, psychic rewards, trust, and control.

Brady and Cronin [25] originated an integrated conceptualization of service quality as a unifying theory of the preceding concepts (especially [17] and [18]). Interaction quality (attitude, behavior, and competence), the physical environment (atmosphere, design, social factors) and results (waiting time, property, and value) are considered as impact factors.

Grönroos and Ojasalo [26] analyzed the productivity of services to come up with a service productivity model. The providers' use of people, technology, systems, information, time and the customers' contribution with regard to their own participation and the involvement of other customers are important elements.

An analysis of productivity in service organizations combined with defining productivity, efficiency and usage has been performed by Johnston and Jones [27]. They distinguish between on the one hand, operational productivity (provider perspective) which includes material, customer, employee, costs as inputs and customer, applied resources, income as outputs, on the other hand customer productivity that includes the inputs time, effort, cost and the outputs experience, results and benefits.

Payne et al. [28] provided a process-based framework that focusses i.a. on service development and customer relationship development. They differentiate between customer value-creating processes (where customers use "information, knowledge, skills and other operant resources"), supplier value-creating processes (where providers have to understand customer's value creating processes) and encounter processes (focusing on communication, usage and service).

Füller and Matzler [29] did an empirical study on the role of product and service attributes of basic, performance and excitement factors in different market segments with different impact on the customer satisfaction. Regarding the service setting they pointed out psychometric properties as information, friendliness (employees), offers and accessibility.

Lee [30] did a comparative analysis of service characteristics of different service industries (telecommunications, retail, banking, food, public transport). Based on a customer survey service materials, service operators, service procedures, the service environment and service equipment have been presented as impacting aspects.

Yi and Gong [31] analyzed i.a. customer participation behavior and provided a multidimensional scale for value co-creation. They pointed out information sharing as the "key of success of value co-creation". Focusing on customer participation behavior they derived information seeking, information sharing, responsible behavior, and personal interaction as the main important factors.

Xu and Huang [32] did a structural analysis of knowledge-intensive business services. They focused on the effect of client cooperation on the service result in terms of performance and innovativeness. It was shown, that the client's contribution affects information exchange, cooperation in general, as well as adaptive adjustment.

Jaakkola and Alexander [33] focus on customer engagement behavior from a service system perspective. In their work, they complement theoretical perspectives on customer engagement with qualitative results of a case study. Besides the providers opportunities "of providing effective platforms for information exchange and interaction", they highlight the potential of voluntary resource contributions by the customer that "go beyond what is fundamental to transactions" (ibid.).

It is important to keep in mind that analyzing the papers discussed it is not possible to explain all aspects of value co-creation. In the following chapter, we derive "influence factors" considering the importance the papers presented above attest specific aspects.

3 Derivation of the Framework

In the following, the discussed influence categories are supplemented with influence factors that have been reflected in the literature analysis. Because provider and customer are seen as equal partners from a service system perspective [28], the describing attributes should be comparable. Extending the structure introduced above (Fig. 1), we slightly differentiate between the way a service provider typically is involved in the value creation and that one of the customer. While providers operate increasingly interlinked with other partners [7], especially end-customers are not always part of further economic systems. Whereas B2B customers are always involved in further ecosystems, end-customers may act on their own. Therefore we state the provider and his network as one interaction partner in our service system and the customer (and his network, which is optional) as the other interaction partner.

We obtain the factors within the categories provider and customer from the initial service system components "people, technology, other internal and external service systems, and shared information" [1]. The exchange of information forms the basis of value co-creation. Therefore, we define an information influence factor for IP and IC. Since the exchange of information increasingly depends for instance on information and telecommunication technology (ICT) we introduce the interaction underlying 'Infrastructure Technology' as an influence factor, accordingly. Spohrer et al. [1] describe people and technology as important components of service systems. Therefore, we add materials of the partners and physical aspects of further service systems as 'resources'. As we do not expect further supporting service systems with personnel on the customer's side, we contrast the provider's class 'personnel' with the customer's 'cooperation'. In the case of end-customers the class 'cooperation' address the (personal) cooperation of the customer (not necessarily with the support of further service systems) - in the case of business customers, we assume as well the involvement of customer's personnel.

Furthermore there are influencing factors, which are neither directly set within the realm of responsibility of the provider nor the customer. In her work, Bitner [34] shows the high impact of environmental factors on relationships in service organizations – exemplary temperature, noise, or layout. "Because service encounter environments are purposeful environments [...], spatial layout and functionality of the physical surroundings are particularly important" (ibid.). Therefore, we also added the 'layout' as an additional factor class to the environmental influence factors. As stated by [35] the involvement of the customer by the provider and their relationship is important for the value co-creation. We aggregated those external factors under the 'influence of the service environment' (SE) as follows: (E) the environment in which a services is provided, (L) the layout how a service is provided and (RI) the relationship between provider and customer. The resulting framework is shown in Fig. 2.

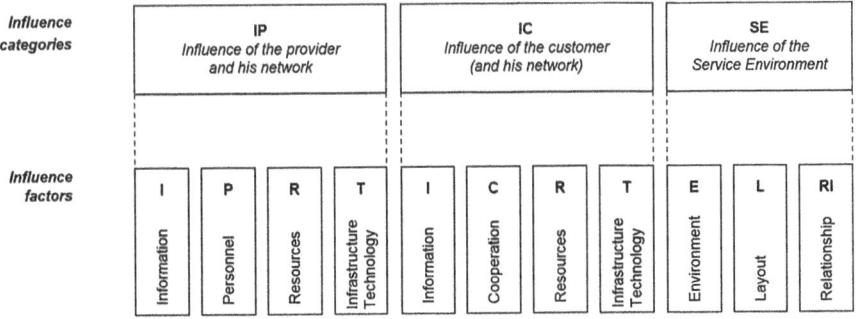

Fig. 2. The framework of influence on value co-creation in service systems complemented with classes of contribution factors.

While contribution factors have to be defined for each specific service setting, the classes of contribution factors are generally applicable throughout different service settings. By performing a comparison of the analyzed papers and the identified foci, it gets obvious, that certain parts of the framework are not as much reflected in empirical studies as others (Table 1).

Table 1. Identification of thematic focal points on co-creation in service science literature.

	Author(s) and Year	Provider				Customer				Service environment		
		I	P	R	T	I	C	R	T	E	L	Rl
[17]	Grönroos (1984)	x			x							
[18]	Parasuraman et al. (1988)		x		x							x
[19]	Woodside et al. (1989)	x	x									x
[20]	Bolton and Drew (1991)					x						
[21]	Danaher and Mattsson (1994)		x		x					x		x
[6]	Liljander and Strandvik (1995)	x				x				x		x
[22]	Dabholkar et al. (1996)		x		x						x	x
[23]	De Ruyter et al. (1997)	x				x				x	x	x
[24]	Lusch et al. (1992)		x	x								x
[25]	Brady and Cronin (2001)					x				x	x	x
[26]	Grönroos and Ojasalo (2004)	x	x	x			x					
[27]	Johnston and Jones (2004)			x			x	x				
[28]	Payne et al. (2007)	x	x			x	x	x			x	x
[29]	Füller and Matzler (2008)	x	x									x
[30]	Lee (2011)	x		x	x					x	x	
[31]	Yi and Gong (2013)	x	x			x	x					x
[32]	Xu and Huang (2013)	x				x	x			x		x
[33]	Jaakkola and Alexander (2014)	x				x	x	x	x			x

This could be due to the actual intention of the examined studies – the studies have not been conducted to show influence of all relevant factors from inside a service system as well as from its direct environment, on the service setting and the value co-creation.

Nevertheless, the examined studies have shown a clear focus on the provider's side as well as on the service environment. Aspects as the information that is provided from the customer, as well as the infrastructure of the customer, to provide information – here infrastructure technology – are only hardly focused. As we stated in the introduction, the knowledge about the customer's ability to contribute is essential for providers to formulate value propositions that really meet their customer's requirements.

4 Conclusions and Future Work

In this paper, we have discussed the applicability of the service science foundational concept 'value co-creation', where providers and customers act as partners in a service relationship. The contribution of our work is twofold:

On the one hand side, we derived a framework for co-creation influencing factors based on the fundamental concepts of service science. The basic structure of the framework, derived from the foundational definitions of service systems, with the influence categories and the identified influence factors are generally applicable to service settings with a customer contribution. These influence factors have to be adapted and operationalized for each service episode individually, according to specific specialty of involved providers, customers and service environment.

On the other side, we conducted an extensive literature analysis on value co-creation influencing factors. We recognized that there are no established frameworks on value co-creation that consider the influence of the provider and his network, the influence of the customer (and his network) as well as environmental influences. We stated that for providers, however, the understanding of those influencing factors, especially of customers' abilities and willingness to contribute to value co-creation, are essential to formulate value propositions, which meet customers' requirements.

In this paper, we could neither present the instantiation nor the evaluation of our framework. In future works, we will describe the selected application of the framework in real-world business-to-business cases. Furthermore, we aim to demonstrate the influence of provider, customer and exogenous effects from the service environment on a variation of the co-creation as it was initiated in [36], where the influence of different types of customer contribution on the utilization of provider's personnel has been examined.

In addition, to understand cause-effect relationships of influencing factors on process measures, such as interaction quality, or outcome measures, such as customer satisfaction, we will analyze historical data of those service settings. Based on that, we expect to determine a functional correlation between the impact of each influence category and the change in value co-created.

References

1. Spohrer, J., Maglio, P.P., Bailey, J., Gruhl, D.: Steps toward a science of service systems. IEEE Comput. Soc. **40**, 71–77 (2007)
2. Vargo, S.L., Lusch, R.F.: Evolving to a new dominant logic for marketing. J. Mark. **68**(1), 1–17 (2004)
3. Spohrer, J., Vargo, S.L., Caswell, N., Maglio, P.P.: The service system is the basic abstraction of service science. In: Proceedings of the 41st Annual Hawaii International Conference on System Sciences, pp. 104–113 (2008)
4. Lusch, R.F.: Reframing supply chain management: a service-dominant logic perspective. J. Supply Chain Manag. **47**(1), 14–18 (2011)
5. Vargo, S.L., Maglio, P.P., Akaka, M.A.: On value and value co-creation: a service systems and service logic perspective. Eur. Manag. J. **26**(3), 145–152 (2008)
6. Liljander, V., Strandvik, T.: The nature of customer relationships in services. In: Swartz, T.A., Bowen, D.E., Brown, S.W. (eds.) Advances in Services Marketing and Management, vol. 4, pp. 141–168. JAI Press, London (1995)
7. Kwan, S.K., Hottum, P.: Maintaining consistent customer experience in service system networks. Serv. Sci. **6**(2), 136–147 (2014)
8. Unterharnscheidt, P., Kieninger, A.: Service level management – challenges and their relevance from the customers' point of view. In: Proceedings of the Sixteenth Americas Conference on Information Systems (AMCIS), Lima, Peru (2010)
9. Satzger, G., Kieninger, A.: Risk-reward sharing in IT service contracts – a service system view. In: Proceedings of the Forty-Fourth Annual Hawaii International Conference on System Sciences (HICSS 44), Kauai, USA (2011)
10. Kwan, S.K., Müller-Gorchs, M.: Constructing effective value propositions for stakeholders in service system networks. In: Proceedings of SIGSVC Workshop. Sprouts: Working Papers on Information Systems 11(160) (2011)
11. Anderson, J.C., Narus, J.A., van Rossum, W.: Customer value propositions in business markets. Harvard Bus. Rev. **84**(3), 90–99 (2006)
12. Lengnick-Hall, C.A.: Customer contributions to quality: a different view of the customer-oriented firm. Acad. Manag. Rev. **21**(3), 791–824 (1996)
13. Von Bertalanffy, L.: The history general and status of systems theory. Acad. Manag. J. **15**(4), 407–426 (1972)
14. Grönroos, C., Voima, P.: Critical service logic: making sense of value creation and co-creation. J. Acad. Mark. Sci. **41**, 133–150 (2013)
15. Prahalad, C.K., Ramaswamy, V.: Co-opting customer competence. Harvard Bus. Rev. **78**(1), 79–87 (2000)
16. Webster, J., Watson, R.T.: Analyzing the past to prepare for the future: writing a literature review. MIS Q. 26(2), xiii–xxiii (2002)
17. Grönroos, C.: A Service Quality model and its marketing implications. Eur. J. Mark. **18**(4), 36–44 (1984)
18. Parasuraman, A., Zeithaml, V.A., Berry, L.L.: SERVQUAL: A Multiple-item scale for measuring consumer perception. J. Retail. **64**(1), 12–40 (1988)
19. Woodside, A.G., Frey, L.L., Daly, R.T.: Linking service quality, customer satisfaction, and behavioral intention. J. Health Care Mark. **9**(4), 5–17 (1989)
20. Bolton, R., Drew, J.: A longitudinal analysis of the impact of service changes on customer attitudes. J. Mark. **55**(1), 1–9 (1991)
21. Danaher, P.J., Mattsson, J.: Customer satisfaction during the service delivery process. Eur. J. Mark. **28**(5), 5–16 (1994)

22. Dabholkar, P.A., Thorpe, D.I., Rentz, J.O.: Measure of service quality for retail stores: scale development and validation. J. Acad. Mark. Sci. **24**(1), 3–16 (1996)
23. De Ruyter, K., Wetzels, M., Lemmink, J., Mattson, J.: The dynamics of the service delivery process: a value-based approach. Int. J. Res. Mark. **14**(3), 231–243 (1997)
24. Lusch, R.F., Brown, S.W., Brunswick, G.J.: A general framework for explaining internal vs. external exchange. J. Acad. Mark. Sci. **20**(2), 119–134 (1992)
25. Brady, M.K., Cronin, J.J.: Some new thoughts on conceptualizing perceived service quality: a hierarchical approach. J. Mark. **65**(3), 34–49 (2001)
26. Grönroos, C., Ojasalo, K.: Service productivity - towards a conceptualization of the transformation of inputs into economic results in services. J. Bus. Res. **57**(4), 414–423 (2004)
27. Johnston, R., Jones, P.: Service productivity: towards understanding the relationship between operational and customer productivity. Int. J. Prod. Perform. Manag. **53**(3), 201–213 (2004)
28. Payne, A.F., Storbacka, K., Frow, P.: Managing the co-creation of value. J. Acad. Mark. Sci. **36**(1), 83–96 (2007)
29. Füller, J., Matzler, K.: Customer delight and market segmentation: an application of the three-factor theory of customer satisfaction on life style groups. Tour. Manag. **29**, 116–126 (2008)
30. Lee, P.-M.: A framework of sector-specific service characteristics. In: Proceedings of the 5th International Conference on New Trends in Information Science and Service Science (NISS), Singapore, pp. 400–403 (2011)
31. Yi, Y., Gong, T.: Customer value co-creation behavior: scale development and validation. J. Bus. Res. **66**(9), 1279–1284 (2013)
32. Xu, Z., Huang, X.: The impact of client coproduction on service innovation performance. In: Proceedings of the 6th Annual Conference of the Academy of Innovation and Entrepreneurship. Oxford, UK (2013)
33. Jaakkola, E., Alexander, M.: The role of customer engagement behavior in value co-creation: a service system perspective. J. Serv. Res. **17**(3), 247–261 (2014)
34. Bitner, M.J.: Servicescapes: impact of physical surroundings customers and employees. J. Mark. **56**(2), 57–71 (1992)
35. Habryn, F., Blau, B., Satzger, G., Kölmel, B.: Towards a model for measuring customer intimacy in b2b services. In: Morin, J.-H., Ralyté, J., Snene, M. (eds.) IESS 2010. LNBIP, vol. 53, pp. 1–14. Springer, Heidelberg (2010)
36. Hottum, P., Reuter, M.: Ideas on customer-oriented queuing in service incident management. KIT Scientific Working Papers, 24 (2014)

Towards Contributory Development by the Means of Services as Common Goods

Anastasiya Yurchyshyna(✉)

Institute of Services Science, University of Geneva, Battelle,
Batiment A, 7 Route de Drize, 1227 Carouge, Geneva, Switzerland
Anastasiya.Yurchyshyna@unige.ch

Abstract. This paper describes our exploratory approach to enable and sustain the environments-oriented creation of services as common goods. We first discuss the characteristics of services, which allow them to be envisaged as engines of innovation and we study the role of economy of contribution in this innovative development. Second, we present an approach supporting the collaborative innovation-oriented work of actors from multiple domains, which facilitates concretizing services. This is achieved by virtue of "Tiers-Lieu", collaborative environments of service innovation, where services are envisaged as common goods. To illustrate the organization of Tiers-Lieu, we present its conceptual framework, and discuss an example from the domain of mHealth. The paper is concluded with the perspectives of the ongoing work for contributive development within service society.

Keywords: Service exploration · Services as common goods · Economy of contribution · Co-creation of services · Tiers-Lieu · Co-creative environments

1 Introduction

The role of technologies is well-established as a dominant factor in the development of contemporary society. Information and communication technologies (ICT) have been integrated into all spheres of contemporary life and established their leading role as an engine for development of the world's economy, guided by an exponential growth of innovations. Developing societies which lagged behind the technological revolution can also gain the potential to leap directly into the connected world with the introduction of mobile technology. Innovations often help to simplify the implementation and usage of traditional services in different sectors of the economy (e.g. supporting services in transport, education, health care sectors) and are the main factors allowing the creation of a conceptually new range of information-based services (e.g. Internet providers, mobile communications, social media, etc.).

The phenomena of facing new, challenging situations and finding ways to address them reveals the importance of innovations in, for example: economical science, management, informatics, technologies and social networking.

Society today is guided by creation, distribution, diffusion, use, integration and manipulation of information and knowledge [1], and it is crucial to investigate all the factors defining the progress of Society and tackle them to optimize such a development.

Moreover, this analysis should go beyond simply admitting the leading role of services in our economy to explore how interactive exchange and functioning of interoperable services [2] enable services to become the main engine for co-creative development within the service-oriented society.

This paper is organized as follows: in Sect. 2, we discuss how the requirements of service orientation within our society are addressed by Service Science. The role of services as engines of innovation is argued in Sect. 3. By analyzing collaborative development and environments supporting innovation, Sect. 4 discusses how innovative ideas are concretized with the help of services. In Sect. 5, we present our exploratory approach for contributory development of services by envisaging them as common good and suggest supporting this by Tiers-Lieu, collaborative environments of service innovation. The conceptual framework of Tiers-Lieu is consequently introduced. To conclude, this exploratory paper synthesizes the discussed principles of supporting creative development of services and identifies the scope of future research.

2 Service-Oriented Society and the Role of Service Science

Even in the early days when the existence of a new type of Society was recognized, it was clear that some definite scientific ground was needed, on which one could perceive, investigate and develop this new type of Society, something that could integrate the main disciplines and non-disciplinary approaches enabling development. This role was taken by Service Science, first introduced by a team of IBM researchers in 2007 [3].

The notion of Service Science, or as it was initially referred to as Service Science, Management, and Engineering (SSME) by IBM, is a term to describe an interdisciplinary approach to the study, the design, and the implementation of service systems. SSME includes three parts: Science, Management and Engineering parts and is, in fact, the science exploring the complex interdependence of these parts. Today, Service Science exceeds the scope of SSME and integrates all the aspects related to: (i) Service Oriented Technologies; (ii) Business Architecture and Process Innovation; (iii) Complex Service Systems Modeling and Simulation; (iv) Service Quality and Experience; (v) Service Business Design and Strategy; (vi) Business Componentization; (vi) Business Modeling, Monitoring & Management; (vii) Service Delivery and Operations; (viii) Business aspects of Service Composition; (ix) People in Services; (x) Service Innovation Management [4].

Service Science offers a scientific framework to tackle new challenges of Society, thanks to its methods of transforming ideas into concrete services. Service Science requires account to be taken of social and economic contexts at the design level, thanks to Service-Dominant Logics [5, 6], and its focusing on knowledge and skills. Service Science allows Society to leave the passive "static" position, where Society only passively contemplates or applauds ICT successes, and to take the active "dynamic" position, in which Society has to actively re-design its organizational parts. It is a great challenge of innovation to open information through services and create new economic values, by respecting the principles of cognitive social responsibility [2] to strengthen the sense of inclusion and to contribute to social stability.

In its complexity, such service orientation is introduced at different levels of service science from traditional project management dimensions (e.g., scheduling, quality management, service marketing, etc.) to unique topics that are specific for idea development and management [7]. Services are incorporated into the core of all economic processes and are widely used in paradigms of conceptual modeling and technical implementation. As a result, it becomes possible to conduct a multi-dimensional analysis of innovation activities, by tying their economic, business, social and IT aspects, so that timely, friendly, proactive services are sought to enhance future business or economic growth from one hand, and from the other, to ensure their dynamic adaptability for the environment.

In other words, services are now seen as the utilizations of specific competences such as the knowledge, skills and technologies of one economic entity for the benefit of another economic entity [8]. As value creation occurs when a resource is turned into a specific benefit, it is now a service system which becomes the main value creation entity. Consequently, the traditional supply chain is re-conceptualized as a network of service systems, called a service value creation network [5].

3 Services as Engines for Innovation

Despite the importance of information in design and innovations, on its basic level it is somewhat arid, which can inhibit human innovations. Thus, the concept of informational service offers the means of comprehensive appropriation. Even if an informational service is defined upon the concept of information, it provides deeper conceptual semantics by describing how to access information, as well as some easy ways to execute its treatments.

Generally, an information service is seen as a part of an information system that serves data/knowledge/information to customers and collects it from its contributors, to manage and store it by optionally using administrators.

Services are characterized by four main factors [8, 9]. They are as follows:

- information is the core element of the design, production and management of services; so services are information-driven;
- customers are co-producers of services, they may require the adaptation or the customization of services, so services are customer-centric;
- digital orientation of services is explained by the achievements in information and communication technologies, the (semi)automation of main services-oriented activities and the creation of new domains: e.g. e-commerce, e-business, e-collaboration, e-government, e-environment; and
- services are driven by their performance criteria and as such are productivity-focused.

We argue that these phenomena related to services can be analyzed in the wider context of a service-oriented society in general and as such, are seen as characteristics of this service society.

Guided by the current experiments in developing economies and the evolution of the underlying technologies, our society is based on information and knowledge that becomes the main sources for value creation. New, emerging situations lead to new challenges we should now face; and new ideas addressing these challenges require to be identified, analyzed and – more important – concretized. This is achieved thanks to services [10]. Generally speaking, the phenomenon of service innovation mirrors the requirements of the knowledge society where knowledge is both the primary production resource and the tool of value (co-)creation and in which information lies in the centre of service creation and functioning. We point to the practical importance of this phenomenon that is implemented by informatics: it supplies not only the tool for IT development but also guarantees the consistency of the sustainable co-creation of its fundamental concepts [11].

4 Collaborative Development Supporting Innovation

The next questions, which naturally arise in the context of our servitized society, are the dynamics of the society, the engines that move its development, and the new aspects of innovation guided by knowledge and spread by virtue of networking.

An idea of joint efforts aiming to develop our society or its different domains is not new. Indeed, a large number of collaborative groups, public-private partnerships (PPP), and other forms of organizations have already proved to be a successful answer in innovative projects [12]. It is also noticeable that these recent works are not exclusively focused on the institutional principles of PPP functioning [13], but particularly address the core elements of different types of partnerships, which guarantee their success: skills and knowledge from both private and public sector [14].

Traditional PPP are beneficial for complex projects involving the government and the private sector. In this context, what are the challenges and advantages brought by industrialization and globalization, and by open and big data, that become more and more important for the development of enterprises and society?

To analyze this phenomenon of collaborative development, we investigate the 3 levels of classical PPP. From one side, PPP represent a tool to structure and maintain PPP projects. From the other side, PPP are working environments allowing the definition and examination of different processes leading to the creation of projects-oriented PPP. Thirdly, PPP are defined by their concrete aim: achieving a defined result. By its dynamics, PPP help to make our society "stable", in the meaning of guiding and controlling its sustainable development, according to the current working environments.

We also underline that classical collaborative partnerships are mainly focused on infrastructure projects, when the return on investments is not expected at the moment of signing the PPP contracts or even finalizing the projects. It is throughout a certain number of years after the projects are terminated that the private partners have an exclusive right to exploit and/or maintain the results of the project and as such, receive the return on their initial investments. (Indeed, a private company financing the construction of the public road that does not have its investments returned during and after the project is finished will be benefiting from exclusive rights on its maintenance and/or receipt of pay tolls during its functioning).

The principles of collaborative development within classical PPP create a solid background for extending this vision of exploring the process of service creation, where results are intangible and often more complex to be valorized.

To do this, we first refer to the principles of development of services, or more precisely, sustainable services. In [11], a sustainable service is defined as a service that is capable of adapting to its environment, to dynamically integrate the ever-changing conditions of this environment and as such, to be sustainably coherent with its evolving challenges. It is important to underline that, according to this approach; sustainable services are dynamically built by virtue of all the relevant semantics: i.e. the information kernel that relies on domain, legal and knowledge ontologies and defines the semantics of services. This semantics is verified and enriched through usage-based validation and existing by practices of usage and as such, a new semantics will be identified and integrated into the information kernel.

This implies that service creation relies on its sustainable development, enabled by co-creation of its members; the process similar to the one traditional to PPP. As such, those PPP, which are oriented towards creation of services (PPPS), have naturally become sources of sustainable creation through a service capacitating process for all the involved actors and stakeholders. Indeed, such PPPS benefit not only from the advantages of traditional PPP, but also enable contributory service empowerment process for all their partners (the government, private partners, individual experts, etc.).

By their composition and through their functioning, PPPS create an innovation-oriented environment and as such, are themselves both the source and the result of innovation. Moreover, the results of contributory development within PPPS are increased, thanks to contributions of actors interested in developing new services. Furthermore, the resulting new services are themselves likely to be sustainable, as they are developed on the basis of sustainable services within PPPS.

In other words, PPPS extend the advantages of traditional PPP: when the government provides direction, the private sector provides the drive to ensure success, and people (actors) provide initiatives and skills to concretize ideas. As the result, PPPS allow concretization of initiatives through services.

Following the increasing impact of collaborative development, it is important to underline that it is mainly due to the creativity and motivation of actors (individual persons, formal working groups, as well informal groups of civil society) in PPPS, that innovation-oriented processes are now not restricted by the "desired" pre-defined results, and are as such, given the freedom of exploration, such development represents the common interest and turns to be more sustainable within the developing society.

In this context, the services developed through PPPS are, in fact, common goods (i.e. rivalrous and non-excludable goods shared by and beneficial for all or most members of a community), or more precisely, the myriad of common goods, which serve the common interest and are free.

5 Towards Contributory Development of Services

Whilst the central concept of innovative approaches is a service, the main innovative activities are focused on service design with its major goal: to establish the consonance between activities and ICT. For this purpose, it is essential to establish the context of any service. In particular, it requires the determination of the activities which will be executed through the intentioned service; to explore their legitimacy and their soundness considering their environment, the new forms aiming to execute and to coordinate them; the new business models and the new values being created. Often, it is necessary to invent new activities and new ways of coordinating them. Such exploration endeavors to research and find out upon which foundations services will be built. These foundations can be expressed in terms of knowledge, as well as in terms of culture. Thus, services can establish a more or less appropriate consonance between activities and ICT, depending on their design. However, behind this concordance, the issue is in fact the concordance between persons and institutions in charge of these activities, the cognitive serenity of each involved person and the cognitive unity and identity of each involved institution.

5.1 Services as Common Goods, or Why We Should Share

In the context of the traditional economy, guided by added value and the copy-right principles of protecting the rights for the goods developed by businesses, it becomes unclear why they should be encouraged to contribute "free of charge"; why the actors need to share their own knowledge, skills and make efforts to develop something, the results of which do not belong to them.

Indeed, in the world of commercialized services, the notion of a service as common good seems to be lacking sense. The hot questions from the traditional businesses are focused on the following:

- Who is the "consumer" of free services?
- Who "pays" for service creation?
- What outcome can the businesses have from them?
- Which are human and economic values of services?
- Why are Enterprises interested in having co-creators?
- Why should Enterprises agree to pay for creating anything, from which they cannot profit?

By implementing the vision of the traditional economy, no positive answers to these questions can be given. Instead, we argue that this problematic from be addressed from a different viewpoint.

According to our exploratory approach of Service Science, we change the accents of this discussion from seeking the answers to these questions within the traditional economic vision and focus on the analysis of how to address the existing situations.

Indeed, with the growing impact of services in identifying and enabling our society, one cannot ignore the importance of creating services. However, the lifecycle of services is very different from that of tangible goods, it is impossible to have clear criteria on the material value of services, neither to have classical return on investments from their creation. Consequently, it is impossible for the private sector to accurately evaluate the risk of participating in projects of service creation, or to estimate the expected income as the result of creating a free common good service.

We argue that this, in fact, is not needed... In the context of our knowledge-based and service-enabled society, the main risk is not the one of not returning one's investments, but the risk of "no innovation"; the risk of being outside the revolutionary tendencies identifying the dynamics of society and participating in innovations arising around them, the risk of losing the knowledge and skills allowing sustainable leadership in each domain.

5.2 Economy of Contribution: Can It Really Work?

It is first important to underline that the economy of contribution does not aim at putting into question the traditional market economy but to broaden its vision by taking into account the new phenomena, such as technological progress, networking, and social media, allowing more possibilities to create and share value.

The economy of contribution is described in [15] as the one having the following characteristics:

- No longer is there separation between economic actors as producers and consumers; all actors are now seen as contributors
- The value produced by contributors is not totally monetizable, it is a 'positive externality'
- It is as much an economy of existence (as the production of 'savoir vivre') as it is an economy of subsistence.

It is remarkable that the economy of contribution does not exclude alternative means of production and exchange, but rather combines with them, whilst its contributors participate in chosen activities, creation of social value and have an interest in selflessness [16].

The main challenge here, in comparison to the traditional approach, is to accept the vision that a service is not a product, that PPP oriented products cannot be applied, and that this classical vision should be extended.

In other words, each actor (private, public or individual) is not any more seen as just a consumer or creator of a service, but has become a co-creator: "paying" by their commitment and efforts in service development and by being "paid" through an exclusive right to define the dynamics of the development of the domain, access to the most recent technologies and methods, as well as initiatives of various actors, and finally by forming the cognitive unity in service creation. In other words, in its complexity, the contributory approach in service development through PPPS allows the creation of a new market for initially planned and completely new services, which is not dependant on the initial estimation of the utility of a service but coordinates itself sustainably, according to new situations and guided by democratically developed initiatives.

In this context, Internet and new technologies offer collaborative multicultural environments whose actors are put in the position of active participants, supported by free and open source software. It thus represents the source of collective creative practice and new value-creating mechanisms, whilst digital technologies have intensified the exchange of information and knowledge.

Creating a new market for services as common goods has a crucial effect for commercial activities of the involved actors. Indeed, "free" services allow the development of a new market, which offers an environment for further development of a vast amount of commercialized services with economically defined added value, based on and disseminated by virtue of the initial common goods services.

5.3 Tiers-Lieu of General Interest for Creating Services as Common Goods

Creating services of the "common good" nature can be possible thanks to a collaborative environment which offers the possibility to identify the initiatives-oriented common goods, and detail them and develop the corresponding services for commercial projects, research or business-oriented methodologies.

The first results were discussed in our previous research [10], which introduces the concept of Tiers-Lieu (extending the initial concept of "third place" from [17]) and argues the characteristics of Tiers-Lieu, which reveal its added value in comparison to other collaborative environments.

In our approach, Tiers-Lieu are envisaged as an open environment that motivates collaboration, intellectual creativity and surpasses the limits of traditional disciplines-defined collaborative spaces, by allowing defining new services. We underline that all initiatives of Tiers-Lieu must be:

- inter-organisational (by representing a general interest),
- inter-disciplinary (not related to the only domain, but aiming to address interdisciplinary situations),
- take into account international/intercultural aspects; lead to value creation in human, social and economic spheres and, finally,
- all initiatives must be concretized in the form of one or several trans-organizational and trans-disciplinary services.

The participants of Tiers-Lieu share "think contribution" vision, supporting creating services of the "common good" nature, which are also characterized by human added value.

This also includes understanding by all the participants that these services are created under Creative Common License [18], and no exclusive ownership rights can be demanded by any actor of such service innovation environments.

5.4 Organization of Tiers-Lieu

Firstly, it is important to underline that Tiers-Lieu are developed as collaborative environments, which aim to overcome the typical problems potential actors may face. This includes the so called "resistance to change" when actors are invited to change their way of work, communication, usage of systems, in order to find a "better" way of doing (even if they do not particularly want to change them). Instead of this, in Tiers-Lieu actors receive a possibility to take part in co-creation as active participation in changes, and as such define by being which (if any) changes are really needed.

Moreover, within Tiers-Lieu, absence of immediate tangible results is not seen as blockage, since all actors share "think contribution" vision, with added human value, and the results are, in fact, achieved through concretization their initiatives as services.

The activities that are supported by Tiers-Lieu are naturally discussed during the meetings of co-operative nature concerning strategic questions typical for complex competition-based environments. As an example, we refer to the domain of mobile healthcare (mHealth) [19], and more precisely, analyze the actors involved into defining services for aged people (Fig. 1).

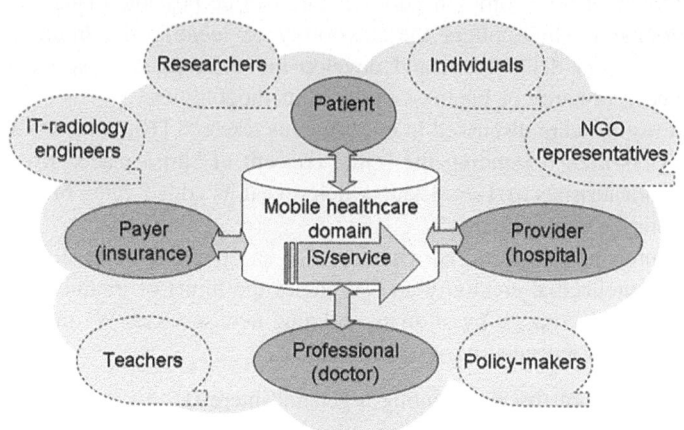

Fig. 1. mHealth actors

There are 4 main groups of actors, 4P:

- Patient
- Provider (hospital, care house)
- Payer (insurance companies)
- Professional (doctors, nurses, other medical professionals).

Along with these 4P actors, we should also consider other involved actors. They are providers of technology (IT-radiology specialists), policy-makers, researchers, actors related to education, representatives of different organisations, legal administration officers, or just interested people, who would like to participate in developing services (for example for aged people).

Despite certain contradictions between the value intentions of each actor, Tiers-Lieu are characterized by a high level of collaboration in achieving common objectives. For example, while introducing new forms of medical services, IT standards or compliance norms, the necessity of coherent collaboration between direct competitors (e.g., leading companies in the sector), standardization organizations, policy-making bodies and other interested parties has become a crucial factor.

The forms of meetings within Tiers-Lieu are multiple: they can be face-to-face, diffused by Internet, supported in real-time or asynchronous, or a mixture of different forms. The participation is open for other contributors: actively interested people, and is highly beneficial if various interesting – and multi-domain – ideas are exchanged.

In this context, it is important to underline that the participations in Tiers-Lieu are based on the acceptance of its members of the main principles of team creativity, their desire and ability to create collectively, to share the expert knowledge and the acquired results, to avoid innovation resistance [20] and to ensure participative safety, to improve the quantity and quality of attempts to introduce or develop new ideas.

One of the most important conventions within Tiers-Lieu are the mutual agreements between all the involved actors that innovative ideas are represented through initiatives which can dynamically change, according to the discussions. Each actor should share the interest in selflessness [16]: before being selected and approved by all actors, initiatives can be modified, reorganized, abandoned, etc.

In order to guarantee smooth functioning of Tiers-Lieu in creation and implication of initiatives for service creation, it is necessary to establish its infrastructure, allowing tracking the history and dynamics of ideas exchange, some principles for regulating roles and access of actors.

A few crucial aspects should be underlined.

Firstly, Tiers-Lieu are motivated by the spirit of the PPPS approach: they are supported by private (P), public (P) partnerships (P) and are oriented to service (S) creation.

Secondly, to ensure the balanced organization of discussions and the effectiveness of taken decisions, there should be a system of roles within Tiers-Lieu.

We start by identifying the following 6 roles:

- Initiators: actors, who come with a new innovative idea, define an initiative and invite other actors to discussions. Initiators are those who take the final decision, once the initiative is discussed and developed by others. For example, there is an initiative to develop a special watch for aged people, which would evaluate their blood pressure, as well as speed and amplitude of their movements, analyze the results and trigger the other related services, if necessary.
- Participants: actors, who actively contribute in discussions and help to develop the proposed initiative. These can be patients, psychologists, IT-developers, etc.
- Moderators: actors supporting the process of Tiers-Lieu functioning, i.e., "neutral" actors who guide the discussion towards concretization of initiatives.
- Observers: actors, who assist at discussions and follow them, but are not actively participating in them, i.e., the ones who do not have a word. Observers might have educational purposes (e.g., students in medicine) or just share the general interest for the discussed subject, without offering any concrete solutions (e.g., public who would like to participate in creating services for aged people).
- Historians (or secretaries): actors who play a supporting role: helping to register and track discussions and contributions of participants, introducing required information, keeping in order the agreed planning, etc.
- Developers: actors, whose aim is to develop a service, once the initiative has been defined and validated. These can be the same actors as initiators and participants, after having accepted the validated initiative and acting within the defined framework for service creation.

The role of the initiator is characterized by a high level of responsibility and is crucial for functioning of Tiers-Lieu. Indeed, it is the initiator who not only introduces a new initiative as a subject of innovation, but also defines the scope of participation within the scope of Tiers-Lieu. The initiator is also the one who evaluates the expressed ideas and has the final word on accepting or refusing them.

To facilitate the discussion procedure and to minimize the uncertainty in discussions, the initiator has a set of measures to keep the discussions fruitful, by attributing the participants a yellow card (warning about the semantic inconsistency or non-respect of the ethics of Tiers-Lieu) or a red card (serious breach of the rules or consistent contradiction with the main idea of the current initiative; this leads to the exclusion of the participant from this Tiers-Lieu). Analogically to football rules, two yellow cards in the same meeting constitute a red card.

A participant with a red card (or in fact any participant at any time) may leave this initiative and eventually launch an alternative initiative and a different Tiers-Lieu, which might have the same participants of the initial Tiers-Lieu. All initiatives are launched under the Creative Commons License [18], used when an author wants to give people the right to share, use, and even build upon a work that they have created.

It is remarkable that there are no limitations for the participants to contribute for multiple initiatives, as well as to leave them at any time.

It is important to develop a balanced system of ethics principles concerning the supported activity, and, consequently, the ethics principles defining the developed service.

Despite the self-motivation of the actors to participate in Tiers-Lieu, there should be developed a balanced approach for supporting their interest in sharing and increasing their knowledge about complex situations which require common effort, even under the risk of competition. Tiers-Lieu are thus becoming a good choice for a neutral environment, which can put together various actors for their "winning-winning" collaboration.

6 Conclusion and Future Work

This exploratory paper addressed the challenge of supporting creative development of services, in order to ensure sustainable development of the service society.

In order to do this, we discussed the main aspects of the economy of contribution, analysed the environments oriented service creation and proposed to develop Tiers-Lieu (collaborative environments for service creation) of different domains. This allowed us to address different situations facing our society, to develop situational method components, which would offer the possibility to all the actors to collaboratively and effectively co-create services, in particular services of "common good" nature.

We described the conceptual aspects of organization of Tiers-Lieu and illustrated it with the example from the mHealth domain.

Our ongoing and future works include the further conceptualization of Tiers-Lieu within the economy of contribution and the analysis of the impacts of the proposed approach for societal development. We also aim at developing multiple Tiers-Lieu in different domains: mobile health, relationships between the University and service society, and green transport, to mention but a few. We envisage Tiers-Lieu becoming a sustainable environment for exploring the phenomena of service society and all the situations we face, by offering all the actors the possibility to collaboratively create services of "common good" nature.

References

1. Webster, F.: Theories of the Information Society. Routledge, Cambridge (2002)
2. Demirkan, H., Kauffman, R., Vayghan, J., Fill, H., Karagiannis, D., Maglio, P.: Service-oriented technology and management: perspectives on research and practice for the coming decade. Electron. Commer. Res. Appl. **7**(4), 356–376 (2008)
3. Spohrer, J., Maglio, P., Bailey, J., Gruhl, D.: Steps toward a science of service systems. IEEE Comput. (IBM Almaden Research Center) **40**(1), 71–77 (2007)
4. Web resource IBM. http://researcher.watson.ibm.com/researcher/view_group.php?id=1230. Accessed June 2014
5. Lusch, R.F., Vargo, S.L., Wessels, G.: Toward a conceptual foundation for service science: contributions from service-dominant logic. IBM Syst. J. **47**, 5–14 (2008)
6. Vargo, S.L.: Service-dominant logic reframes (service) innovation. In: Isomursu, M., Toivonen, M., Kokkala, M., Pussinen, P. (eds.) Highlights in Service Research. VTT Technical Research Centre of Finland, Espoo (2013)
7. Barnaby, W.: Science, technology, and social responsibility. Interdisc. Sci. Rev. **25**(1), 20–23 (2000)
8. Le-Dinh, T., Léonard, M.: A conceptual framework for modelling service value creation networks. In: 1st International Workshop on Information Technology for Innovative Services (ITIS-2009), IEEE 12th International Conference on Network-Based Information Systems (NBiS-2009), August 2009, Indianapolis, Indiana, USA (2009)
9. Tien, J.M., Berg, O.: A case for service systems engineering. J. Syst. Sci. Syst. Eng. **12**(1), 13–38 (2003)
10. Yurchyshyna, A., Opprecht, W., Leonard, M.: Collaborative decision constructing supported by cross-pollination space. In: Proceedings of the International Conference on Advanced Collaborative Networks, Systems and Applications, COLLA 2011, Luxembourg (2011)
11. Opprecht, W., Yurchyshyna, A., Khadraoui, A., Léonard, M.: Governance of initiatives for e-government services innovation. In: Proceedings of Electronic Government and Electronic Participation: Joint Proceedings of Ongoing Research and Projects of IFIP EGOV and ePart, pp. 203–210 (2010)
12. Web resource UNCITRAL United Nations Commission on International Trade Law, International Colloquium on PPPs Discussion Paper. http://daccess-dds-ny.un.org/doc/UNDOC/GEN/V13/821/00/PDF/V1382100.pdf?OpenElement. Accessed June 2014
13. UNECE: Guidebook on Promoting Good Governance in Public-Private Partnerships. UN, New York, Geneva (2008)
14. Web resource UNECE PPP ICoE (International PPP Centre of Excellence). http://www.unece.org/ceci/ppp.html. Accessed June 2014
15. Web resource Bernard Stiegler (2013). http://www.samkinsley.com/2013/02/06/bernard-stiegler-we-are-entering-an-era-of-contributory-work/comment-page-1/. Accessed September 2014
16. Web resource Sam Kinsley. http://www.samkinsley.com/2012/12/02/economy-of-contribution/. Accessed September 2014

17. Oldenburg, R.: The Great Good Place: Cafes, Coffee Shops, Community Centres, Beauty Parlors, General Stores, Bars, Hangouts, and How They Get You Through the Day. Paragon House, New York (1989)
18. Web resource Creative Common Licenses. http://creativecommons.org/licenses/. Accessed September 2014
19. Tsiourti, C., Joly, E., Ben Moussa, M., Wings-Kolgen, C., Wac, K.: Virtual assistive companion for older adults: field study and design implications. In: 8th International Conference on Pervasive Computing Technologies for Healthcare (PervasiveHealth), Oldenburg, Germany (2014)
20. Sheth, J.N.: Psychology of innovation resistance: the less developed concept (LDC) in diffusion research. In: Sheth, J.N. (ed.) Research in Marketing, vol. 4, pp. 273–282. Jai Press Inc., Greenwich (1981)

Knowledge Sharing and Value Co-creation: Designing a Service System for Fostering Inter-generational Cooperation

Sabrina Bonomi[1(✉)], Stefano Za[1], Marco De Marco[2], and Cecilia Rossignoli[3]

[1] e-Campus University, Novedrate, CO, Italy
{sabrina.bonomi,stefano.za}@uniecampus.it
[2] Uninettuno University, Rome, Italy
marco.demarco@uninettunounversity.net
[3] University of Verona, Verona, Italy
cecilia.rossignoli@univr.it

Abstract. This paper highlights the necessity of knowledge transfer and sharing between young and old people, to avoid skills and expertises loss by the organizations and for co-creating value. The paper depicts how the use of a digital platform providing a common place in which people act and interact could facilitate the exchange of knowledge and experience between these two generations, thus fostering value co-creation. A case study describing the "5020 project" is presented in which this kind of a digital platform is developed. In this scenario, mixed work groups, composed by young and old people, are created, in which people, working together, share the knowledge acquired in the past (respectively at school and on the job by experiences), co-creating value and providing good solutions to requests of enterprises.

Keywords: Knowledge transfer · Knowledge sharing · Inter-generational cooperation · Value co-creation · Service system

1 Introduction

In today's economy, sometimes it is difficult to grasp how enterprises modify the environment in which they act. Very often, it is the environment that modifies behaviours of enterprises and encourages their changes [1]. Anyway, in both cases there is always an interaction between organizations and their environment, as emphasised by many organizational theories [2]. There are several, various and also complex factors affecting environment as well as enterprises [3]. These factors change continuously and rapidly, causing uncertain situations, in which knowledge becomes one of the most important competitive factors for enterprises. [4, 5]. In this scenario businesses tend, then, to become more and more information-intensive and networked [6]. Moreover, the most part of that knowledge reposes in the mind of older workers, especially if they acting in the same enterprise for a long time [7].

On the other hand, the continuing technological improvement and development, combined with other reasons, increase the unemployment rate [8]. For instance, in the

Italian context, this situation penalizes especially two categories of people: (i) young people who are looking for a job[1] (and often they don't find it due to the lack of experience) and (ii) elderly workers not retired yet and expelled from work by downsizing or other types of enterprises transformations, that have also difficulty to find a new employment due to the lack of updated competencies and flexibility [9].

Furthermore, people belong to the second category, also known as "baby boomer generation", have built up a huge amount of knowledge [10] that could be no simple to transfer to the succeeding generation, since it has different behaviours and communication style. Consequently, the knowledge and the skills acquired by older workers during their work life are neglected. At the same time, nowadays young people with no work experiences risk to remain unemployed without the possibility to exploit their knowledge acquired mainly through academic training and/or university courses.

On the basis of these assumptions, considering the two categories of unemployed people, the issue on which this work seeks to bring a contribution is twofold:

- how it is possible to avoid the waste of the knowledge reposing in the older workers' minds;
- how it is possible to improve the possibilities for young people to exploit their academic knowledge.

For facing these two aspects, there should be a way to allow:

- older workers to become "upgradable" and "flexible";
- young workers to acquire experiential knowledge without too much experiences.

To face this issue, this paper presents preliminary results of a project designing a digital platform [11] for providing a meeting place in which the two categories of people can get to know one another, working together and "mixing" and "combining" their knowledge to solve problems. Those problems or tasks are provided by Italian enterprises especially micro, small, medium[2] and non-profit organizations, involved in this design project. In this way, the two kind of unemployed people transfer their knowledge reciprocally in informal way, co-creating value [12]. Value co-creation is defined as a special case of collaboration where the intent is to create something that is not known in advance [13]. The interaction at work between young and old people, that constitute the same team, reciprocally could foster the transfer of knowledge, offering to enterprises a new complete approach to solve problems. These are the staring points for the definition of "meta-requirements", in compliance with the Design Research model of Walls et al. [14], adopted for designing this particular e-service environment [15]. The first part of the research path provides: (i) a taxonomy of the aspects (formal and informal) that foster knowledge sharing and knowledge transfer among individuals inside an organization, (ii) the different motivations that lead elderly and young people to share knowledge; (iii) a description of changes produced in this field by using digital

---

[1] The unemployment rate of "under 24" people is about 30 % in Italy (Istat - http://www.istat.it/en/); in 2013 people "over 50" were 438.000, increased from 2008 by 261.000, equal to 146 % - (Censis – http://www.censis.it/).

[2] In Italy they are the majority; the micro enterprises are 6,5 million and Small and medium enterprises are about 265.000 (Confindustria, http://www.confindustria.it/).

artefacts or platforms. According to Walls et al., these contents will contribute to the definition of the so-called "Kernel Theories". The research project, called "5020 – Fifty Twenty", aims at creating a digital environment to support the not-formal-knowledge transfer process between elderly and young workers and to avoid the "waste of skills", considering the organizational and social needs of the context under investigation.

In particular, the workers taken into account act in the IT/IS context, so the knowledge content concern mainly to IT/IS competencies and capabilities. The digital platform in which both categories of workers act and interact for solving specific problem is one of the outcomes of the design research process. Currently the experimentation phase is still in progress, but this paper can already shows some preliminary results.

2 Value Co-creation

Value co-creation can be defined an interaction among people, a relationship, a special case of collaboration where the intent is to create something that is not known in advance [16]. Vargo et al. [17] argue that value is fundamentally derived and determined in use, the integration and application of resources in a specific context. The interaction through mutual service exchange relationships creates an integration of resources and the actors involved in value co-creation, also mutually benefice of them [18].

According to Sanders and Simon [19], it is possible to individuate three types of value co-creation: monetary, use/experience and social. The key actors can be several and they can bring to the value creation process different resources. Knowledge can be one of them, especially its flow and sharing.

The people's creativity and empathy, inside companies and organizations, create value that they can utilize themselves. The roles of producers and consumers are not distinct; value is always co-created, jointly and reciprocally, in interactions among providers and beneficiaries through the integration of resources and application of competences [20]. In this way, the service system can improve the adaptability and survivability by allowing integration of resources that are mutually beneficial.

3 Knowledge Economy and Italian Situation

Organisations interact with their environment and reshape the environment and even themselves through the process of knowledge creation [21]. The knowledge takes place through the action and the social interaction between individuals and organisations and it could be tacit or explicit. Thanks to the conversion process, based on the interaction between these two forms, knowledge grows in both quality and quantity [5]. The dynamic capability of knowledge creation could sustain the competitive advantage of enterprises [22].

Hence in a dynamic and knowledge-based economy, how the knowledge is managed could represent both a way to create a competitive advantage of organizations or to avoid loss of organizational knowledge [4, 23–26].

3.1 Knowledge Sharing and Knowledge Transfer

We are living in a "Knowledge based society" [21, 27], where innovation and dynamic process of knowledge create value for the firms [5] and determine their competitive advantage. Furthermore it is necessary to combine internal and external competences [28], integrating and applying Knowledge [29]. Enterprises are constituted by set of productive resources and competence [30–32], therefore the knowledge process must permeate in all the organization with the dynamic capability to continuously create new knowledge [5].

According to Nonaka, the knowledge-creating process arises in dialectical thinking, which transcends and synthesizes some contradictions. Indeed, it is not always so easy to communicate tacit knowledge to others, since it is an analogue process that requires a kind of "simultaneous processing" [5]. Often people don't realize that they have tacit knowledge; they can transfer it only if there is trust. If there isn't, tacit knowledge could atrophy in each one. On the contrary, from an organisational viewpoint, if enterprises don't promote sharing knowledge, they lose expertise. It is necessary to have relational knowledge to build organizational sense [5, 33]. The process of embodying explicit knowledge into tacit knowledge is called "internalization". Through internalisation, related to "learning by doing", explicit knowledge created is shared throughout an organisation and converted into tacit knowledge by individuals [5]. Business relations between colleagues, and friendship relationships between the members, could enlarge the possibility of knowledge exchange [34, 35] and promote the informal learning of new competences [36]. Hence the colleagues' experience is an important source of knowledge [37], in particular for the more creative ideas that the exchange of experience can bring out. In addition to a good trust climate, openness in the business culture is also a precondition in order that knowledge exchange occurs [38].

3.2 Elderly and Younger Workers

The "baby boom generation" is constituted by people, which were born between 1946 and 1964 and have built up a considerable amount of knowledge about how things work, how to get things done and who calls when problems arise. Their knowledge comes especially from their own experience. Many organizations are going to lost a lot of knowledge and their gaps in skills and capabilities grow, largely due to the baby boomer retirements [10]. The knowledge transfer process from baby boom generation to the next generation is necessary because young people need to be helped to acquire work experience. [39]. On the other hand, it is extremely hard because it has been developed in an era of unprecedented technological and scientific advance [10]. Furthermore, elderly and young workers unlikely have business relationships and friendship relations that could create the necessary confidence to transfer tacit knowledge. They have different characteristics, habits, values and expectations; they determine different working dynamics that ask an organisational transformation and a working method change.

Moreover, they are two most disadvantaged generations and, at the same time, antagonistic in the working world. However, the non-use of professional skills can "atrophy" skills, and, on the other hand, the rapid change of technology increases the risk of obsolescence and could decreases progressively their value.

The young people are looking for their first job while the workers "over 50" are prematurely expelled from the companies. Both are in difficult because younger are missing experience, older are missing update and often their salaries are too high due to their seniority. So it could be profitable for both of them, find a common space of personal relationship to share and transfer tacit knowledge, filling the gap between academic/theoretical competences and capabilities built on long work experiences.

3.3 The Italian Landscape

In the Italian context, it is possible to identify at least two main issues that can hinder diffusion of knowledge, exacerbated also by the economic and financial crisis of the recent years:

1. The market is constituted over ninety per cent by many micro, small and medium-sized enterprises (SMEs), in which the knowledge creation process is especially based on the training on the job for reasons of efficiency and economic sustainability [40]. Small and Medium-sized enterprises are important drivers of economy but often they neglect knowledge management issues and investments in information system and technologies. Due to the lack of resource, SMEs in Italy have more difficulties than larger enterprises to employ experts or hire external consultants.
2. There is a growth of third sector and non-profit organizations and also they have to manage the generational shift and need to improve their knowledge organization and transfer.

In general SMEs and non-profit organizations rarely make investments in process of knowledge creation, especially in ICT [26]; they do it only if they are conveniently "stimulated", for example by funding, as it is arisen in the recent few years. [41]. Therefore this research work wants to study the problem of knowledge transfer between elderly and younger workers that especially is relevant for these two important sectors of the Italian economy.

4 A Design Research Model

The use of specific innovative technologies may represent an effective solution for fostering that knowledge transfer process [42]. According to Walls et al. (2004), design theories should be based on natural and social science theories (referred to as "kernel theories") since the "laws" of the natural and social world govern the components that comprise an information system.

The "5020 Fifty-Twenty" project aims at creating a technological environment for whom that work in IT/IS area, such as: IS Manager, IS Designer, IS Auditor, IT System Administrator, etc. Considering this specific sector, the good practices learned (also informally) by the elderly worker and the IT competences related to IT innovations acquired by the younger generation attending specific courses (e.g. master, official university courses, etc.) could represent for an organization the right component to mix for gaining a competitive advantage combining both kind of knowledge.

On the basis of these assumptions, in according with the Design Research model of Walls et al. [14], it is possible to identify the following requirements:

- create a network to promote knowledge sharing and knowledge transfer between senior and junior employees;
- provide opportunities of employment to elderly workers who have lost their job and the younger who are seeking it in Information Technologies;
- promote the training on the job of younger workers;
- bring up to date the older, giving them the opportunity to upgrade technology;
- provide high-level skills;
- enable workers who live in remote or poor areas or to get in labour market;
- provide good product /service but low-cost to the enterprises, especially SMEs and non-profit, who need to review their processes or improve their efficiency or that need improving their information technology;
- reduce the cost /time of transfer (and the consequent pollution).

In keeping with the kernel theory of knowledge creation this Information Systems Design Theories (ISDT) is not specific but it could be connect to the concept of "ba", i.e. a shared space that could be a combination of physical, virtual and mental area or only one of them; it is more than an ordinary human relation the cause of knowledge creation [43]. Ba provides a platform to create and improve individual and/or collective knowledge.

4.1 The "5020 – FiftyTwenty" Project

This project is an intergenerational agreement for work and training, made through a platform that promotes cooperation of recruitment and work team creation, between baby boomer and next generations.

The platform is a combination of a technological platform and a virtual and mental area (see the "ba" concept), looking at young and "over Fifty" workers who live a particularly disadvantage and sometimes dramatic social problems of unemployment. It promotes employment in information system sector by spreading the culture of innovation and knowledge transfer. The project indeed considers that skills acquired in both learning and job experiences are a valuable asset that can't and should not be wasted.

In this context, value is co-created by three key actors: (i) young people that doesn't work because of their lack of experience; (ii) older people that are prematurely thrown up from work and that with difficulty can be reinstated because of the lack of upgrade, and (iii) organizations – public administration, SME or no-profit – that can hire them and improve themselves. These actors bring a resource, their knowledge, for supporting the value creation process, especially through knowledge transfer and sharing.

The platform is designed to recruit non-occupied people, younger and older and to distribute few of them into the same team, depending on requires of the enterprises participating to this project. Fostering by the a common space (virtual) provided by 5020 platform, they can transfer and share their knowledge. Both, younger and older, have indeed an absorptive capacity and a teaching skill, concerning respectively the college-prep and the work experience; they learn and explain each other. The appropriation affects the flow and the knowledge transfer.

The project proposes the use of that platform as organizational solution to improving expertise, experience and innovation of SMEs and non-profit organizations. These enterprises can obtain tools and methodologies saving cost and improving their efficiency (Fig. 1).

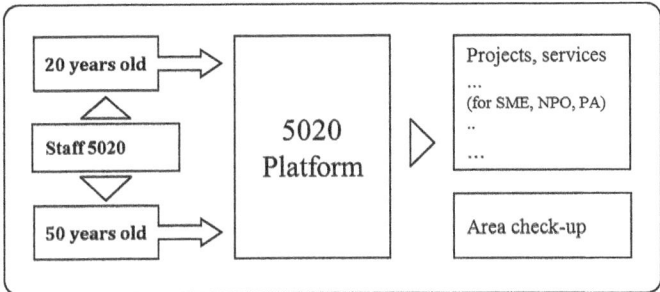

Fig. 1. The "5020 project": an intergenerational agreement for work and training, made through a platform of recruitment and work team creation.

One small staff, also working in 5020 spirit (the managing team is constituted by 2 senior and 2 young), selects the senior and the young people each time. The digital platform supports planning, operational and organizational processes. It is also a showcase to present the job opportunity and it is the tool to select the most appropriate people.

The 5020 project uses a dynamic recruitment (in collaboration with local Universities for the selection of new graduates). The platform organizes the team and controls the progress of activities too. It creates a real learning community and upgrading as well as representing the first channel of communication and promotion. The wide number of job applicants permits to identify the most suitable job profile and allows the composition of highly specialized teams. In this way the team member's skills increase: young people complete their training, taking the "best practices" from senior; elderly upgrade their knowledge, learning from the younger.

4.2 Preliminary Results

Knowledge originates and resides in people's minds, but its sharing requires a common place to exchange knowledge and create it [43]. The "5020 project" would want to be that place. It is more important that all the stakeholders (i.e. policy makers, enterprises, employers and employees) need to be interested to the age-group relationships in regard to workplace practices [44, 45].

In the 5020 project it is possible to identify seven main activities fostering directly or indirectly knowledge transfer, depicted below:

1. Interview: the job interviews is made generally by the management team 5020 and, certainly, they were always between people of different age and/or experience. The team, to fully understand the candidate's experience and to address him/her towards

the enhancement of the skills that the market requires, based on the experience of 5020. Sometimes the 5020 staff suggests attending to institutional courses (e.g. organized by region or province institutions), online training or participation in free courses organized by 5020.
2. Training: the 5020 staff organizes free courses combining for each one people of different generations to facilitate the knowledge transfer starting from the moment of the training;
3. Post Training: the 5020 staff organizes sessions of practice exercises on the product of the course, for people who have not found immediate employment in 5020 neither on the labour market, by developing applications that could be presented to the market;
4. Design activity: the project activities are composed by mixed teams that operate at the customer or during the feasibility study or preparation of the bid. The 5020 staff spends time and pays attention to young people, to identify the critical points of the phase that they are facing and to prevent any mishaps. Similarly, evaluates all the innovative proposals;
5. Lessons on Soft skills: 5020 staff also organizes horizontal or soft skills courses (e.g. customer relationship, clarity of exposition, consumptive activities, project management, etc.).
6. Management issues: the meetings to organizing the activities occur with high frequency during each month, and they are often occasions to illustrate and compare management practices.
7. Team building: the organization of mixed teams senior / junior is confirmed, where possible. However, analysing the people profiles, we found a greater number of unemployed over 50 and a significant presence into the intermediate band (40–50 years old), and in general a growing interest in the initiative 5020 especially young people who want to improve their skills.

Davenport and Prusak (1998) assert that technology is a tool that enables knowledge behaviours and Hendriks (1999) states that it can facilitate knowledge transfer. Thanks to "5020 project", 3 courses were made (81 days in all) of learning for 20 people, on the average 42 years old. Furthermore, since knowledge resides in people, not in technology, it is necessary to act toward and with people. According to Deng and Weight (2001) rewards and encouragements can represent an essential motivation. In this particular case it is necessary to act towards and with younger and elderly workers.

Finally, 69 % of learning people was employed post learning or job experience. Six teams are employing in four different organizations: one enterprise (Pirelli S.p.A.), one public administration (Veneto Region), one non – profit organization (ASD US-Acli), and one small cooperative company (Cooperativa Lavoro).

5 Conclusion

Thanks to the conversion process, based on the interaction between of tacit and explicit forms, knowledge grows in both quality and quantity [5]. In a dynamic and knowledge-based economy, the knowledge is managed could represent both a way to create a competitive advantage of organizations or to avoid loss of organizational knowledge [4, 23–26]. However in Italian market, small and medium sized enterprises and non-profit organizations, which are the majority, have some difficulties to create process for retaining and growing knowledge. The knowledge transfer from baby boom generation and younger workers is not so easy and lot of skills and competences could be wasted. Some authors above mentioned assert that knowledge transfer and sharing behaviours can be facilitating, and technologies could be a useful tool. The "5020 project" could be one of those solutions.

The literature review and the preliminary results of the case study underline that knowledge sharing is facilitated when elderly and young workers find a common space with a good trust climate or/and if they are motivated to share (e.g. in 5020 project, some unemployed people can get work). This research is still in progress; at the moment the first results shows that some proposed objectives are achieved or reachable.

Finally this work contributes to the literature on the technology mediated employee organization relationship and on the technology impact on work flexibility [46].

Future works should verify if and how fostering intergenerational knowledge sharing could be really useful or not for SMEs and non-profit organizations, gathering information using the 5020 platform in the next years. Furthermore, further steps could be related to investigate (i) on which factors motivate Knowledge transfer from baby boom generation to younger people and (ii) on the possible role-played by digital artefacts/platform in supporting the value co-creation. According to Hendriks [47], the use of ICT, indeed, can be an important instrument to foster knowledge sharing among people but it cannot work alone.

References

1. Golinelli, G.M., Gatti, M.: L'impresa sistema vitale. Il governo dei rapporti inter-sistemici. SYMPHONYA Emerg. Issue Manag **2**, 53–81 (2002)
2. Baum, J.A., Singh, J.V.: Organization-environment coevolution. In: Baum, J.A., Singh, J.V. (eds.) Evolutionary Dynamics of Organizations, pp. 379–402. Oxford University Press, Oxford (1994)
3. Dore, R.P.: Flexible Rigidities: Industrial Policy and Structural Adjustment in the Japanese Economy, pp. 1970–1980. Stanford University Press, Stanford (1986)
4. Drucker, P.: The coming of the new organization. Harvard Bus. Rev **66**, 45–53 (1998)
5. Nonaka, I., Toyama, R., Konno, N.: SECI, Ba and Leadership: a Uni ® ed model of dynamic knowledge creation. Long Range Plan. **33**, 5–34 (2000)
6. Ricciardi, F., De Marco, M.: The challenge of service oriented performances for chief information officers. In: Snene, M. (ed.) IESS 2012. LNBIP, vol. 103, pp. 258–270. Springer, Heidelberg (2012)
7. Hoffman, R.R., Ziebell, D., Fiore, S.M., Becerra-Fernandez, I.: Knowledge management revisited. Intell. Syst. IEEE. **23**, 84–88 (2008)
8. Baumol, W.J., Wolff, E.N.: Side effects of progress. Public Policy Br. 41 (1998)
9. Encel, S., Studencki, H.: Older workers: can they succeed in the job market? Australas. J. Ageing. **23**, 33–37 (2004)

10. De Long, D.W.: Lost Knowledge: Confronting the Threat of an Aging Workforce. Oxford University Press, New York (2004)
11. Resca, A., Za, S., Spagnoletti, P.: Digital platforms as sources for organizational and strategic transformation: a case study of the Midblue project. J. Theor. Appl. Electron. Commer. Res. **8**, 71–84 (2013)
12. Maglio, P.P., Spohrer, J.: Fundamentals of service science. J. Acad. Mark. Sci. **36**, 18–20 (2007)
13. Spohrer, J., Maglio, P.P.: The emergence of service science: toward systematic service innovations to accelerate co-creation of value. Prod. Oper. Manag. **17**, 238–246 (2008)
14. Walls, J.G., Widmeyer, G.R., El Sawy, O.A.: Assessing information system design theory in perspective: how useful was our 1992 initial rendition? J. Inf. Technol. Theory Appl **6**, 43–58 (2004)
15. Spagnoletti, P., Za, S.: A design theory for e-service environments: the interoperability challenge. In: Snene, M. (ed.) IESS 2012. LNBIP, vol. 103, pp. 201–211. Springer, Heidelberg (2012)
16. Roig, A., San Cornelio, G., Sanchez-Navarro, J., Ardevol, E.: The fruits of my own labour: a case study on clashing models of co-creativity in the new media landscape. Int. J. Cult. Stud. **17**, 637–653 (2013)
17. Vargo, S.L., Maglio, P.P., Akaka, M.A.: On value and value co-creation: a service systems and service logic perspective. Eur. Manag. J. **26**, 145–152 (2008)
18. Depaoli, P., Za, S.: Towards the redesign of e-business maturity models for SMEs. In: Baskerville, R., De Marco, M., Spagnoletti, P. (eds.) Designing Organizational Systems, pp. 285–300. Springer, Heidelberg (2013)
19. Sanders, L., Simons, G.: A social vision for value co-creation in design. Open Source Bus. Resour. (2009)
20. Gronroos, C.: Value co-creation in service logic: a critical analysis. Mark. Theory. **11**, 279–301 (2011)
21. Nonaka, I.: The knowledge-creating company. Harvard Bus. Rev. **69**, 96–104 (1991)
22. Zahra, S., George, G.: Absorptive capacity: a review, reconceptualization, and extension. Acad. Manag. Rev. **27**, 185–203 (2002)
23. Ruggle, R.: The state of the notion: Knowledge Management in Practice. Calif. Manage. Rev. **40**, 80–89 (1998)
24. Bollinger, A.S., Smith, R.D.: Managing organizational knowledge as a strategic asset. J. Knowl. Manag. **5**, 8–18 (2001)
25. Treleaven, L., Sykes, C.: Loss of organizational knowledge: from supporting clients to serving head office. J. Organ. Chang. Manag. **18**, 353–368 (2005)
26. Boccardelli, P., Fontana, F., Manzocchi, S.: La diffusione dell'ICT nelle piccole e medie imprese. Luiss University Press, Rome (2007)
27. Toffler, P.: Knowledge, Wealth and Violence at the Edge of the 21st Century. Bantam Books, New York (1990)
28. Nelson, R.R., Winter, S.G.: The Schumpeterian tradeoff revisited. Am. Econ. Rev. **72**, 114–132 (1982)
29. Grant, R.M.: Toward a knowledge-based theory of the firm. Strateg. Manag. J. **17**, 109–122 (1996)
30. Barney, J., Wright, M., Ketchen, D.J.J.: The resource based view of the firm: ten years after 1991. J. Manage. **27**, 625–641 (2001)
31. Peteraf, M.A.: The cornerstones of competitive advantage: a resource-based view. Strateg. Manag. J. **14**, 179–191 (1993)
32. Dagnino, G.B.: I paradigmi dominanti negli studi di strategia d'impresa: fondamenti teorici e implicazioni manageriali. Torino (2005)

33. Argiolas, G.: Il valore dei valori. La governance nell'impresa socialmente orientata (2014)
34. Argote, L., McEvily, B., Reagans, R.: Managing knowledge in organizations: an integrative framework and review of emerging themes. Manage. Sci. **49**, 571–578 (2003)
35. Varriale, L.: Mentoring and technology in the learning process: E-mentoring. In: Spagnoletti, P. (ed.) Organizational Change and Information Systems. LNISO, vol. 2, pp. 371–379. Springer, Heidelberg (2013)
36. Za, S., Spagnoletti, P., North-Samardzic, A.: Organisational learning as an emerging process: the generative role of digital tools in informal learning practices. Br. J. Educ. Technol. **45**, 1023–1035 (2014)
37. Werr, A., Stjernberg, T.: Exploring management consulting firms as knowledge systems. Organ. Stud. **24**, 881–908 (2003)
38. Von Krogh, G., Ichijo, K., Nonaka, I.: Enabling knowledge creation: how to unlock the misteery of tacit knowledge and release the power of innovation. Oxford University Press, Oxford (2000)
39. Quintini, G., Martin, S.: Starting well or losing their way?: the position of youth in the labour market in OECD Countries. OECD social employment migration working paper no. 39. OECD, Paris (2006)
40. Federighi, P., Campanile, G., Grassi, C.: Il Modello dell'Embedded Learning nelle PMI (2009)
41. Acquati, E.: Il non profit in rete (2013)
42. Dameri, R.P., Sabroux, C.R., Saad, I.: Driving IS value creation by knowledge capturing: theoretical aspects and empirical evidences. In: D'Atri, A., Ferrara, M., George, J.F., Spagnoletti, P. (eds.) Information Technology and Innovation Trends in Organizations, pp. 73–81. Physica-Verlag HD, Heidelberg (2011)
43. Nonaka, I., Konno, N.: The concept of "Ba". Kalifornia Manag. Rev. **40**, 40–54 (1998)
44. Booke, L., Taylor, P.: Older workers and employment: managing age relations. Ageing Soc. **25**, 415–429 (2005)
45. Depaoli, P., Sorrentino, M., De Marco, M.: E-services in the ageing society: an Italian perspective. J. e-Governance **36**, 105–118 (2013)
46. Imperatori, B., De Marco, M.: E-work and labor processes transformation. In: Bondarouk, T., Oiry, E., Guiderdoni-Jourdain, K. (eds.) Handbook of Research on E-Transformation and Human Resources Management Technologies: Organizational Outcomes and Challenges, pp. 34–54. Hershay, PA (2009)
47. Hendriks, P.: Why share knowledge? the influence of ICT on the motivation for knowledge sharing. Knowl. Process Manag **6**, 91–100 (1999)

Towards a Cyberinfrastructure for Social Science Research Collaboration: The Service Science Approach

Thang Le Dinh[✉], Van Thai Ho, Theophile Serge Nomo, and Ayi Ayayi

Research and Intervention Laboratory on Business Development in Developing Countries, Université du Québec à Trois-Rivières, C.P 500, Trois-Rivières, QC G9A 5H7, Canada
{Thang.Ledinh,Ho.Van.Thai,Theophileserge.Nomo, Ayi.Ayayi}@uqtr.ca

Abstract. Research collaboration in a globalized world has become one of the most important challenges for higher-education today. Collaboration between researchers all over the world is still an intricate and difficult challenge, which is the motive for this study that aims at filling this gap in the field of social science research. Based on the review of the literature, we propose a conceptual framework for designing a cyberinfrastructure to promote the collaboration among researchers across institutions. We present an example to illustrate the application of the framework that supports international collaboration between a research laboratory in a developed country and its partners in developing countries. Future work and research directions are also suggested in order to apply and extend the framework at a broader scale.

Keywords: Research collaboration · Cyberinfrastructure · Social science · Service science

1 Introduction

Nowadays, the knowledge economy requires a stronger focus on the production and the distribution of knowledge, especially in the field of research and development. Research collaboration is defined as cooperation among researchers to attain the mutual objective of producing new scientific knowledge [17]. The need for research collaboration has increased in the past few years with requirements from funding agencies and governments. Research collaboration has become important for researchers, research institutes, and policy makers [3]. The motivations for research collaboration are to verify research proposals, to make the research results available to the public, to enable others to extend the research data, and to advance the state of research and innovation [5]. Further, motivations are also to save costs and to promote interaction among researchers in various fields and in different countries [17].

Research collaboration may positively affect research outputs and research quality since a researcher may widen his understanding and achieve better outcomes with other researchers' contributions [23]. With research collaboration, researchers may share their experience, expertise, skills and resources and may create fresh ideas [3]. The high degree of collaboration intensity is a strong driver for achieving higher levels of research quality. The more a researcher uses the collaboration network, the higher research quality he or she can gain [23].

To promote collaboration among researchers over the world, *e-science*, also called *cyberinfrastructure*, was introduced as the emergent infrastructure supporting the next wave of collaboration in knowledge communities [16]. The term e-science evolved as a new research field that concentrates on collaboration in key areas of science using next generation computing infrastructures to extend the potential of scientific computing [29]. E-science is also used to describe computational intensive science that is conducted in highly distributed network environments, which use immense data sets requiring grid computing, and technologies for enabling distributed collaboration [27]. E-science is related to large-scale science that is being conducted through collaborations among researchers all over the world by using the Internet [10]. In general, e-science has the potential to revolutionize research and learning in the digital world [1].

Recent studies showed that much of the current e-science effort was mostly oriented towards supporting natural science and technology-oriented research in order to access large data sets, to provide greater computing resources and to broaden the uses of new instruments and sensors [32]. We believe that e-science in the field of social science research needs the same motivations and means for social researchers to work together across time and space while pursuing larger scientific problems. Indeed, the social science is undergoing a transformation from studying problems to solving them, from a purely academic pursuit to having a major impact on public and industry, and from isolated scholars to larger scale, collaborative, interdisciplinary, and lab-style research teams [18].

This paper focuses particularly on a special need for more collaboration between social researchers all over the world, especially those in developing countries and those in developed countries. Developing countries have suffered from the lack of both financial and human resources in R&D. There is a need for improving higher-education institutions in developing countries to strengthen their research activities and international collaboration [31]. The purpose of this paper is to present a conceptual framework for designing a cyberinfrastructure for promoting social science research collaboration. In the context of scientific research, a cyberinfrastructure is a technological and sociological system to efficiently connect research laboratories, information systems, and people to promote novel scientific theories and knowledge [4]. The objective of a cyberinfrastructure is to allow researchers to collaborate in doing their research activities with researchers all over the world in the digital age.

The paper seeks to answer the following research question: *"How to design a cyberinfrastructure for promoting collaboration in social science research?"*

To respond to this question, this paper introduces a conceptual framework that can be used to design a specific cyberinfrastructure for an institution or a network of institutions for promoting social science research collaboration. In our approach, design is the creation of a roadmap for the construction of a cyberinfrastructure. Therefore, the main objectives of the framework are to clarify the key elements of a generic cyberinfrastructure and to specify relationships between them [15]. Each institution can adapt the framework to build its own cyberinfratructure by identifying and specifying the specific elements according to its business priority, processes, and management styles.

The remainder of this paper is structured as follows. Section 2 continues with a theoretical background. Section 3 introduces a conceptual framework for designing a cyberinfrastructure for social science research collaboration based upon the perspective of service science. The paper also presents the applicability of the framework by illustrating an application for a research laboratory. Section 4 concerns with related work and discussion. Section 5 ends with conclusions and outlook.

2 Theoretical Background

2.1 E-Science and Research Collaboration

E-science is, firstly, defined as computationally intensive science that is carried out in highly distributed network environments. Consequently, collaborative research in e-science is the emerging trend in the 21st century science, since it brings new possibilities and challenges in various aspects, including technical, social and legal [10, 16]. For instance, the collaboration norms and procedures are important challenges for research collaboration among researchers [10].

Recent trends towards an e-science offer the following approaches: data mining and analysis, information visualization, observation tools, knowledge organization and collaboration services. Data used by social science research have been stored and analyzed digitally, while new research tools have emerged and become the prospects for social science research in a large scale [14].

Firstly, *data mining and analysis* is a method used in the analysis of big datasets and establishment of meaningful models using computer-based tools. In particular, network data analysis is a method used in social science research to discover relationships between individuals, communities, or organizations. Secondly, *information visualization* is used to create images, graphs, charts, or animations to communicate, understand, and improve the results of large data sets' analysis. Thirdly, *observation tools* such as living lab introduce new ways of managing innovation processes that support the observation, measurement and fabrication of services [6]. Fourthly, *knowledge organization* encompasses all types of schemes for organizing information and promoting knowledge management [22]. Finally, besides email and chat that are often used as media of communication, various *collaboration services* may be used to support research collaboration, including video conferencing, telephone, and periodic project meetings assessing progress using these forms of communication [2].

2.2 Service-Oriented Cyberinfrastructure

Service-orientation is a design paradigm to build systems in the form of services. *Service-oriented science* is a new way of doing research that leads to an ideal opportunity to promote research collaboration among researchers from various departments, institutions, and countries [30]. Consequently, researchers may produce quality research outputs by using computational tools to share information and data. Moreover, knowledge has become collective knowledge, which is not only stored and shared exclusively in the scientific literature but also documented in different databases [12].

In our approach, we consider higher-education organizations as knowledge-intensive organizations that offer to the market knowledge-intensive services, which are defined as services and business operations heavily reliant on professional knowledge [25]. These services are both sources and carriers of knowledge that influence and improve the performance of people, organizations, and value-creation networks. In a knowledge-intensive organization, knowledge-intensive services are supported by two categories of application services: dependent and independent services. Dependent services need the cooperation with other service systems for their realization; meanwhile, independent services can be performed inside the organization without outside cooperation [22].

A service-oriented cyberinfrastructure for a knowledge-intensive organization needs to support the knowledge business value chain that covers different categories of services that support both organizational and information systems activities. Figure 1 presents the principal architecture of a cyberinfrastructure that serves several domain-specific knowledge communities in their knowledge-intensive work.

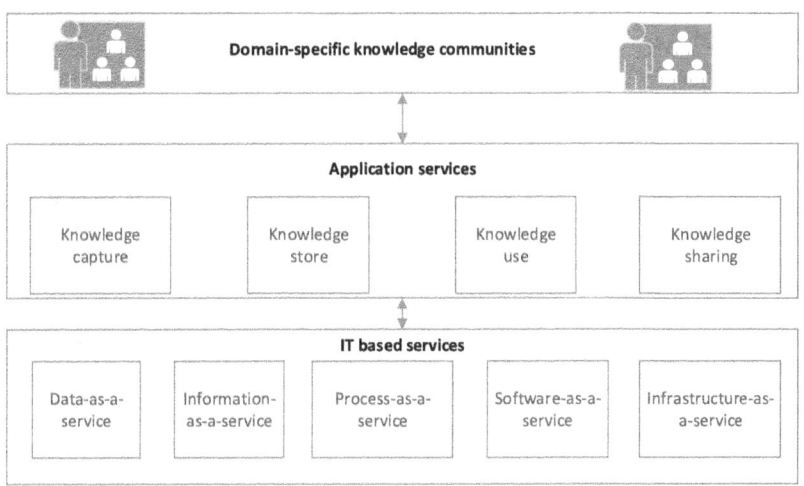

Fig. 1. General architecture of a service-oriented cyberinfrastructure

A cyberinfrastructure provides application services offered in e-science such as data mining and analysis services and observation services for knowledge capture, knowledge organization services for knowledge store, visualization services for knowledge use, and collaboration services for knowledge sharing. These application services then use IT based services such as data-as-a-service, information-as-a-service, process-as-a-service, software-as-a-service and infrastructure-as-a-service [11].

3 Framework for Social Science Research Collaboration

Service science is a term used to describe a new science that encompasses all the aspects that relate to service systems. A service system is defined as a "value-coproduction configuration of people, technology, other internal and external service systems, and shared information" [34].

The framework for promoting social science research collaboration (SSRC framework) needs to cover all the three dimensions of service science, including management, science and engineering. The management dimension, corresponding to *Service proposal*, adds more value to existing services and provides new innovative services in a network of service systems. The science dimension, corresponding to *Service creation*, defines the structure of service systems and clarifies the process of service creation. The engineering dimension, corresponding to *Service operation*, covers the invention of new technologies to improve the quality of services [21]. Some key elements were derived from the earlier versions of this framework for business interoperability based on conceptual specifications of information systems [19, 20].

In our approach, a cyberinfrastructure aims at serving a network of service systems that efficiently connects institutions, organizations and people in order to promote a new way of doing research and collaboration in the digital age. Figure 2 introduces the different dimensions of the framework and principal elements of each dimension.

The section continues with the details of the principal elements of the SSRC framework in accordance to the different levels of abstraction: network of service systems, service system and service. At the network of service systems level, the service proposal relates to the role, the collaboration and the value of services. At the

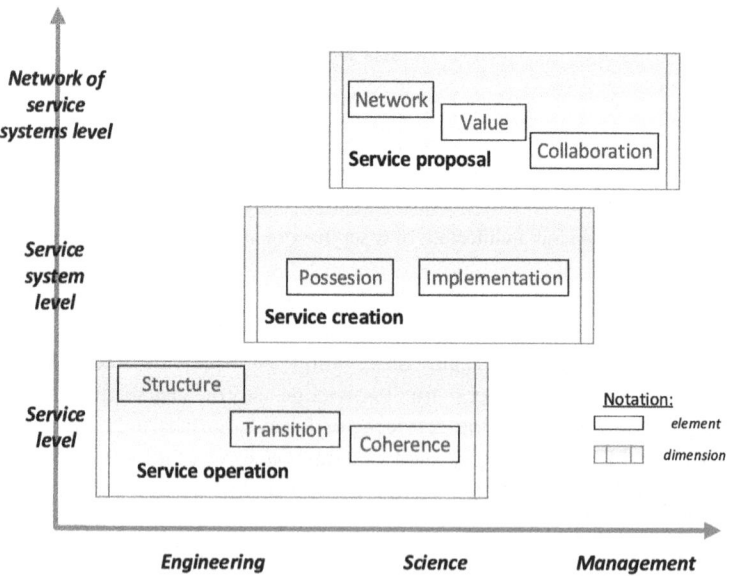

Fig. 2. Dimensions and elements of the SSRC framework

service system level, the service creation element deals with the possession and technical implementation of services. At the service level, the service operation element includes the three principal elements: the structure, the transition and the coherence of knowledge-intensive services.

3.1 Network of Service Systems Level

At the network of service systems level, the focus of the framework is to create and increase service values. Its principal elements correspond to the network, value and collaboration aspects to specify the network configuration and operation as well as the representation of value creation and exchange [21]. Accordingly, the following concepts are proposed to specify a network of service systems: economic entity, service, role, contract and overlap situation.

A network of service systems is comprised of a variety of *economic entities,* which assumes a subset of roles and their respective responsibilities in the network. A *service* is defined as "a change in the condition of a person or a good belonging to some economic entities brought about as the result of the activity of other economic entities, with the approval of the first person or economic entity" [8]. A service requires at least two roles: one *service provider* and one *service client*. A service offers a value proposal defined as a value produced by transferring things or by improving some states of service clients [24]. A *contract* defining what to offer and to whom, will be performed by one or several economic entities. Depending on the value-creation process, there are co-creation activities in which value is exchanged or co-created [28]. An *overlap situation* occurs when there is at least one component of a service shared by some economic entities, which perform together a co-creation activity. An *overlap protocol* is a protocol that allows each economic entity to perform its own activities locally but also to guarantee the coherence and consistency of the network globally [20].

In social science research, there are two traditions commonly referred to as quantitative and qualitative research [9]. The quantitative research concentrates on behaviour; meanwhile, the qualitative research concentrates on meanings. Moreover, action research is proposed to explore how the research findings can be used to make a difference to the situations of those involved in the study [9].

Figure 3 illustrates economic entities involved in a cyberinfrastructure as a network of service systems. The cyberinfrastructure provides a research collaboration service as a knowledge-intensive service that includes various research activities in social science research [9]. Recently, social researchers have begun to use IT based services in e-science for carrying out research activities such as online surveys, statistical analysis, simulation and forecasting tools, data explore and visualization, dataset integration and sharing, and web-based interview and intervention [14].

Let us discuss about an example, which is extracted from a real-world application of the SSRC framework for supporting social research collaboration. A medium-size university in a developed country is interested in promoting its collaboration in social science research with its partners in developing countries. The university has built a cyberinfrastructure to carry out the delocalization of MBA program with research thesis option.

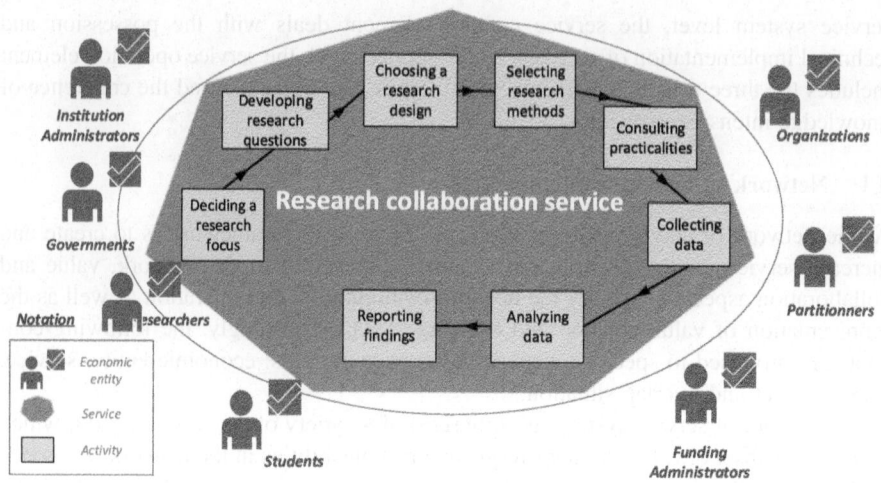

Fig. 3. A generic cyberinfrastructure for social research collaboration

Thanks to this cyberinfrastructure, researchers from this university can validate their hypotheses with organizations in developing countries by performing their research activities remotely in collaborating with their partners. In particular, the project concentrates on building certain cyberinfrastructure-enabled knowledge communities related to specific domains such as microfinance, women's entrepreneurship, industrial upgrading program, and ICT for development.

Figure 4 illustrates the network configuration for an action-research project performed by a MBA student. The research collaboration service in this case is the "thesis supervision" service. This network is comprised of a set of economic entities such as the university, the partner, the organization, the supervisor, the examiner and the student. The organization is the enterprise that performs the action-research project. The university and the partner are the service providers. The student is the service client. The "thesis supervision" service helps a student to change his state, becoming a "graduated" student. The "thesis supervision guidelines" document is a contract of the service that clarifies the responsibilities of each economic entity.

There is an overlap situation related to the "research thesis" component between the university, the partner and the organization. Those economic entities work together on the information and documents related to the thesis based on the "network-based" overlap protocol [20]. This protocol is used to operate overlap situations by authorizing economic entities as co-owners to monitor the effects caused by other co-owners' actions.

3.2 Service System Level

At the service system level, the framework focuses on service creation, which involves the two principal elements: the configuration and the implementation of services. The objective of this level is to ensure that services have adequate resources for efficiently implementing as well as sufficient technological support.

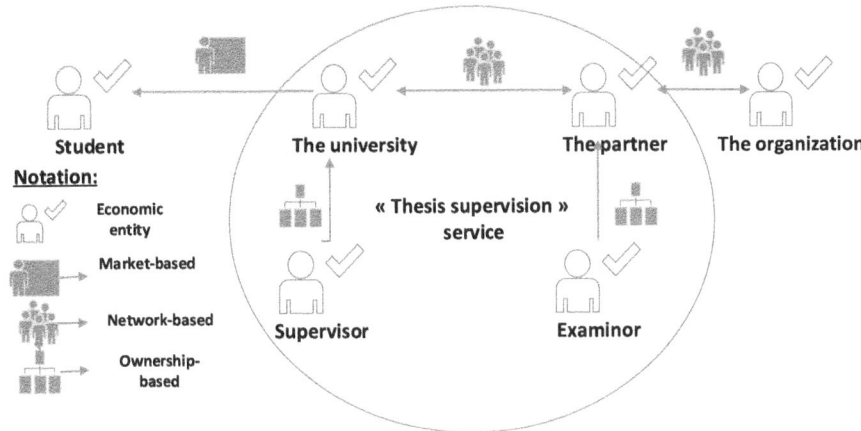

Fig. 4. Network configuration for the "thesis supervision" service

In our approach, a service is provided by an economic entity and represented by a unit of shared information. A service is operated by a subset of business activities and requires resources for the technical implementations of those activities. A *technical implementation* of a business activity is the use of a set of IT based services so that this business activity can be operated [21]. Business activities may consume or produce products and services whose information is represented by business objects (BO). A *unit of shared information* covers a subset of interconnected business objects. Each business activity of a unit of shared information can be implemented by one or several technical implementations, and each technical implementation may use a set of IT based services.

Concerning technical implementation of services, firstly, data mining and analysis services can be useful to capture explicit knowledge. Secondly, observation services such as living lab tools can be used to experiment, observe, and measure results of a research project, especially action-research.

Thirdly, knowledge organization services can organize knowledge inside the cyberinfrastructure according to the different knowledge components [13] (such as know-what, know-how, know-why and know-who) to promote different types of innovations and to facilitate knowledge visualization [22]. *Know-what* corresponds to the structure of knowledge focusing on business objects and their relating concepts. *Know-how* corresponds to the transition of knowledge focusing on processes and activities. *Know-why* corresponds to the coherence of knowledge focusing on business rules, which are the reflection of the raison d'être inside a service system [10]. *Know-who* corresponds to the possession of knowledge by economic entities that may provide resources related to domain knowledge.

Fourthly, data visualization can be performed according to the semantic relation between knowledge components. Taxonomy tools can be used to organize the structure of knowledge according to the knowledge components.

Finally, collaboration services provided in e-collaboration systems can be helpful to capture tacit knowledge, to promote knowledge transfer and to improve the quality of explicit knowledge [22]. Awareness tools are useful to acquire a deep understanding of current research topics related to knowledge components, and workflow tools can be used to enforce the coherence of knowledge.

Continuing with our example, the university assumes responsibilities such as providing professors for thesis supervision, hosting and managing the cyberinfrastructure, and granting degrees to graduated students. The "thesis supervision" service is represented by a unit of shared information called "research thesis context" that covers the "research thesis" business object and the "Carrying out a research thesis" process.

Table 1 introduces the detailed implementations of the "Deciding on a research focus" activity, the first activity of the "Carrying out a research thesis" process.

Table 1. Implementation of the "Deciding on a research focus" activity.

Business activity	Technical implementation	Required resources
Deciding on a research focus	Following blogs of professors	Blog, comments
	Requesting an online meeting	Web-based interview, professor
	Checking CVs and publications of professors	Online repository for scientific publications, Email
	Participating in a seminar	Online seminar, professor
	Following a course	E-learning, professor

3.3 Service Level

The service level focuses on service operation that presents what is provided and how it is provided [21]. Its principal elements are the aspects representing the knowledge structure of a service, including the structure of knowledge, transition of knowledge and coherence of knowledge [22].

The structure of knowledge is represented by business objects, which refer to facts and artefacts relating to services [21]. A *business object* is defined as a type of an intelligible entity being an actor inside the business architecture. In social science research collaboration, there are BOs related to a scientific paper, a subvention proposal, a service contract, a team-teaching project, or a thesis co-supervision. An *attribute* of a BO is a function corresponding to every instance of this BO and to a set of instances of other objects.

The transition of knowledge is represented by processes that refer to the understanding of the generative operations constituting a service [21]. A *process* can be triggered by an event and uses a set of business activities. A process in social science research collaboration describes a submission process of a paper, an application process of a grant, steps of a service contract, a syllabus of a course, or a roadmap for a thesis. A *business activity* is an operation of a service used to transit from a dynamic state to another dynamic state. A *dynamic state* of a BO expresses a condition of a service in which certain business activities are enabled and others are disabled.

The coherence of knowledge is represented by business rules that refer to the understanding of the principles underlying a service [21]. A *business rule* (BR) constrains certain components of services. BRs in social science research are connected with eligibility criteria and constraints related to time, quality, and conformity. *Scopes* of a BR represent the context of a business rule that covers a subset of relative BOs. *Risks* of a BR are the possibilities of suffering from incoherent information that may lead to fail points of business activities or to the incoherence of business objects.

In our example, the "thesis supervision" service transforms a student status from a "graduating" into a "newly graduated" student. Service operation concentrates on the three dimensions of knowledge: structure, transition and coherence.

Concerning the structure of knowledge, the key business object is the "research thesis" BO. Figure 5a illustrates an excerpt of the structure of knowledge related to the "research thesis" BO and its attributes. Concerning the transition of knowledge, the process states the roadmap of a research thesis is the "carrying out a research thesis" process. Figure 5b depicts an excerpt of the "Carrying out a research thesis" process, including its business activities and dynamic states. Concerning the coherence of knowledge, there are business rules extracted from the guidelines and procedures of the MBA program. For example, there is a BR, called BR#1, indicates that "the period of thesis fulfillment (determined by start-date and end-date) must not exceed two years". The risk of the BR#1 is the operation related to the "end-date" of the "research thesis" BO.

4 Related Work and Discussion

According to our literature review, recent studies that attempt at applying e-science for promoting research collaboration have presented the following inputs: semantic e-science, infrastructure interoperability reference model, social research network sites, and document practice focus.

Semantic e-science is an approach supporting research collaboration in which all the services of data access, integration, provenance, and data processing need semantic representation. As a matter of fact, semantic e-science is insufficient for complete data discovery [26]. The *infrastructure interoperability reference model* (IIRM) was based on the OGSA (Open Grid Services Architecture) so that researchers can access multiple interoperable infrastructures [12, 29]. The *social research network sites* (SRNS) are used as a web-based service [7]. This service allows individual researchers to perform the research collaboration functions such as identity, communication, information and collaboration [7]. The *document practice focus* approach concentrates on a common platform where research resources can be stored and shared across researchers [32, 33].

Research studies related to e-science have demonstrated the importance of social science research collaboration. Different from natural sciences, social science research requires different methods and different tools, such as survey method, case study and action research. With the development of the large-scale data in social science research, a specific cyberinfrastructure framework is useful to support collecting and analyzing large-scale data sets. Compared with the other approaches mentioned above, the SSRC framework addresses the cyberinfrastructure in an integrated manner, more coherent and more complete. Indeed, the framework takes into account all of the three levels of a service, including the service, service system and network of service systems levels. Moreover, it covers all the three dimensions of service science: the engineering (service

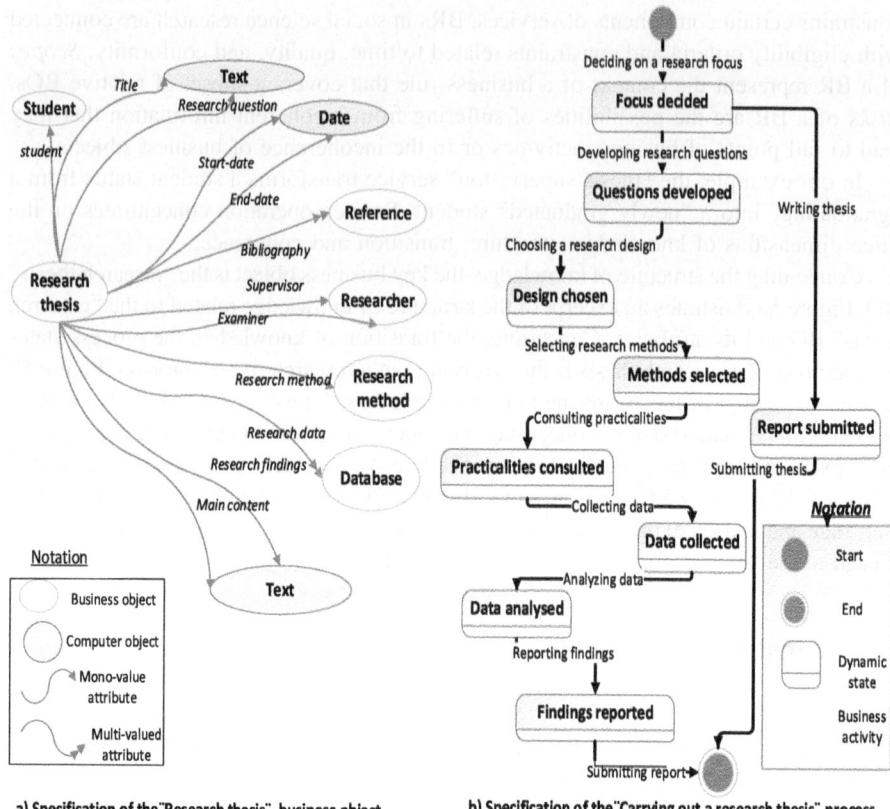

Fig. 5. Specifications of the framework elements

operation), science (service creation) and management (service proposal). Table 2 compared the focal points, including the focused levels and elements of the SSRC framework with the other approaches.

Table 2. Comparison of the SSRC framework with the other approaches.

Approach	Author(s)	Focused levels	Focused elements
Social research network sites	Bullinger et al. [7]	Network of service systems	Service proposal
Semantic e-science	Narock and Fox [26]	Service	Service operation
Infrastructure interoperability reference model	Riedel et al. [29]	Network of service systems	Service proposal
Document practice focus	Sawyer et al. [32] Sharma et al. [33]	Service system	Service creation

5 Conclusion and Outlook

In this paper, we address the general lack of e-science literature and the special need for a foundation for building a cyberinfrastructure for social science research collaboration.

We, therefore, propose a conceptual framework for designing a cyberinfrastructure for social science research collaboration, called the SSRC framework, in order to promote collaboration among researchers as well as new ways of doing social science research in the digital age. To the best of our knowledge, this approach is one of the first that concentrates on applying the service science perspective on e-science to promote social science research collaboration. The paper presents a theoretical foundation for identifying, specifying and implementing different aspects of knowledge-intensive services based on the main dimensions of service science (engineering, science and management) and on the different levels of a service (service, service system and network of service systems). Concerning the applicability of the framework, an example extracted from an experimentation of the framework is illustrated. The purpose of this experimentation is to build a cyberinfrastructure for an institution in a developed country that intends to delocalize its MBA program with research thesis option to developing countries.

With regard to practical implications, our approach aims at supporting institutions to build their cyberinfrastructure to promote social science research collaboration. Due to the variety of requirements of research collaboration, it is suggested that the artefacts of our framework could be adapted and customized to fit real-world scenarios. With regard to theoretical implications, the framework can be extended to discover new ways of doing social research in the digital age.

Currently, we are developing a prototype based on an open-source platform supporting the social science research collaboration based on the SSRC framework. The objective of the prototype is to allow higher-education organizations to build their own network at a low cost but high flexibility.

Our future research direction focuses on applying and experimenting data science and living lab in social science research. Indeed, we believe that working on big data or data science is an interesting direction for new survey methods. Furthermore, the new research landscape such as living lab can promote a more proactive role of enterprises in the R&D process in doing case study and action-research methods remotely.

Acknowledgements. The authors would like to thank the reviewers for their valuable suggestions for improvement on a previous version of this article. The authors also express their sincerely thanks to the FRQSC (Fonds de recherche sur la société et la culture) of the Government of Quebec, Canada for the partial financial support for this research.

References

1. Atkins, D.: Revolutionizing science and engineering through cyberinfrastructure. Report of the National Science Foundation Blue-ribbon Advisory Panel on Cyberinfrastructure (2003)
2. Balliet, D.: E-research Collaboration and the Free-rider Problem: Communication Solutions to Social Dilemmas in Computer Mediated Research Collaborations. E-research Collaboration, pp. 277–288. Springer, Heidelberg (2010)

3. Bammer, G.: Enhancing research collaborations: three key management challenges. Res. Policy **37**(5), 875–887 (2008)
4. Berman, F.D., Brady, H.E.: Final report: NSF. SBE-CISE workshop on cyber-infrastructure and the social sciences. National Science Foundation, Arlington, VA (2005)
5. Borgman, C.L.: The conundrum of sharing research data. J. Am. Soc. Inf. Sci. Technol. **63**(6), 1059–1078 (2012)
6. Birgitta, B.K., Stahlbrost, A.: living lab: an open and citizen-centric approach for innovation. Int. J. Innovation Reg. Dev. **1**(4), 356–370 (2009)
7. Bullinger, A.C., Hallerstede, S.H., Renken, U., Soeldner, J.H., Moeslein, K.M.: Towards research collaboration: a taxonomy of social research network sites. In: Proceedings of the Sixteenth Americas Conference on Information Systems, Lima, Peru, 12–15 Aug 2010
8. Chesbrough, H., Spohrer, J.: A research manifesto for services science. Commun. ACM **49**(7), 35–40 (2006)
9. Colin, R.: Real World Research, 3rd edn. Wiley Publications, Chichester, West Sussex, United Kingdom (2011)
10. David, P.A., Spence, M.: Towards institutional infrastructures for e-science: the scope of the challenge. Research Report No. 2, Oxford Internet Institute (2003)
11. Demirkan, H., Delen, D.: Leveraging the capabilities of service-oriented decision support systems: putting analytics and big data in cloud. Decis. Support Syst. **55**(1), 412–421 (2013)
12. Foster, I.: Service-oriented science. Science **308**(5723), 814–817 (2005)
13. Garud, R.: On the distinction between know-how, know-what, and know-why. In: Huff, A., Walsh, J. (eds.) Advances in Strategic Management, pp. 81–201. JAI Press, Greenwich (1997)
14. Halfpenny, P., Procter, R.: The e-social science research agenda. Philos. Trans. Roy. Soc. A Math. Phys. Eng. Sci. **368**(1925), 3761–3778 (2010)
15. Hevner, A.R., March, S.T., Park, J., Ram, S.: Design science in information systems research. Manage. Inf. Syst. Q. **28**(1), 75–105 (2004)
16. Hey, T., Trefethen, A.E.: The UK e-science core programme and the grid. Future Gener. Comput. Syst. **18**(8), 1017–1031 (2002)
17. Katz, J.S., Martin, B.R.: What is research collaboration? Res. Policy **26**(1), 1–18 (1997)
18. King, G.: Restructuring the social sciences: reflections from harvard's institute for quantitative social science. PS Polit. Sci. Politics **47**(1), 165–172 (2014). Cambridge University Press version
19. Le Dinh, T.: Towards a new infrastructure supporting interoperability of information systems: the Information system upon information systems. In: Proceedings of the First International Conference on Interoperability of Information Systems, Geneva, Feb 2005
20. Le Dinh, T., Léonard, M.: Conceptual framework for modelling service value creation networks. In: Proceedings of the 12th IEEE International Conference on Network-Based Information Systems, Indianapolis, USA, 19–21 Aug 2009
21. Le Dinh, T., Pham Thi, T.T.: Information-driven framework for collaborative business service modelling. Int. J. Serv. Sci. Manage. Eng. Technol. (IJSSMET) **3**(1), 1–18 (2012)
22. Le Dinh, T., Rinfret, L., Raymond, L., Dong Thi, B.T.: Towards the Reconciliation of Knowledge Management and e-collaboration Systems. Interact. Technol. Smart Educ. **10**(2), 95–115 (2013)
23. Liao, C.H.: How to improve research quality? Examining the impacts of collaboration intensity and member diversity in collaboration networks. Scientometrics **86**(3), 747–761 (2011)
24. Ma, C., Zhongjie, W., Xiaofei, X.: Preliminary discussions on several characteristics of service value. Int. J. Serv. Sci. Manage. Eng. Technol. **1**(3), 50–62 (2010)

25. Muller, E., Doloreux, D.: What we should know about knowledge-intensive business services. Technol. Soc. **31**(1), 64–72 (2009)
26. Narock, T., Fox, P.: From science to e-science to semantic e-science: a heliophysics case study. Comput. Geosci. **46**, 248–254 (2012)
27. Nishihara, K., Fukuda, Y., Shimada, K., Taniguchi, M., Zhakhovskii, V., Fujioka, S., Shigemori, K., Sakane, E., Shimojo, S., Ueshima, Y., Okamoto, T., Sasaki, A., Sunahara, A., Nakajima, T.: e-science in high energy density science research. Fusion Eng. Des. **83**, 525–529 (2008)
28. Payne, A.F., Storbacka, K., Frow, P.: Managing the co-creation of value. J. Acad. Mark. Sci. **36**(1), 83–96 (2008)
29. Riedel, M., Wolf, F., Kranzlmüller, D., Streit, A., Lippert, T.: Research advances by using interoperable e-science infrastructures: the infrastructure interoperability reference model applied in e-science. Cluster Comput. **12**, 357–372 (2009)
30. Russell, R.S.: Collaborative research in service science: quality and innovation. J. Serv. Sci. (JSS) **2**(2), 1–8 (2011)
31. Sanyal, B.C., Varghese, N.V.: Research capacity of the higher education sector in developing countries. In: Second International Colloquium on Research and Higher Education Policy, UNESCO Headquarters, Paris (2006)
32. Sawyer, S., Kaziunas, E., Østerlund, C.: Social scientists and cyberinfrastructure: insights from a document perspective. In: Proceedings of the ACM 2012 Conference on Computer Supported Cooperative Work, pp. 931–934 (2012)
33. Sharma, S., Snyder, J., Østerlund, C., Willis, M., Sawyer, S., Brown, M., Szkolar, D.: Document practice as insight to digital infrastructures of distributed, collaborative social scientists. In: iConference 2014 Proceedings, pp. 1021–1024 (2014)
34. Spohrer, J., Maglio, P., Paul, P., Bailey, J., Gruhl, D.: Steps towards a science of service systems. IEEE Comput. **40**(1), 71–77 (2007)

Evolution and Overview of Linked USDL

Jorge Cardoso[1,2](✉) and Carlos Pedrinaci[3]

[1] Technical University of Dresden, Dresden, Germany
jcardoso@dei.uc.pt
[2] Department of Informatics Engineering, CISUC, University of Coimbra, Coimbra, Portugal
[3] Knowledge Media Institute, The Open University, Milton Keynes, UK
c.pedrinaci@open.ac.uk

Abstract. For more than 10 years, research on service descriptions has mainly studied software-based services and provided languages such as WSDL, OWL-S, WSMO for SOAP, and hREST for REST. Nonetheless, recent developments from service management (e.g., ITIL and COBIT) and cloud computing (e.g. Software-as-a-Service) have brought new requirements to service descriptions languages: the need to also model business services and account for the multi-faceted nature of services. Business-orientation, co-creation, pricing, legal aspects, and security issues are all elements which must also be part of service descriptions. While ontologies such as e^3service and e^3value provided a first modeling attempt to capture a business perspective, concerns on how to contract services and the agreements entailed by a contract also need to be taken into account. This has for the most part been disregarded by the e^3 family of ontologies. In this paper, we review the evolution and provide an overview of Linked USDL, a comprehensive language which provides a (multi-faceted) description to enable the commercialization of (business and technical) services over the web.

Keywords: Linked USDL · Service description · Service management

1 USDL Overview

Linked USDL (Unified Service Description Language) [15] was developed for describing business and software services using computer-readable and computer-understandable specifications to make them tradable on the web/ Internet [6]. Linked USDL takes the form of a reference vocabulary which is an approach used in many fields to facilitate the exchange of data and integration of information systems. For example, online social networks rely on FOAF[1] to describe people and relationships; computer systems use WSD[2] to describe distributed software-based services; GoodRelations[3] is used to mainly describe products; and business-to-business systems use ebXML[4] to describe transactions,

---
[1] http://www.foaf-project.org/.
[2] http://www.w3.org/TR/wsdl.
[3] http://purl.org/goodrelations/v1.
[4] http://www.ebxml.org/.

orders, and invoices. Adding to these existing standards, Linked USDL describes services in a comprehensive way by providing a business or commercial description around services. Therefore, Linked USDL is seen has one of the foundational technologies for setting up emerging infrastructures for the Future Internet, web service ecosystems, and the Internet of Services.

The objective of this paper is to provide a retrospective on the development of the service description language Linked USDL; the various technologies that have been used to support the evolving models; the current models and documentation available; and the projects that are using and evaluating Linked USDL. This will enable to ease future developments on the field of the web of services by providing an important overview to reduce ramp-up time.

This paper is organized as follows. Section 2 describes the evolution of USDL which started in 2007. Section 3 discusses our findings and the experience gained from modeling services over the years. Section 4 describes the various modules that have already been developed (e.g., core and pricing) and the ones that are in development. It also discusses the benefits of Linked USDL and the standardization efforts that were carried out in the past. Section 5 provides an example of how to describe a service using Linked USDL. We have chosen to model last.fm since it is a good example of an emerging type of services which are part of the so-called Web API economy. ProgrammableWeb, the world's leading directory of Internet-based APIs, shows a dramatic growth of APIs since 2005 and has as of July 2014 more than 11.500 entries. Section 6 describes the related work and the alternatives to using Linked USDL. Finally, in Sect. 7 the conclusions are presented and discussed.

2 Evolution of USDL

The initial main driving organization behind the first two versions of USDL was SAP Research. Developments were carried in conjunction with other research partners such as Siemens, Forschungszentrum Informatik (FZI), and Fraunhofer Institut für Arbeitswirtschaft und Organisation (IAO). Funding for the research was part of the Theseus project and supported by the German Federal Ministry of Education and Research (BMBF).

The two initial versions of USDL (versions 1.0 and 2.0) started to be developed in 2007 and were ready in 2009. They were built using XML Schema. Later, in 2011, based on the experience gained from the first developments, a W3C Incubator group[5] was created and USDL was extended leading to version 3.0. This version was built using the Ecore metamodel and the Eclipse Modeling Framework (EMF) to define UML modules for capturing the "master data" of a service. It included extensions for pricing, legal, functional, participants, interactions, and SLA aspects. The extensions resulted from the use of USDL in several European academic and industrial projects (e.g., RESERVOIR, SLA@SOI, and SOA4ALL).

---

[5] http://www.w3.org/2005/Incubator/usdl/.

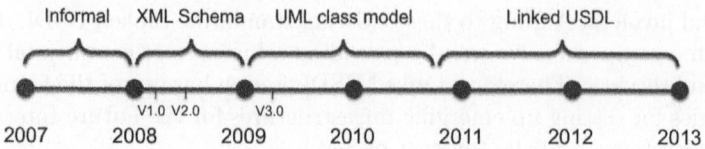

Fig. 1. The evolution of USDL and Linked USDL (2007–2013)

In 2012, version 4.0 was created and renamed to Linked USDL since its development followed Linked Data principles [4] due to the rather inflexible and close nature of previous technologies (e.g., XML, Ecore, and UML). Currently, Linked USDL is the version most often used to develop infrastructures and applications to manage services. The objective is to shift from a closed solution to a language which enabled the large scale, open, adaptable, and extensible description of services using a decentralized management. The use of Linked Data enabled USDL to inherit many distinctive aspects such as unique service addresses on the web via the use of URIs and the description data about services is published in a computer-readable and -understandable format.

The rationale behind the use of Linked Data is the requirement that USDL descriptions should be shared between interested parties and linked to other descriptions, standards, and vocabularies. Linked Data technologies are particularly suitable for supporting and promoting this level of web-scale interlinking. Globalization truly happens only when people, devices, processes, and services are all connected into a global network. As with its predecessors, Linked USDL was also conceived, explored, and evaluated in several research projects including FI-Ware (smart applications), FInest (logistics), and Value4Cloud (value-added cloud services).

Figure 1 provides an overview of the evolution of Linked USDL and Table 1 describes the various versions of the USDL language and their main characteristics.

Versions 1.0, 2.0, and 3.0 of USDL have been discontinued and are no longer supported. Linked USDL introduces many changes and follows a different philosophy when compared to its predecessors. While the core and pricing models for Linked USDL are finalized, work on developing and aligning several modules of the specification (e.g. legal, security, and service level) with various use cases (e.g., higher education, cloud computing, and human-based services) is still in progress. The modular approach followed, separating the different service aspects into independent vocabularies, has proved to be efficient, flexible, and easy to be processed by service delivery platforms. The following sections cover USDL version 4.0, i.e., Linked USDL, since it offers a larger spectrum of advantages to build a large-scale web of services.

3 Lessons Learned

The development of four versions of USDL to model human-driven and software-based services taught us many lessons about service modeling. Table 2 summarizes

Table 1. The main characteristics of USDL languages

Name	Ver	Year	Characteristics
USDL [7]	1.0	2008	Introduces the notions of business, operational, and technical perspectives. The model is serialized with an XML Schema (in this paper it will be also referred to as USDL/XML)
USDL [6]	2.0	2009	The model is extended. It addresses the first set of concrete requirements for service description languages (e.g., extensibility, multiple views, and variability)
USDL [3]	3.0	2011	The model is divided into various modules, and Ecore and the Eclipse Modeling Framework (EMF) are used for modeling (also referred as USDL/ECore)
Linked USDL [15]	4.0	2013	The model is represented using Linked Data principles and RDFS. The core model is rebuilt to provide a simpler view on services and better coverage (also referred as Linked USDL/RDFS)

our findings over the years and provides conclusions, which can be useful for future developments indispensable to create a web of services' infrastructure. We discuss the four most relevant findings: *model extensibility*, *data interoperability*, and *instance identification*.

Model extensibility [2] refers to the capability to create new service models as extensions/derivations from a base model. Data interoperability [8] is the ability of two or more systems to exchange service information and to use the information that has been exchanged. Data integration [12] refers to the capability to combine service data coming from different sources to provide a unified view of these data. Instance identification [14] is related to the creation of unique identifiers to identify service instances.

3.1 Model Extensibility

A web of services requires more than a one-size-fits-all model and, thus, the extensibility of service models was important. USDL/XML and USDL/Ecore provided a schema for service descriptions with a rather fixed structure. XML Schema does not provide an elegant mechanism to enable providers to add new elements to a data schema to better describe their services. In USDL/XML, the solution implemented consisted in using a place holder that captured a list of pairs attribute-value. Both attribute and value where elements of type string, which enabled providers to add new descriptive attributes to their services. Clearly, this type of approach is not practical either from a syntax or semantic perspective.

An attribute-value approach can support extensibility (since any attribute can be added) but it is not suitable for interpretation (and integration) since attributes are just "strings" with no meaning attached. RDFS allows the same

Table 2. The main lessons learned

Lesson learned	Description
Model extensibility	Linked USDL/RDFS has the highest extensibility capabilities. USDL/Ecore and USDL/XML only provided extensibility via the creation of new attribute-value pairs.
Data interoperability	Due to the adoption of XML by businesses, USDL/XML has the highest degree of data interoperability. Ecore, despite its XMI serialization, does not enjoy this popularity. RDFS has a growing base of adopters, which makes Linked USDL/RDFS part of a new generation of web specification languages. This movement corresponds to an interoperability through adoption.
Data integration	USDL/XML and USDL/Ecore generate self-contained instances. In other words, the meaning or semantics of instance data is not shared across stakeholders via the model specification. It is given by the entity (e.g., provider) creating a service description instance. On the other hand, Linked USDL/RDFS enables to create instances which are integrated with external data managed and shared by linked data registries (e.g., dbpedia). Anyone can reuse preexisting instances/data defined by 3rd parties which enables data reuse (saving effort) but also enhances interoperability.
Instance identification	While Linked USDL/RDFS relies on URIs to provide a simple way to create unique global identifiers for services, USDL/XML and USDL/Ecore did not provide such a decentralized and scalable mechanism.

kind of extensibility but every new attribute added comes with its own semantics ready to be interpreted by software.

3.2 Data Interoperability

While USDL/XML enables to archive a high degree of data interoperability, since XML has been adopted and used for many years by businesses and many tools exist, Ecore does not enjoy this popularity. While a serialization to XMI exists, the objective of Ecore is not to foster the exchange of data but to provide a metamodel to implement object-oriented programs. It can be used to model packages, classes, attributes, references, etc. to facilitate dynamic code generation. In other words, Ecore is suitable for the automated generation of code to develop applications that use the model (e.g., editors, service marketplaces, matchmakers, etc.). With respect to data interoperability, XML was more adequate than Ecore to support a web of services. When analyzing the difference of interoperability between USDL/XML and Linked USDL/RDFS, it is clear that XML has also a higher degree of data interoperability due to its dissemination and adoption level. Nonetheless, RDFS is gaining popularity for knowledge modeling and its adoption was strategic.

3.3 Data Integration

USDL/XML and USDL/Ecore specify a model that contains attributes (e.g., integers, longs, strings, or other structures) to which values (e.g., 232, 1.4, "ITIL Incident Management") are assigned. This means that the data associated with a service instance has only an established meaning to the entity providing the data. RDFS, on the other hand, enables to reuse data that already exists on the web in the form of Linked Data. For example, when creating a description for the service `ITIL_IM_service`, the company providing the service can be specified by assigning the unique URI http://dbpedia.org/resource/Cloudera maintained at `dbpedia.org`. This URI holds a lot of data interlinked to many other data sources. Thus, it is possible to know the number of employees, the address, the economic sector, etc. of the service provider.

Using USDL/XML and USDL/Ecore, the string "Cloudera" would be assigned to an attribute. Thus, its meaning would remain with the entity that provided it. As we converge to an interconnected world of data, the integration of data and services will be important. Thus, and when compared to USDL/XML and USDL/Ecore, Linked USDL/RDFS incorporates Linked Data mechanisms that are valuable to support data integration initiatives as part of a web of services.

3.4 Instance Identification

The result of describing a service with a model is an instance. For the global trading of services, each instance needs to be uniquely identified. USDL/XML and USDL/Ecore proposed to use universally unique identifiers (UUID) [14]. Problems associated with this approach include the need for a central management of identifiers and "hiding" service information, e.g., service name and provider, into a number via an encoding mechanism. On the other hand, Linked USDL/RDFS relies on URIs to provide a simple way to create unique global identifiers for services. Compared to UUID, Linked USDL URIs are more adequate to service distribution networks since they are managed locally by service providers. The same URI, which provides a global unique identifier for a service, also serves as endpoint to provide uniform data access to the service description. A Linked USDL URI can be used by, e.g., RDFS browsers, RDFS search engines, and web query agents looking for cloud service descriptions.

4 Linked USDL Family

Linked USDL[6,7] is segmented into modules that together form the Linked USDL family. The objective of this division is to reduce the overall complexity of service modeling by enabling providers to only use the modules needed. Currently, five modules exist but they have different maturity levels. The modules identified with one star (⋆) have been developed only as a proof of concept. The modules

---
[6] http://www.linked-usdl.org/.
[7] http://github.com/linked-usdl/.

identified with two stars (⋆⋆) have passed the proof-of-concept stage and are being finalized. The modules identified with three stars (⋆ ⋆ ⋆) are ready and have been validated.

- usdl-core (⋆ ⋆ ⋆). The core module covers concepts central to a service description. It includes operational aspects, such as interaction points that occur during provisioning, and the description of the business entities involved.
- usdl-price (⋆ ⋆ ⋆). The pricing module provides a range of concepts which are needed to adequately describe price structures in the service industry.
- usdl-agreement (⋆⋆). The service level module gathers functional and non-functional information on the quality of the service provided, e.g., availability, reliability, and response time.
- usdl-sec (⋆). This module aims at describing the main security properties of a service. Service providers can use this specification to describe the security features of their services.
- usdl-ipr (⋆). This module captures the usage rights of a service, which are often associated with the concept of copyright.

For example, the usdl-agreement module is being reconstructed with the objective to align it with the WS-Agreement specification. Customers and providers can use usdl-agreement to create service level agreements to, afterwards, monitor whether the actual service delivery complies with the service level agreed terms. In case of violations, penalties or compensations can be directly derived.

Linked USDL Core can be regarded as the center of the Linked USDL family since it ties together all aspects of service descriptions distributed across the USDL modules. Figure 2 shows the conceptual diagram of the core module. Classes are represented with an oval, while properties with an edge. Linked USDL Core has 12 classes and 13 properties (the reader is referred to [15] to understand the purpose of using external vocabularies such as GoodRelations, SKOS, and MSM).

Other modules are being developed as proofs of concept. For example, Linked Service System USDL (LSS USDL)[8] provides modeling constructs to capture the concepts of a service system. While Linked USDL looks into the external description of a service, i.e., a service is seen as a black box, LSS USDL looks inside the'box' to describe its elements.

4.1 Standardization Efforts

Service standards are expected to drive the industrialization of the service market, to increase transparency and access, to lead to higher trading of services across countries, and to contribute to a new level of service innovation by aggregation or composition. Linked USDL fills the gap by proposing a specification language which enables the unified formalization of business and technical aspects.

---

[8] https://w3id.org/lss-usdl/v2/.

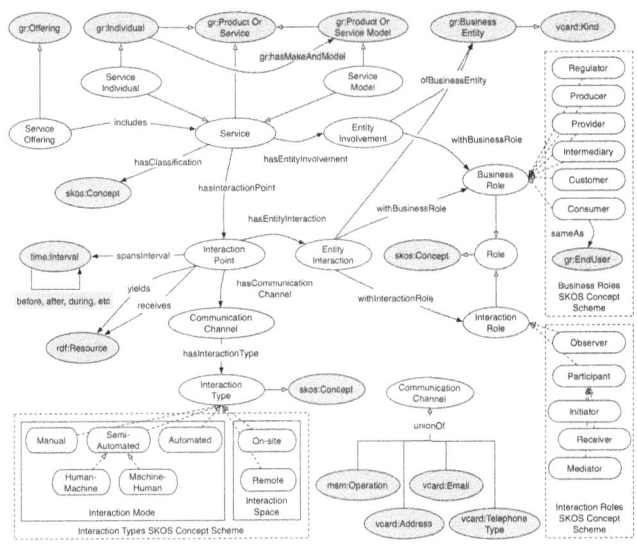

Fig. 2. Linked USDL Core schema [15]

A W3C Unified Service Description Language Incubator Group was initiated by Attensity, DFKI, SAP, and Siemens on September 2010. The group concluded its activities on October 2011. The objectives were to investigate related standards and approaches; re-design USDL to include feedback, requirements, and related work, and define and implement reference test cases to validate USDL. The final outcome was a report and a reworked USDL specification: USDL V3.0 of Table 1.

While USDL did not reach to become a W3C standard after the Incubator Group concluded its activities, the working group agreed that creating a Linked Data version was one of the steps forward for the possible standardization and wider adoption. Linked USDL can evolve toward a language that can fill the gap existing in various fields requiring service modeling such as cloud computing. In fact, in 2012, a report requested by the German Federal Ministry of Economics and Technology [5] indicated that the potential contained in USDL to model services could be adapted to become an important contribution for cloud computing to describe cloud services.

5 Modeling Example

The objective of this modeling exercise is to describe part of the Last.fm service using Linked USDL. Last.fm is a music recommendation service which can be accessed using a browser or programmatically by accessing a Web API. Only part of the service will be described because showing the complete modeling would require a considerable space. Most of the information used for the modeling was

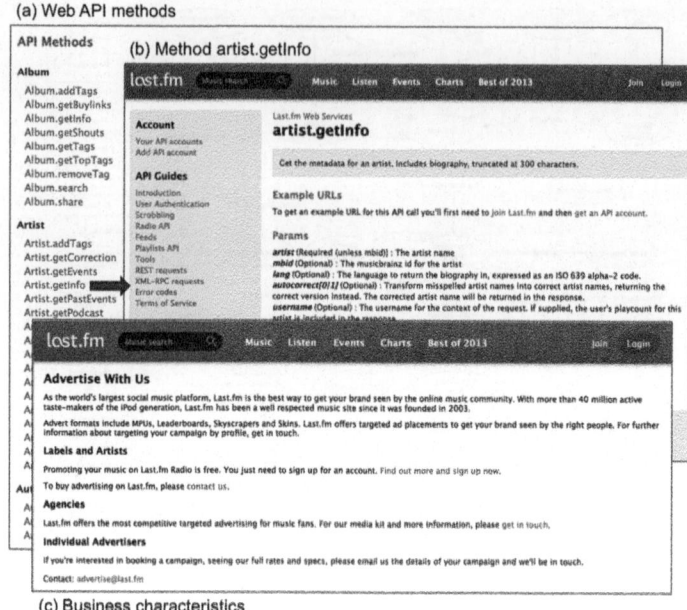

Fig. 3. LastFM web site description and Web API

retrieved from the web site http://last.fm and is shown in Fig. 3. The description was written using the Turtle language[9].

The class `usdl:Service` provides the entry point for the description. As shown in Listing 1, the new service was named `service_SLastFM`. The specification also includes:

- Associating a service model with the service.
- Specifying the business entities participating during service provisioning.
- Enumerating the interaction points provided by the service.

The class `usdl:ServiceModel` is used to create groupings of services that share a number of characteristics. For example, a service model for the S-LastFM service can group services characterized for supplying online music services. In the same line of thought, the service "Vodafone unlimited internet service" may belong to the grouping "Internet provisioning service". The example from Listing 1 associates the service `service_SLastFM` with the grouping `onlineMusicServiceModel`[10] (Line 4).

---

[9] Turtle – Terse RDF Triple Language (http://www.w3.org/TR/turtle/).
[10] The definition of the model `onlineMusicServiceModel` is not provided in this running example.

```
1  :service_SLastFM a usdl:Service ;
2    dcterms:description"A semantic recommendation service for music.";
3
4    usdl:hasServiceModel :onlineMusicServiceModel ;
5    usdl:hasEntityInvolvement [
6      a usdl:EntityInvolvement ;
7      usdl:ofBusinessEntity :be_SLastFM_Ltd ;
8      usdl:withBusinessRole usdl-br:provider
9    ];.
10   usdl:hasInteractionPoint :ip_Advertise ;
11   usdl:hasInteractionPoint :ip_Artist_GetInfo .
```

Listing 1. The S-LastFM service class

The class usdl:EntityInvolvement captures the usdl:BusinessEntities involved in the service delivery and the usdl:Role they play (lines 5–9). This enables specifying, for instance, that a given music service is provided by a certain company or that a third party is involved in the service delivery chain.

In Listing 1, the business entity is defined with the class be_SLastFM_Ltd and its role is defined as usdl-br:provider. Linked USDL provides a reference taxonomy of basic business roles that cover the most typical ones encountered during service modeling such as regulator, intermediary, producer, and consumer. The prefix usdl-br identifies the taxonomy usdl-business-roles[11] which defines the default roles available.

Listing 2[12] illustrates the description of the company providing the S-LastFM service and described with the class be_SLastFM_Ltd. The description include the ISIC (International Standard Industrial Classification of All Economic Activities) code for S-LastFM: 5920 – sound recording and music publishing activities. It also specified the NAICS (North American Industry Classification System) code, legal name, tax ID number, and country where the company is located.

```
1  :be_SLastFM_Ltd a gr:BusinessEntity ;
2    foaf:homepage <http://Slast.fm/> ;
3    foaf:logo <http://cdn.last.fm/flatness/badges/lastfm_red.gif> ;
4
5    gr:hasISICv4 "5920"^^xsd:string ;
6    gr:hasNAICS "512220"^^xsd:string ;
7    gr:legalName "SLast.fm Ltd."^^xsd:string ;
8    gr:taxID "830 2738 46"^^xsd:string ;
9
10   vcard:hasAddress
11     [ a vcard:Work ;
12       vcard:country-name "UK"@en ] .
```

Listing 2. Description of the business entity providing the S-LastFM service

---

[11] http://linked-usdl.org/ns/usdl-business-roles.
[12] The prefixes :gr, :dcterms, :foaf, and :vcard refer to relevant vocabularies such as GoodRelations and Dublin Core.

The extract from Listing 1 also defines two interaction points ip_Advertise and ip_Artist_GetInfo for the service service_SLastFM. An interaction point (usdl:InteractionPoint) represents an actual step in performing the operations made available by a service. On a personal level, an interaction point can model that consumer and provider meet in person to exchange service parameters or resources involved in the service delivery (e.g., documents that are processed by the provider). On a technical level, this can translate into calling a web service operation. An interaction point can be initiated by the consumer or the provider.

Listing 3 describes the interaction point ip_Advertise which enables customers to book advertising campaigns and inquire about rates and specs. Interaction points define four main pieces of information:

- The communication channels that customers or applications can use to interact with a service.
- The entities that are involved during the interaction.
- The resources that are needed for an interaction.
- The resources that are generated from an interaction.

Communication channels are additionally characterized by their interaction type. Linked USDL provides two reference taxonomies covering the main modes (e.g., automated, semi-automated, and manual) and the interaction space (e.g., on-site and remote).

The specification describes how customers can ask for information to advertise a campaign with S-LastFM. This can be done by using traditional mail, a telephone, or email. All the communication channels require a manual (usdl-it:manual) and remote (usdl-it:remote) interaction. This means that humans, not software applications, will be involved in the interaction.

The example also indicates the role of the two entities that will interact (lines 29–39): both will be participants. This information is represented using the class usdl:EntityInteraction which links interaction points to business entity types (e.g., provider, intermediary, and consumer), and the role they play within the interaction (e.g., initiator, mediator, and receiver).

```
1  :ip_Advertise a usdl:InteractionPoint ;
2     dcterms:title "S-LastFM Advertisement"@en ;
3     dcterms:description "If you are interested in booking a campaign,
          seeing our full rates and specs, please send us the details of
          your campaign and we will be in~touch."@en ;
4
5     usdl:hasCommunicationChannel [
6        a usdl:CommunicationChannel ;
7        vcard:country-name "UK";
8        vcard:locality "London";
9        vcard:postal-code "SE1 0NZ";
10       vcard:street-address "Last.fm Ltd., 5-11 Lavington Street" ;
11       usdl:hasInteractionType usdl-it:manual ;
12       usdl:hasInteractionType usdl-it:remote
13    ];
```

```
14
15    usdl:hasCommunicationChannel [
16      a usdl:CommunicationChannel ;
17      vcard:telephone "tel:+61755555555" ;
18      usdl:hasInteractionType usdl-it:manual ;
19      usdl:hasInteractionType usdl-it:remote
20    ];
21
22    usdl:hasCommunicationChannel [
23      a usdl:CommunicationChannel ;
24      vcard:hasEmail <mailto:advertise@slast.fm> ;
25      usdl:hasInteractionType usdl-it:manual ;
26      usdl:hasInteractionType usdl-it:remote
27    ];
28
29    usdl:hasEntityInteraction [
30      a usdl:EntityInteraction ;
31      usdl:withBusinessRole usdl-br:provider ;
32      usdl:withInteractionRole usdl-ir:participant
33    ];
34
35    usdl:hasEntityInteraction [
36      a usdl:EntityInteraction ;
37      usdl:withBusinessRole usdl-br:customer ;
38      usdl:withInteractionRole usdl-ir:participant
39    ];
40
41    usdl:receives dbpedia:Advertising ;
42    usdl:yields dbpedia:Contract .
```

Listing 3. An interaction point involving human interaction

Listing 3 shows that the interaction point receives (`usdl:receives`) and yields (`usdl:yields`) resources (lines 41–42). Receives is the input required and yields corresponds to the outcome yielded by an interaction point. The example shows that the interaction point ip_Advertise receives an `dbpedia:Advertising` and yields a `dbpedia:Contract`. Naturally, other computer-processable data sources such as freebase.com can be used.

While the previous example of an interaction point involved only human participants, the example from Listing 4 illustrates a fully automated interaction which does not require human intervention. Linked USDL covers the most widely used human-based communication channels (e.g., email, phone, and mail) by means of vCard (a standard for electronic contact details), and application-driven channels (e.g., SOAP and REST Web services) by relying on the Minimal Service Model (MSM).

```
1  :ip_Artist_GetInfo a usdl:InteractionPoint ;
2      dcterms:title "Artist metadata"@en ;
3      dcterms:description "Get the metadata for an artist. Includes
           biography, truncated at 300 characters."@en ;
4
5      usdl:hasCommunicationChannel  :ArtistGetInfo ;
6
7      usdl:hasEntityInteraction  :ei_provider ;
8      usdl:hasEntityInteraction  :ei_customer ;
9
10     usdl:receives dbpedia:Artist ;
11     usdl:receives dbpedia:Software_license_server ;
12     usdl:yields dbpedia:Record_software .
13
14 :ei_provider a usdl:EntityInteraction ;
15     usdl:withBusinessRole usdl-br:provider ;
16     usdl:withInteractionRole usdl-ir:participant .
17
18 :ei_customer a usdl:EntityInteraction ;
19         usdl:withBusinessRole usdl-br:consumer ;
20         usdl:withInteractionRole usdl-ir:initiator ;
21         usdl:withInteractionRole usdl-ir:receiver .
```

Listing 4. An interaction point for an application-driven interaction

The first interaction point ip_Advertise established a remote communication channel between the provider and the customer. The interaction is manual from both sides of the channel. Nonetheless, the interaction point ip_Artist_GetInfo shown in Listing 4 is different: it is automated. This means that in both sides of the communication channel, applications will be involved during service provisioning by exchanging data. This requires a well-defined programming interface which must be understood by applications.

A usdl:ServiceOffering is an offering made by a gr:BusinessEntity of one or more usdl:Service to customers. An offering usually associates a price, legal terms of use, and service level agreements with a service. In other words, it makes a service a tradable entity. Listing 5 illustrates an offering named offering_SLastFM for the service service_SLastFM (Lines 1 and 10). A service offering may have limited validity over geographical regions or time. The offering adds various pieces of information such as temporal validity, eligible regions, and accepted payment methods (Lines 2-9).

```
1 :offering_SLastFM a usdl:ServiceOffering ;
2     gr:validFrom "2014-01-17T09:30:10Z"^^xsd:dateTime ;
3     gr:eligibleRegions "DE"^^xsd:string, "US-CA"^^xsd:string ;
4     gr:acceptedPaymentMethods gr:VISA, gr:ByBankTransferInAdvance ;
5     gr:eligibleDuration [
6         a gr:QuantitativeValue ;
7         gr:hasValueInteger "1"^^xsd:int ;
8         gr:hasUnitOfMeasurement "MON"^^xsd:string
```

```
9     ] ;
10    usdl:includes :service_SLastFM ;
11
12    usdl:legal :legal_SLastFM ;
13    usdl:price :price_SLastFM .
```

Listing 5. A concrete offering of a service

Finally, the last part of the example indicates that the classes `legal_SLastFM` and `price_SLastFM` describe the legal aspects and the price of the S-LastFM service, respectively (lines 12–13).

6 Related Work

In the past, schemas have been explored to describe (web) services. For example, WSDL, a W3C standard, focused on describing technical aspects of web services such as interaction interface and protocols. Since WSDL was essentially a specification for the syntax to describe services it was insufficient, the accuracy of service search algorithms was inadequate, especially at a global scale. Therefore, there was research streams towards the semantic representation of web services. Service descriptions were annotated with semantics to improve not only search but also composability and integration. As a result, new description languages, such as OWL-S [13], Semantic Annotation for WSDL (i.e., SAWSDL) [11], and WSMO [16], were proposed. The research has only tackled the semantic enrichment of function-based services, such as WSDL and REST, by using domain knowledge describing mainly technical interfaces.

In fact, legal aspects, pricing models, and service levels are all elements which need to be explicitly described when dealing with cloud services. Therefore, efforts were redirected to the development of new languages to capture business and operational perspectives beside the technical one. USDL [6] and Linked USDL [15] are probably the most comprehensive attempts.

The most notable effort able to represent and reason about business models, services, and value networks is the e^3 family of ontologies which includes the e^3service and e^3value ontologies [1,9]. This research has, however, not been much concerned with the computational and operational perspectives covering for instance the actual interaction with services. Likewise, the technical issues related to enabling a Web-scale deployment and adoption of these solutions were not core to this work. GoodRelations [10] (GR) on the contrary is a popular vocabulary for describing semantically products and offerings. Although GR originally aimed to support both services and products, it is mostly centred on products to the detriment of its coverage for modelling services, leaving aside for instance the coverage of modes of interaction, or the support for value chains.

7 Conclusion

Services and service systems, such as cloud services and digital government services, are showing increasing interests from both academia and industry. Among the many aspects which still require to be studied, such as service innovation, design, analytics, optimization, and economics, service description is one of the most pressing and critical components since it is a keystone supporting a web of tradable services.

While several service description languages have been developed over the past 10 years to model software-based service descriptions, such as WSDL, OWL-S, SAWSDL, e^3service, and e^3value ontologies, a language that also covers business and interaction aspects is missing. This paper summarizes our efforts to create USDL and, more recently, Linked USDL, a family of languages providing a comprehensive view on services to be used by providers, brokers, and consumers when searching, evaluating, and selecting services.

References

1. Akkermans, H., Baida, Z., Gordijn, J., Peña, N., et al.: Value webs: ontology-based bundling of real-world services. IEEE Intell. Syst. **19**(4), 57–66 (2004)
2. Barbero, M., Jouault, F., Gray, J., Bézivin, J.: A practical approach to model extension. In: Akehurst, D.H., Vogel, R., Paige, R.F. (eds.) ECMDA-FA. LNCS, vol. 4530, pp. 32–42. Springer, Heidelberg (2007)
3. Barros, A., Oberle, D.: Handbook of Service Description: USDL and Its Methods. Springer, New York (2012)
4. Bizer, C., Heath, T., Berners-Lee, T.: Linked data - the story so far. Int. J. Semant. Web Inf. Syst. **4**(2), 1–22 (2009)
5. BMWi. The standardisation environment for cloud computing. Technical report, Germany Federal Ministry of Economics and Technology, February 2012
6. Cardoso, J., Barros, A., May, N., Kylau, U.: Towards a unified service description language for the internet of services: Requirements and first developments. In: IEEE International Conference on Services Computing (SCC), pp. 602–609, July 2010
7. Cardoso, J., Winkler, M., Voigt, K.: A service description language for the internet of services. In: International Symposium on Services Science (ISSS'09) (2009)
8. Geraci, A.: IEEE Standard Computer Dictionary: Compilation of IEEE Standard Computer Glossaries. IEEE Press, Piscataway (1991)
9. Gordijn, J., Eric, Y.: e-service design using i* and e3value modeling. IEEE Softw. **23**, 26–33 (2006)
10. Hepp, M.: GoodRelations: an ontology for describing products and services offers on the web. In: Gangemi, A., Euzenat, J. (eds.) EKAW 2008. LNCS (LNAI), vol. 5268, pp. 329–346. Springer, Heidelberg (2008)
11. Kopecky, J., Vitvar, T., Bournez, C., Farrell, J.: SAWSDL: semantic annotations for WSDL and XML schema. IEEE Internet Comput. **11**(6), 60–67 (2007)
12. Lenzerini, M.: Data integration: a theoretical perspective. In: Proceedings of the 21st Symposium on Principles of Database Systems, pp. 233–246. ACM (2002)
13. Martin, D., Burstein, M., Hobbs, J., Lassila, O., McDermott, D., et al.: OWL-S: Semantic markup for web services. W3C Member submission, 22, 2007–04 (2004)
14. Paskin, N.: Toward unique identifiers. Proc. IEEE **87**(7), 1208–1227 (1999)
15. Pedrinaci, C., Cardoso, J., Leidig, T.: Linked USDL: a vocabulary for web-scale service trading. In: Presutti, V., d'Amato, C., Gandon, F., d'Aquin, M., Staab, S., Tordai, A. (eds.) ESWC 2014. LNCS, vol. 8465, pp. 68–82. Springer, Heidelberg (2014)
16. Pedrinaci, C., Domingue, J., Sheth, A.: Semantic web services. In: Handbook on Semantic Web Technologies. Semantic Web Applications, vol. 2. Springer, New York (2010)

An Agile BPM System for Knowledge-Based Service Organizations

José António Faria^(✉) and Henriqueta Nóvoa

Faculdade de Engenharia, Universidade do Porto, Rua Dr. Roberto Frias,
4200-465 Porto, Portugal
`{jfaria,hnovoa}@fe.up.pt`

Abstract. This paper presents a business process management (BPM) system aimed at knowledge-based service organizations. The core activity of these organizations consists on the delivery of high-valued services tailored to each customer. When compared to product-based organizations, service organizations have more dynamic and diversified business portfolios and business processes, due to the need to adapt to evolving customer needs. The efficiency of business process management (BPM) solutions is widely recognised as far as high volume standardized processes are concerned, but the unsuitability of these systems to handle customizable service requests is also widely acknowledged. With this in mind, a new BPM platform, hereafter referred to as the soBPM platform, was designed and deployed. This platform is intended to offer a higher degree of flexibility, both at process design-time and process run-time. The platform implements a soft-automation process management approach that will be discussed in the first part of the paper. Then, the deployment of the platform at the Shared Service Center of a large University will be presented.

Keywords: Business process management · Knowledge based services · Adaptive and emergent processes

1 Introduction

This paper presents a business process management system aimed at knowledge-based service organizations (KBSO) that was primarily designed to manage the activity of a newly created Shared Service Center (SSC) of a large public University. Every day the Center has to handle a large number of requests coming from the academic community and addressed to one of its main activity areas.

A large part of the requests are served by routine procedures supported by the automatized workflow systems embedded in the transactional information system of the University. However, as it will be discussed in Sect. 5, due to the diversity and heterogeneity of the requests, a significant part of the processes dealt by the Center can hardly be classified as routine work, a situation common to all knowledge-based service organizations. Some authors [1, 2] introduced the concept of knowledge work to differentiate it from traditional administrative work, the first target of traditional BPM solutions.

The real challenge for a service organization such the SSC is to manage effectively business processes whose course of action depends on multiple factors that can't be fully anticipated at process design time, and, at the same time, to ensure a strict compliance to the mandatory constraints imposed by internal and external regulation.

The paper starts by introducing the key features of knowledge-based service organizations in Sect. 1, highlighting the major differences from product-oriented organizations. In Sect. 2, the shortcomings of standard BPM approaches for service organizations are discussed, whereas in Sect. 3 the conceptual framework of the soBPM platforms is introduced, highlighting its key features when compared to standard BPM platforms. Section 4 introduces the organization where soBPM was firstly implemented: the Shared Service Center of a large university, as well as the reasoning for the adoption of a human-based flexible process management system. Section 5 introduces the service life cycle at the Center and shows how it is supported by the soBPM system. Finally, the results achieved so far with this new approach of soBPM at this shared service's Center and the envisioned developments are discussed.

2 Knowledge-Based Service Organizations

Knowledge-based intensive services is not a straightforward concept, as different researchers use different terms [2]. Typical examples of KBSO are companies providing technical services, computer and IT services, research and development services, patent offices, legal and economic consulting, training, education and recruiting services or education and recruiting services.

KBSO are guided by different principles and have different characteristics than more traditional product-oriented companies. In order to design a process management platform targeted at KBSO, it is important to have in mind their distinguishing characteristics [3], namely, (i) a greater focus on the quality of service as the paramount factor for business effectiveness; (ii) a closer relation with the stakeholders all along the value creation processes; (iii) a higher dynamics of the service portfolio; (iv) a larger number of service variants and (v) more flexible internal procedures in order to be able to accommodate specific requirements for each request.

A fundamental dimension of the quality of service in a KBSO is the ability to cope with the specific needs, expectations and preferences of the clients, which requires a higher flexibility, not only at service delivery, but all along the value creation chain. This means that it may not be enough to introduce local changes and adaptations in the normal flow of the processes, but the inner structure of a process, handling a particular service request at a given time, may have to be reshaped according to the specific needs of the request. This requirement can only be attained in organisations with empowered workers, the cornerstone of every knowledge-based work system [1].

From a process management perspective, it can be pointed out that a KBSO needs a deeper structural flexibility of the process model, as opposed to local flexibility as discussed in [4].

3 The Standard BPM Approach

Business process management systems (BPMS) have been recognized as a substantial extension to the legacy of workflow management systems (WFMS) [3]. A standard

BPM implementation normally seeks the improvement of organizational efficiency through a combination of three main principles: process normalization, process formalization and process automation.

Process normalization is based on the assumption that a standard and optimized process flow can be derived from a suitable business analysis. Process formalization assumes that it is possible to externalize into a formal model the knowledge required to manage a process. Finally, process automation draws on the idea that task enactment, assignment, routing and control may be performed automatically by a computer application based on such formal process model. It is also assumed that the combination of these three elements is the cornerstone to leverage process efficiency and process controllability, thus improving dramatically organizational performance.

The effectiveness of this approach in unquestionable as far as high-volume processes are concerned. However, there are many situations in which the above principles may not apply. When a business process is expected to handle highly customizable requests, it may not be feasible to accommodate the full complexity of the process in the computer application. Very likely, the model that is actually implemented will be a rather simplified version of reality. As stated by [3], whereas one fundamental aspect of BPMS and its predecessor WFMS, is to provide control and coordination of business activities, there is another equally demanding aspect of ensuring that the control does not prohibit the operational flexibility, to unacceptable levels.

In the end, the models resulting from a trade-off between conflicting requirements don't fit the actual needs of any request and offer a sub-optimal solution in all the situations.

Another usual difficulty relies on the fact that the course of action of a knowledge-based process always depends on idiosyncratic factors and on the judgement of the people involved which, in turn, depends on their knowledge and previous experience.

In [5] these processes are denoted as artful processes in the sense that there is an art to their execution that would be extremely difficult, if not impossible, to codify in an enterprise application.

For specialized knowledge based processes, such as those mentioned in [6], trying to capture all the relevant knowledge in a formal model may be a vain exercise because, (i) the process has many variants and so the final model would become too complex to be of practical interest, (ii) the organization is constantly evolving and so are its processes or, (iii) because a significant part of the knowledge engaged in the management of the process is intrinsically tacit.

As it is not possible to develop a formal model holding all the management rules, process automation is no longer viable, and a different approach has to be devised. For example, Adams [7] has implemented an approach for dynamic flexibility and evolution in workflows, using a Service Oriented Architecture, through the support of flexible work practices.

In fact, the lack of flexibility of the standard BPM solutions as far as knowledge based processes are concerned, is widely recognized and documented in the technical literature [8], limiting its deployment in some domains. According to Stavenko [9], the shortcomings of standard BPM solutions are the models' inherent lag from the practice, unsuitability for dynamically changing and multi-version processes, a gap between the company's IT services and managers and employees, and, hence, a failure to account for the fact that processes in the company may often run (and do run) in a way that is completely different from what is reflected in the analyst's model.

Many strategies have been attempted to bring flexibility to BPM solutions as, for example [10], but it has become evident that there is no "one size fits all" solution, and that, depending on the application, different types of flexibility are needed [10]. For the most part, those attempts tried to enhance the modelling notations and workflow engines in order to handle more complex rules, but they resulted in complex modelling notations and execution engines having a limited practical interest [11, 12].

As discussed in the next section, a different approach was adopted in the soBPM platform.

4 The soBPM Approach

The soBPM platform retains the fundamental traits of process management, namely the focus on (i) client oriented value creation, (ii) end-to-end process management and (iii) process level performance assessment. However it diverges from standard BPM on the fact that it is not assumed that there is a predefined predictable formal model fully specifying the management rules susceptible of being automated through a computer application.

Instead of trying to externalize the knowledge about a process into a formal model, it is assumed that part of this knowledge is, and should remain, tacit, i.e. knowledge that lies in the mind of the experienced process managers. This approach may seem to be less effective than standard BPM. However, when flexibility and adaptability are the paramount factors, the additional management overhead is largely compensated by the significant increase on these attributes.

In order to understand the design of soBPM it is important to have in mind the different types of business processes, ranging from structured workflows to semi-structured and ad hoc business processes [9].

There are many definitions for business processes but here will be assumed: that a process consists on an ordered set of tasks that are executed after a trigger event with the intent of producing a valuable result to a client (in this definition, *client* should be understood in the broad sense of those interested in the result of the process). There are three main types of business processes compatible with this definition: predictable, adaptive and emergent, being critically important to understand their main features.

A predictable process is one such that the sequence of tasks is previously known in advance. The flow of the process may contain alternative paths, but the conditions that determine the actual path that the process follows are strictly defined at process design time.

However, as remarked in [5, 13], many processes do not posses such a deterministic behavior.

An adaptive process is a process where it is possible to identify a main flow of steps and tasks, but its actual execution is subject to many factors that impose changes and adaption of the process flow. Consider, for example, a hiring process. The major flow of the process will certainly be known and there will be some regulatory constraints that have to be respected. However, many aspects of the process (e.g., disclosure, procedures for the assessment and selection of the applicants) may be tailored depending on the particular circumstances of the processes at hand. For these processes, it is not feasible to represent in a model all the alternatives paths that the process might actually unfold. Typically, there will be a reference model that specifies the main course of action (e.g. phase, steps, the actors, deadlines, main alternative paths) and imposes some constrains. Then, during process execution, there will be a continuous adaptation of the process flow taking account the events that occur meanwhile [14, 15].

In an emergent process it is not even possible to identify a main flow. The next action is planned and, then, executed. As soon as it is completed, the next course of action will be decided.

In a predictable process, all the rules that govern its execution may be externalized into a formal process model and so these processes are prone to computerized automation. In an adaptive process, some parts of it might be automated, but full process automation would not be feasible. In an emergent process, the core management of the process should be handled by a human and just auxiliary functions, such as sending of notifications and alerts, may be automated.

It is important to highlight the fact that, although the above classification proves to be useful, there isn't a clear boundary between the different types of processes. For example, in a workflow application there is always room for human decision. However, the underlying paradigm puts the control of the process on the computer application whereas, in adaptive and emergent processes, the computer application plays a subsidiary role.

The following figure sketch the management model for the tree types of processes (Fig. 1). In a predictable process, the model of a process instance is a direct instantiation of the standard process model and the model does not change during process execution (Fig. 1a). In an adaptive process, the process model is a template that has to be configured for each case. Also, the model may change along the execution of processes, e.g., new tasks may be added to the process and other skipped (Fig. 1b). Finally, in an emergent process there isn't even a template for the process flow, so that once a new step is achieved, the next step is planned (Fig. 1c).

The following table (Table 1) summarizes some key features of the three process types.

Software vendors offer a wide array of tools targeted to the different types of processes: BPM suites and workflow management systems are widely used to manage predictable processes, case management systems are the effective solution for adaptive and knowledge-intensive business processes [1, 16] and, finally, open collaboration platforms providing services for task management, document sharing and messaging, may be an effective solution to handle emergent processes.

In a knowledge-based service organization the three types of processes will co-exist and the same knowledge worker may have to manage processes ranging from unstructured emergent processes to highly structured predictable processes. Thus being, the use of specialized tools to handle the different types of processes would not be an effective solution. Instead, the same management tool should be able to accommodate all the processes of the organization irrespectively of their nature.

When designing such overall management system, it is also important to notice that work management is just one of the three management dimensions that has to be

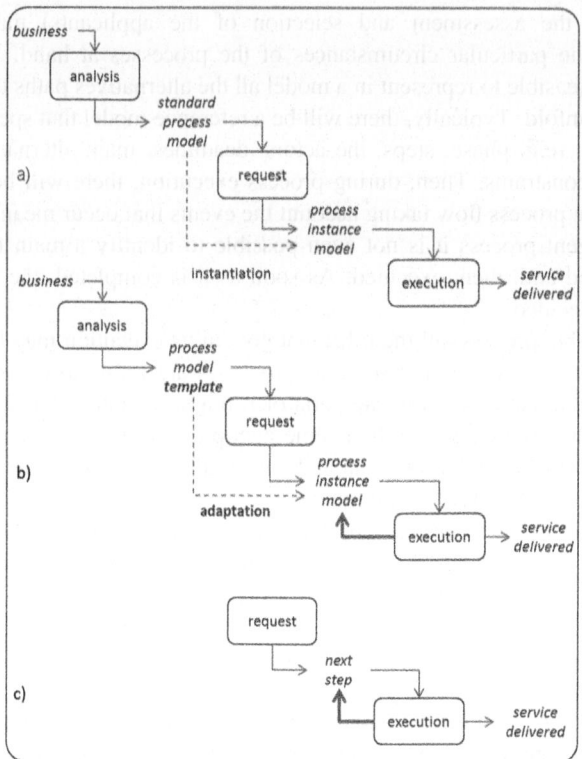

Fig. 1. Predictable, adaptive and emergent process models

Table 1. Process characteristics

	Predictive	Adaptive	Emergent
Process model	Drives execution	Provides guidance	N/A
Collaboration	Structured	Semi-structured	Ad hoc
Automation	Hard	Soft	Manual
Management system	BPM suites	Case management systems	Collaboration platforms (e.g. wiki's)

considered, the other two being the management of the information (documents and data) produced along the execution of the processes, and the management of the communication between the participants in the processes.

Work management deals with the normal assignment and control of tasks, due dates and plans. Within work management, two main levels should be considered: (1) the process level dealing with the orchestration of tasks within a process instance (this is the main target of any workflow application) and, (2) the overall work system level dealing with the overall management of the set of running processes in a particular moment.

When analyzing more closely the information management dimension, we find information with different levels of structure: from highly structured data, normally stored in databases, till unstructured information in office documents. The overall management system should be able to cope with such disparate types of information. Within this dimension we also have to consider reference documents (e.g. regulations, procedures, templates, work instructions) that are assigned to process types, as well as documents that are produced during the execution of each process instance.

The management of a process always involves the collaboration between different actors. In order to ensure process reliability, the communication between these different actors should be properly managed within the work management system and it may range from explicit messages to implicit communication through shared resources such as a dashboard or a task list.

In summary, an overall process management system of a knowledge-based service organization should address the management of work, information and communication, for the full range of processes identified, assuring the alignment with the collaboration and enterprise content management requirements, as discussed in [17].

5 Application Case

The soBPM was primarily developed to support the operation of the newly created SSC at the University of Porto. This section briefly introduces the University and explains why it was considered that a standard BPM solution would not fit the needs of SSC and why it was decided to engage in the development of the soBPM platform.

The University of Porto (UP) is a large institution, encompassing three campus in different regions of the city of Porto, housing 15 schools, and tens of research units [18]. All the 15 schools are internationally recognized by its peers but have very disparate backgrounds and history, so within the University there is a large heterogeneity in its processes and practices. The Rectory of the UP oversees this federate organization, balancing at every moment the righteous aspiration of autonomy of each of the schools, with the need to improve the overall efficiency of the University. Thus, the streamlining of the administrative processes is a critical and challenging issue for the University.

The mere existence of distributed services and different cultures at every single school, as well as the fact that laws and regulations are often being altered both by national and European authorities, heavily increases the complexity of management of the University and the effective implementation of improvement actions. Aware of this challenge, the University decided to create a new unit Shared Services Center (SSC) with the goal of improving the quality of services delivered to the academy, as well as reducing the costs associated with these functions. In order to overcome the natural resistance to change of the different schools, the new center had to quickly demonstrate its ability of providing superior quality services adapted to the specific needs of each school.

It was soon recognized that to accommodate this challenge it was crucial to develop an information system that could streamline transversal processes, supplying at any point in time all the required information to anyone involved in a particular process, irrespectively of its physical location. At SSC there is a large number of routine processes, highly standardized. These processes are supported by workflow applications embedded in the legacy information system of the University. This system provides access to all the relevant information of the institution, either of pedagogical, scientific, technical or administrative nature, as well as streamlines internal cooperation and collaboration with the academic and business communities outside UP [19]. This system actually supports several business processes of the University, such as all those related to the registration and grading of students, as well as the processes related to expenses and incomes. Nevertheless, it was quickly perceived that the traditional workflow engines embedded couldn´t cope with the heterogeneity of processes and cultures of the different schools, thus leading the University to the decision of developing the soBPM platform, for handling adaptive and emergent processes.

This means that, instead of putting a workflow engine coordinating the processes, as in traditional BPM, a human process manager will now be in charge of process coordination. The recognition of the need of having empowered workers or "information workers" for adaptive and emergent processes is widely referred in the literature [1, 20, 21]. Other authors have also referred to this shift as "the democratization of processes" [5]. This approach implies a much more demanding culture of service delivery, accountability and empowerment of the process managers, with a vision focused in the overall development of the organization. Information systems are a fundamental support tool, but the distinctive characteristic of this approach lies in the fact that people are at the center, orchestrating all the actors involved in the successful execution of the process. For each process type there is an indicative stream of tasks that is known a priori. However, during the execution of a particular instance of the process there are several factors that may intervene in the flow of events of that instance.

The soBPM platform includes a vast array of functionalities grouped on three main areas: work management, document management and communication management. In order to introduce these functionalities, the service life cycle implemented by the soBPM platform is detailed in the next section.

6 The Service Life Cycle

Figure 2 represents the three main phases of the service lifecycle at SCC together with the three main management functions supported by the soBPM platform.

The first stage of the lifecycle is the Service Request (Fig. 3). To enter his request, the user accesses the service catalog web page. This page exposes the services provided by the units of the SSC grouped in categories.

For each service, there is a fully customized web form (Fig. 4).

Once a new request is entered by a member of the academia, the next stages of the lifecycle is Scheduling. The new request is routed to the area manager. After validation, the manager may change the default deadlines for the process (which are configured for

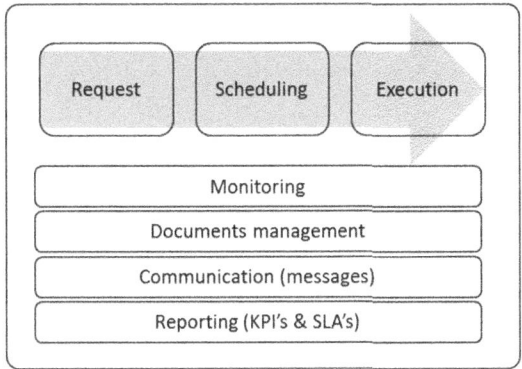

Fig. 2. The service life cycle

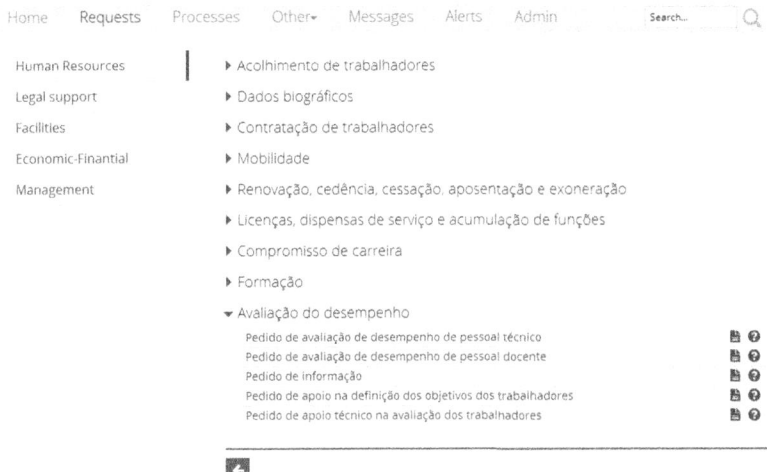

Fig. 3. Service catalog

each process type) and assign the process to an element of his staff. The nominee receives a notification and has explicitly to acknowledge his nomination as the process manager for that request. Doing it, he commits to handle the process end-to-end, to provide information at any time about the process status to all the interested parties, and do his best effort to ensure that the service is delivered within the planned deadlines and accordingly to the University regulations. Once the process is accepted, the requester receives a notification with the contacts of the process manager.

To help on the management of the process at hand, the soBPM platform instantiates a new checklist detailing the corresponding set of tasks and the milestones (Fig. 5). This checklist is a very useful tool that not only provides important guidance to the process manager, but also holds the current state of the process, acting as a log of the execution dates (start and end dates for each task are logged automatically, and the manager can also add ad hoc annotations).

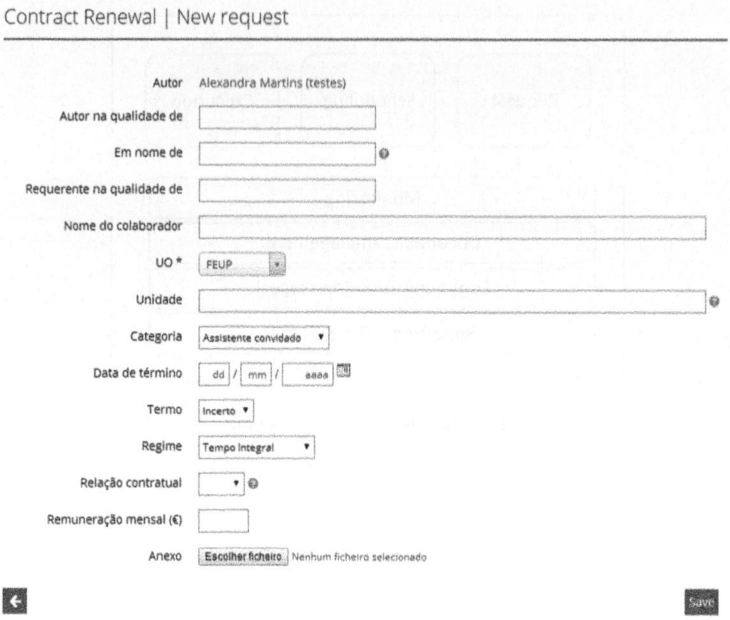

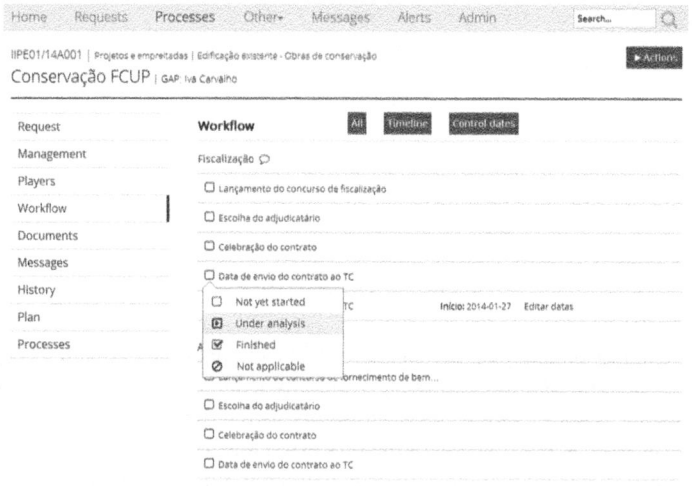

Fig. 4. Service web form

Fig. 5. Process checklist

The checklist is the main tool for the process manager. For the area manager, the main management tool is the process dashboard.

By accessing the dashboard, the area manager may monitor the current state of the tens of processes (sometimes more than one hundred) running in his area at any point in time. The dashboard highlights those that require immediate attention. The dashboard integrates a wide variety of tools (filtering, grouping, ordering and searching) offers a timeline view and highlights those processes that require immediate attention (Fig. 6). The dashboard also integrates a set of functionalities designed to improve its usability and effectiveness as a work management tool, namely, automatic alerts on close deadlines (yellow) or a delayed deadline (red); ad hoc alerts created by the users; automatic alerts on message delays; a detailed view of the pending task for each process; a in-place summary of the process status.

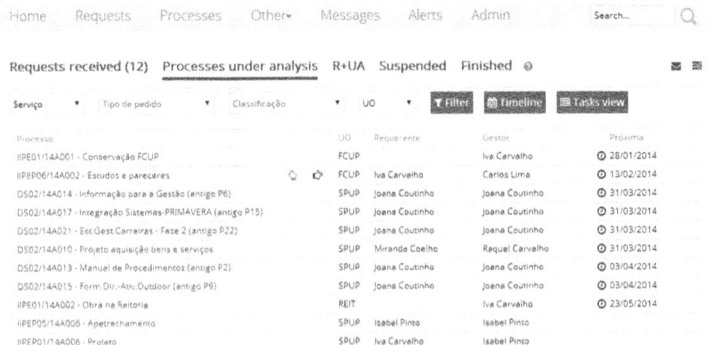

Fig. 6. Process dashboard

The data collected during the execution of a processes is registered in the checklists. Afterwards, it is consolidated in activity reports containing and key performance indicators and service level agreements (KTI's & SLA's). These activity reports show in tabular and graphical format the volume of activity, including performance indicators that allow a quick assessment of the fulfillment of the service level agreements (Fig. 7).

6.1 Document and Communication Management

The soBPM platform also integrates a document management system. For each process instance, a new dossier is instantiated from a template configured for the process type. The template defines the internal folder structure and the models for the documents that are expected to be produced along the execution of the process. Depending on their permissions, users may change the structure of the dossier, upload and delete documents, for example. The system also handles managed document that have a tighter access and version control. These documents inherit the attributes of the enclosing process instance and are searchable based on standard metadata such as the process type, the document type, the author and the date, for example.

It was recognized the importance of maintaining all the stream of messages related to one process easily and quickly accessible, which was quite difficult to accomplish in traditional email systems. The soBPM platform includes an embedded messaging system so that the messages exchanged in the context of a process instance are automatically assigned to that instance (Fig. 8).

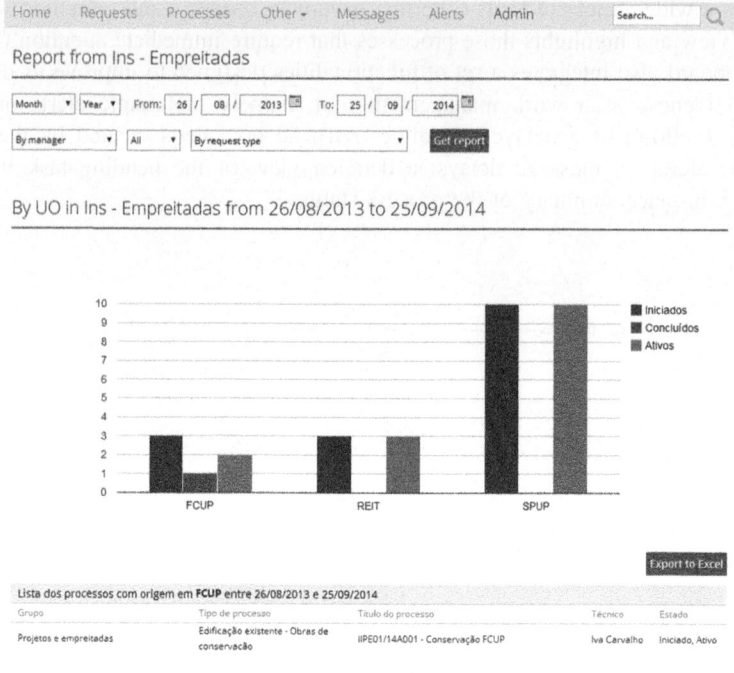

Fig. 7. Automatic reporting example

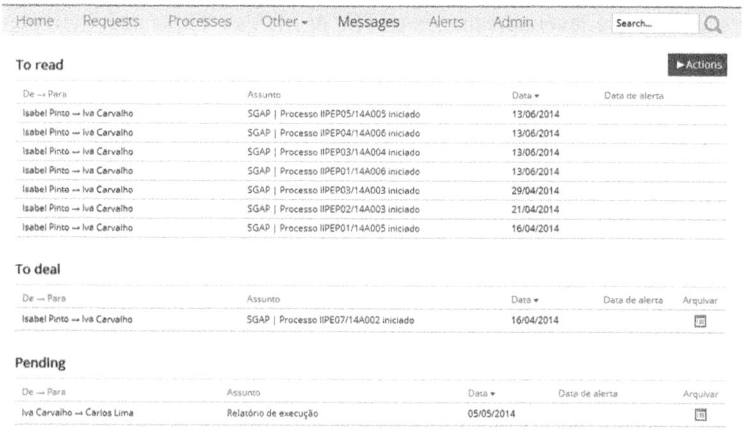

Fig. 8. Messaging System

The stream of messages within a process is organized in talks (or threads). Each talk conveys a sequence of messages relating to a particular topic. When sending a new message, the user may specify an expected date to receive an answer. This way, the sent message will remain in a pending folder of the sender. If he got the answer within the expected due time, the sent message is removed from the pending folder and the incoming message will appear at the inbox folder; otherwise, an automatic alert will be generated. This is a very useful feature that gathers process control and process log in the same user interface. Much as managed documents, messages are always sent within the context of a process from which they inherit the main attributes, i.e. they may be searched based on standard metadata.

7 Conclusions

In the first part of the paper, it was claimed that a distinctive characteristic of a service oriented organization is the ability to handle specific user requirements. In such organizations, a large part of the business processes will be either adaptive or emergent. As discussed in the paper, this statement is particularly true for the Shared Service Center of the University of Porto due to the diversity and dynamics of its procedures.

The flexibility embedded in the *soBPM* platform was an essential factor to achieve a successful implementation of a process based management system. In order to achieve it, a semi-formal and human–interpretable business process approach was adopted, instead of a formal and machine interpretable workflow, as in conventional BPM. For knowledge based organizations, this soft automation approach proves to be more effective not only at the development and maintenance stage, but also at the execution stage. This approach was not devised as an intermediate step towards full automated processes, but as the most effective way to address the righteous balance between the agility required to adapt to specific user requests and the efficiency on the usage of the available resources.

Any process management application may be seen as tool for structured collaboration. In a conventional BPM application, collaboration is managed by the computer application according to the rules pre-defined in the process model. Being much more flexible and simplifying the communication between the participants in a process, the *soBPM* platform eases collaboration between service providers (staff) and service requestors (academia members) and boosts value co-creation, while safeguarding the hard organizational constraints imposed by law and regulations.

In knowledge-based service organizations, both service portfolios and business processes are highly dynamic, so their management system have to be highly reconfigurable. Some of the features of the soBPM platform that were designed according to this key requirement are now summarized:

- The entries and the web forms of the service catalogue are fully customizable so that new services may promptly be added to the catalogue;
- The items in the checklist are also fully customizable for each process type. Managers may specify reference delays for each task, or group of tasks, that as a basis for setting-up and assess the service level agreements;
- It is possible to an area manager to fine tune the permissions assigned to each member of his staff according to his seniority (uploading and updating documents, introduce or skip tasks, etc.). It is possible to define area level access permissions (that apply to all the processes and to all the staff of a given area) and process level permissions, where authorized users can grant permissions on a process instance basis;

- For each process type, it is also possible to define a template for the document dossier, as well as specify pre-defined messages and assign them to a process type or to specific tasks. These messages may be sent automatically or may require an explicit user confirmation.

All these features were essential to achieve a successful implementation of a process oriented management system at the SSC.

Acknowledgments. The authors would like to thank Nuno Almeida, Miguel Fernandes for their invaluable work in developing the soBPM platform.

References

1. Swenson, K.D.: Mastering the Unpredictable: How Adaptative Case Management Will Revolutionize the Way that Knowledge Workers Get Things Done, p. 337. Meghan-Kiffer Press, Tampa (2010)
2. Kemppilä, S., Mettänen, P.: Innovations in knowledge intensive services. In: The 5th International CINet Conference, Sydney, Australia, 22–25 Sept 2004
3. Lu, R., Sadiq, S., Governatori, G.: On managing business processes variants. Data Knowl. Eng. **68**(7), 642–664 (2009)
4. Weber, B., Reichert, M., Rinderle-Ma, S.: Change patterns and change support features - enhancing flexibility in process-aware information systems. Data Knowl. Eng. **66**, 438–466 (2008)
5. Hill, C., Yates, R., Jones, C., Kogan, S.L.: Beyond predictable workflows: enhancing productivity in artful business processes. IBM Syst. J. **45**(4), 663–682 (2006)
6. Bider, I.: State-oriented business process modeling: principles, theory and practice. Royal Institute of Technology and Stockholm University (2004)
7. Adams, M., Hofstede, A.H.M., Edmond, D., van der Aalst, W.M.P.: Implementing dynamic flexibility in workflows using worklets (2006)
8. Mangan, P., Sadiq, S.: On building workflow models for flexible processes. J. Aust. Comput. Sci. Commun. **24**(2), 103–109 (2002)
9. Stavenko, Y., Kazantsev, N., Gromoff, A.: Business process model reasoning: from workflow to case management. Procedia Technol. **9**, 806–811 (2013)
10. van der Aalst, W.M.P., Adams, M., ter Hofstede, A.H.M., Pesic, M., Schonenberg, H.: Flexibility as a service. In: Chen, L., Liu, C., Liu, Q., Deng, K. (eds.) DASFAA 2009. LNCS, vol. 5667, pp. 319–333. Springer, Heidelberg (2009)
11. Mangan, P.J., Sadiq, S.: A constraint specification approach to building flexible workflows. J. Res. Pract. Inf. Technol. **35**(1), 21–39 (2003)
12. Kammer, P.J., Bolcer, G.A., Taylor, R.N., Hitomi, A.S., Bergman, M.: Techniques for supporting dynamic and adaptive workflow. Comput. Support. Coop. Work **9**(3–4), 269–292 (2000)
13. Alter, S.: Service system fundamentals: work system, value chain, and life cycle. IBM Syst. J. **47**(1), 71–85 (2008)
14. Sadiq, S.W., Orlowska, M.E., Sadiq, W.: Specification and validation of process constraints for flexible workflows. Inf. Syst. **30**(5), 349–378 (2005)
15. Pesic, M., Schonenberg, H., van der Aalst, W.M.P.: DECLARE: full support for loosely-structured processes. In: 11th IEEE International Enterprise Distributed Object Computing Conference (EDOC 2007), pp. 287–287 (2007)

16. van der Aalst, W.M.P., Weske, M., Grünbauer, D.: Case handling: a new paradigm for business process support. Data Knowl. Eng. **53**(2), 129–162 (2005)
17. Brocke, J.V., Becker, J., Braccini, A.M., Butleris, R., Hofreiter, B., Kapočius, K., de Marco, M., Schmidt, G., Seidel, S., Simons, A., Skopal, T., Stein, A., Stieglitz, S., Suomi, R., Vossen, G., Winter, R., Wrycza, S.: Current and future issues in BPM research: a European perspective from the ERCIS meeting 2010. Commun. Assoc. Inf. Syst. **28**(1), 393–414 (2010)
18. University of Porto: Universidade do Porto (2014). http://www.up.pt [Online]
19. TIC: SIGARRA - information system for the aggregated management of resources and academic records (2014). https://sigarra.up.pt/up/en/WEB_BASE.GERA_PAGINA?P_pagina=2418 [Online]
20. Swenson, K.: Workflow for the information worker. In: Fischer, L. (ed.) Workflow Handbook 2001. Workflow Management Coalition, Future Strategies Inc., Lighthouse Point (2000)
21. Malhotra, Y.: Integrating knowledge management technologies in organizational business processes: getting real time enterprises to deliver real business performance. J. Knowl. Manag. **9**(1), 7–28 (2005)

A SoaML Approach for Derivation of a Process-Oriented Logical Architecture from Use Cases

Carlos E. Salgado[1]([✉]), Juliana Teixeira[1], Nuno Santos[1],
Ricardo J. Machado[1], and Rita S.P. Maciel[2]

[1] Centro ALGORITMI, Universidade do Minho, Guimarães, Portugal
carlos.salgado@algoritmi.uminho.pt,
{juliana.teixeira,nuno.santos}@ccg.pt,
rmac@dsi.uminho.pt
[2] DCC, Universidade Federal da Bahia, Salvador, Brazil
ritasuzana@dcc.ufba.br

Abstract. Designing logical architectures for cloud computing environments can be a complex endeavor, moreover when facing ill-defined contexts or insufficient inputs to requirements elicitation. Existing solutions are no longer enough to embrace challenges brought by complex scenarios and multi-stakeholder realities, as in Ambient Assisted Living ecosystems. As new concepts and cross-domain solutions emerge, these problems are tackled by connecting evermore the world of requirements and architectures, of business and technology, through service-oriented approaches. This due, we propose to extend the Four-Step-Rule-Set (4SRS) method, which has proven successful in generating a proper candidate logical architecture for an information system in ill-defined contexts, to a Service-Oriented Architecture approach for greater business integration, flexibility, and agility, by using the SoaML language. We present the result of a demonstration project, based in an industrial live setting where the 4SRS-SoaML reshaped method was applied, by generating the architectural participants, and respective channels of services and requests.

Keywords: Service-Oriented architectures · Logical architectures · Requirements elicitation · Componentization · Ambient assisted living

1 Introduction

As our digital life and work increases the need for more specific services, nowadays cloud oriented, the pressure is on for software architectures to lead the development of these services. However, designing logical architectures for cloud computing environments can be a complex endeavor, moreover when facing ill-defined contexts or insufficient inputs to requirements elicitation.

Building systems with well-defined component interfaces, ready for effective reuse and maintenance, requires a robust and realistic development process, where both requirements engineers and system architects work concurrently and iteratively to describe and align the artifacts they produce. In fact, candidate architectures constrain designers from meeting particular requirements and the choice of requirements influence the architecture that designers select or develop, in an iterative process that produces progressively more detailed requirements and design specifications [1].

Also, continued research on service-oriented technologies and management brings new conceptual frameworks and theoretical perspectives to firms that adopt and implement them, helping to address the major challenges faced with technology, information and strategy. Recent growing research supports companies on delivering new, more flexible business processes that harness the value of the services approach from a customer's perspective, needed to leverage technology in response for greater business integration, flexibility and agility [2].

The Four-Step-Rule-Set (4SRS) method has proven successful in generating a proper candidate logical architecture, in ill-defined contexts and with multiple stakeholders [3], by eliciting and managing requirements from a process-perspective in an Ambient Assisted Living (AAL) project. Nevertheless it failed to provide a more clear business and strategic view of the system, with its large, complex architecture and oversimplified architectural elements.

Due to the increased complexity and challenges posed by new realities and the emergence of more robust, cross-domain, solutions, we felt the need to improve the 4SRS method in order to answer these issues. In this sense, our proposal is to extend the 4SRS method by adapting its steps while taking advantage of the Service oriented architecture Modeling Language (SoaML) concepts, in order to build a stronger, Business-Information System/Technology (IS/IT) aligned solution.

We tested the new method on a demonstration project, in an AAL industrial live setting, where the method was applied by generating the architectural participants and respective channels of services and requests, and present its results comparatively to a previous existing solution.

This paper follows with related research on the topics of this work, and in Sect. 3 we present the description of the changes proposed in the steps involved in the new 4SRS-SoaML method, highlighting the differences to the conventional approach. In Sect. 4, a demonstration of the proposed method, applied in an AAL project is presented and, in Sect. 5, a brief analysis on the ongoing research and preliminary results obtained is performed. Finally, some conclusions are drawn for this work.

2 Related Research

In this section, we present research on the topics of Service-Oriented Computing (SOC) and Service-Oriented Architectures (SOA), where related or with relevance to the use of the Object Management Group (OMG) SoaML notation, and Business Process Management (BPM). Also, some notes regarding the conventional 4SRS method are presented for reader positioning.

2.1 Services on Business and Information Systems

Service support can help in reducing the gap between Business and IS/IT, ensuring a good connection and mapping between models of both sides, thus easing the communication and understanding between them. As the concepts of SOA apply both to business and system architectures, they can help the business and system stakeholders to align their business requirements and the IS/IT architecture implementations.

Attesting this, works by Delgado [4] and Elvesaeter [5] provide solutions for the service oriented development of business processes, relying on the SOA paradigm closeness to business models while integrating concepts, methodologies and tools that combine the application of SOC and Model-Driven Development (MDD) paradigms to support BPM. These last through the use of OMG 'standards' to model business processes and services, such as BPMN [6] and SoaML [7].

Applying SOC and BPM paradigms in conjunction is an important but not trivial step to take, involving different visions of business and technological challenges, and demanding a service oriented methodology for the derivation of software services from business process models [8]. Moreover, when in a collaborative context, the integration of different partners deeply depends on the ability to use a collaborative architecture to interact efficiently and to help bridge the requirements gap between the business analyst and the IS/IT analyst developer levels. Using business models to design a logical model of a solution is an essential step to reach a collaborative solution and support practices in the development of systems integration [9].

A model-driven approach for direct generation of services from business processes provides several advantages such as reuse of the knowledge embedded in the correspondences defined between the involved metamodels and traceability between their elements, allowing for better Business-IS/IT alignment. The realization of business processes by means of services becomes more important, since it is common for participants to collaborate within an organization. In this context, transformations to generate SoaML service models from use cases models are required in order to obtain service-oriented systems to realize business processes. Delgado [10] presents a proposal to define a framework for the Model-Driven specification of Software Architectures, which uses the concepts behind Service-Orientation for its definition.

Another solution to the problem of architecting the existing gap between the high-level configuration of a software system, describing business entities and relationships required by a software solution, and its low-level representation, in which the technological aspects determine the final shape of the system, is presented by López-Sanz [11]. Here, the definition of a framework for the Model-Driven specification of Software Architectures, using concepts behind Service-Orientation for its definition, showed a tendency towards the use of a hybrid approach as the most suitable choice, following a 'pure' UML-based approach for architecture specification where SoaML is worth mentioning.

2.2 Four-Step-Rule-Set (4SRS) Method

The conventional 4SRS method, included in the larger V-Model method [3], is organized in four steps to transform use cases (UC) into architecture elements (AE), namely: **Step 1, AE creation**; **Step 2, AE elimination**; **Step 3, AE packaging & aggregation**; and **Step 4, AE association**. AE refers to the pieces from which the final logical architecture (LA) can be built, it is used to distinguish these artifacts from the components, objects or modules used in other contexts, like in UML structure diagrams.

The 4SRS method takes as input a set of leaf UC in the problem space, describing the requirements for the processes that tackle the initial problem, which are then refined trough successive 4SRS iterations (by recurring to tabular transformations), producing progressively more detailed requirements and a design specification, in the form of a LA representation of the system, representing the intended cloud concerns of the involved business and technological stakeholders.

These tabular transformations [12] are supported by a spreadsheet where each column has its own meaning and rules. Some of the steps have micro-steps, of which some can be completely automated. Correct application of the tabular transformations assures alignment and traceability, between the derived LA diagram and the initial UC representations, and at the same time allows adjusting the results of the transformation to any changing requirements.

3 4SRS-SoaML: A Method for Deriving a SOA Architecture

Although the 4SRS method has proven successful in generating a proper candidate logical architecture, in ill-defined contexts and with multiple stakeholders, it failed to provide a more clear business and strategic view of the system. Its large, complex architecture and oversimplified architectural elements call for more full-bodied, cross-domain solutions, with in-depth detailed elements, as the ones found in SOA, namely through the definition of different levels of architectures, composed of services and requests, and their properties, as specified by SoaML.

Although SoaML allows building a complete service architecture, for now our work will focus solely on using system requirements to identify participants (P) and its associated requests and services, enabling the design of a logical architecture based only on these participants. The process-level 4SRS method seems capable of supporting such design by maintaining its main steps but changing some rationale.

Here, our purpose is to focus on how SOA concerns – by using the SoaML notation – are treated during the execution of the four steps of the method and focus on the main differences to the conventional method execution, rather than exhaustingly describing the full method's steps and micro-steps. This application differs from the conventional approach by defining a set of added rules that must be observed when reasoning about the execution of the method steps.

The starting point of our approach is the elicitation of UC using refinement techniques (Fig. 1a). The leaf UC of this model are used as inputs for the 4SRS-SoaML method execution (Fig. 1b), where throughout it, participants (P instead of the conventional AE) are derived, as well as their respective requests, services and properties (Fig. 1c). Participants are used to define the service providers and consumers in a system, where they may play the role of service provider, consumer or both [7], communicating between service/request channels. After aggregating participants in super participants (SP), later described in Step 3 of the method, the main service/request channels are identified and ready to be thoroughly specified (Fig. 1d).

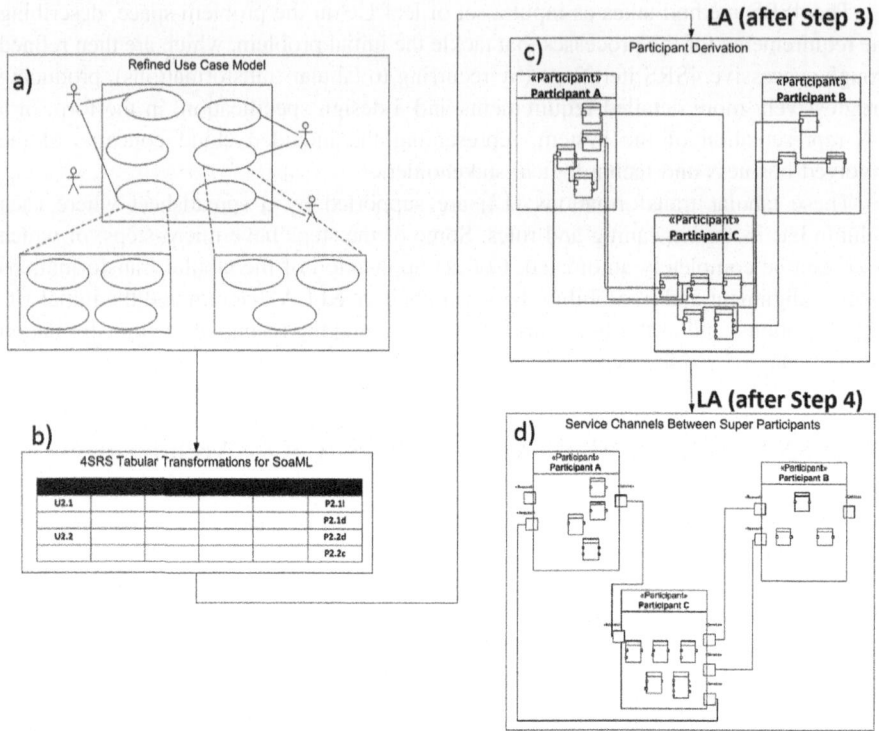

Fig. 1. From use cases to service/request channels

3.1 Step 1 – Participant Creation

Now called Participant Creation, instead of AE Creation, wherein the conventional method automatically derived at least three types of AE classified as interface, data or control (referred using i-type, d-type, or c-type stereotypes). Within this new approach, the same reasoning is used but rather to automatically derive at least three types of P. Other small difference within this step regards the prefix reference that identifies the derived participant, "P" instead of the conventional process-level 4SRS "AE", with the suffix regarding the given type having no changes (e.g., {P1.1.i} instead of {AE1.1.i}, where 1.1 refers to the UC number and i to an interface type).

3.2 Step 2 – Participant Elimination

Composed by the equivalent eight micro-steps of the conventional method, the "new" issues for eliciting a SoaML participant-based logical architecture are dealt with in non-automatic micro-steps (only micro-steps ii and vi are automatic). The main differences on reasoning are in micro-steps iv, v and viii (Participant Description, Participant Representation and Participant Specification, respectively). The remaining micro-steps (i, iii and vii) are executed applying the same reasoning as in the conventional method execution, the only difference is to deal with P rather than AE.

| | Step 2 - participant elimination ||||
	2i - use case classification	2ii - local elimination	2iii - participant naming	2iv - participant description
{0b.1.2}	ci			
{P0b.1.2.c}		T	Health Monitoring Decisions	Short Description: Makes decisions on how the measured information from {P0b.1.2.i} is used within the AAL4ALL Node. The information can be used by the platform for preventing abnormalities... Requests: Monitoring Configurations (0b.1.1.i.s) Receive Current Vital Signs (0b.1.2.i.s) User Validation (0b.6.1.1.c.s) Services: Health Monitoring Decisions (0b.1.2.c.s) Properties/Resources: Configurations User's Activities Vital Signs Values
{P0b.1.2.i}		T	Receive Current Vital Signs Information	Short Description: Receives the current values for vital signs (e.g., blood pressure, heart rate, etc.) measured by the health monitoring devices. The information is published. Requests: Services: Receive Current Vital Signs (0b.1.2.i.s) Properties/Resources:

Fig. 2. Micro-steps i to iv of Step 2 of the 4SRS-SoaML method

Micro-step iv – Participant Description. Regarding micro-step iv, our proposal provides an extended structure for the required description of the P's role for the service behavior. This information has as input the textual description of the original use case from the UC model. The P's description includes an overall description of its behavior (as in the conventional method), where there must be defined how it acts to provide or consume a given service/request, if it has any properties, etc. (Fig. 2). Additionally, from the use case's textual description, it is possible to identify some requests, services and properties.

Micro-step viii – Participant Specification. Micro-step v purpose remains from the conventional method, i.e., to identify a participant whose role can be represented by another participant from the global architecture. This micro-step signals P that can be eliminated without losing coherence within the architecture. The decision to identify if a participant represents another participant, or if it can be represented in the system by another one, is based solely on their overall description. If any P under analysis (to be represented or not by others) have different requests or services regarding the participant that will for now on represent them, that does not allow to directly infer the representation of these P into a single participant at this moment. Rather, the mixing of requests, services and properties regarding these given P are only dealt with in micro-step viii.

	2v - participant represented by	2v - participant represents	2vi - global elimination	2vii - participant renaming	2viii - participant and service specification
{0b.1.2}					
{P0b.1.2.c}	{P0b.1.2.c}	{P0b.3.3.1.c}	T	Health Monitoring Decisions	**Short Description:** Makes decisions on how the measured information from {P0b.1.2.i} is used within the AAL4ALL Node. The information can be used by the platform for preventing abnormalities in User's wellbeing while he is at home (routines, sport exercises, during sleep etc.). The information is also used by the Formal Caretaker (Doctor) ... Requests: Monitoring Configurations (0b.1.1.i.s) Receive Current Info (0b.1.2.i.s) User Validation (0b.6.1.1.c.s) Services: Health Monitoring Decisions (0b.1.2.c.s) Properties/Resources: Configurations User's Activities Vital Signs Values
{P0b.1.2.d}					
{P0b.1.2.i}	{P0b.1.2.i}	{P0b.1.3.i} {P0b.1.4.i} {P0b.3.3.1.i}	T	Receive Current Information	**Short Description:** This Participant is responsible for receiving all monitoring-related information from the several monitoring devices. Receives the current values for vital signs, the current information regarding equipment usage and User's steps. The information is published in the AAL MQ. ... Requests: Remind Meds (0b.3.2.1.c.s) Remind Consults (0b.3.3.3.c.s) Remind Events (0b.4.4.1.2.c.s) Services: Receive Current Vital Signs (0b.1.2.i.s1) Receive Equipment Information (0b.1.2.i.s2) Receive Routines Information (0b.1.2.i.s3) Properties/Resources:

Fig. 3. Micro-steps v to viii of Step 2 of the 4SRS-SoaML method

Micro-step viii – Participant Specification. Micro-step viii is still similar to micro-step iv, since it intends to describe P that, in micro-step v, were considered to represent other P without losing any information (role and objective of the participant, requests, services and properties), and were meanwhile eliminated in micro-step vi. Thus, for defining the Participant Specification, it must be taken in consideration that only redundant overall description of the behavior of the participant, requests, services and properties are eliminated, and that any of these fields that differ from the P to be represented should be incorporated in this "new" specification that represents them (Fig. 3).

	Step 3 - packaging & aggregation		Step 4 - participant association
	3i - super participant identification & naming	3ii - super participant description	
{0b.1.2} Check			
{P0b.1.2.c}	{SP2} Home Gateway	**Description:** central node where different services (provided by several service providers) that will compose the AAL4ALL ecosystem, are aggregated, **Kind:** Software Application **Interfaces:** AAL Devices Cloud; Events and Transports Private Cloud; Health Care Private Cloud; **State Variables:** **Requests:** Monitoring Configuration Requirements; User Monitoring Configuration; Home Emergency Alert Requirements; Outdoor Emergency Alert Requirements; Health Monitoring Decisions; Equipment Monitoring Decisions; User Indoor Position; Show Routes; ... **Services:** Provider Validation; User Validation; Publish Business Info **Realization options:** Ethernet, AMQP and HTTP **Prerequisites:** **NFR's:**	
{P0b.1.2.d}			
{P0b.1.2.i}	{SP4} Sensors	**Description:** sensor devices that will compose the AAL4ALL ecosystem ... **Kind:** Device **Interfaces:** Home Gateway; **State Variables:** **Requests:** Home Emergency Alert Requirements; Outdoor Emergency Alert Requirements; Health Monitoring Decisions; Equipment Monitoring Decisions; Routines Monitoring Decisions; User Indoor Position; User Outdoor Position **Services:** Receive Current Vital Signs, Receive Equipment Information, Receive Routines Information, ... **Realization options:** Bluetooth, HTTP, WiFi, IEE 802.11, ... **Prerequisites:** **NFR's:**	{P0b.1.2.c} {P0b.1.3.c} {P0b.1.4.c}

Fig. 4. Steps 3 and 4 of the 4SRS-SoaML method

3.3 Step 3 – Participant Aggregation

In Step 3, the enduring P (those that were maintained after executing the entire Step 2), for which there is an advantage in being treated in a unified process, should give origin to aggregations of semantically consistent P. In the conventional method (both process- and product-level) this step outputs packages for aggregating AE, objects or components, in the new approach this step outputs SP instead. A super participant represents a group of assigned P, which may or may not represent a software product from the services ecosystem in question. The aggregation performed can also reflect identified product classes or other aggregated types of service suggested by reference architectures or models. The notational representation of SP in SoaML remains the same as for P, only viewed one level up.

In this new approach, there is the addition of dividing this step in two new micro-steps. Besides the conventional identification and naming of the super participant, with the inclusion of the P, here performed in micro-step i, its characterization, similar to a description of a product class, is performed in micro-step ii (Fig. 4). This last micro-step can be performed by defining the descriptions in a structural way, following guidelines as, for instance, the European Telecommunications Standards Institute (ETSI) [13], namely defining the super participant description by: Name, Brief Description, Kind, Interfaces, State Variables, Requests, Services, Realization options, Prerequisites and Non-functional requirements.

3.4 Step 4 – Participant Associations

Regarding Step 4 on the conventional method (both process- and product-level), associations between AE, objects and components, respectively, are derived based on the AE objects or components originated by the same use case or based on textual descriptions of UC. In our new approach, this step formalizes the requests and services that were previously identified in micro-steps iv and viii of Step 2, but only those regarding the P that were not aggregated in the same super participant in Step 3, i.e., belonging to a different one. Our purpose in this step is to generate the main communication channels between the different SP, by exposing their services and requests in the final architecture.

4 Demonstration Case

The AAL4ALL project [14] arises from the need to create an oriented national market to products and services for AAL given the trend of an aging population and the need to respond positively to the increasing availability of better health care and wellness. At the same time the concept of Cloud Computing appears in the AAL4ALL domain with the opportunities for developing new products and services that can be available on the Internet. This project presents an idea for an answer through the development of an ecosystem of products and services for AAL associated to a business model and validated through large scale trial.

AAL refers to electronic environments that are sensitive and responsive to the presence of people and provide assistive prepositions for maintaining their lifestyle. It is primarily concerned with the individual in its immediate environment by offering user-friendly interfaces for all sorts of equipment at home and outside, taking into account that, sometime in their life, people have impairments in vision, hearing, mobility or dexterity [15]. These AAL solutions intend to monitor and facilitate health, safety and well-being of individuals in specific scenarios such as within their home, in mobility, in care centers, at work and even during recreational activities, promoting independency, mobility, safety and social contact through increased communication, inclusion and participation, using ICT [16].

The AAL4ALL project aims to develop a core platform that allows an aggregation of all stakeholders systems to enable the composition of the AAL services that will be provided to end-users in both home and in mobility environment, where several types of devices are installed to gather data form user environments and to provide AAL services. Therefore the AAL4ALL platform development should aim at providing a SOA and a cloud-based solution, capable of ensuring a set of services for the ecosystem. This project has defined four main Life Settings (LS): Independent Living; Health and Care in Life; Occupation in Life and Recreation in Life. A number of scenarios in each LS and their potential impact on the roadmap implementation are included as a starting point.

Another element of implementation is the identification of the main participants to be involved in the project, for idealization of the kind of needs specified in each scenario. The scenarios' descriptions, alongside the participating Personas, actors that represent users that interact with the projects IS, were elicited and gave origin to UC diagrams with the actors and their interactions by LS and Canonic Activities (CA) criteria, from a process point of view. The process-level UC allowed a better understanding of the projects IS related activities.

Using this information, it was possible to characterize the necessary UC for representing the high level processes related to the project. Each UC has a textual description allowing process requirements to be captured and described. It was decided to use two orthogonal views of the system under analysis: the {0a} LS and the {0b} CA (Fig. 5), which existence in user requirements higher abstraction level has enabled to cope with the inherent complexity when dealing with both.

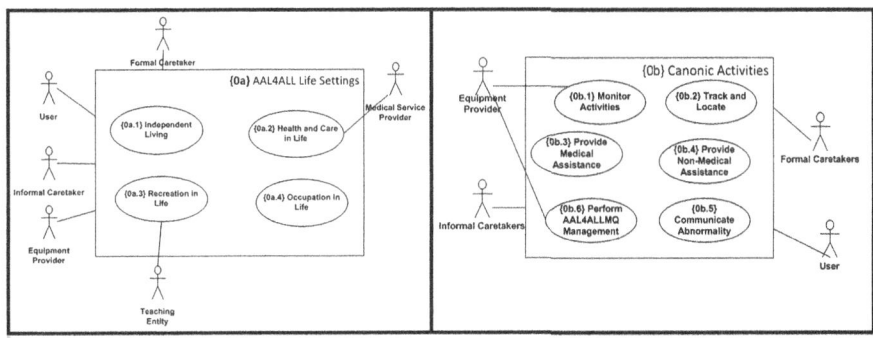

Fig. 5. The use case model by two orthogonal views

The process-level logical architecture of the project ecosystem has previously been developed recurring to the conventional 4SRS method [17]. That perspective allowed capturing the intentionality's presented in the desired activities that the ecosystem sustains. However, the need for a clearer business and strategic view of the system, by identifying the communication channels between the products and services within the AAL4ALL ecosystem, raised the need for deriving a logical architecture now based in a SoaML notation. This logical architecture should allow depicting a set of services channels between the participants and, in a higher view, the super participants.

An excerpt of the demonstration case, throughout the four steps of the method execution, is included in Sect. 3 (Figs. 2, 3, 4). Namely, the derivation of Use Case

{0b.1.2} Check Health Values, until participants in super participants **{SP2} Home Gateway** and **{SP4} Sensors** (Fig. 4) is presented throughout the steps execution and this last in the zoomed area of the process-level logical architecture for the AAL4ALL project (Fig. 6), after the execution of the 4SRS-SoaML method for deriving a logical architecture. Also depicted in the zoomed area is a subset of the architecture, where the super participant **{SP4} Sensors** and its associated requests and services are presented, with the rest of the super participants that compose the remainder of the logical architecture in the background.

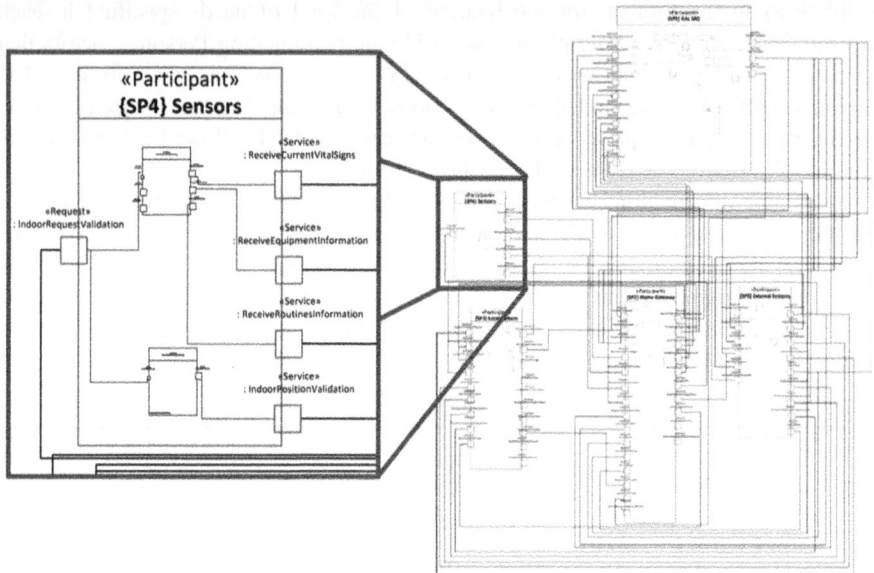

Fig. 6. Subset of the AAL4ALL logical architecture using SoaML

The execution of Step 3 in the AAL4ALL project was based on the product classes identified in [17], where the logical architecture was mapped and a new iteration of the architecture arose by following the **Continua** reference model [18]. The identified super participants in the AAL4ALL projects were the following: **{SP1} AALMQ** (cloud platform for service orchestration); **{SP2} Home Gateway** (home and mobile application hosting devices); **{SP3} Local System** (home private cloud); **{SP4} Sensors** (PAN/LAN devices, either sensors or actuators); and **{SP5} External systems** (other public or private health clouds). The super participants of the AAL4ALL logical architecture (Fig. 6) regard the aggregated participants that relate to the functionalities elicited from the orthogonal view of the CA and LS.

The adoption of the 4SRS-SoaML method allowed the SoaML architectural model composed by participants, requests and services, representing the system requirements, to be derived from and aligned with the initial user requirements, resulting in an identification of elements in a non ad hoc approach, thus less prone to errors of design. AAL4ALL logical architecture (Fig. 5) also shows some of the complexity regarding the project ecosystem that has justified the adoption of process-level, to support the elicitation efforts and the definition of the services channels.

5 Discussion

In this paper, the SoaML modeling language was used to support process-level logical architectures and, as such, to provide a baseline modeling language for specification of any services within a service-oriented environment, which includes cloud-based services. This work demonstrated that the SoaML profile supports the range of modeling requirements of the logical architecture, including the specifications of systems of services, individual service interfaces and service implementations.

According to our experience, at the end of the requirements elicitation phase (considering the traditional development macro-processes Analysis, Design, Implementation, Test and Deployment) implementation teams experience difficulties interpreting and implementing the generated conventional process-level logical architecture, composed by AE. The purpose of this architecture artifact is to provide information regarding the software system functionalities, regardless of the implementation techniques and technologies the team uses.

This is due to the fact that functional requirements are elicited, but technical decisions regarding messaging, protocols, amongst others are lost along the way, being unclear at this point. The authors believe that SoaML notation is more adequate for relating business and system information, leveraging the business requirements and transporting them to implementation phase. By eliciting P and its associated requests, services and properties, instead of simple AE, the provided artifacts are richer and clearer for better interpretation and implementation by the teams.

Also, associations between AE were not always understandable, since typically teams interpreted them as interactions between AE, not depicting the type of information within, as well as the course of the flows. In fact, for depicting the course, stereotyped sequence diagrams had to be developed (as in [9]). These issues are tackled in our approach by explicitly defining P's requests and services. The combination of the 4SRS method with the SoaML language helps to strengthen the associations in terms of services and requests channels across the architectural elements, either P or SP.

The previous architecture was composed by 110 AE and ours was composed by the same amount of P, since they have a somewhat direct correlation. However:

- in the 4SRS-SoaML architecture, there are 171 requests and 143 services, which results in an addition of 61 requests and of 33 services.
- in the previous architecture there were depicted 159 associations, i.e., communication flows of any kind between the AE, in our architecture there are 139 associations, i.e., services that are requests between P.

This means that this new approach was indeed able to provide more detailed information regarding the services provided, with the excess in number of services and requests discovered. Additionally, the architectural representation was also improved due to the decrease number of associations, providing a clearer depiction of the architecture and aggregating the main communication channels information.

5.1 Lessons Learned

As previously stated, the authors believe that using the SoaML notation at the requirements elicitation phase is more useful for implementation teams since it allows including more information for the future system to be implemented, like technical data regarding the software services. Within our approach it was possible to early identify requests and services directly from the use case's textual descriptions.

Step 3 of the 4SRS-SoaML method allowed identifying possible aggregations of semantically consistent P into SP, according to the proposal of the intended system. Somehow in this step, the logical architecture can be divided into subgroups according to the ultimate goals of the desired system, in terms of functional groups and product categorizations.

Changes made in Step 4, where we only consider requests and services between the SP, are useful for depicting the service channels required for communications between different products that will be integrated in the future. In cases of software implementations made by multiple and distributed teams, each nominated to implement one of the SP, the service channels hidden inside the same product are no longer relevant in the overall project management.

5.2 Future Work

Within our approach to elicit a SoaML architecture, we derived participants with their constituent requests, services and properties. Albeit complete Service Choreographies are depicted by RUP's Basic Flow and Alternative Flow information from the UC's textual descriptions, only generic information was derived in this work, so the model derivation has several points to be improved. In the future we intend to include in our approach the derivation of other SoaML diagrams like Service Contracts, Service Architectures and Interfaces.

Here, we derived a candidate logical architecture in an ill-defined context by executing a 4SRS method that was tailored for SoaML diagrams, which constitutes one of the steps in the V-Model [3] approach, within other models successive derivations. This approach is composed by UML models, like use cases, stereotyped sequence diagrams, logical architectures, amongst others. As future work, we intend to use SoaML notation throughout the entire V-Model, in order to obtain information regarding services until the product-level side of the requirements elicitation phase.

Finally, we intend to improve these service channels with business information, usually hidden in non-functional requirements, as business goals and rules. In order to do so, we intend to include the processing of this information within our approach, supported on the OMG Business Motivation Model (BMM) link with SoaML. This would strengthen the channels business information, associated to the connection between the requests and services of P and SP, so supporting the quality characteristics of the derived service-oriented logical architecture.

6 Conclusion

SOA is a top concern in todays IS research, where the growing use of the SoaML notation can help to strengthen the link between business and technological worlds, ever more interconnected and involved in issues of requirements elicitation, process modeling and business strategy.

Our work integrates all of these topics and proposes a way to generate, align and maintain a service-oriented logical architecture for a desired information system, based on the elicitation of use cases and their transformation to participants at the end of the 4SRS-SoaML method execution.

In this paper, we put forward a visualization to support the connection between each problem-side, leaf-level use case, building a strong focus on the requirements elicitation, retaining business information along the way, and aiding in the Business-IS/IT alignment and requirements traceability. Therefore, we can consciously build a logical architecture based in participants and super participants, supported in the SoaML notation, identifying requests and services as communication channels.

Acknowledgments. This work has been supported by Project AAL4ALL (QREN 13852) and by *FCT – Fundação para a Ciência e Tecnologia* in the scope of the project: PEst-OE/EEI/UI0319/2014.

References

1. Nuseibeh, B.: Weaving together requirements and architectures. Computer (Long. Beach. Calif.) **34**, 115–119 (2001)
2. Demirkan, H., Kauffman, R.J., Vayghan, J.A., Fill, H.-G., Karagiannis, D., Maglio, P.P.: Service-oriented technology and management: perspectives on research and practice for the coming decade. Electron. Commer. Res. Appl. **7**, 356–376 (2008)
3. Ferreira, N., Santos, N., Machado, R.J., Fernandes, J.E., Gasevic, D.: A V-model approach for business process requirements elicitation in cloud design. In: Bouguettaya, A., Sheng, Q.Z., Daniel, F. (eds.) Advanced Web Services, pp. 551–578. Springer, New York (2014)
4. Delgado, A., de Guzmán, I.G.R., Piattini, M.: From BPMN business process models to SoaML service models: a transformation-driven approach. In: 2nd International Conference on Software Technology and Engineering (ICSTE), pp. 314–319 (2010)
5. Elvesaeter, B., Panfilenko, D.: Aligning business and IT models in service-oriented architectures using BPMN and SoaML. In: Proceedings of the First International Workshop on Model-Driven Interoperability, pp. 61–68 (2010)
6. OMG: Business process model and notation (BPMN) specification (2011). http://www.omg.org/spec/BPMN/2.0
7. OMG: Service oriented architecture Modeling Language (SoaML) specification (2012)
8. Delgado, A., Ruiz, F., de Guzmán, I.G.R., Piattini, M.: Towards a service-oriented and model-driven framework with business processes as first-class citizens. In: BPSC, pp. 19–31 (2009)
9. Touzi, J., Benaben, F., Pingaud, H., Lorré, J.P.: A model-driven approach for collaborative service-oriented architecture design. Int. J. Prod. Econ. **121**, 5–20 (2009)
10. Delgado, A., Ruiz, F.: Model transformations for business-IT alignment: from collaborative business process to SoaML service model. In: Proceedings of the 27th Annual ACM Symposium on Applied Computing, pp. 1720–1722 (2012)
11. López-Sanz, M., Marcos, E.: ArchiMeDeS: a model-driven framework for the specification of service-oriented architectures. Inf. Syst. **37**, 257–268 (2012)

12. Santos, N., Machado, R.J., Ferreira, N., Gašević, D.: Derivation of process-oriented logical architectures: an elicitation approach for cloud design. In: Dieste, O., Jedlitschka, A., Juristo, N. (eds.) PROFES 2012. LNCS, vol. 7343, pp. 44–58. Springer, Heidelberg (2012)
13. ETSI: European Telecommunications Standards Institute. http://www.etsi.org/
14. AAL4ALL: AAL4ALL (Ambient Assisted Living for All) project. http://www.aal4all.org/
15. Pieper, M., Antona, M., Cortes, U.: Ambient assisted living (2011). www.ercim.eu
16. Magjarevic, R.: Home care technologies for ambient assisted living. In: 11th Mediterranean Conference on Medical and Biomedical Engineering and Computing 2007, pp. 397–400. Springer (2007)
17. Santos, N., Teixeira, J., Pereira, A., Ferreira, N., Lima, A., Simões, R., Machado, R.J.: A demonstration case on the derivation of process-level logical architectures for ambient assisted living ecosystems. In: Garcia, N., Rodrigues, J., Dias, M.S., Elias, D. (eds.) Ambient Assisted Living Book. Taylor and Francis/CRC Press (USA) (2012). (accepted for publication)
18. Continua Health Alliance. http://www.conntinuaalliance.org/

A Service Oriented Architecture for Total Manufacturing Enterprise Integration

Theodor Borangiu[1], Cristina Morariu[1], Octavian Morariu[1],
Monica Drăgoicea[1(✉)], Silviu Răileanu[1], Iulia Voinescu[1],
Gheorghe Militaru[2], and Anca-Alexandra Purcărea[2]

[1] Faculty of Automatic Control and Computers,
University Politehnica of Bucharest,
313 Splaiul Independenţei, 060042 Bucharest, Romania
theodor.borangiu@cimr.pub.ro,
monica.dragoicea@acse.pub.ro

[2] Faculty of Entrepreneurship, Business Engineering and Management,
University Politehnica of Bucharest, 313 Splaiul Independenţei,
060042 Bucharest, Romania

Abstract. The paper describes a, framework and implementing issues addressing service orientation in the management and control of enterprises. A hybrid, semi-heterarchical control model based on the paradigm of holonic manufacturing is proposed; it switches its operating mode from hierarchical to heterarchical in the presence of perturbations to ensure both global optimization and agility to changes in batch orders, while featuring robustness to disturbances in the production environment. In order to ensure these conflicting functionalities, a service oriented architecture is proposed and implemented, whose structure includes a distributed fault-tolerant Resource Service Access Model. Besides the design of a generic structural and dynamic model, a real implementation solution is proposed using a multi-agent framework.

Keywords: SOEA · Manufacturing integration framework · HMES

1 Introduction

Service orientation is emerging nowadays at multiple organizational levels in enterprise business, leveraging technology in response to growing needs for business integration, flexibility and agility of manufacturing enterprises. The environment of the manufacturing industry is characterized by radical changes and companies are facing today more than ever great challenges that result from alterations in the global framework. Not only do technological changes (particularly in ICT) have a big impact on manufacturing companies, but also the market registers dramatic, unpredictable variations in size and types of product batches. To be competitive, manufacturing should adapt to changing conditions imposed by the market. The greater variety of products, the possible large fluctuations in demand (from mass production to short lots), the shorter lifecycle of products, and the increased customer expectations in terms of quality and delivery time are challenges that production companies have to deal with to remain competitive. Besides market-based challenges, manufacturing firms also need constantly to be flexible – adapt to newly developed processes and technologies, and agile – reconfigure at market and shop-floor disturbances [1].

A particularly critical element in the shop floor reengineering process is the control system, which lacks agility in general, because any process or resource team change requires programming modifications, implying the need for qualified programmers, usually not available in manufacturing SMEs. Even small changes (e.g. rush orders) might affect the global system architecture which clearly increases the programming effort and the potential for side-effect errors [2, 3].

Agent-oriented and Holonic Manufacturing Execution Systems (HMES) have been used to manage not only the correct and autonomous execution of a plan of activities or schedule, but also to efficiently respond to production changes and occurrence of unexpected disturbances [4–6]. Among the main benefits of HMES are adaptability and flexibility when facing changes on the shop floor, and efficiency when using the available resources. Most of the theoretical research done during the last two decades addressed centralized batch scheduling systems (SS), which have the main drawbacks of their lack of reactive capabilities and the inability to provide robust and efficient solutions in real time when disturbances occur (e.g., resource breakdown). To efficiently address the mixed batch planning and product scheduling problem found in real manufacturing domains, the horizontal integration (the collaboration between centralized SS and distributed HMES) is a challenge that needs to be faced.

In addition to providing shop floor agility to business changes (market dynamics, rush orders, new product recipes, highly scalable mass customization), shop floor reengineering, based on dynamic reconfiguration rather than on reprogramming must be possible in HMES control/supervision architectures [7, 8]. This is feasible by using a resource-related, agent-based control architecture characterized by: modularity, configuration rather than programming, high reusability, legacy systems migration, predictive maintenance of resources and sustainability (resource timeliness, operation accuracy, power footprint and real-time consumption are continuously monitored) [9–11]. Current HMES development frameworks are based on implementing holonic reference architectures and applying the delegate multi-agent system pattern [12, 13].

The total integration approach of manufacturing enterprises (vertical integration of business processes and shop floor control processes, and horizontal collaboration of centralized scheduling systems - SS and distributed manufacturing execution systems - dMES) represents a new concept for enterprise process integration, agility to market changes and customer requirements, service orientation and robustness to technical disruptions in the context of sustainability [14, 15].

The methodology presented for enterprise reengineering compensates for the deficiencies of both hierarchical and heterarchical management and control systems, and is based on new concepts such as Service Oriented Architecture [16], Web services, distributed intelligence with service-oriented agents and holonic manufacturing.

The rest of the paper is organized as follows: Sect. 2 proposes a model for total, service-oriented integration in the manufacturing enterprise, considering business and shop-floor processes in semi-heterarchical production control topology. Section 3 discusses a Service Oriented Enterprise Architecture (SOEA) using a Manufacturing Integration Framework (MIF). Section 4 describes implementing issues. Section 5 reports experimental results. Final conclusions are presented in Sect. 6.

2 The Manufacturing Integration Framework (MIF)

The primary goal of Service Oriented Architecture in the context of manufacturing enterprises is to align the business layer information flow with the technology specific information flow - the latter being partitioned on two layers: (1) the business layer (management of customer orders); (2) the shop floor layer (execution of customer orders). SOA is the bridge that creates a symbiotic and synergistic relationship between the two layers; it is an IT system model providing flexibility to the enterprise in the way business applications are created. SOA is not just focused on application integration, but also on application construction from existing IT assets [17, 18]. This type of architecture allows for the creation of composite business applications from independent, self-describing, and inter-changeable code modules called services. These services are available for use on a services bus, and they can be arranged together into a business process or composite application using process choreography. Thus, the major components of SOA are: (1) services; (2) services bus; (3) process choreography - composite applications; (4) message transformation, mediation and routing; (5) services registry.

2.1 Service-Oriented Business Process Integration for Manufacturing

The Service Oriented Enterprise Architecture (SOEA) for the generic business layer of a manufacturing enterprise is an emerging concept that represents a business approach to SOA governance. The set of business processes and business services that a given business user (consumers of processes and services) will consume, are: Offer Request-, Production Order-, Rush Order-, Customer- and Supplier Relationship- Management.

Business processes should be treated as compositions of other business processes and services and therefore be decomposed into their subordinate sub-processes and services [19]. Services (including business processes as services) can then be detailed in service components - converted into a detailed set of definition metadata that will describe that service to the information system. The Enterprise Service Bus (ESB) is a flexible connectivity infrastructure for integrating applications and services. One of the objectives of an ESB is to reduce the number, size and complexity of interfaces in a SOA. An ESB performs the following actions between requestor and services:

- Intelligent message routing between parties;
- Conversion of transport protocols between service consumer and provider;
- Transformation of message formats between service consumer and provider;
- Handling business events from various sources.

When SOA is employed as an integration strategy, it brings about a catalogue of self-describing, atomic business services that are used together to create a business process. Often, a business event (for example: one rush order arriving at the customer order management module) will need to trigger interactions between many different business and/or shop floor manufacturing systems. These interactions are achieved using process choreography within an SOA. Process choreography allows for multiple business services to be combined and used together to implement a business process; in the present SOA it is realized via BPEL (Business Process Execution Language).

From a SOA perspective, the Holonic Manufacturing System (HMS) was seen as a layered architecture, as illustrated in Fig. 1.

1. **Business Layer**: includes two main components - the offer request management module (ORM) and the customer order management module (COM).
2. **Manufacturing Execution Layer** (MES): encapsulates the production scheduler (PH), production monitor (PM) and the product knowledge base.
3. **Shop Floor Layer**: represents the actual shop floor processes and structure. There are two types of active entities: intelligent products and shop floor resources.

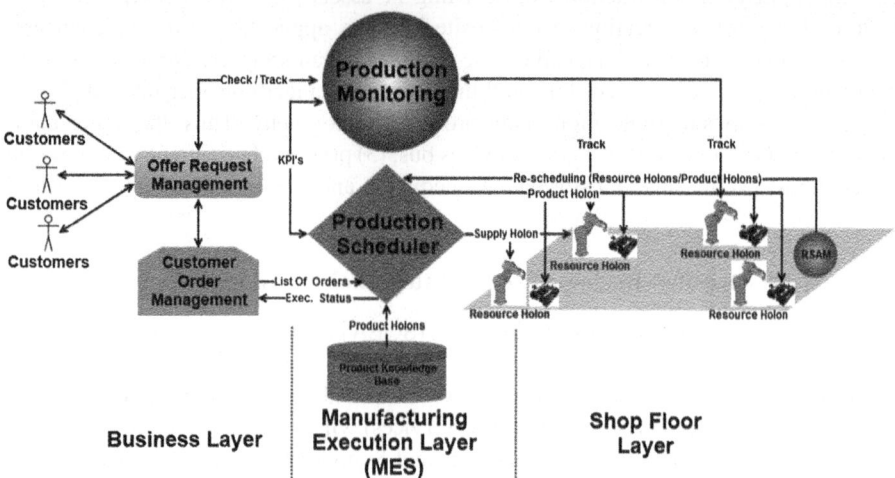

Fig. 1. Block architecture of the SOA components for total HMS integration

Figure 2 shows the proposed architecture of the Customer Order Management (COM) module related to an implementation based on SOA and the integration with the HMS system. The COM presented in this section is built on top of a standard SOA engine capable of executing BPEL processes as a SCA application. The customer interacts with the COM application in two scenarios, first by creating an order for a product batch and secondly by tracking the execution of the order.

The COM developed in this project is built on top of a standard SOA engine capable of executing BPEL processes as a SCA application. The customer interacts with the COM application in two scenarios, first by creating an order for a product batch and secondly by tracking the execution of the order.

The COM application has three Web Service endpoints that integrate with the customer portal application and with the HMS. The Customer Order is initiated from the Portal web application and in the COM module is triggering the execution of a BPEL process instance. Essentially each Customer Order is represented by a BPEL process instance, which tracks the order lifecycle from creation and until the order is completed. The portal user can interrogate the state of the BPEL process representing the customer order at any time by invoking the TrackCO endpoint, allowing real time tracking of the production status.

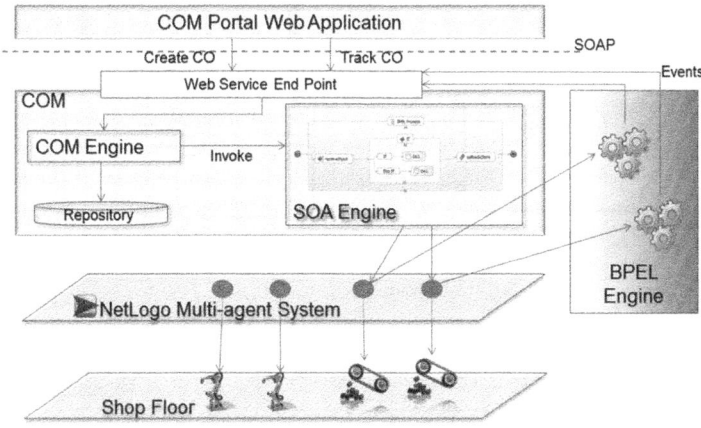

Fig. 2. Customer Order Management architecture

The CreateCO endpoint is responsible for starting an instance of the BPEL process representing the customer order (Fig. 3).

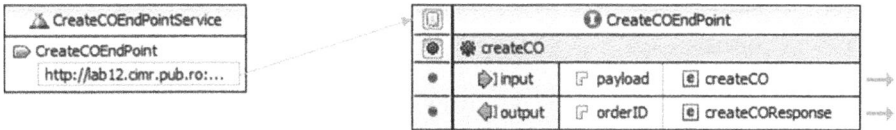

Fig. 3. Service definition: CreateCO EndPoint Service

The CreateCO method accepts the customer order details as a parameter, creates the payload for the BPEL process and invokes the CO BPEL process in the SOA engine. Once the process is invoked, it returns synchronously the BPEL process_ID to the portal application. The portal application will store this process_ID in the customer order object for tracking purposes.

2.2 Monitoring Resource Services for SS-DMES Horizontal Integration

For the MES layer, an interaction model was defined allowing the cooperation between two different subsystems: a centralized scheduling system (SS) based on a selectable mixed planning & scheduling technology (e.g. constraint programming, production rules) and a decentralized manufacturing execution subsystem (dMES) based on the PROSA holonic reference architecture and applying the delegate multi-agent pattern.

This interaction model was defined considering: events triggering new planning requests to the SS; bidirectional switching sequence between hierarchical and heterarchical scheduling modes and switching mechanism between scheduling modes; resource service access model weighting the resources' participation in work teams function of cost, cumulated load, power consumption, timeliness and quality of

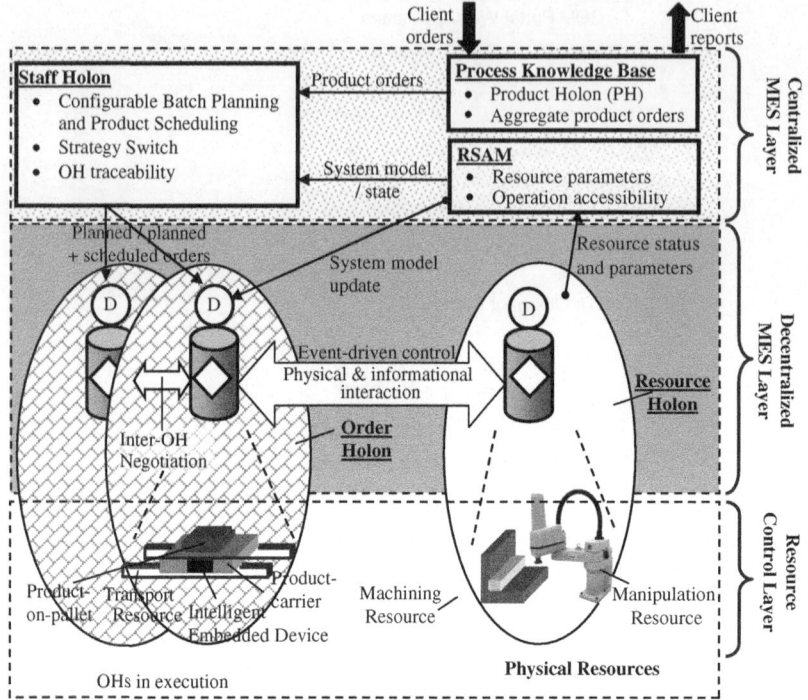

Fig. 4. Generic 2-layer architecture (SS, dMES) for semi-heterarchical shop-floor control

performed services. The tuning of the collaborative MES model will be also considered: nervousness, centralized guidance level, mode switching and performance measure. The collaborative model for SS - dMES interaction has two layers which are depicted in Fig. 4.

The centralized scheduling system (includes the SS) is in charge of generating a good quality global solution for a set of orders (batch) that must be processed in the shop floor. The system ensures that the main constraints related with the domain are satisfied (timing, assignment and topological restrictions). On the other hand, the decentralized execution system (dMES) processes all tasks involved in the problem, including not only the manufacturing activities already scheduled by the SS, but also other relevant activities as transport, routing and storage tasks.

The MES executes the schedule - based on a certain predefined level of guidance - as it is initially delivered by the SS. The execution is carried out until a disruptive event occurs. At this point, because the current agenda is no longer feasible to be performed (because of alterations caused by unexpected situations), the MES should profit from new advice (on request) from the SS in order to continue the execution.

The proposed semi-heterarchical control architecture is based on the PROSA [20] reference architecture from which it takes the basic holon structure (Product, Order, Resource) and extends it with: (i) automatic strategy switching performed by a multifunctional Staff Holon entity and (ii) *service orientation of operation scheduling and resource allocation* by aggregating the information about the quality of services performed by resources into an aggregate entity (agent) called Resource Service Access Model (RSAM), replicated on several workstations (resource terminals) for fault tolerance. This control architecture is generic because its structure is designed in terms of composing entities and their computing tasks, with no reference at technical implementation aspects; such aspects are only taken into account in the instantiation phase when the equipment is selected to provide the necessary functionalities.

The control architecture of the MES is organized on two loosely coupled decision layers: centralized MES (includes the SS), and decentralized MES (dMES). The interconnection between the layers uses standardized, SOA-specific messages (scheduled/planned orders, system model update, resource status and behaviour).

The RSAM is designed as an aggregate, replicated autonomous entity in charge of collecting information about the resources' behaviour (timelines, accuracy of performed operations, power consumption, a.o.) and using it for the collaborative in line decision on resource allocation and preventive maintenance of resources.

This entity is initially created using a Graphical User Interface, resources being manually added to create an initial set of competencies needed for the current client order; then RSAM acts as an aggregate, replicated intermediate that will constantly be updated with data from resources (status and parameters, specific behaviour, and QoS) and consulted on a regular basis (status and QoS update). RSAM offers two types of information for manufacturing resource service management:

- Information related to the *accessibility of services*;
- Resource *service history*.

3 Bus-Oriented MIF Integration

Software busses have a built-in messaging system allowing message passing between every module in a publish-subscribe fashion, which can be one to one, represented by a simple queue or one to many, represented by a topic. This allows decoupling between modules at communication level, by enabling asynchronous communication.

The *Enterprise Service Bus*, first proposed as software architecture, has a set of key characteristics [19]:

- Message routing and control across enterprise components;
- Decoupling of various modules by asynchronous messaging, replacing point to point communication with the common bus architecture;
- Promote reusability of utility services, reducing the number of redundant services across the enterprise;
- Provide transformation and translation of messages to allow easy integration of legacy applications;
- Provide an engine for workflow execution.

The *Manufacturing Service Bus* (MSB) integration model introduced in this development is an adaptation of ESB for manufacturing enterprises and introduces the concept of bus communication for the manufacturing systems. The MSB acts as an intermediary for data flows, assuring loose coupling between modules at shop floor level. We have identified and used the following main characteristics of a MSB, in addition to the ones inherited from the ESB:

- Event driven communication;
- Workflows;
- High number of messages;
- Message transformation;
- Message Validation;
- Synchronous and asynchronous communication;
- Message persistence;
- Intelligent message routing;
- Service directory;
- Distributed execution (Fig. 5).

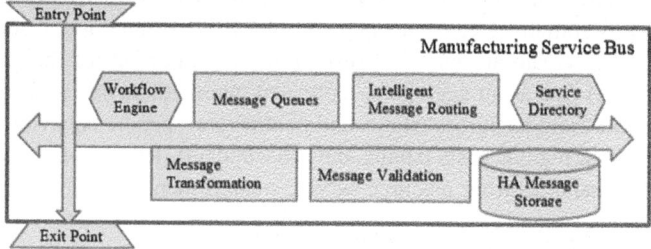

Fig. 5. Manufacturing Service Bus logical view

The integration framework is given in Fig. 6. The lower level MSB integrates the shop floor components, while MIF is used to integrate the business level components of a manufacturing enterprise. The two buses are linked together by the Mediator Agent. This agent is plugged in both busses and contains a set of rules for message passing between the two buses. The shop floor model consists in the following entities represented by their corresponding agents:

- **Product Holon** (PH): agent representing the intelligent product; consists in product pallet, product being assembled and an Intelligent Embedded Device (IED) able to support the agent execution and wireless communication;
- **Order Holon** (OH): is a dynamic data structure initialized by the MIF layer and consists in the product batch characteristics associated with a customer order. The OH has two components: a metadata component containing the features and supported by each product in the batch and a data component containing the target make span of the batch and the bindings to the expertise holon;
- **Expertise Holon** (EH): a data structure that records manufacturing execution and outcomes for each product type. This information is used during initial scheduling to assure an optimum allocation. In heterachical mode, these EH data structures are used to decide the online resource allocation for each PH based on previous outcomes of similar operations (QoS, power consumption).
- **Resource Holon** (RH): agent representing the physical resource on the product line (conveyor, robot, CNC machine).

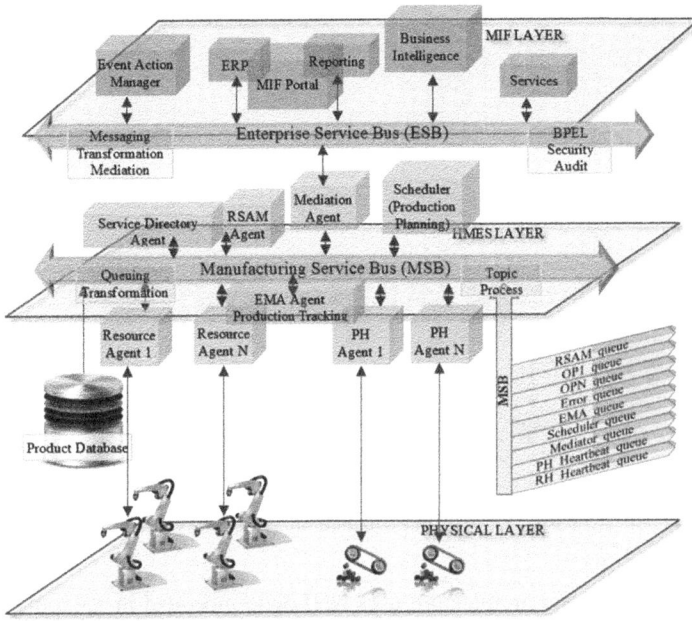

Fig. 6. Business and shop-floor layers - MSB integration with Mediation Agent

- **Product Database**: agent that stores and retrieves data from a structured storage containing information about products and operations.
- **Resource Service Access Model** (RSAM): agent that acts as a resource broker, where RHs can publish their state and capabilities. This information is used by PH (s) during execution;
- **Execution Monitoring Agent** (EMA): agent that centralizes PH states; it executes process monitoring at PH level, being responsible for generating periodic events that are sent through the Mediator Agent to the upper layer ESB and consumed by the Audit services. This activity enables the business layer to have real time data of the production schedule. This information can also be routed to the CRM module to enable customers to track the execution status.

4 Implementation Issues

The MES system architecture used for validating the COM module design is shown in Fig. 7. The implementation is based on NetLogo multi agent system. As most multi agent simulation environments, NetLogo platform allows to model agents and the world in which the agents live. This 2D world consists of patches, links and turtles.

- *Links* allow turtles to connect with each other to form networks, graphs and other structures.
- *Turtles* are the mobile agents in the NetLogo world and are used to model the products in the manufacturing line.

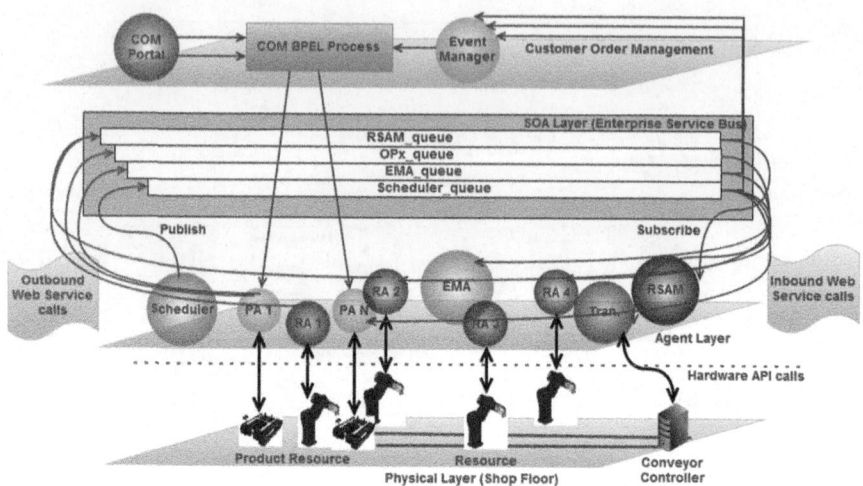

Fig. 7. MIF implementation at MES level

The execution system architecture uses NetLogo embedded in an application server. The application server role is to provide a J2EE environment for web service deployment. The application server starts the NetLogo instance in the same Java Virtual Machine, using the NetLogo API. This is done using an EJB Service that is deployed at start-up inside the application server and as part of its state initialization starts the NetLogo application. The EJB provides a remote, external interface that is used by the Web Services deployed in order to communicate with the agents in the NetLogo world. The design includes the usage of a SOA Server, running a BPEL engine. The BPEL process is deployed dynamically by the COM module for each product agent when the customer order is componentized.

For the decisional part of the HMES control (the Agent layer in Fig. 7) the Java Agent Development Framework (JADE) is used since it was specially designed for developing multi-agent systems conforming to FIPA standards for intelligent agents (www.fipa.org) [20]. The core of the 2-layer command and control model contains three decisional entities: OH, RH and RSAM agents. These agents implemented in JADE and running on Java Virtual Machines are interfaces used to integrate products being assembled and manufacturing resources into the control architecture (Fig. 8).

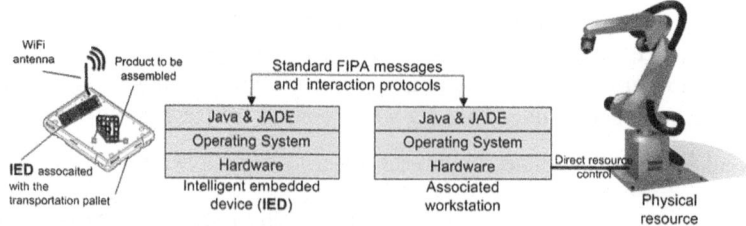

Fig. 8. Resource and order integration in the HMES control architecture using JADE

The core of the 2-layer command and control model in contains three decisional entities (Fig. 9), implemented as agents in JADE running over generic cross platform Java Virtual Machines (VM):

- *Order Holon agent*, in charge of production scheduling and tracking, and product routing. OH agents are located on each of the intelligent embedded units (IED) that are attached to the physical pallets (acting as product carriers).
- *Resource Holon agent*, located on the PCs attached to the resource controllers; this agent is an intermediate, its main task being to offer a standard interface to heterogeneous equipment (e.g. industrial controllers).
- *RSAM agent* running on a Start-up Monitoring Agent, whose responsibilities are: initial manual set up of the RSAM, periodic update of the RSAM using RH information, and point of information to all the entities that need to know the structure of the system. It is located on a high availability cluster consisting of PCs linked via Ethernet to the resource controllers and the cell server – head of the cluster.

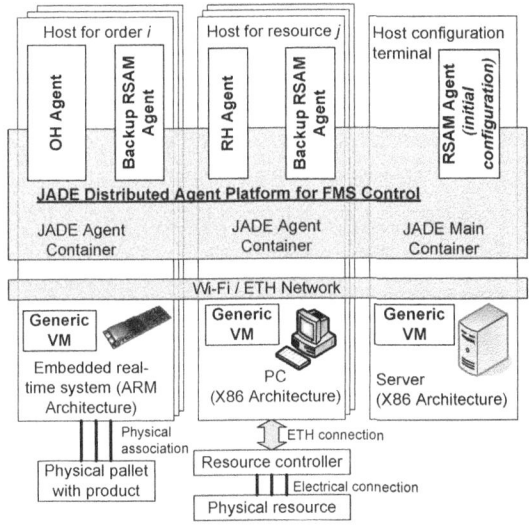

Fig. 9. Software system controlling shop-floor processes in the dual HMES mode: SS-dMES

5 Experimental Results

Experiments concerning SOA for Total Manufacturing Enterprise Integration have been carried out on the industrial pilot FMS platform in the Robotics & AI Lab of the University Politehnica of Bucharest.

The experimental scenario consists of a comparative performance analysis of the hierarchical, heterarchical and semi-heterarchical types of control strategies in the presence of resource failure. Experiments have been carried out using a batch of 200 orders in 3 cases (Fig. 10): **1 – pure hierarchical operation** with perturbation where orders are entirely replanned and rescheduled at the centralized MES level (with production stop), **2 – semi-heterarchical operation** consisting of hierarchical **to temporary heterarchical commuting with recovery of hierarchical mode**: when a perturbation occurs (resource failure) the remaining orders are rescheduled on 2-time intervals: orders in execution are scheduled online while all remaining batch orders are replanned and rescheduled offline at global level, **3 – hierarchical to permanent heterarchical commuting** when a resource failure occurs.

The results obtained from this experiment (Fig. 10) show that in the presence of perturbations (not critical resource failure – operations done on this resource are relocated on other available resources) there is a clear advantage of using a 2-time interval scheduling and planning (9567 sec in case 2 compared to 12053 sec in case 3). This result is justified by the fact that in the 2nd case production is still running with local optimization at packet level until the centralized re-planning and rescheduling are performed and the hierarchical mode is resumed, whereas in the 3rd case, after resource failure there is no more local or global optimization and the cell operates in the heterarchical strategy.

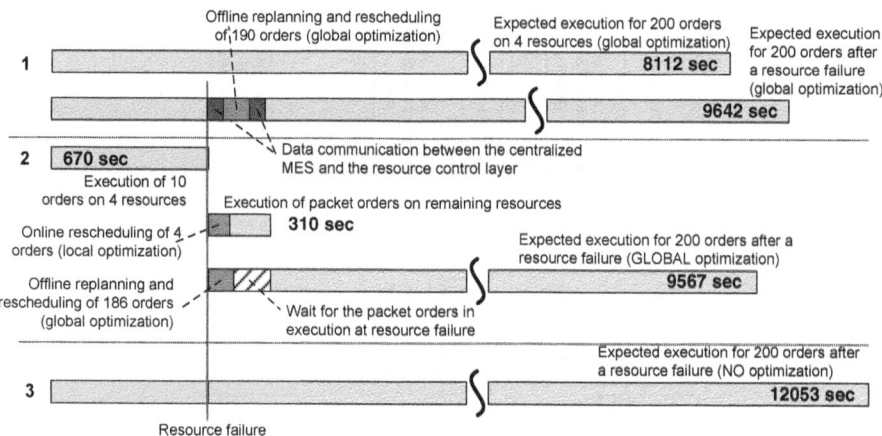

Fig. 10. Comparison of makespans for different execution strategies

On the other hand, compared to the purely hierarchical operation the 2nd method has the advantage that it reacts faster to resource failures due to rapid local scheduling while maintaining a global optimization view and thus minimizing makespan (9567 sec in case 2 compared to 9642 sec in case 1). The online re-planning and finishing of the packet orders and the offline re-planning of the remaining orders are done in parallel, saving thus time as compared with the pure hierarchical strategy which inserts an important production stop.

Because of the latency of the communication protocols (few minutes for 200 orders) the data transfer time between the resource control layer and the centralized MES layer makes the purely hierarchical method undesirable especially if perturbations occur frequently. This is also the case for FMS with heterogeneous control and communication resources which do not support open-interfaces. In such situation the hierarchical to permanent heterarchical commuting is preferred.

6 Conclusion

The paper proposes a Service Oriented Architecture for Total Manufacturing Enterprise Integration used for supporting both the business and control operation of manufacturing systems. At the business level it facilitates the integration of functionalities like Offer Request-, Production Order-, Rush Order-, Customer- and Supplier Relationship-Management. At control level it provides a flexible switching between hierarchical and heterarchical strategies called semi-heterarchical control.

This model greatly simplifies the resource allocation process during heterarchical mode, and also allows for dynamic reconfiguring of resource consortia depending on the quality of the services they provide. The capacity of a semi-heterachical control system to switch back to a global optimal mode without stop (with on line optimization of orders in execution while computing a centralized re-planning) solves the long term optimization problem, making the system more reactive since global planning and scheduling are decoupled from local scheduling, the two being done in parallel.

This behaviour is also confirmed by results obtained from real experiments which have shown the benefit of dynamically changing the control architecture: following centralized planning and scheduling recommendations as long as possible (for cost efficiency), and switching at resource failure or performance degradation to decentralized scheduling (for agility).

References

1. Verstraete, P., Valckenaers, P., Van Brussel, H., Saint Germain, B., Haldeli, K., Van Belle, J.: Towards robust and efficient planning execution. Eng. Appl. Artif. Intel. **21**(3), 304–314 (2008)
2. Kaminsky, P., Kaya, O.: centralized versus decentralized scheduling and due date quotation in a make-to-order supply chain. In: Proceedings of the MSOM'05 Conference, North-Western University Evanston, Illinois (2005)
3. Murillo, J., Muñoz, V., Busquets, D., López, B.: Schedule coordination through egalitarian recurrent multi-unit combinatorial auctions. Appl. Intel. J. **34**(1), 47–63 (2009) (published online, Springer)
4. Babiceanu, R.F., Chen, F.F., Sturges, R.H.: Framework for control of automated material-handling systems using holonic manufacturing approach. Int. J. Product. Res. **42**(17), 3551–3564 (2004)
5. Barata, J.: The cobasa architecture as an answer to shop floor agility. In: Kordic, V. (ed.) Manufacturing the Future, Concepts, Technologies and Vision, ARS Germany, pp. 908–923 (2006)
6. Leitão, P., Restivo, F.: Implementation of a holonic control system in a flexible manufacturing system. IEEE Trans. Syst. Man Cybern. Part C Appl. Rev. **38**(5), 699–709 (2008)

7. Leitão, P.: An agile and adaptive holonic architecture for manufacturing, control. Ph.D. Thesis (2004)
8. Leitão, P., Restivo, F.: A holonic approach to dynamic manufacturing scheduling. In: Shen, W. (ed.) Information Technology For Balanced Manufacturing Systems. IFIP, vol. 220, pp. 37–46. Springer, Boston (2006)
9. Sallez, Y., Berger, T., Raileanu, S., Chaabane, S., Trentesaux, D.: Semi-heterarchical control of FMS: from theory to application. Eng. Appl. Artif. Intel. **23**(8), 1314–1326 (2010)
10. Ulieru, M., Doursat, R.: Emergent engineering: a radical paradigm shift. Int. J. Auton. Adapt. Commun. Syst. (IJAACS) **4**(1), 39–60 (2011)
11. Valckenaers, P., Hadeli, K., Saint Germain, B., Verstraete, P., Van Brussel, H.: MAS coordination and control based on stigmergy. Comput. Ind. **58**(7), 621–629 (2007)
12. Claes, R., Holvoet, T., Wyns, D.: A decentralized approach for anticipatory vehicle routing using delegate multiagent systems. IEEE Trans. Intel. Transport. Syst. **99**, 364–393 (2011)
13. Novas, J.M., Bahtiar, R., Van Belle, J., Valckenaers, P.: An approach for the integration of a scheduling system and a multi-agent manufacturing execution system. towards a collaborative framework. In: Proceedings of the 14th IFAC Symposium INCOM'12, Bucharest, IFAC PapersOnLine, pp. 728–733 (2012)
14. Kusiak, A.: Intelligent Manufacturing Systems. Prentice-Hall, Englewood Cliffs (1990)
15. Sauer, O.: Automated engineering of manufacturing execution systems – a contribution to "adaptivity" in manufacturing companies. DET 2008 Nantes, France, pp. 181–193 (2006)
16. Borangiu, T., Gilbert, P., Ivanescu, N.A., Rosu, A.: An implementing framework for holonic manufacturing control with multiple robot-vision stations. EAAI, **22**, 4–5, 505–521 (2009) (Elsevier)
17. Morariu, O.: Resource monitoring in cloud platforms with tivoli service automation management. In: Proceedings of the IFAC Symposium Information Control Problems in Manufacturing (INCOM'12), IFAC PapersOnLine, vol. 14, no. 1, pp. 1862–1868 (2012)
18. Morariu, O., Morariu, C., Borangiu, T.: Transparent Real Time Monitoring for Multi-tenant J2EE Applications. J. Control Eng. Appl. Inf. **15**(4), 37–46 (2013)
19. Boyd, A., Noller, D., Peters, P., Salkeld, D., Thomasma, T., Gifford, C., Pike, S., Smith, A.: SOA in Manufacturing Guidebook. MESA International, IBM Corporation and Cap-gemini co-branded white paper (2008)
20. Van Brussel, H.V., Wyns, J., Valckenaers, P., Bongaerts, L., Peeters, P.: Reference architecture for holonic manufacturing systems: PROSA. Comput. Ind. **37**(3), 255–274 (1998). Special Issue on IMS

On the Necessity and Nature of E-Mobility Services – Towards a Service Description Framework

Carola Stryja[✉], Hansjörg Fromm, Sabrina Ried, Patrick Jochem, and Wolf Fichtner

Karlsruhe Service Research Institute,
Englerstraße 11, 76131 Karlsruhe, Germany
{carola.stryja,hansjoerg.fromm,sabrina.ried,
patrick.jochem,wolf.fichtner}@kit.edu

Abstract. After years of focusing exclusively on the technological side of electric mobility (e-mobility), services are getting more and more in the focus of scientists. Many recent works concentrate on the identification and analysis of the potential of new business models in this field. Although the relevancy of services for the success of e-mobility is becoming more obvious among industry and science, there is still a lack in scientific contributions when asking for a comprehensive overview of existing e-mobility services. With this paper, we try to bridge this gap by providing a framework that enables the description and classification of services around the usage of an electric vehicle (EV). The framework captures six dimensions which allows to characterize and compare different services. This enables the identification of commonalities and differences between the services and provides an interdisciplinary playground for developing new services and further research in this field.

Keywords: E-Mobility · Services · Description framework · Service dimension

1 Introduction

In order to limit global warming to 2 °C above pre-industrial levels, mitigation of greenhouse gas (GHG) emissions is on the agenda of many countries and organizations around the world [1, 2]. For Germany, the Federal Ministry for the Environment, Nature Conservation, Building and Nuclear Safety has calculated that the GHG emissions of passenger cars should be reduced by 80 % between 2005 and 2050 [3].

This reduction target cannot be reached with efficiency improvements of conventional combustion engines alone. It can only be reached with a bundle of measures. One main measure is the electrification of vehicles [3] going along with an increase of electricity generation by renewable energy sources (e.g. [4, 5]).

Electric vehicles (EV) can generally be distinguished into three groups [6] (see Fig. 1): (a) vehicles relying on continuous electric supply from an off-board generation system, (b) vehicles relying on stored electricity from an off-board generation system, and (c) vehicles relying mainly on on-board electric generation to supply their needs. Examples for group (a) vehicles are electric trains or trolley buses powered by overhead wires. Group (b) includes *battery-electric vehicles* (BEV) and group (c) includes hybrid-electric vehicles (HEV) which have an electric motor and an internal combustion engine. Electric hybrids can be further distinguished into hybrids without a vehicle inlet for electricity, *range-extended electric vehicles* (REEV), and *plug-in hybrid electric vehicles* (PHEV). Thus, electric cars fall into groups (b) and (c).

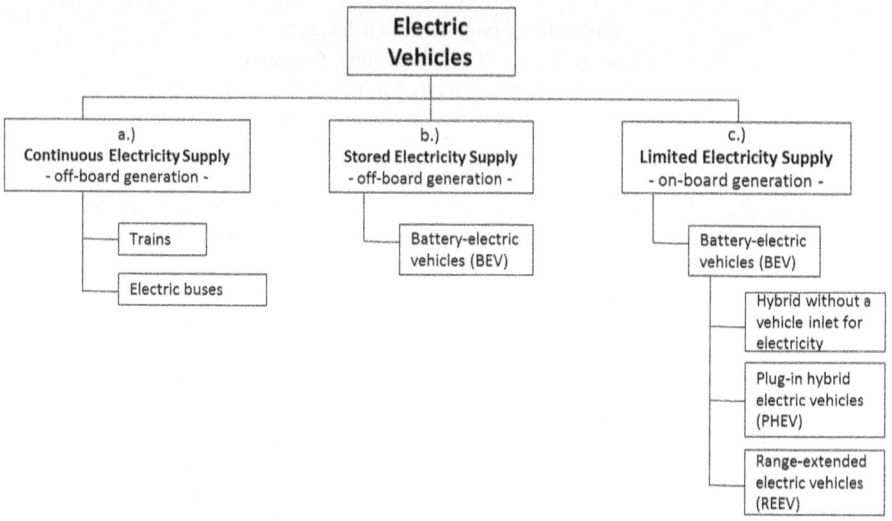

Fig. 1. Typology of electric vehicles (based on [6])

In the interest of this paper are *plug-in electric vehicles* (PEV) including BEV, REEV, and PHEV which allow a recharging of the battery from the external grid. Many governments have set targets for the market dissemination of PEV. For example, the United States are aiming for one million PEV on their roads by 2015 and Germany aims at one million PEV by 2020 [7].

In general, the success factors for market penetration of PEV are manifold. Some factors are (based on [8, 9]):

(a) adequate purchase prices of EV (highly dependent on battery prices), especially in comparison with traditional vehicle prices;
(b) similar total cost of ownership of EV vs. traditional vehicles (largely determined by gasoline, diesel, and battery prices);
(c) monetary and non-monetary incentives;
(d) reduction of driving range limitations, charging time, and increasing green image as well as adequate availability of a convenient charging network; and finally
(e) services which make the use of electric vehicles as easy and comfortable as possible.

The last success factor in the list, "services", has been widely neglected in literature and research landscape so far [15, 16].

Traditional automotive mobility could be seen as a complex but rather static ecosystem consisting of a product – the car – and a multitude of services surrounding this product. Examples are gas stations, maintenance and repair services, car wash services, but also insurance, financing, leasing, and services within the car like traffic information and navigation. We are typically not much concerned about these services, because they are widely available and functioning well. If we run short of gas, the next gas station is most often not far away.

This is quite different for electric mobility (*e-mobility*). Charging stations for PEV are not found at every arterial road or major intersection. This means that services have to be provided to locate charging stations – offline, or integrated into the navigation systems. Charging a PEV takes much longer than filling up gasoline today – even though fast charging stations allow an 80 % charging in less than 15 min. To make sure that an unoccupied charging station is available, a reservation is desirable. If someone wants to travel a larger distance with a PEV, the navigation system should consider stops that are necessary for charging. Intelligent systems might combine the stop with the recommendation of a restaurant or shopping mall, so that the battery could be recharged while the driver and companions make the best use of their time. These service scenarios are all related to travelling, but other services for e-mobility might be offered much earlier in the "PEV life cycle". First, services are being offered that give the owner of a traditional automobile an indication, if a PEV would fit to his or her mobility needs. This indication can be based on GPS data from trips with a conventional car that the driver shares with the service provider and that are being statistically evaluated to characterize the driver's mobility pattern (distances travelled, parking times and locations, geography). Thus recommendations for very individual mobility requirements can be given.

These examples demonstrate that for e-mobility new services need to be provided (e.g., reserving a charging station, evaluating the fit of a PEV) and existing services need to be extended (e.g., navigation considering charging locations and times). Many conventional services (e.g., maintenance and repair, financing) remain the same, but need to take the special characteristics of PEV into account. Furthermore, the current trend to intermodal mobility in many countries (and the increasing services in this field) seems to fit well to EV. Their low variable costs, local emission free driving in rural areas and their limited range makes them to a very attractive link within intermodal trip chains. Car sharing programs are a good example for an ideal application environment for PEVs. Combined with a train ride or flight, PEV are ideally suited to cover the "last mile". Such an offering is more likely to be accepted if the customer can book the entire trip from one provider. Other mobility "bundles" are already offered by automotive companies for customers who buy a PEV: for weekend or vacation trips, they have the option to use a conventional (long-range) car.

A mobility system providing all necessary services for PEV differs strongly from the long-established conventional automotive system. It is a system that includes players from the automotive industry (e.g., car manufacturers, suppliers), the energy sector (e.g., utilities, grid operators), the public sector (e.g., public transportation, cities, authorities), other players in the transportation sector (e.g., rental car companies, logistics service providers), the IT industry and in the middle: the user (e.g., driver or owner of a car). Much more than the traditional system, it is more dynamically and an *open system* in which new players are continuing to enter. The system requires interaction between players which traditionally were not closely related (e.g. automotive and energy industry). New business models, pricing mechanisms and revenue sharing models need to be developed. Information and communication technology (ICT) plays an important role in providing platforms for connectivity and innovation and attractive end-user solutions. The availability and intelligent use of data becomes an important factor.

In this open system it is still not clear who will provide the individual services for e-mobility. The system is highly dynamic and competitive maneuvering can be observed. To understand these dynamics, it is first necessary to understand the nature of services around the use of PEVs. In this context, the following two research questions arise:

RQ 1: Which services are necessary for a convenient PEV usage?
RQ 2: How can they be described in a short and structured manner?

The description and mapping of services is an important basis for all forthcoming research. Further studies will be necessary to get clear of the impact services have on user acceptance and how far conventional companies will be able to offer these services by themselves or whether they need to form alliances.

The paper is organized as follows: Sect. 2 discusses several scientific works which focus on e-mobility and related services while Sect. 3 explains the exploratory study, we used for this work. In Sect. 4, the description framework is introduced by proposing relevant e-mobility services as well as dimensions to describe them in further detail. At the end, a summary and outlook section provides insight to limitations and further research potentials of this work.

2 State of Research and Related Work

Since the research on e-mobility services is still at its beginning, studies and publications in this domain are rare and distributed over various disciplines, often without linkages between them, e.g. automotive engineering, energy economics, information systems or transportation and logistics.

The research of e-mobility services is also a research of service systems. According to Maglio and Spohrer [10] a service system is "a configuration of people, technologies, organizations and shared information, able to create and deliver value to providers, users and other interested entities, through service" (p. 18). This is also defined in the main principles of service science introduced by Spohrer et al. [11], in which service systems are connections of service entities as nodes and value propositions as their ties. These networks are shaped by the exchange of resources, collaborative advantages as well as cooperative strategies [12, 13]. An example in the field of e-mobility networks and business models is the study by Kley et al. [14]. The authors provide a foundation for a structured analysis of business models. By listing and analyzing examples of existing business models, the authors state that there are a lot of initiatives in many domains which, however, are often in a too early stage. To address this problem, they use the methodology of morphological boxes to capture different aspects of the e-mobility business model and derive a descriptive model for a structured characterization of business models for e-mobility [14]. By explicitly addressing e-mobility services, Busse et al. [15] are the first who provide an overview of the research domain. However, they limit their work to information systems (IS) services only. In this context, they define service groups in a technical way as collections that "combine(s) a homogeneous concentration of properties required for operation, business and other additional support purposes" (p. 914). Furthermore, the unclear distinction and description of each service group makes it difficult to identify the different services which are allocated to the group. Driven by its IS-focus, the framework thus ignores services that are important for running e-mobility but are not touched by the IS domain as such. The customer as individual with needs and expectations is not captured by this work.

In contrast, the relevance of addressing the customer role in this field has been emphasized by Klör et al. [16]. Their approach does not have the goal to provide a description of the overall e-mobility ecosystem but rather strives for drawing a research agenda for future IS research. Nevertheless, their work is a valuable foundation for our study since the authors emphasize the missing system perspective in current publications on e-mobility services. They state that studies on e-mobility services are too often too much focused on the resources involved rather than on the system in which they are used. Klör et al. highlight the customer acceptance as one of the "core challenges" of e-mobility. Today, there is already a broad literature on this issue [17–20]. However, many studies are still analyzing ways to enhance customer acceptance only by focusing on price and overall usage costs or at least with a strong economic background. By this, the understanding of the customer is too often a picture of a completely rational individual ("homo oeconomicus") which could be convinced just by reducing price and total cost of ownership (TCO) and improving the charging infrastructure. In fact, the customer is far more than this – especially during the car purchase decision [21–24]. Every user is a human being whose decision for or against the use of e-mobility is influenced by various factors concerning his or her mindset. Besides economic considerations this is especially the social network, the income, the mobility patterns, the culture in which the customer grew up etc.

A missing point in all studies we analyzed is the comprehensive and interdisciplinary view on e-mobility services. Those services usually address many actors and activities whose interactions have not been considered by current research yet. To bridge this gap, we aim for providing a more comprehensive and service science-based view on the topic of e-mobility services. The core concept of the service science domain is the co-creation aspect between service provider and service consumer [11]. The provision of a service typically involves the contribution of the customer who expects the fulfillment of a value proposition made by the service provider. To address this issue, studies on e-mobility services which claim to give an overview of existing services have to include co-creation aspects in their service description.

3 Methodology

The framework we present in the following sections has been derived by insights gained within a small exploratory study of nine interviews with experts of the e-mobility industry and the research fields of service science, information systems and energy economics. All experts are either part of e-mobility service research projects or work in leading positions (e.g. head of business development, head of strategy) of the e-mobility actors. The expert sample consists of employees from one main car manufacturer, one IT-service provider, one roaming (billing) provider, one energy provider, one fleet software start-up as well as four representatives of research projects in this field, with background in different disciplines.

Each interview has been conducted by using a semi-structured interview guideline with questions concerning various aspects of e-mobility services. These were characteristics of successful e-mobility services, their network structure as well as the customer and provider aspect. The duration of all interviews varied between forty-five and ninety minutes. Each interview has been transcribed and analysed by using the open coding method of the grounded theory methodology. Open coding is defined as a systematic comparison of unstructured qualitative data in order to find conceptual similarities which allow a categorization in groups and related subgroups. Referring to our study, we tried to identify recurring e-mobility service characteristics in our interview material [25]. Afterwards, two workshops with a focus group of ten researchers from the domains of service science, energy economics and e-mobility were initiated to evaluate the characteristics collected in the interview phase and to derive suitable dimensions for the description framework.

4 Describing E-Mobility Services

Analyzing and designing e-mobility services require a profound knowledge about the different facets by which a service can be characterized. Description frameworks help to structure existing data and information about the entities of interest in a way that knowledge can emerge. The objective of this paper is to propose an intuitive, i.e. applicable and reasonable description framework for e-mobility services along several dimensions. This allows other researchers to test the framework by adding other services in the field of e-mobility and, thus, further validating and eventually improving this framework.

The intention of this work is to provide to give a comprehensive understanding of how the term "e-mobility service" can be described in a more tangible and applicable way than existing theoretical approaches may offer. This might be the basis for future research on the relationships between players and the overall system.

4.1 Identification of E-Mobility Services

The following list provides a collection of services which are useful for driving a PEV. The services have been sorted along four contexts in which a customer might get in touch with during the lifetime of the car. These service contexts are briefly described in the following section with a list of non-exhaustive examples that has been named in interviews and the focus group involved and repeatedly identified in literature research.

Group 1: Services in the context of buying a PEV are services concerning the acquisition of a PEV and managing the ownership either as proprietor or as user when choosing leasing contracts.

- Car leasing
- Car financing
- Battery leasing
- Insurance (traditional, pay-as-you-drive)
- Safety and theft protection

Group 2: Services in the context of using a PEV encompass all services around the direct usage of PEV.

- Battery changing/swapping
- Billing and roaming (of charging)
- Car usage information (private, fleet)
- Charging station finder
- Navigation (including charging)
- Reservation of charging station
- Roadside assistance
- Fleet analysis and consulting
- Information services (weather, sightseeing)
- Automatic emergency call in case of accident
- Entertainment services

Group 3: Services in the context of maintaining a PEV concern technical maintenance and battery care.

- Battery recycling, battery testing
- Car washing
- Car maintenance and repair

Group 4: EV services in a system context encompass all services which integrate the PEV in a larger system context such as Smart Grid or as part of a multimodal service offering.

- Intermodal navigation
- Vehicle-to-grid services (battery as storage)
- Conventional vehicle option for PEV owners
- Car sharing services
- Yard and plug sharing service platform (for private households)
- E-mobility consulting services (for private persons and fleet operators)

Since the services in the list are very heterogeneous, the current clustering approach is insufficient for a profound analysis. In order to better understand the services, i.e. its provider, customer and delivery structure, further dimensions seem to be necessary. The next section will introduce the fundamental framework approach as well as propositions for potential dimensions that have been emerged as a first appropriate foundation for an e-mobility service description.

4.2 A Multidimensional Approach for Describing E-Mobility Services

In this section, six exemplary dimensions are introduced which have been considered by the focus group as appropriate initialization of the framework. Appropriate literature has been selected to support the results of the focus group work. At the end of the section, two exemplary services have been chosen to show the dimensional functionality. As guiding principle for selecting the dimensions, established works in the field of service classification have been used.

Several approaches for description and categorization of services have been suggested by researchers in the past (e.g. [26, 27]). The intended result is to get a brief but clear description of each e-mobility service in the system. The selection of the dimensions is significant to ensure the applicability of the framework.

4.2.1 Description According to the Value Proposition

One essential part of service transactions is the value proposition which defines the service setting, its delivery and the expectations that customers have of the service [11]. This dimension is important to capture the fundamental intention that is aligned with the service, i.e. value added by delivering the service. A categorization of services according to their customer value has been suggested e.g. by Westphal et al. [28] who state that product-oriented services can add value through product individualization, improvement of the customer-supplier relationship, the support of customers regarding product-related processes such as vehicle usage, and through services in the context of product financing. Dimensional entities are "energy service", "mobility service", "installation service", "charging service", "financial service".

An alternative approach for assessing the service value might be to analyze whether the e-mobility service enables PEV a similar customer value known from conventional vehicles and thus compensating for current disadvantages of e-mobility or whether the service even increases the customer value with respect to current utility. Today, since most of the current e-mobility services rather can be allocated to the first category, e.g. the localisation of charging stations or an online estimation of the remaining range, this does not seem suitable for the description framework.

4.2.2 Description According to the Service Position in the Vehicle Lifecycle

We base our understanding of the lifecycle according the German standard DIN 9241-210 for user experience with "product-related processes". The standard distinguishes three stages (entities): before usage, during usage and after usage. Since some services may affect the whole product lifecycle, we introduce a further dimension "concerning whole lifecycle" in our framework. Therefore, dimensional entities are "before usage", "during usage", "after usage", "whole lifecycle".

4.2.3 Description According to the Nature and Recipient of the Service Act

According to Lovelock [27], services can be distinguished according to their nature and the consumer of the service. Similarly, Hill [29] mentions the categories services affecting persons vs. those affecting goods. Also Shostack [30] and Sasser et al. [31] use the share of goods or intangible services for categorizing a product. For the framework, the following three categories of [27] have been adapted.

Consequently, the dimensional entities are "tangible actions" (services directed at goods and other of the physical possessions, such as maintenance and repair), "intangible actions" (services directed at people's minds, such as navigation/charging station finder), and "intangible services" (services directed at intangible assets such as financing or insurance).

4.2.4 Description According to the Nature of Provider and Recipient

Each service transaction is an exchange between a service provider and a service recipient. Rathmell [26] suggested the service categories type of seller, type of buyer, buying motives, buying practice and the degree of regulation. For this work, the first two categories "seller" and "buyer" have been adapted, since the knowledge on the market players involved in the transaction is a prerequisite for a later description of the whole e-mobility service system (e.g. alliance structures, business models). This dimension therefore describes the relationship of provider and customer regarding the question who offers and who receives the service. However, both service provider and service recipient can have more than one role for a service. For example: a plug sharing service platform can be offered by a small IT- Start up or an established energy provider. Dimensional entities are "IT services provider", "OEM", "auto repair shop", "energy provider", "charging service provider", "roaming services provider", "financial services provider", "consultancy provider", "fleet operator", "driver" (normally end-user, but provider in a V2G context), "car owner", "others".

4.2.5 Description According to the End User Closeness

The fifth summarizes the overall closeness to the end user. This dimension is chosen since the knowledge about the service's position in the service value chain is a prerequisite for deriving a service network. Services which are directly addressing the end user need a different service setting than support services inside the service system. While in the first case the service delivery focuses more on the personal interaction and the customer experience aspect, the supporting (often business to business) service is more characterized by economic aspects and service level contracts. Dimensional entities are "supporting service", "end user service".

4.2.6 Description According to the Degree of Service Modification

Some of the services discussed and introduced for PEV are not transferrable to conventional vehicles, such as the reservation of a charging station, mainly because there is no need for them. However, other e-mobility services, e.g. separated leasing, rental or sales contracts for the vehicle and its battery, are already known from conventional vehicles but modified for the electric car. The sixth and last dimension "service modification degree" describes the degree of novelty of a service. Often e-mobility services are simply adaptations of classical car service offerings such as maintenance, navigation or insurance services. The framework distinguishes between two possible properties of a service: "developed for PEV" and "modified for PEV".

To illustrate the principle of the framework, two selected services from the service groups of Sect. 4.1 are described and represented by using a morphological box [32]. In the morphological box, the leading dimensions are placed on the outer left side while the dimensional entities are organized on the right side (see Fig. 2). When describing a service, the corresponding dimensional entity (or entities) is marked for each dimension. For developing further services, potential contradictions of dimensional entities can be identified. This decreases the complexity of the problem. The working principle is illustrated in the following figures that show four selected description examples from the service groups of Sect. 4.1.

Description Dimensions	Dimensional Entities				
Value proposition	energy service	mobility service	(de)installation service	charging service	financial service
Position in EV lifecycle	before usage	during usage	after usage	complete life cycle	
Nature of the service act	tangible action directed at goods		intangible actions directed at people	intangible actions directed at intangible assets	
Nature of service provider	OEM	IT services provider	auto repair shop	energy provider	charging service provider	roaming services provider
Nature of service recipient	car owner	driver	fleet operator	...	
Closeness to end user	supporting service			end user service	
Service modification degree	developed for PEV			modified for PEV	

Fig. 2. Description framework as morphological box

In an electric car, the battery is one of the most expensive parts. However, the lifetime of the battery does not necessarily correspond to the lifetime of the vehicle. In order to reduce the risks of the vehicle users, there is the option to rent the battery from a battery leasing company. This company might maintain, withdraw and replace (if necessary) the battery. This "Battery Leasing" service shall be the first illustrating example to demonstrate the framework application (cf. Fig. 3).

The value proposition which comes along with the battery service is some kind of a charging service. The service is used usually while using the car actively, hence the field "during usage" is marked in the framework. Further is the service a tangible action which means that a car workshop or even the leasing provider itself put the old battery out of the car and the new one in. This is a visible action concerning a tangible good, the battery. The provider of the service is the battery leasing provider which is here understood as sort of a charging service provider. As service recipients, all "forms" of customers are possible so all of them are marked in the framework. The service itself is

Group 1: Battery Leasing					
Value proposition	energy service	mobility service	(de)installation service	charging service	financial service
Position in EV lifecycle	before usage	during usage	after usage	complete life cycle	
Nature of the service act	tangible action directed at goods		intangible actions directed at people	intangible actions directed at intangible assets	
Nature of service provider	OEM	IT services provider	auto repair shop	energy provider	charging service provider	roaming services provider
Nature of service recipient	car owner	driver	fleet operator	...	
Closeness to end user	supporting service			end user service	
Service modification degree	developed for PEV			modified for PEV	

Fig. 3. Description of "Battery Leasing"

a service provided for the end user – that means, it is not an intermediate and background service such as many IT services are. At least, leasing a battery is a service developed exclusively for electric cars. There is no equivalent offering so far for conventional cars.

In Fig. 4, one service of group 2 "Services in the context of using an EV" has been selected. The reservation of charging stations is an important tool to guarantee the charging process at the required time and at the desired place. Since there is usually a limited amount of charging stations at highly frequented places such as shopping malls or public parking slots, a well working reservation system is inevitable. Here, the value proposition of the service is to enable mobility for people by getting their electric cars charged while they are working, shopping etc. The service itself is offered via the internet and is characterized by its intangible accomplishment. The customers expect the service to be done when they arrive at the charging station. Usually, the service is offered by the charging service provider, i.e. owner of the charging stations. The service is especially relevant for the driver of the electric car but also important for car owner or fleet operators in the case of integrating the service in their own infrastructure. We consider the service as end user service since the customer directly interacts with the reservation system.

We applied our categorization framework exemplary with two services. It becomes obvious, that at least for these examples our framework delivers a good mapping of services and it might be used as a basis for further developments of the services. However, since the framework has not been evaluated by any empirical study, this will be the next step in the research process. Therefore, several case studies with existing e-mobility services may be a possibility to test the applicability of the framework.

Group 2: Reservation Service for Charging Stations						
Value proposition	energy service	mobility service	(de)installation service	charging service	financial service	
Position in EV lifecycle	before usage	during usage	after usage	complete life cycle		
Nature of the service act	tangible action directed at goods		intangible actions directed at people	intangible actions directed at intangible assets		
Nature of service provider	OEM	IT services provider	auto repair shop	energy provider	charging service provider	roaming services provider
Nature of service recipient	car owner	driver	fleet operator	...		
Closeness to end user	supporting service			end user service		
Service modification degree	developed for PEV			modified for PEV		

Fig. 4. Description of "Reservation Service for Charging Stations"

5 Summary and Outlook

This paper describes potential synergies of services and the usage of electric cars. We identified a research gap in the field of structured analysis of electric mobility services and develop a first framework for describing and categorizing them.

By using insights from a literature review and an exploratory study conducted with practitioners from industry and science, relevant e-mobility services have been identified and described. Building on these services, six appropriate categorization dimensions have been introduced and applied to two example e-mobility services. The development and application of the framework is an important step towards an e-mobility service system description model. By filtering the services along certain dimensions, new insights into the e-mobility service landscape, e.g. "white spots" or the identification of patterns in customer/provider relationships would be possible.

However, our exploratory study only consists of nine expert interviews. Thus, the insights gained may not be representative and comprehensive enough to sketch the current e-mobility service market. Consequently, we suggest the proposed framework as a first attempt of shedding light on the research agenda in this field.

Further expert interviews (from other sectors and disciplines) tests and refinements of our framework as well as the inclusion of further services and dimensions will complete this research. Further research could also focus on the relationships between the market players, i.e. the form of alliance building, existing business models between the players.

References

1. Edenhofer, O., Pichs-Madruga, R., Sokona, Y., Farahani, E., Kadner, S., Seyboth, K., Adler, A., Baum, I., Brunner, S., Eickemeier, P., Kriemann, B., Savolainen, J., Schlömer, S., von Stechow, C., Zwickel, T., Minx, J.C. (eds.) Climate Change 2014: Mitigation of Climate Change. Contribution of Working Group III to the Fifth Assessment Report of the Intergovernmental Panel on Climate Change (IPCC). Cambridge University Press, Cambridge (2014)
2. European Commission: Roadmap to a single European transport area—towards a competitive and resource efficient transport system. White Paper COM (2011), March 2011
3. Federal Ministry for the Environment, Nature Conservation and Nuclear Safety (BMU): Renewably mobile. Marketable solutions for climate-friendly electric mobility, April 2013
4. Torchio, M.F., Santarelli, M.G.: Energy, environmental and economic comparison of different powertrain/fuel options using well-to-wheels assessment, energy and external costs – European market analysis. Energy **35**(10), 4156–4171 (2010)
5. Thomas, C.E.S.: How green are electric vehicles? Int. J. Hydrogen Energy **37**(7), 6053–6062 (2012)
6. Faiz, A., Weaver, C.S., Walsh, M.P.: Air Pollution from Motor Vehicles: Standards and Technologies for Controlling Emissions. World Bank Publications, Washington, DC (1996)
7. Progress Report of the German National Platform for Electric Mobility, Third report, May 2012
8. Pfahl, S., Jochem, P., Fichtner, W.: When will electric vehicles capture the German market? And why? In: Proceedings of the EVS27 International Battery, Hybrid and Fuel Cell Electric Vehicle Symposium, Barcelona, Spain (2013)
9. Sierzchula, W., et al.: The influence of financial incentives and other socio-economic factors on electric vehicle adoption. Energy Policy **68**, 183–194 (2014)
10. Maglio, P.P., Spohrer, J.: Fundamentals of service science. J. Acad. Market. Sci. **36**(1), 18–20 (2007)
11. Spohrer, J., Anderson, L., Pass, N., Ager, T.: Service science and service-dominant logic. In: Otago Forum, vol. 2 (2007)
12. Allee, V.: Reconfiguring the value network. J. Bus. Strategy **2**(4), 36–39 (2000)
13. Barile, S., Polese, F.: Smart service systems and viable service systems: applying systems theory to service science. Serv. Sci. **2**(1–2), 21–40 (2010)
14. Kley, F., Lerch, C., Dallinger, D.: New business models for electric cars—a holistic approach. Energy Policy **39**(6), 3392–3403 (2011)
15. Busse, S., Runge, S., Jagstaidt, U., Kolbe, L.M.: An ecosystem overview and taxonomy of electric vehicle specific services. In: MKWI Tagungsband, pp. 908–920 (2014)
16. Klör, B., Bräuer, S., Beverungen, D., Matzner, M.: IT-basierte Dienstleistungen für die Elektromobilität – Konzeptioneller Rahmen und Literaturanalyse. In: MKWI Tagungsband, pp. 2048–2066 (2014)
17. Hackbarth, A., Madlener, R.: Consumer preferences for alternative fuel vehicles: a discrete choice analysis. Transp. Res. Part D: Transp. Environ. **25**, 5–17 (2013)
18. Dütschke, E., Schneider, U., Peters, A., Paetz, A.-G., Jochem, P.: Moving towards more efficient car use - what can be learnt about consumer acceptance from analysing the cases of LPG and CNG? In: ECEEE 2011 Summer Study Proceedings (2011)
19. Peters, A., Dütschke, E.: How do consumers perceive electric vehicles? A comparison of German consumer groups. J. Environ. Policy Plan. **16**(1) (2014)

20. Ensslen, A., Jochem, P., Schäuble, J., Babrowski, S., Fichtner, W.: User acceptance of electric vehicles in the French-German transnational context. In: Proceedings of the 13th WCTR, Rio de Janeiro, pp. 15–18 (2013)
21. Propfe, B., Kreyenberg, D., Wind, J., Schmid, S.: Market penetration analysis of electric vehicles in the German passenger car market towards 2030. Int. J. Hydrogen Energy **38**(13), 5201–5208 (2013)
22. Mueller, M.G., de Haan, P.: How much do incentives affect car purchase? Agent-based microsimulation of consumer choice of new cars—Part I: Model structure, simulation of bounded rationality, and model validation. Energy Policy **37**(3), 1072–1082 (2009)
23. de Haan, P., Mueller, M.G., Scholz, R.W.: How much do incentives affect car purchase? Agent-based microsimulation of consumer choice of new cars—Part II: Forecasting effects of feebates based on energy-efficiency. Energy Policy **37**(3), 1083–1094 (2009)
24. Eggers, F., Eggers, F.: Where have all the flowers gone? Forecasting green trends in the automobile industry with a choice-based conjoint adoption model. Technol. Forecast. Soc. Change **78**(1), 51–62 (2011)
25. Corbin, J.M., Strauss, A.: Grounded theory research: procedures, canons, and evaluative criteria. Qual. Sociol. **13**(1), 3–21 (1990)
26. Rathmell, J.M.: Marketing in the Service Sector. Winthrop, Cambridge (1974)
27. Lovelock, C.H.: Classifying services to gain strategic marketing insights. J. Market. **47**, 9–20 (1983)
28. Westphal, I., Nehls, J., Wiesner, S., Thoben, K.-D.: Steigerung der Attraktivität von Elektroautomobilen durch neue Produkt-Service-Kombinationen. Ind. Manag. **5**, 19–24 (2013)
29. Hill, T.P.: On goods and services. Rev. Income Wealth **23**(4), 315–338 (1977)
30. Shostack, G.L.: Breaking free from product marketing. J. Market. **41**, 73–80 (1977)
31. Sasser, W.E., Olsen, R.P., Wyckoff, D.D.: Management of Service Operations: Text, Cases, and Readings. Allyn and Bacon, Boston (1978)
32. Zwicky, F., Wilson, A. (eds.): New Methods of Thought and Procedure: Contributions to the Symposium on Methodologies. Springer, Berlin (1967)

Towards the Alignment of a Detailed Service-Oriented Design and Development Methodology with ITIL v.3

Bertrand Verlaine[(✉)], Ivan Jureta, and Stéphane Faulkner

PReCISE Research Center, University of Namur, Rempart de la Vierge 8,
5000 Namur, Belgium
{bertrand.verlaine,ivan.jureta,stephane.faulkner}@unamur.be

Abstract. Many organizations providing IT services try to be service-oriented at the business layer and at the IT layer. To do so, these organizations follow a service-orientation for their management and business processes while working with a service-oriented system (SOS). This should improve, i.a., their work organization during the service implementation projects and the exchange of information between the stakeholders. However, a very few papers bring solutions for aligning an IT service management (ITSM) framework –which represents the business layer– with a service implementation methodology –which stands for the IT level.

In this paper, we detail the Papazoglou's service design and development methodology in order to align it with ITIL v.3, which is probably the most used ITSM framework. This work should help the staff of companies respecting the ITIL v.3 best practices and owing an SOS in their communication and in their project management, leading to the implementation and the composition of services.

Keywords: Enterprise architecture · IT service management · ITIL v3 · Service-oriented paradigm · Service implementation methodology

1 Introduction

The *enterprise architecture* seeks to bring together the Information Technologies (IT) layer and the business layer in organizations [1]. This requires an alignment of the vision, the strategy and the business processes of an organization with its Information System (IS) supporting its business activities. In this paper, we focus on organizations creating and selling IT services, whether it is a company or an internal IT department of a company whose the core business is not selling IT services. Of course, this narrow the scope covered regarding the business layer. This decision is motivated by the fact that many IT organizations aim at becoming service-oriented, i.e., applying service-oriented approaches both at the IT and business layers [2,3]. They are called *service-oriented organizations* by Gartner [4].

Regarding the architecture of their IS, several IT organizations follow the service-oriented paradigm. The latter is "a paradigm for organizing and utilizing distributed capabilities that may be under the control of different ownership domains." [5]. It leads to the implementation of Service-oriented Systems (SOS). An SOS combines the computational means to manage distributed and independent software functionalities named services which perform the functionalities required by the stakeholders [6]. The creation and the management of an SOS require to follow a Service-oriented Software Engineering (SOSE) model. As with the Traditional Software Engineering (TSE), SOSE is the application of a systematic and structured approach to the analysis, the design, the conception, the implementation, the operation and the maintenance of SOSs. Unlike TSE, SOSE has to organize the creation, the publication, the discovery, the composition, the evaluation and the monitoring of services [7]. However, "the existing SOSE methodologies focus mainly on the design and analysis part of the SOSE process, but pay little or not sufficient attention to the constructing, delivering and management part" [8]. This lack of organizational models for the management of the SOS creation is also underlined in [9]: its authors claim for more abstractions and management methods during the implementation and the composition of services. Therefore, aligning the SOS creation with the management of the IT organization using this SOS becomes one key issue.

In the literature, some works tackle this problem by focusing on the company governance aspects. The governance has to ensure that the stakeholders' point of view is taken into account to determine the organization vision and objectives, which are then monitored and measured [10]. At a lower level in the organization, the management refers to the planning, the building and the monitoring of the activities which should be aligned with the vision and the enterprise objectives set by the governance [10]. Although the organization governance is needed, a process alignment at the management level should help the IT teams and leaders in charge of the SOS implementation to coordinate their work with the rest of the IT organization and its processes, and conversely.

In order to reach this objective, we identify and analyse the relations between the steps of a detailed version of the Papazoglou's service-oriented design and development methodology [11] –we name it the *detailed service-oriented design and development methodology* (DSDDM)– with the ITIL V.3 processes. ITIL V.3 is an Information Technology Service Management (ITSM) framework composed of organizational best practices for providing IT services. The result of this work is an alignment between the business layer of an IT organization –represented by the ITIL V.3 best practices– and its IT layer managing an SOS –corresponding to DSDDM. This work also contributes to solve an issue left open in ITIL V.3 [12, Sect. 3.10]: *How to integrate the ITIL framework with a service implementation methodology?* This paper details how the ITIL V.3 framework can be aligned with a service implementation model which can be used to create and to compose services in an SOS.

The rest of this paper is organized as follows. Firstly, the lack of relations between ITIL V.3 and the service creation in an SOS is analysed in Sect. 2 (in which we also discuss the related work). Then, in Sect. 3, the service-oriented design and development methodology of Papazoglou is detailed in order to become its detailed version abbreviated by DSDDM. This enables to align the DSDDM steps with the ITIL V.3 processes (Sect. 4). The conclusion and future work end this paper (Sect. 5). Note that this publication is a shortened version of our work; see the technical paper [13] for a more complete and detail version of this paper.

2 An Analysis of the Current Identified Relations Between Service Implementation Methodologies and ITIL v.3

In this section, we first describe ITIL V.3 and the reference service-oriented design and development methodology (Sect. 2.1). Then, we pinpoint some of the issues coming from the lack of identified relations between them (Sect. 2.2). We finally analyse the related work in order to discuss the already proposed relations in the literature (Sect. 2.3).

2.1 A Brief Introduction to ITIL v.3 and to the Reference Service-Oriented Design and Development Methodology

The third version of ITIL, which has been revised in 2011, is the organizational framework used in the scope of this work. It is indeed one of the most used ITSM framework in the IT industry [15]. An ITSM framework provides best practices and recommendations to manage organizations providing IT services. One of the main ITIL objectives is to integrate the requirements of the customers and the users into many activities of IT organizations. The latter have to provide value to these customers and users in their own business processes.

ITIL V.3 is structured into five phases: Service Strategy [14], Service Design [12], Service Transition [16], Service Operation [17] and Continual Service Improvement [18]. Each of these phases is composed of processes –the latter are written down and associated to their phases in Fig. 1. For more information on ITIL V.3,

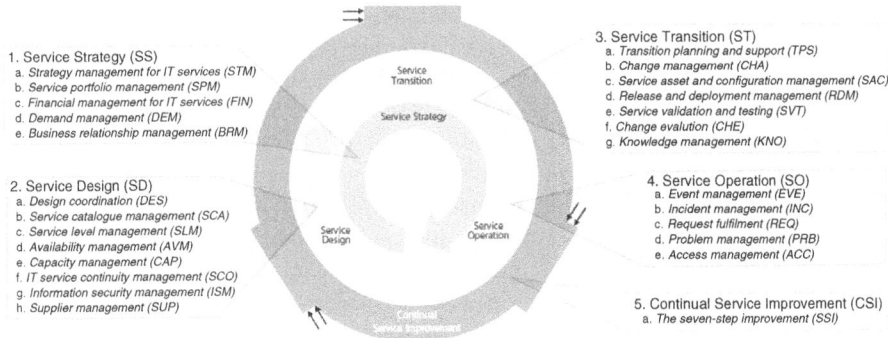

Fig. 1. ITIL V.3 life cycle (based on an official illustration of ITIL [14])

see [12,14,16–18] or the technical paper [13]. ITIL recommends, i.a., "that business processes and solutions should be designed and developed using a service-oriented architecture approach" [12, Sect. 3.10]. However, the relations between ITIL and a service implementation methodology are not detailed nor identified in the official ITIL publications. Some initiatives in the scientific literature address both the service-oriented paradigm and ITIL, but they mainly discuss the governance issue. In the scope of this work, we only focus on the management level.

Concerning the SOSE methodology, we refer to the one of Papazoglou called the service-oriented design and development methodology [11]. The main reason of this choice lies in its good evaluations compared to similar initiatives [8]. This methodology is his answer to the need for specific tools and methods taking into account the distinctive features of the service-oriented computing. The phases proposed are the Planning, the Analysis & Design, the Construction & Testing, the Provisioning, the Deployment and the Execution & Monitoring. For more information on this methodology, see [11] or the technical paper [13].

The Papazoglou's methodology is mainly composed of guidelines to specify, build and compose the services. One of the primary objectives is to support dynamic business processes with an IS. However, current companies also require a global view on the management of their services, i.e., they want to adopt an ITSM framework [19] such as ITIL. While the service-oriented design and development methodology is more about the implementation of services, the reusability and the composability, ITIL focuses on the organizational processes to follow in order to deliver value to the customers and users of services by applying a proper service delivery and support. Even though the service-oriented paradigm and ITIL seem to be complementary in an organization, the combined use of ITIL and the service-oriented design and development methodology raises several problems and issues. The main ones are discussed hereafter in Sect. 2.2. Then, this paper brings some solutions in Sect. 4.

2.2 Main Issues When Comparing ITIL v.3 and the Service-Oriented Design and Development Methodology

The first issue is related to the service notion which is differently comprehended. In ITIL, a service, called an IT service, is defined as the "means of delivering value to customers by facilitating outcomes customers want to achieve without the ownership of specific costs and risks" [14]. Although the definition of the service concept in the service-oriented paradigm varies somewhat, the one proposed by Papazoglou is often cited: a service "is a self-describing, self-contained software module available via a network [...] which completes tasks, solves problems, or conducts transactions on behalf of a user or application. [...] Services constitute a distributed computer infrastructure made up of many different interacting application modules trying to communicate [...] to virtually form a single logical system" [20, Chap. 1]. Other concepts share the same problem such as the notion of SLA. This will be discussed in Sect. 4.

A second observation concerns the lack of understanding between the management of organizations and the technical teams in charge of the IT. From one side, ITIL helps to establish, structure and improve the management of organizations. From the other side, the service-oriented paradigm mainly focuses on the IS structure and its technical management. Both of these two layers recommend to adopt a service-orientation. However, how to combine them in order to create a full service-orientation in organizations is not clear [21]. As an example, we can mention the notion of service registry in an SoS, and the notion of service portfolio and service catalogue in ITIL. How to associate these related notions in order to use them as a whole in the organization? A second example lies in the possible confusion between the notion of service design package in ITIL and the notion of service description used in the service-oriented computing.

Thirdly, the service life cycle has a different structure. In ITIL, the Continual Service Improvement phase organizes the improvement of the service solutions and processes based on, i.a., the changing and new business needs. In an SoS, the service monitoring phase focuses on the quality measurement of the service characteristics [11]. Therefore, using ITIL to manage the services of an SoS should help to improve the services by taking into account the new and changing business requirements.

2.3 Related Work

In the literature, the relations proposed between ITIL and the service-oriented paradigm are often based on the organizational concepts of ITIL, and on the SoS concepts and implementation steps. First initiatives combining the SoS with management practices and organizational aspects focus on SOSE (see [22] for more details). In the scope of this work, we only consider the relations established at a management level between ITIL best practices and SoS implementation activities of IT organizations.

In [1], the authors propose a meta model of an enterprise service based on the service concept of ITIL v.2 and of the service-oriented paradigm. They do not tackle the possible relations between the ITIL processes and the activities of the SoS implementation and composition. Other works such as [23] use ITIL v.3 concepts to build a service-oriented and organizational framework. But they do not align the processes of ITIL with processes or activities of an SoS implementation and composition methodology.

In [24], the author favours the use of an SOA integrated with ITIL in order to improve the agility of IT in organizations. This integration helps to relate the management of IT service with their supportive technical layers, which are assimilated to the SOA components. They use the second version of ITIL –the third one was not yet finished when the work has been published. Most of the ITIL v.2 processes are related to the SOA concepts. A particular attention is paid to the CMDB management and the operational activities, i.e., the management of the services configuration, the incidents, the requests and the problems. A second work shares a similar objective, i.e., improving the IT agility by combining an SOA and ITIL [25]. Its authors claim for a clear distinction between the SOA concepts and the ITIL concepts, although they underline some connections between these two organizational domains.

Compared to [24,25], our work goes one step further by aligning the steps of a service-oriented design and development methodology and the ITIL processes. Of course, the scope of our work is narrowed since we only focus on the creation and composition of services. The operational management of the built services is left for future work. A third work is very close to this idea. In [26], the authors describe the technical platform used by IBM to manage the services in an SOS. They clearly refer to ITIL best practices and principles. Of course, the use of the alignment between the SOS components and ITIL is only possible if the IBM software tools are purchased. Moreover, these relations are not publicly described neither justified.

Other works propose to associate the service-oriented paradigm with an organizational framework which is not ITIL. For instance, Li et al. design a high level organizational framework and structure which are then compared and aligned to the SOA implementation [27]. They consider that the SOA is a mirror of real organizations. This choice is motivated by the need for a technology independent framework. We meet this requirement by using ITIL as the reference organizational framework which is independent of any specific technologies. The detailed description of ITIL is an advantage compared to the use of a high level and less described organizational framework. A second example is the Service-Oriented Analysis and Design method (SOAD) [28]. The authors cover the business and organizational layers in their model, but without reference to a detailed organizational framework.

3 Foundations of the Detailed Service-Oriented Design and Development Methodology

In this section, we first detail the steps of the service-oriented design and development methodology in order to align them with the ITIL v.3 processes (the DSDDM is depicted in Fig. 2). To do this, we use the structure of the Spiral Model [29,30]. This model helps to answer the two following questions: *What are the objectives and the output of the current stage?* and *After this stage, what should we do?* It does not aim at explaining how each stage can be completed. ITIL v.3 solves this issue once the alignment described. The structure of the Spiral Model used is close to the initial model proposed by Boehm [29] and the revised version [30]. Nevertheless, we lightly adapt it for the service-oriented paradigm –the flexibility was one of its main strengths [30]. The structure used is composed of five parts numbered with Roman numerals (see Fig. 2). Note, before the beginning of each cycle, its planning is always carried out by placing the tasks on a timeline, identifying the resources and then allocating them to the tasks.

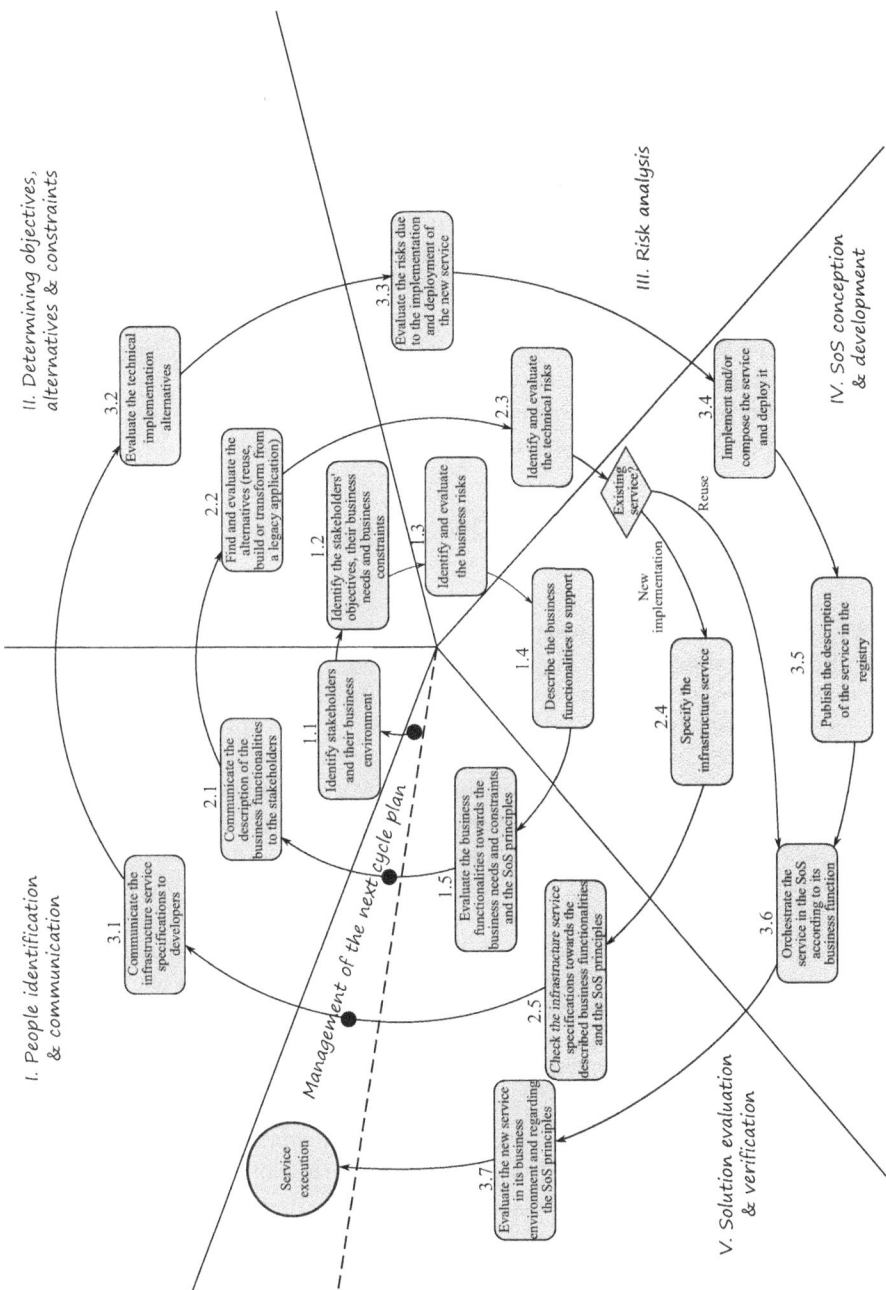

Fig. 2. Illustration of the detailed service-oriented design and development methodology

I **People identification & communication:** The steps included in this part focus on the stakeholders. The latter are first identified. Based on an efficient communication framework, they are kept informed about the progress of the projects.

II **Determining objectives, alternatives & constraints:** This section facilitates the establishment of the vision and the direction of the project by determining the objectives, scope and constraints of the project. It also helps to solve design conflicts after their communication to the stakeholders.

III **Risks analysis:** This part focuses on the risk management. Once the vision determined and the choices made, their underlying risks are identified and analyzed. A good risks management will help to achieve the steps of the next section.

IV **sos conception & development:** The steps of this section help to define, design and implement the services.

V **Solution evaluation & verification**: This fifth and last section includes the steps related to the output evaluation of each cycle.

4 Alignment of the DSDDM Steps with the ITIL v.3 Processes

The detailed model of Papazoglou's methodology –abbreviated by DSDDM– is the process leading to the analysis, the design, the implementation and the composition of services. It is depicted in Fig. 2. This model should be covered for each required business service –a business service is a logical part of an SoS aligned on an activity of a business process which represents some required business functionalities [31]. In the scope this work, another important concept is the notion of infrastructure service. It is defined as a container associated with the service management and monitoring infrastructure that encapsulates computational resources [31]. Once combined, these infrastructure services can provide the business functionalities required by the stakeholders. In ITIL, the notion of IT service –defined in Sect. 2.2– is close to the notion of business service. Indeed, supporting the functionalities of the business processes should provide some value to the stakeholders by facilitating their business outcomes. Moreover, the use of a service provided by an SoS allows the transfer of some costs and risks from the stakeholders to the technical staff maintaining the SoS. In the definition of an IT service, the term "means" refers to, i.a., the infrastructure services supporting the business service. We recommend to only use the notion of IT service and infrastructure service given that the notion of business service is redundant with the notion of IT service.

The next three sections (Sects. 4.1 to 4.3) respectively detail the first, the second and the third cycle of the DSDDM spiral model –illustrated in Fig. 2– along with the justified relations of each DSDDM step with the corresponding ITIL V.3 processes. Tables 1, 2 and 3 summarize this alignment.

Table 1. Alignment of the first DSDDM cycle with ITIL v.3

	1.a STM	1.b SPM	1.c FIN	1.d DEM	1.e BRM
1.1 Identify stakeholders and their business environment				v	v
1.2 Identify the stakeholders' objectives, their business needs and business constraints	v				v
1.3 Identify and evaluate the business risks		v	v		
1.4 Describe the business functionalities to support		v		v	
1.5 Evaluate the business functionalities towards the business needs and constraints, and the SoS principles	v	v			

Table 2. Alignment of the second DSDDM cycle with ITIL v.3

	1.b BRM	2.b SCA	2.c SLM	2.d AVM	2.e CAP	2.f SCO	2.g ISM	2.h SUP
2.1 Communicate the description of the business functionalities to the stakeholders	v							
2.2 Find and evaluate the alternatives (reuse, build or transform from a legacy application)		v						
2.3 Identify and evaluate the technical risks				v	v	v	v	
2.4 Specify the infrastructure service				v	v	v	v	v
2.5 Check the infrastructure service specifications towards the described business functionalities and the SoS principles			v					

Table 3. Alignment of the third DSDDM cycle with ITIL v.3

	2.b SCA	2.c SLM	3.a TPS	3.b CHA	3.c SAC	3.d RDM	3.e SVT	3.f CHE
3.1 Communicate the infrastructure service specifications to developers			v					
3.2 Evaluate the technical implementation alternatives				v	v		v	
3.3 Evaluate the risks due to the implementation and deployment of the new service			v					v
3.4 Implement and/or compose the service and deploy it				v	v	v		v
3.5 Publish the description of the service in the registry	v	v				v		
3.6 Orchestrate the service in the SoS according to its business function				v	v			
3.7 Evaluate the new service in its business environment and regarding the SoS principles							v	

4.1 Description and Alignment of the First DSDDM Cycle

The first DSDDM cycle focuses on the analysis of the business environment –i.e., the analysis of the stakeholders, their requirements, the business risks and the business constraints– that the future IT service will support. Its alignment with ITIL v.3 is summarized in Table 1 and illustrated in Fig. 3. The illustrations of the alignment of the two other DSDDM cycles with ITIL v.3 processes are available in [13] or by sending an email to the first author.

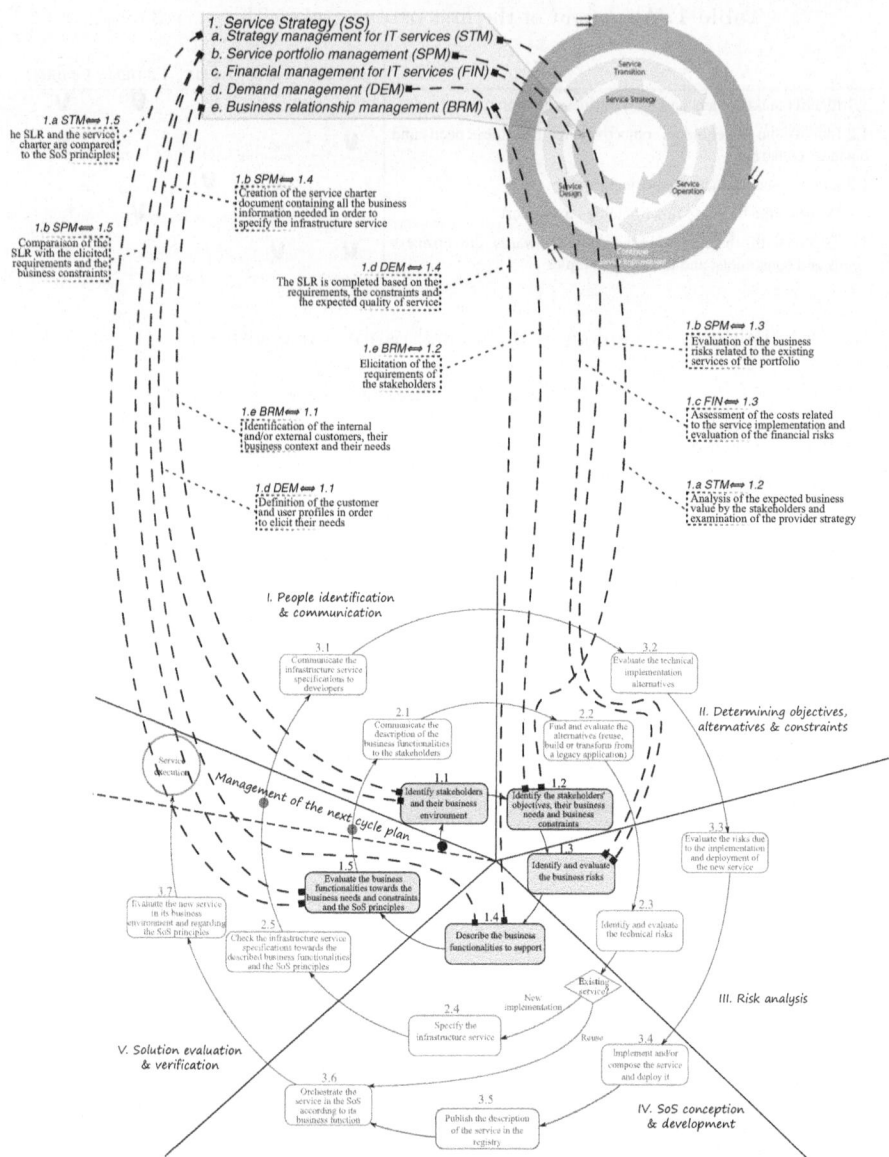

Fig. 3. Alignment between the first DSDDM cycle and the ITIL V.3 processes

Before the first step numbered 1.1, the whole cycle is organized, i.e., planning and structuring the tasks, allocating the resources needed and monitoring the achievement of each step (see "Management of the next cycle plan" in Fig. 2). Regarding the alignment with ITIL V.3, this planning work has to be achieved in accordance with the company strategy (defined thanks to the ITIL V.3 process 1.a

STM). These activities leading to the description of the business functionalities of the future service are detailed hereafter.

1.1 Identify stakeholders and their business environment: This step aims at having a first contact with the stakeholders once they are identified (related to 1.e BRM). One of the key aspects to analyse is their business context in order to understand what their job is and how they work (related to 1.d DEM and 1.e BRM).

1.2 Identify the stakeholders' objectives, their business needs and business constraints: This step helps to clarify the business environment of the stakeholders as well as their requirements and business constraints (related to 1.e BRM). The identification and the analysis of the business constraints should help to design a feasible service solution which complies with the strategy of the service provider (related to 1.a STM).

1.3 Identify and evaluate the business risks: This step focuses on the analysis of the risks due to the future use of an IT service and its possible consequences on the business processes, including the financial considerations (related to 1.b SPM and 1.c FIN).

1.4 Describe the business functionalities to support: Based on the stakeholders' objectives, the business constraints and the business risks analysis (managed by the process 1.b SPM), this step leads to the business design of the future service (related to 1.d DEM).

1.5 Evaluate the business functionalities towards the business needs and constraints, and the SoS principles: This step ends the first DSDDM cycle. The quality of the IT service specifications is evaluated by comparing the specifications of the IT service with the business needs expressed by the stakeholders (related to 1.b SPM) and the SoS principles (managed by the process 1.a STM).

4.2 Description and Alignment of the Second DSDDM Cycle

The second cycle focuses on the analysis of the technical alternatives that match the business functionalities described and validated during the first cycle. This consists in analyzing the implementation alternatives and the risks of these alternatives, and in specifying the future service. Its alignment with ITIL V.3 is summarized in Table 2. Note, in case of service reuse –i.e., the business needs can already be satisfied by an existing (composed) service–, a part of the second and the third cycle is skipped. Indeed, the flow to follow between the steps 2.3 and 2.4 depends on the alternative chosen: reused service or new service implementation (see Fig. 2).

First of all, the activities of the second cycle are organized based on the results obtained at the end of the first cycle. This lies in planning and structuring the tasks, allocating the resources and monitoring the achievement of each step. The ITIL process 2.a DES is in charge of the organization of the service design activities which lead to the creation of the service design package. These activities are detailed hereafter.

2.1 Communicate the description of the business functionalities to the stakeholders: The evaluation achieved during the step 1.5 as well as the specifications of the future service are communicated to the stakeholders, including the IT staff (related to 1.e BRM).

2.2 Find and evaluate the alternatives (reuse, build or transform from a legacy application): Based on the exchanged information during the previous step, the possible solutions are considered (related to 2.b SCA). They are three alternatives: (i) service reuse –an existing service will be used; it can be provided by the existing SoS or by an external service provider– (ii) building of the service from scratch –the service functionalities will be built from scratch, and/or existing services will be composed to support the functionalities needed to provide the IT service specifications– or (iii) building of the service from a legacy application –the legacy software component will be encapsulated.

2.3 Identify and evaluate the technical risks: This step aims at identifying and evaluating the risks raised by the alternative previously chosen. These risks are associated to the existing ISs, the other ongoing implementation projects and the other existing services in use (related to 2.d AVM, 2.e CAP, 2.f SCO and 2.g ISM). This technical risk analysis completes the business risk analysis carried out during step 1.3.

2.4 Specify the infrastructure service: The analysts have to specify the IT service functionality(ies) in order to implement the corresponding infrastructure service during the subsequent steps (related to 2.d AVM, 2.e CAP, 2.f SCO, 2.g ISM and 2.h SUP).

2.5 Check the infrastructure service specifications towards the described business functionalities and the SoS principles: During this step, the specifications of the infrastructure service are compared to the IT service description (related to 2.c SLM).

4.3 Description and Alignment of the Third DSDDM Cycle

The third cycle focuses on the implementation and the deployment of the specified infrastructure service, i.e., the evaluation of the technical choices, the management of the implementation and deployment risks, the coding of the service, the publication of its description and its orchestration. The alignment of the third DSDDM cycle with ITIL V.3 is summarized in Table 3.

First of all, the activities of the third cycle are organized based on the results of the second cycle. This means planning and structuring the tasks, allocating the resources needed and monitoring the achievement of each next step. The ITIL process 3.a TPS is in charge of this work, which is detailed in the rest of this section.

3.1 Communicate the infrastructure service specifications to developers: The validated specifications of the infrastructure service are communicated to the IT staff in charge of its implementation and publication (related to 3.a TPS).

3.2 Evaluate the technical implementation alternatives: The technical choices are made after their evaluation and comparison (related to 3.b CHA, 3.c SAC and 3.e SVT). This step should also take into account the constraints due to the use of legacy software component(s) to build the new infrastructure service (related to 3.c SAC).

3.3 Evaluate the risks due to the implementation and deployment of the new service: This step focuses on the identification and on the management of the technical risks raised by the implementation of a new service in the SoS (related to 3.a TPS and 3.f CHE).

3.4 Implement and/or compose the service and deploy it: During this step, the infrastructure service will be implemented according to its specifications (related to 3.b CHA, 3.c SAC and 3.f CHE). This new service is, eventually, composed with other existing services. Then, this new service is deployed (related to 3.d RDM).

3.5 Publish the description of the service in the registry: The functional and non-functional characteristics of the built service as well as its communication procedure are described (related to 2.c SLM and 3.c SAC). These documents are then published in a registry which enables the discovery of the new service (related to 2.b SCA).

3.6 Orchestrate the service in the SoS according to its business function: This step consists of the orchestration of the new or reused service in order to integrate it in the existing composite application (related to 3.b CHA and 3.c SAC). If the composite application does not exist, it should be built. This possibility is not covered in this paper since it is not directly related to the service creation.

3.7 Evaluate the new service in its business environment and regarding the SoS principles: This last step focuses on the validation of the implemented service once orchestrated in its composite application (related to 3.e SVT). This validation is based on the service built (or reused) compared to the underlying business processes and the SoS principles.

4.4 Concluding Remarks on the Alignment of the DSDDM Steps with the ITIL v.3 Processes

After the service implementation into the SoS, the next stage is the service execution (see the end of the third cycle in Fig. 2). It corresponds to the use of the service functionalities. Note that the alignment of the service execution with the ITIL V.3 processes is not in the scope of this paper, although this issue deserves further investigations. The possible relations between the improvement of the created services and the Continual Service Improvement phase in ITIL are also out of the scope of this paper.

The last remark concerns the Knowledge management process (3.g KNO) that supports all the DSDDM steps detailed previously. Indeed, this process aims at sharing and providing the information and knowledge needed in the organization.

5 Conclusion and Future Work

A global service-orientation in IT organizations requires a service-oriented management framework (such as ITIL v.3) and an SoS. Although this kind of IS structure is recommended in the ITIL official literature, the relations between the ITIL v.3 processes and the service implementation methodologies for creating the SoS are not defined. In other words, the organizational processes of ITIL v.3 do not correspond to the activities of the existing models followed to implement and provision services in SoSs. This could lead to some problematic situations during the service implementation projects. For instance, several similar concepts have different names, or similar syntaxes are differently understood. We can also mention a service life cycle which is different in the current version of ITIL and in the existing SoS implementation models.

In order to tackle this issue, we first detail and expand the Papazoglou's service-oriented design and development methodology based on the structure of the Spiral Model. This work enabled to present the DSDDM model. Then, we align it with the ITIL v.3 processes by identifying and describing their relations. This alignment is also shaped in three graphical illustrations, one by DSDDM cycle. This work, associated with the illustrations of the proposed relations, should help the IT staff and managers to organize their work, the communication and the exchange of information during the service implementation projects. Indeed, it clarifies the relations between the main ITIL v.3 concepts and those of the detailed service-oriented design and development methodology. It also detailed the interactions between the organization management activities and the service implementation and composition steps.

As part of our work, we shape a validation framework which can be used to generate hypotheses about the use of this work in a real environment (available in the technical paper [13]). Indeed, the current version of our work lacks of empirical validation. Once this exploratory study achieved, a second phase of the validation work should be the confirmation of these hypotheses. Of course, one of our future work is to achieve an exploratory study based on the validation framework proposed.

Another main future work lies in the analysis of the service execution and improvement steps in order to identify the possible relations between them and the ITIL v.3 processes and concepts.

References

1. Braun, C., Winter, R.: Integration of IT service management into enterprise architecture. In: Cho, Y., Wainwright, R.L., Haddad, H., Shin, S.Y., Koo, Y.W. (eds.) Proceedings of the 2007 ACM Symposium on Applied Computing (SAC 2007), pp. 1215–1219. ACM (2007)
2. Keel, A.J., Orr, M.A., Hernandez, R.R., Patrocinio, E.A., Bouchard, J.: From a technology-oriented to a service-oriented approach to IT management. IBM Syst. J. **46**(3), 549–564 (2007)

3. Khoshafian, S.: Service Oriented Enterprises. Auerbach Publications, Boca Raton (2007)
4. Buytendijk, F.: Last Call for DATATOPIA - Four Future Scenarios On The Role of Information and Technology in Society, Business and Personal Life, 2030. Technical report, Gartner, Inc. (2014). http://www.gartner.com/imagesrv/summits/docs/emea/business-intelligence/Gartner_LastCallforDatatopia.pdf
5. MacKenzie, C.M., Laskey, K., McCabe, F., Brown, P.F., Metz, R.: Reference Model for Service Oriented Architecture 1.0. Technical report, Organization for the Advancement of Structured Information Standards (OASIS), October 2006
6. Huhns, M.N., Singh, M.P.: Service-oriented computing: key concepts and principles. IEEE Internet Comput. **9**(1), 75–81 (2005)
7. Zhou, J., Niemela, E.: Beyond application-oriented software engineering: service-oriented software engineering (SOSE). In: Stojanovic, Z., Dahanayake, A. (eds.) Service-Oriented Software System Engineering: Challenges and Practices, pp. 27–47. IGI Global, Hershey (2005)
8. Gu, Q., Lago, P.: Guiding the selection of service-oriented software engineering methodologies. Serv. Oriented Comput. Appl. **5**(4), 203–223 (2011)
9. El-Sheikh, E., Reichherzer, T., White, L., Wilde, N., Coffey, J., Bagui, S., Goehring, G., Baskin, A.: Towards enhanced program comprehension for service oriented architecture (SOA) systems. J. Softw. Eng. Appl. **6**(9), 435–445 (2013)
10. Board, I.C.M.: COBIT 5 - A Business Framework for the Governance and Management of Enterprise IT. ISACA (2012)
11. Papazoglou, M.P., van den Heuvel, W.J.: Service-oriented design and development methodology. Int. J. Web Eng. Technol. **2**(4), 412–442 (2006)
12. Hunnebeck, L., Rudd, C., Lacy, S., Hanna, A.: ITIL V3.0 - Service Design. 2nd edn. TSO (The Stationery Office) (2011)
13. Verlaine, B., Jureta, I.J., Faulkner, S.: Aligning a Service Provisioning Model of a Service-Oriented System with the ITIL v. 3 Life Cycle. Technical report, University of Namur - PReCISE Research Center, September 2014. http://arxiv.org/abs/1409.3725
14. Cannon, D., Wheeldon, D., Lacy, S., Hanna, A.: ITIL V3.0 - Service Strategy. 2nd edn. TSO (The Stationery Office) (2011)
15. Marrone, M., Gacenga, F., Cater-Steel, A., Kolbe, L.: IT service management: a cross-national study of ITIL adoption. Commun. Assoc. Inform. Syst. **34**(1), 865–892 (2014)
16. Rance, S., Rudd, C., Lacy, S., Hanna, A.: ITIL V3.0 - Service Transition. 2nd edn. TSO (The Stationery Office) (2011)
17. Steinberg, R., Rudd, C., Lacy, S., Hanna, A.: ITIL V3.0 - Service Operation. 2nd edn. TSO (The Stationery Office) (2011)
18. Lloyd, V., Wheeldon, D., Lacy, S., Hanna, A.: ITIL V3.0 - Continual Service Improvement. 2nd edn. TSO (The Stationery Office) (2011)
19. Galup, S.D., Dattero, R., Quan, J.J., Conger, S.: An overview of it service management. Commun. ACM **52**(5), 124–127 (2009)
20. Papazoglou, M.: Web Services: Principles and Technology. Prentice Hall, Upper Saddle River (2007)
21. Fischbach, M., Puschmann, T., Alt, R.: Service lifecycle management. Bus. Inf. Syst. Eng. **5**(1), 45–49 (2013)
22. Karhunen, H., Jantti, M., Eerola, A.: Service-oriented software engineering (SOSE) framework. In: Proceedings of International Conference on Services Systems and Services Management (ICSSSM'05), vol. 2, pp. 1199–1204. IEEE Computer Society (2005)

23. Najafi, E., Baraani, A.: CEA framework: a service oriented enterprise architecture framework (SOEAF). J. Theoret. Appl. Inform. Technol. **40**(2), 162–171 (2012)
24. Waring, J., Shum, A.W., Dhillon, A.: Achieve IT agility by integrating SOA with ITIL based BSM. In: Proceedings of the 31th International Computer Measurement Group Conference, pp. 479–488. Computer Measurement Group (2005)
25. Izza, S., Imache, R.: An approach to achieve IT agility by combining SOA with ITSM. Int. J. Inform. Technol. Manag. **9**(4), 423–445 (2010)
26. Ganek, A., Kloeckner, K.: An overview of IBM service management. IBM Syst. J. **46**(3), 375–385 (2007)
27. Li, Z., Zhang, H., O'Brien, L.: Towards technology independent strategies for soa implementations. In: Maciaszek, L.A., Zhang, K. (eds.) Proceedings of the 6th International Conference on Evaluation of Novel Approaches to Software Engineering (ENASE 2011), pp. 143–154. SciTePress (2011)
28. Zimmermann, O., Krogdahl, P., Gee, C.: Elements of service-oriented analysis and design - an interdisciplinary modeling approach for soa projects. Technical report, IBM, June 2004
29. Boehm, B.W.: A spiral model of software development and enhancement. IEEE Comput. **21**(5), 61–72 (1988)
30. Boehm, B.W., Egyed, A., Kwan, J., Port, D., Shah, A., Madachy, R.J.: Using the WinWin spiral model: a case study. IEEE Comput. **31**(7), 33–44 (1998)
31. Papazoglou, M.P., Traverso, P., Dustdar, S., Leymann, F.: Service-oriented computing: a research roadmap. Int. J. Coop. Inf. Syst. **17**(2), 223–255 (2008)

How Social Responsibility Influences Innovation of Service Firms: An Investigation of Mediating Factors

Gheorghe Militaru[1], Anca-Alexandra Purcărea[1], Theodor Borangiu[2], Monica Drăgoicea[2(✉)], and Olivia Doina Negoiță[1]

[1] Faculty of Entrepreneurship, Business Engineering and Management, Department of Management, University Politehnica of Bucharest, Bucharest, Romania
gheorghe.militaru@upb.ro, apurcarea@gmail.com
[2] Faculty of Automatic Control and Computers, University Politehnica of Bucharest, 313 Splaiul Independenței, 006042 Bucharest, Romania
theodor_borangiu@cimr.pub.ro,
monica.dragoicea@acse.pub.ro

Abstract. The purpose of this study is to extend research on corporate social responsibility and to emphasise the role of this concept on innovation performance of service firms using mediators such as customer collaboration, employee collaboration, and business partners' collaboration. This will help identifying the opportunities to improve the innovation capacity of firms. The results indicate that collaboration relationships played a partially mediating role. It acts as significant intermediate variables between social responsibility and innovation performance of service firms. The findings fill a gap in the literature by demonstrating how social responsibility initiatives influence the collaboration mechanisms of the firms through its positive effects on the collaboration between customers, employees, and business partners. They could also lead to the increase of their innovation potential. The managers of the firms using limited resources can stimulate indirectly the innovation by stimulating social responsibility initiatives because these have a multiplicative role in increasing the service firms' innovation potential.

Keywords: Corporate social responsibility · Innovation · Collaboration

1 Introduction

The concept of the corporate social responsibility (CSR) has been studied, both theoretically and empirically, for many decades. CSR continues to gain importance for scholars and managers, and it has become more widespread [1]. Although in the literature there are many studies focusing on the relationship between CSR and the firm performance, a large part of these refer to the relationship between firm performance and CSR such as financial performance, reputation, and trust [2, 3]. Surprisingly, with all these, there is little empirical research investigating whether CSR affects innovation performance of service firms [1, 2, 4]. Consequently, a study in this direction could provide a theoretical model and could show the advantages that service firms could benefit from.

The present study examines the relationship between CSR actions and policies and the innovation performance of service firms in the context generated by the mediation effects of the external collaboration between service firms and their customers or business partners and, also, the internal collaboration among the employees [5]. This study tries to elucidate how collaboration mechanisms can affect the relationship between CSR and innovation performance through the integration of CSR action and policies into the innovation processes so as to generate strategic value [6, 7]. Quite a few studies have provided insight into such underlying processes, remarking that CSR has a "strategic" role in capturing value for the firm [8, 9]. From this perspective, CSR can play a key role in improving the customers trust and in increasing the service firm reputation, and attracting, motivating, and retaining talented employees.

The rest of the paper is organized as follows. First, a literature review is presented that provides a theoretical background to the present research before proposing a set of formal hypotheses. This is followed by a description of the proposed study, research method, and results. Finally, a discussion on obtained results is presented, followed by an examination of the managerial implications, identifying also future research opportunities.

2 Theoretical Foundations and Hypotheses Development

Academic researchers and business managers recognize the importance of service innovation as key driver of organic growth because new offerings yield opportunities to increase business performance [10] and can be a source of sustainable competitive advantage. Service innovation can be considered as an offering not previously available to the firm's customers requiring modifications in the sets of competences applied by service provider and/or customers [11].

The previous studies showed that the firms having higher levels of intangible assets deal more with CSR initiatives than those having lower levels of intangible assets [12]. Larger firms are exposed to bigger risks than their smaller counterparts and should be more willing to engage in CSR initiatives [12, 13]. Firms engaging more actively in CSR activities benefit from higher levels of goodwill with customers, employees, and business partners [14]. This situation is determined by the moral capital derived from CSR initiatives. Thus, CSR engagement provides more benefits for service firms such as obtaining capital from the investors by financing R&D projects. The value service creation is supported by collaboration and interactive processes between customers and frontline employees [15, 16]. Clarifying the role of CSR in service innovation can lead to more effective use of resources and capabilities for new service innovation. This study tested this possibility by examining whether CSR has a positive influence on the innovation performance. Therefore, a theoretical support is proposed following this hypothesis:

Hypothesis 1: *The more a service firm is perceived to be socially responsible, the greater is its innovation performance.*

Customer collaboration mechanism relies on the social relationship facilitating more tacit knowledge which has to be shared between customer and service provider. The customer plays an active role in service innovation by integrating his or her own knowledge, and competences into any activity of the innovation process [17, 18]. An extensive research on customer involvement in service innovation found out that stronger long-term relations, rapid service innovation diffusion or reduced cycle time of innovation can be built [19, 20].

The capability to collaborate with customers during new service development is essential to foster innovation and competitiveness [21]. Customers potentially play an important role in the service innovation process through their knowledge and skills. Thus, customer collaboration mechanism can generate more new ideas and accelerate their implementation [22]. Customer collaboration facilitates better alignment between service innovation and customer needs [19, 20, 23]. To examine whether prior findings on customer collaboration about judgments on innovation performance are true, we advance the following hypothesis:

Hypothesis 2: *A service firm's customer collaboration mediates the positive effect of corporate social responsibility on its innovation performance.*

Employees collaboration of service firm have different expertise, abilities, experience to share tacit knowledge, mental models, and combine individuals' knowledge in new and different ways [24, 25]. The role of employees, and especially frontline employees, in ensuring creativity and firm innovation is very important for service firms [23, 26]. Social interaction and trust play a key role in the willingness of employees to collaborate, to share tacit knowledge, which in turn fosters creativity and innovation [27, 28]. CSR actions and policies contribute to increasing trust among employees, creativity, ethical and improving the innovation-oriented climate [29]. Trust can be developed among employees with good intentions, competent, open-minded and who trust their co-workers actions' [30, 31]. People prefer to work for service firms that demonstrate a high level of ethics and social responsibility. Therefore, CSR activities can attract and retain high-quality employees. On the basis of this theoretical reasoning, we propose the following hypothesis:

Hypothesis 3: *A service firm's employee collaboration mediates the positive effect of corporate social responsibility on its innovation performance.*

Business partner collaboration enables service firms to improve the innovation potential and the combination of existing different complementary skills [32]. Collaboration mechanisms facilitate access to external resources and knowledge through networks of business partners' ties [33]. The collaboration between service firm and its business partner balances the internal and external complementary capabilities [34, 35]. The effort taken by a business partner for service innovation depends on the level of interaction, communication, reputation, and treatment these benefits from the service firm [36, 37]. Thus, the more a service firm is engaged in CSR actions and policies the more it can attract and keep valuable and extremely useful business partners for service innovation. On this background, we hypothesize the following.

Hypothesis 4: *A service firm's partner collaboration mediates the positive effect of corporate social responsibility on its innovation performance.*

Our theoretical arguments and hypotheses are summarized in the conceptual model shown in Fig. 1.

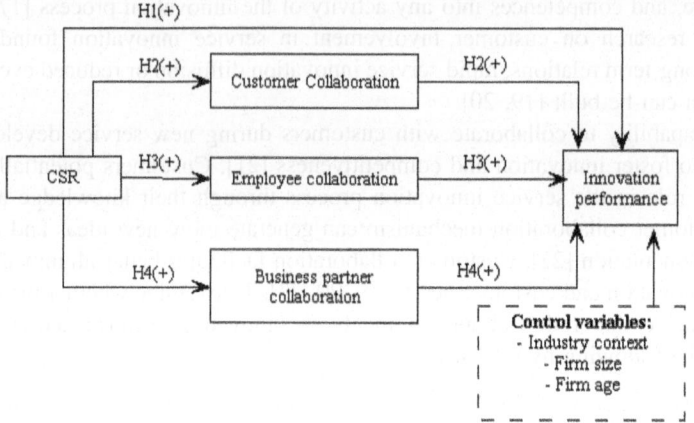

Fig. 1. Hypothesized model

3 Method

A questionnaire survey was designed to test the theoretical model. The questions on the questionnaire are based on the respondents' knowledge about the degree of engagement of service firms in CSR actions and policies and the innovation performance which those firms achieved. The geographical location was Romania. The methodology applied was a structured questionnaire and a procedure stratified sample with proportional allocation. In order to ensure the validity of the study, all the variables included in the questionnaire were obtained from empirical observations and theoretical reviews.

3.1 Sample and Data Collection

Data for the research was collected over a time frame spanning from May to December 2011. The survey sample comprised 540 Romania-based service organizations. In each organization, the manager served as the key informant because he or she has access to the information related to CSR actions and policies and also to the innovation capacity of one's own businesses. Precautions in data collection were taken to ensure reliability.

The sampling frame was stratified by the service industry sector. There are several different classifications of the service industry sector, one of the best-known being the ISIC (Industrial Sector International Classification). We randomly selected 540 service firms from the most important cities of Romania. Out of these 540 firms, we were able to contact 280 managers personally or by phone, and 211 managers agreed to participate in our study. This enabled us to obtain 211 valid responses, an approximate response rate of 39 %.

3.2 Measures

Scales were taken from the existent literature and previous research and adapted to our requirements. All measures were conducted with a 7-point Likert scale with anchors "1 = strongly agree", and "7 = strongly disagree". We are concerned with the degree to which a service firm allows, supports, and encourages innovation through commitment to CSR initiatives. Many researchers analyse organizations' innovation with reliable valid measurement scales [38, 39]. We measured *innovation performance* (dependence variable) through a 5-item scale adapted from [39, 38]. We modified the original instrument to reflect the degree to which a service firm allows, supports, and encourages innovation.

CSR (independent variable) is an important indicator of an organization's reputation for social involvement or social responsibility. We measured *corporate social responsibility* through a 3-item scale adopted from [40]. We modified the original scale to reflect the degree to which a service firm is engaged in CSR actions and policies.

Similar to previous studies *customer collaboration* was measured by using an instrument adapted to measure people's perceptions on customer collaboration [41, 42]. Our measure included 4 items reflecting the intensity and depth of customer interactions. We used a similar scale to assess the extent of *business partner collaboration*. To measure *employee collaboration* in service innovation processes, we used an instrument adapted from [43]. The primary role of the employees in new service development is to integrate new knowledge and customer preferences in service innovation processes. All these variables are mediator variables.

We included three control variables such as industry context, firm size, and firm age that were not of direct interest for testing our hypotheses but could be theoretically related to the innovation performance and might provide plausible alternative explanations for our findings. We take into consideration the nature of the service organization in our study, and this variable is controlled through the *industry context*.

Firm size has a positive effect on performance and also on innovation because the biggest firms usually have more resources to invest in innovation and CSR initiatives. Large organizations have more specialized, professional and skilled workers, who can benefit from transformational leadership [44]. We controlled firm size by taking into account the natural log of the number of full-time employees of individual firms in our sample. The natural log was taken in order to normalize the data

Firm age has an effect on performance and innovation because the experience, reputation, social responsibility, and organizational competencies are formed through time, and these characteristics help service firms to develop their operations more efficiently, including the innovation processes. We measured this variable as the number of years the firm has operated in its business sector. Firm age was operationalized as the logarithm of the number of years since the firms was founded in order to normalize the data.

4 Results

4.1 Data Analysis

All of the mediation hypotheses were tested together within a single model. All measurements of the constructs are based upon the respondent's perceptions. The data were assessed for the extent of missing values. This assessment found missing values for 18 of the 211 possible responses (8.5 %) and determined that these values were missing completely at random. Therefore, the means substitution method was used to replace missing values.

Table 1 shows the means, standards deviations, and correlation matrix relating the all variables used in our model. We can see that correlation coefficients are within acceptable levels. The highest correlation coefficient between the variables is between the extent to which a company is socially responsible and the contribution of the company to society's welfare than other competitors. This correlation coefficient is equal to 0.68. Therefore, no constructs were found to correlate so highly (at .90 or more). That is, no bivariate correlation is greater than 0.68, and there is little threat of common methods in our data. The measures of corporate social responsibility, customer collaboration, business partner collaboration and employee collaboration were positively correlated with the measures of innovation performance, with correlation coefficients ranging from 0.01 to 0.68. The correlation analysis shows that most coefficients are low, well under 0.5, which minimizes concern with multi co- linearity issues in our analysis. Many indicators showed a significant positive correlation.

Reliability of the factors was measured as both Cronbach's alpha and composite reliability (CR). The Cronbach's alphas calculated ranged between 0.811 (for "innovation performance") and 0.823 for "business partner collaboration". The coefficient Cronbach's alpha was calculated for each construct and was found to be greater than the recommended minimum of 0.70 indicating high reliability [45]. We studied the composite reliability of each whole scale by applying the Cronbach's alpha, composite reliability needs to be greater 0.70 (CR > 0.7). The composite reliability values ranged between 0.816 and 0.846. We also found evidence of construct reliability, which measured the stability of the scale on the basis of an assessment of the internal consistency of the items that measured the construct. Reliability measured in both Cronbach's alpha and composite reliability exceeded the minimum of 0.7 as suggested by Fornell and Larker [46]. Therefore, the results indicated satisfactory construct reliability.

The evaluation of the convergent validity of constructs was carried out by analysing the significance of the factor loadings (λ) and the average extracted variance (AVE). All factor loadings need to be statistically significant. We refined the scales by eliminating items with factor loadings below the 0.50 threshold ($\lambda \geq 0.50$). The factor loadings range between 0.53 and 0.88 and they exceed the minimum 0.5. All the estimates for the average variance extracted (AVE) need to be greater than 0.50, in support of convergent validity (AVE > 0.50) as suggested by Fornell and Larker [46]. Our results confirm this requirement less the innovation performance where AVE = 0.47. This particular value is very close to the threshold of 0.5 so that the convergent validity of construct is supported.

Discriminate validity was established between each pair of latent variables by constructing the estimated correlation parameter between them. The average variance extracted measured the variance shared between a construct and its indicators. The square root of the AVE of each construct should be much larger than the correlation of the specific construct within the model and should be at least 0.5 [46]. In our study, all the constructs met this criterion. The AVE for each construct was larger than the squared correlations between constructs, thereby satisfying the discriminate validity criterion.

4.2 Hypothesis Testing

The hypothesized relationships among variables were examined by means of structural equation modelling (SEM) analysis using LISREL 8.80 program. A path-analytic model was developed and tested. Path analysis allows researchers to test direct and indirect effects of multiple independent variables on multiple dependent variables, as illustrated in Fig. 2. In this way, we were able to test all study variables simultaneously. On the predictor side, the structural model included the CSR variable. Three mediating variables (customers, employees, and business partners' collaboration) and one dependent variable (innovation performance) were included.

We followed the procedure suggested by Holmbeck to test our hypotheses [47]. First of all a model is run to test the direct effects of the corporate social responsibility on the innovation performance. As shown in Table 1 (Model 1), the fit statistics for the direct effects model were as follows: χ^2 = 385, df = 220, p < .01, CFI = 0.95, RMSEA = 0.06, SRMR = 0.13. The resulting path coefficient is significant (β = 0.29, p < 0.001).

Next, a full mediation model is tested (Model 2), linking the corporate social responsibility to the mediators and the mediators to the innovation performance. The full mediation model did not have direct paths from predictor to the innovation performance. As shown in Table 1 (Model 2), the fit indices for this structural model provided a good fit to the data, χ^2 = 317.5, df = 218, p < .01, CFI = 0.96, RMSEA = 0.047, SRMR = 0.082.

Following the approach recommended by Anderson and Gerbing [48], we tested a series of nested models against our full mediation model through sequential chi-square tests with the multiple mediators in this study [49, 48]. In Model 3 the path related to Hypothesis 2 was constrained to zero. That is, the link involving CSR, customer collaboration and innovation performance was removed from the full mediation model. A significant change in the chi-square difference would suggest that the constrained path was important and thus support for the full mediation model. The fit indices for this model were as follows: χ^2 = 771.4, df = 223, p < .01, CFI = 0.87, RMSEA = 0.108, SRMR = 0.14.

Similarly, we constrained other two models by successively eliminating the relationships related to business partner collaboration (Model 4) and of the paths referring to employees' collaboration (Model 5). The research results are presented in Table 1. This indicates significant differences between the full mediation model and each of the models reflected by chi-square, RMSEA or CFI. As expected, all of the chi-square differences were significant suggesting that full mediation model best fit our data. The results provide a significant change in the chi-square difference and would suggest that the constrained path was important and thus provides support for the full mediation model.

Furthermore, we compared our full mediation model with a partial mediation model in which one direct path from CSR to innovation performance was added to the former [50, 51]. As shown in Table 1 (Model 6), the chi-square difference between the partial mediation model and full mediation was significant because the chi-square increase, p < 0.001, and CFI = 0.97. CFI ≥ 0.95 is presently recognised as indicative of good fit. The results provide a value of SRMR of 0.081, values for the SRMR as high as 0.08 are

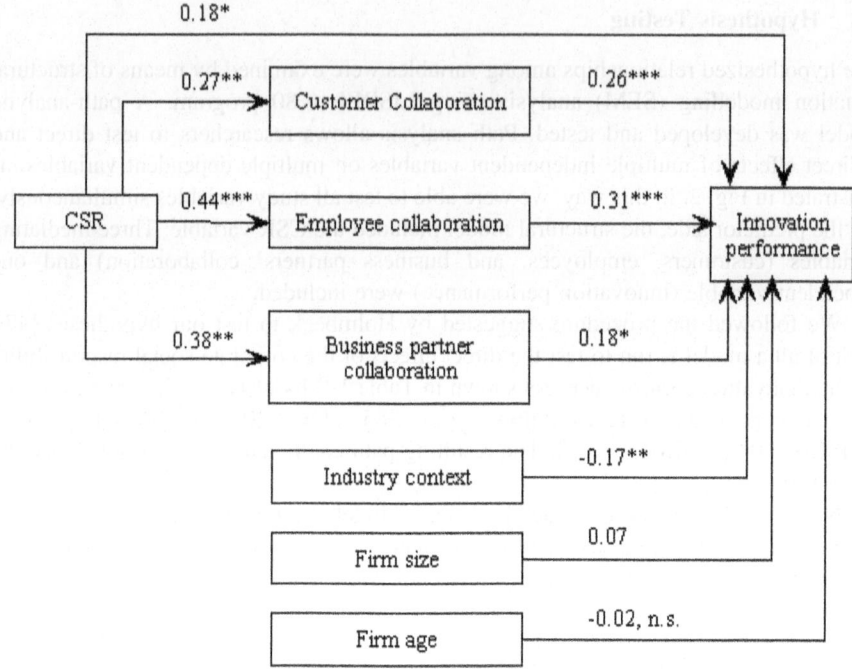

Fig. 2. Estimated path model

deemed acceptable [52]. These findings suggest that adding the direct path (CSR to innovation performance) to the full mediation model significantly improved the model fit [53]. We concluded that the partial mediation model was superior to the full mediation model, and acceptable for further consideration.

Table 1. Summary - results of alternative model comparisons and fit indices measures.

Model and structure	χ^2	df	RMSEA	CFI
Model 1 (Non-mediation model) CSR → Innovation Collaboration → Innovation	385	220	0.060	0.95
Model 2 (Full mediation model) CSR → Collaboration → Innovation	317.5	218	0.047	0.96
Model 3	771.4	223	0.108	0.87
Model 4	778	223	0.109	0.87
Model 5	800.6	223	0.111	0.86
Model 6 (Partial mediation model) CSR → Collaboration → Innovation CSR → Innovation	315.5	217	0.046	0.97
Model 7 (Reverse causality model) Innovation → CSR → Collaboration	355.9	223	0.053	0.96

Another situation can appear when a service firm is innovative and this performance can determine a responsible social behaviour. Consequently, one must check the reverse relationship in which innovation performance is an antecedent of CSR, which, in exchange, is a predictor of the collaboration between customers, business partners and employees. In order to exclude this possibility, we have tested the reverse causality model (Model 7). The results indicate that this alternative model is significantly worse than our hypothesized model. One can notice that RMSEA was 0.053, which is above the value of 0.046, while SRMR was 0.094, above the suggested cut-off value of 0.08 [52]. By examining the chi-square index one notices that the partial mediation model (Model 6) fit the data better than the direct effect model did, since chi-square dropped by 69.5, the degree of freedom varied by 3, and $p < 0.001$.

The final model is presented in Fig. 2. The parameters are standardized parameter estimates and the terms in rectangles are factor names. This model illustrates the best results of the hypothesis testing. Hypothesis 1 states that corporate social responsibility has a significant impact on innovation performance. The results provide support for this hypothesis ($\beta = 0.18$, $p < 0.05$).

Hypothesis 2 states that customer collaboration mediates the relationship between CSR and innovation performance. We note in Fig. 2 that CSR had a positive effect on customer collaboration ($\beta = 0.27$, $p < 0.001$). Customer collaboration in turn had a positive impact on innovation performance ($\beta = 0.26$, $p < 0.001$). This suggests that CSR has an indirect impact on customer collaboration. Therefore, Hypothesis 2 was supported.

We also tested for the mediated effect of employee's collaboration. That is, employee collaboration mediates the relationship between CSR and innovation performance. As shown in Fig. 2, CSR had a positive effect on employee collaboration ($\beta = 0.44$, $p < 0.001$). In turn, employees collaboration had a positive impact on innovation performance ($\beta = 0.31$, $p < 0.001$). This suggests that the CSR has an indirect impact on innovation performance through employee collaboration. We found Hypothesis 3 was supported.

Finally, we tested for the mediated effects of business partner's collaboration (Fig. 2) and found that the impact of CSR on business partner's collaboration was high and significant ($\beta = 0.38$, $p < 0.001$), while business partner collaboration had a positive effect on innovation performance ($\beta = 0.18$, $p < 0.05$). This suggests that CSR has an indirect impact on innovation performance through business partner's collaboration. The results provide strong support for Hypothesis 4. Findings showed that our different models with various paths from the predictors to the outcome provide support for partial mediation effects.

Overall, the results suggest that the partial mediation model best fit our data. Among the three control variables, the moderating effect of industry context on innovation performance is negative and significant ($\beta = -0.17$, $p < 0.01$). Firm size and firm age, which reflect different businesses' stages over time, are not significant for innovation performance ($\beta = 0.07$, $p > 0.1$ and $\beta = -0.02$, $p > 0.1$, respectively).

5 Conclusion

In this study, we examined how CSR initiatives influence directly the service firms' innovation performance. Our findings from the analysis of data provide strong support for Hypothesis 1. We found that CSR actions and policies had a positive influence on innovation performance and were also fully supported. However, this relationship was weaker than the relationships between CSR and innovation performance mediated by collaboration variables (path weight = 0.18). This finding is not surprising given the direct effect of CSR on innovation performance. An explanation regarding this result relies on the fact that CSR initiatives create the framework for stimulating innovation by collaborative mechanisms and catalyze these processes.

As predicted by Hypothesis 4, we found that CSR had a positive and significant effect on business partners' collaboration ($\beta = 0.38$). This indicates that firm reputation and trust between business partners are critical in increasing the collaboration relationships. The CSR initiative would foster business partners' collaboration. This is one of the most effective ways to capture new knowledge or support technology transfer through personal and organizational interactions. Our findings underscore the critical role of business-partner collaboration in improving the innovation potential because knowledge is the very important to improve the firm's dynamic capability by balancing exploration and exploitation activities.

Finally, a great deal of research has been conducted on the relationship between three important mediators in predicting the CSR influence on innovation performance of service firms, as well as whether these influences are moderated by industry context, firm size, and firm age. We found that only the moderating effect of industry context on innovation performance was negative and significant ($\beta = -0.17$, $p < 0.01$). Instead, the others variables, firm size and firm age, are not significant for innovation performance.

Practitioners can benefit from these results by noting the importance of CSR initiatives and the mediating variables reflected by collaboration mechanisms. The managers of the service firms using limited resources can stimulate indirectly the innovation capacity by stimulating CSR actions and policies. One knows that a firm with a good reputation that enjoys the trust of the business partners and the customers' loyalty by the mechanisms discussed in this study can improve its innovation performance. Besides these actions mediated by the collaborative mechanisms, there is another direct effect of the CSR initiatives on innovation materialized in orienting the long term creative efforts so as to lead to sustainable innovation.

Finally, our findings help service firms in developing effective strategies by incorporating CSR actions and policies in their innovation strategy. By aligning the CSR strategy to the firm's general strategy and the target objectives, one can obtain an efficient use of the resources and, at the same time, one can get an increase of the firm's innovation capacity. Practically, the managers can notice that CSR initiatives have a multiplicative role in increasing the service firms' innovation potential. At the same time, by this correlation, one can examine the way in which the firms' efforts destined to the CSR actions are justified or not.

Secondly, we encourage researchers to engage in longitudinal research on mediating the effects of the relationship between CSR and innovation performance, as such research would enable researchers to obtain a fairly detailed understanding of the influence of CSR on innovation performance in service firms. Thus, future research will be needed to examine longitudinal changes in patterns, predictors and outcomes. This work is only a first step in trying to understand the CSR actions and policies and the impact on innovation performance of service firms. We believe that this is a promising research area and our model offers an important point of departure for this.

References

1. Aguinis, H., Glavas, A.: What we know and don't know about corporate social responsibility: a review and research agenda. J. Manag. **38**(4), 932–968 (2012)
2. McWilliams, A., Siegel, D.: Creating and capturing value: strategic corporate social responsibility, resource-based theory, and sustainable competitive advantage. J. Manag. **37**(5), 1480–1495 (2011)
3. McWilliams, A., Siegel, D.: Corporate social responsibility and financial performance: correlation or misspecification? Strateg. Manag. J. **21**, 603–608 (2000)
4. Adler, P.S., Kwon, S.: Social capital: prospects for a new concept. Acad. Manag. Rev. **27**(1), 17–40 (2002)
5. Bell, G.G., Oppenheimer, R.J., Bastien, A.: Trust deterioration in an international buyer-supplier relationship. J. Bus. Ethics **36**(1/2), 65–78 (2002)
6. Mackey, A., Mackey, T.B., Barney, J.B.: Corporate social responsibility and firm performance: investor preferences and corporate strategies. Acad. Manag. Rev. **32**(3), 817–835 (2007)
7. Miller, D., Friesen, P.H.: Strategy-making and environment: the third link. Strateg. Manag. J. **4**(3), 221–235 (1983)
8. Baron, D.: Private politics, corporate social responsibility and integrated strategy. J. Econ. Manag. Strateg. **10**(1), 7–45 (2001)
9. Luo, X., Bhattacharya, C.B.: Corporate social responsibility, customer satisfaction, and market value. J. Mark. **70**(4), 1–18 (2006)
10. Melton, H.L., Hartline, D.M.: Customer and frontline employee influence on new service development performance. J. Serv. Res. **13**(4), 411–425 (2010)
11. Demirel, P., Mazzucato, M.: Innovation and firm growth: is R&D worth it? Ind. Innov. **19**(1), 45–62 (2012)
12. Godfrey, P.C.: The relationship between corporate philanthropy and shareholder wealth: a risk management perspective. Acad. Manag. Rev. **30**(4), 777–798 (2005)
13. Murtha, T.P., Lenway, S.A., Bagozzi, R.P.: Global mind-sets and cognitive shift in a complex multinational corporation. Strateg. Manag. J. **19**(2), 97–114 (1998)
14. Peloza, J.: Using corporate social responsibility as insurance for financial performance. Calif. Manag. Rev. **48**(2), 52–72 (2006)
15. Bhattacharya, C.B., Sankar, S.: Consumer-company identification: a framework for understanding consumer relationships with companies. J. Mark. **67**(2), 76–88 (2003)
16. Hansen, M.T., Birkinshaw, J.: The innovation value chain. Harvard Bus. Rev. **85**(6), 121–130 (2007)
17. Johnson, S.P., Menor, L.J., Roth, A.V., Chase, R.B.: A critical evaluation of the new service development process. In: Fitzsimmons, Fitzsimmons (ed.) New Service Development, pp. 1–32. Sage Publications, Thousand Oaks (2000)
18. Zeithaml, V.A., Bitner, M.J., Gremler, D.D.: Services Marketing: Integrating Customer Focus Across the Firm, 5th edn. McGraw-Hill, New York (2009)

19. Alam, I.: An exploratory investigation of user innovation in new service development. J. Acad. Mark. Sci. **30**(3), 250–261 (2002)
20. Chesbrough, H.: Managing open innovation. Res. Technol. Manag. **47**(1), 23–26 (2004)
21. Vargo, S.L., Lush, R.F.: Evolving to a new dominant logic for marketing. J. Mark. **68**(1), 1–17 (2004)
22. Urban, G.L., John, R.H., William, J.Q., Bruce, D.W., Jonathan, D.B., Roberta, A.C.: Information acceleration: validation and lessons from the field. J. Mark. Res. **34**(1), 143–153 (1997)
23. Agarwal, S., Erramilli, M.K., Dev, C.S.: Market orientation and performance in service firms: Role of innovation. J. Serv. Mark. **17**(1), 68–82 (2003)
24. Nonaka, I.: A dynamic theory of organizational knowledge creation. Organ. Sci. **5**(1), 14–37 (1994)
25. Kaiser, H.F.: An index of factorial simplicity. Psychometrika **39**(1), 31–36 (1974)
26. Godfrey, P.C., Merrill, C.B., Hansen, M.J.: The relationship between corporation social responsibility and shareholder value: an empirical test of the risk management hypothesis. Strateg. Manag. J. **30**(4), 425–445 (2009)
27. Dakhli, M., De Clercq, D.: Human capital, social capital, and innovation: a multi-country study. Entrepreneurship Reg. Dev. **16**(2), 107–128 (2004)
28. Sen, S., Bhattacharya, C.B.: Does doing good always lead to doing better? consumer reactions to corporate social responsibility. J. Mark. Res. **38**(2), 225–244 (2001)
29. Cook, J., Wall, T.: New work attitude measures of trust, organizational commitment and personal need non-fulfilment. J. Occup. Psychol. **53**, 39–52 (1980)
30. Nahapiet, J., Ghoshal, S.: Social capital, intellectual capital, and the organizational advantage. Acad. Manag. Rev. **23**(2), 242–266 (1998)
31. Turban, D.B., Greening, D.W.: Corporate social performance and organizational attractiveness to prospective employees. Acad. Manag. J. **40**(3), 658–672 (1997)
32. Rothaermel, F.T.: Incumbent's advantage through exploiting complementary assets via interfirm cooperation. Strateg. Manag. J. **22**(6), 687–699 (2001)
33. Moran, P.: Structural versus relational embeddedness: social capital and management performance. Strateg. Manag. J. **26**(12), 1129–1151 (2005)
34. Sirmon, D.G., Hitt, M.A., Ireland, R.D.: Managing firm resources in dynamic environments to create value: looking inside the black box. Acad. Manag. Rev. **32**(1), 273–292 (2007)
35. De Luca, L., Atuahene-Gima, K.: Market knowledge dimensions and cross-functional collaboration: examining the different routes to product innovation performance. J. Mark. **71**(1), 95–112 (2007)
36. Parasuraman, A., Berry, L.L., Zeithaml, V.A.: Refinement and reassessment of the SERVQUAL scale. J. Retail. **67**(4), 420–450 (1991)
37. Tuli, K.R., Ajay, K.K., Sundar, G.B.: Rethinking customer solutions: from product bundles to relational processes. J. Mark. **71**(3), 1–17 (2007)
38. Hurley, R.F., Hult, G.T.M.: Innovation, market orientation, and organizational learning: an integration and empirical examination. J. Mark. **62**(3), 42–54 (1998)
39. Garcia-Morales, V.J., Llorens-Montes, F.J., Verdu-Jover, A.J.: The effects of transformational leadership on organizational performance through knowledge and innovation. Br. J. Manag. **19**(4), 299–319 (2008)
40. Brown, T.J., Dacin, P.A.: The company and the product: corporate associations and consumer product responses. J. Mark. **61**(1), 68–84 (1997)
41. Gruner, K.E., Homburg, C.: Does customer interaction enhance new product success? J. Bus. Res. **49**(1), 1–14 (2000)
42. Ordanini, A., Parasuraman, A.: Service innovation viewed through a service-dominant logic lens: a conceptual framework and empirical analysis. J. Serv. Res. **14**(1), 3–23 (2011)

43. Li, T., Calantone, R.J.: The impact of market knowledge competence on new product advantage: conceptualization and empirical examination. J. Mark. **62**(4), 13–29 (1998)
44. Bryant, S.E.: The role of transformational and transactional leadership in creating, sharing and exploiting organizational knowledge. J. Leadersh. Organ. Stud. **9**(4), 32–44 (2003)
45. Hair Jr., J.F., Money, A.H., Samouel, P., Page, M.: Research Methods for Business. Wiley, Chichester (2007)
46. Fornell, C., Larcker, D.F.: Evaluating structural equation models with unobserved variables and measurement error. J. Mark. Res. **18**(1), 39–50 (1981)
47. Holmbeck, G.N.: Toward terminological, conceptual, and statistical clarity in the study of mediators and moderators: examples from the child-clinical and paediatric psychology literatures. J. Consult. Clin. Psychol. **65**(4), 599–610 (1997)
48. Anderson, J.C., Gerbing, D.W.: Structural equation modelling in practice: a review and recommended two-step approach. Psychol. Bull. **103**(3), 411–423 (1988)
49. Podsakoff, P.M., MacKenzie, S., Lee, J.Y., Podsakoff, N.: Common method biases in behavioral research: a critical review of the literature and recommended remedies. J. Appl. Psychol. **88**(5), 879–903 (2003)
50. Kelloway, E.K.: Using LISREL for Structural Equation Modelling: A Researcher's Guide. Sage Publications, Thousand Oaks (1998)
51. Lu, Y., Zhou, L., Bruton, G., Li, W.: Capabilities as a mediator linking resources and the international performance of entrepreneurial firms in an emerging economy. J. Int. Bus. Stud. **41**(3), 419–436 (2010)
52. Hu, L.T., Bentler, P.M.: Cut-off criteria for fit indexes in covariance structure analysis: Conventional criteria versus new alternatives. Struct. Equ. Model. **6**(1), 1–55 (1999)
53. Barret, P.: Structural equation modelling: adjudging model fit. Pers. Individ. Differ. **42**(5), 815–824 (2007)

Verifying the Image-Dominant (ID) Logic Through Value Cross-Creation Between Social and Imagined Communities

Mari Juntunen[✉] and Jouni Juntunen

Department of Marketing, Oulu Business School/University of Oulu,
Oulu, Finland
{mari.juntunen,jouni.juntunen}@oulu.fi

Abstract. This article focuses on examining the existence and impacts of the image-dominant (ID) logic at collective level. The purpose is to test whether social and imagined communities can create value for each other, in other words, can value actively be cross-created between communities. The data was gathered in a service industry from two closely related social communities (SC) (N = 264 and N = 460) where each SC represents the other respondents' imagined community (IC). Structural equation modeling (SEM) is used for analyses. The identical SEMs from both data sets indicate that value can be cross-created between communities: collective awareness among individuals' SC members is discovered to create value to another SC; and the collective image of the other community among individuals' SC members is revealed to create value for their own SC. The contributions produced by the article are the introduction and verification of the concepts image-dominant logic and value cross-creation.

Keywords: Imagined community · Brand meaning · Industry brand equity · Brand cross-creation

1 Introduction

The extant value research present three main logics: goods-dominant (G-D), service-dominant (S-D), and customer-dominant (C-D). The G-D logic focuses on the exchange of operand resources (such as goods) and the basis of value is *value-in-exchange*; and the S-D logic focuses on the action of operant resources (such as knowledge and skills), and the basis of value is *value-in-use* [1]. In CD logic the basis for value is *value-in-experience*, where customers, both at the individual and collective levels, uniquely experience lived and imagined service experiences and create both lived and imaginary value in their everyday life practices and processes through the physical or mental use or possession of these resources [2–4]. As both imagined experiences and imaginary value is recognized, we suggest that it is time to move value discussions toward *image-dominant (ID) logic*. The focus of this article is to test whether ID logic actually exists and influences at collective level.

Value slippage means that value created by one source or at one level of analysis is captured at another [5]. The purpose of this paper is to examine whether value can actively be created for others at collective level. We call this *value cross-creation*.

The extant research differentiates between social communities (SC) where members engage in some form of social interaction with other members, and imagined communities (IC) which exist only in individuals' minds [6, 7]. In this article we test whether social and imagined communities can cross-create value for each other. Our research question is: can value be cross-created between social and imagined communities?

Based on a theoretical view, we create a research model and gather the data from two closely related social communities in the context of educational services in a service industry: apprentices who are currently studying in a school to gain a license to work in the service industry in question (N = 264), and professionals who already work in that particular industry (N = 460). In both groups, the other social community is their respective imagined community; for the apprentices an imagined future community, and for the professionals a past imagined community. The data was analyzed using structural equation modeling (SEM). As a result, identical value cross-creation models for both groups are provided. The contributions produced by the article are the introduction and verification of the concepts image-dominant logic and value cross-creation.

The paper is organized as follows: First, we review the extant research and develop hypotheses. Thereafter, we describe our empirical context, methodological choices, and results. Finally, we conclude the paper by discussing the results and highlighting some possible directions for further research.

2 Theoretical Background

2.1 Toward Image-Dominant (ID) Logic Through Knowledge

The co-creation experience of a customer is a basis of value [8]. Consumer value perceptions can be generated without the product or service being bought or used [9]. In other words, along with lived aspects, customers' service experience may be either consciously or unconsciously imaginary; and experience-based value can contain both lived and imaginary aspects through the physical or mental use or possession of these resources, both at the individual and collective levels [4].

The physical and mental use of resources refers to skills and knowledge, the operant resources of S-D logic. From the psychological viewpoint both are parts of the cognitive but they differ: knowledge refers to an understanding of something and how it is related to other issues, while skills are something we do, like service; an ability to apply the knowledge into the action. Learning may proceed in each way, from knowledge to skills or from skills to knowledge. Although the difference between these is recognized, value research is at its embryonic state concerning knowledge, specifically in collective context.

Researchers have adapted the idea of co-creation into the field of branding [11–13] and say that customers' experience with the service plays a major role in service brand equity formation creating brand meaning [14, 15]. Keller [16] (p. 2) asserts that "Perhaps a firm's most valuable asset for improving marketing productivity is the knowledge that has been created about the brand in consumers' minds" and he calls "the differential effect of brand knowledge on consumer response to the marketing of the brand" as customer-based brand equity (CBBE). In Keller's conceptualization the central concepts of CBBE are brand awareness (BA) and brand image (BI): BA is the customer's ability to recognize and recall the brand under different conditions, and BI is the "perceptions about a brand as reflected by the brand associations held in consumer memory". According to him (p. 3), brand associations "contain the meaning of the brand for consumers". In other words, brand meaning, which is formed by customer's experience, is a lower concept to brand knowledge - or CBBE.

A subjective knowledge structure or subjective truth of individuals can be called image [10]. Therefore, we call the view which concentrates on examining imaginary value aspects both at the individual and collective levels as the *image-dominant (ID) logic*. In this research we will test whether the CBBE measures can be used to measure imagined value aspects at collective level.

2.2 Social and Imagined (Brand) Communities

Brand researchers say that the power of a brand and its value are seen as dynamically constructed through social interactions [18, 19]. Brand communities can be divided into social and imagined ones. Distinction between them lies in the nature of the relationships between members. Social communities are based on a wide range of commonalities like kinship ties or occupational connections and they consist of individuals who acknowledge membership in the community, perceive a psychological sense of community, exhibit shared values and a shared world view, and engage in some form of social interaction with other members, either offline or online; and imagined (or psychological) community is a group of brand admirers who perceive a psychological sense of community with the other brand admirers even though they do not yet hold membership or engage in social interactions [7, 20–22]. Imagined communities exist only in individuals' minds and can be distinguished by the way they are imagined [23]. Individuals who perceive a sense of community with the other brand users are committed to the brand whether involved in social interaction between members or not [7].

Learning often takes place in social communities, where individuals' involvement and relationships are concrete – but students also possess notions of future communities, or imagined future affiliations, where they are not members yet but in which they hope to gain access some day in the future [24, 25]. This prompts us to examine whether value can be cross-created between the above mentioned communities in the context of educational services.

2.3 Value Cross-Creation Between Communities, Hypotheses Development

Lived experience of a particular service forms when customers are actually participating in a service encounter, and *imaginary experiences* of value may either include nostalgic reinterpretations of previous experiences of value or potential future service experiences originating from imagination or from other indirect sources; the *lived value* in the experience forms at present as the service is actually executed (whether being self-service, virtual, or concrete), and the *imagined value* in the experience concerns either past or future as customer's earlier experiences are always present and are continuously updated through new experiences, and customer may imagine future experiences with the provider [4].

The present value in the experience can affect how a customer makes sense of past and future experiences [4]. Thus, based on Keller's CBBE view, we hypothesize:

H1a: Brand awareness of a social community can create value for a past imagined community.
H1b: Brand image of a social community can create value for a past imagined community.
H1c: Brand awareness of a social community can create value for a future imagined community.
H1d: Brand image of a social community can create value for a future imagined community.

In language learning, research has revealed that the students' past has a powerful influence on their present educational practices [26]. In addition, the students' future imagined communities might have an even stronger effect on their current actions, investment and learning than the ones in which they have daily engagement: In other words, what has not happened yet can be a reason and motivation for what students do at present [24, 25, 27]. Additionally, parents envision their children's future affiliations [27] and schools envision imagined future communities for their students, which have an effect on the current policies and practices of schools as well as on the identities of the students [26]. Thus, we hypothesize:

H2a: Brand awareness of a past imagined community can create value for a social community.
H2c: Brand image of a past imagined community can create value for a social community.
H2b: Brand awareness of a future imagined community can create value for a social community.
H2b: Brand image of a future imagined community can create value for a social community.

2.4 Research Model and Measures

To examine value cross-creation between communities, our research model tests whether BA and BI of respondents' social communities (SC) (BA_{SC}, BI_{SC}) influence BE of respondents' imagined communities (IC) (BE_{IC}); and where BA and BI of respondents' IC (BA_{IC}, BI_{IC}) influence BE of respondents' SC (BE_{SC}) (Fig. 1).

BE refers to the differential effect of brand knowledge on community members' response either to their direct or indirect experience with the community brand [16]. In business services context, researchers have found evidence of BE in the form of differential effect of a brand, advantage over others, and respondents' willingness to

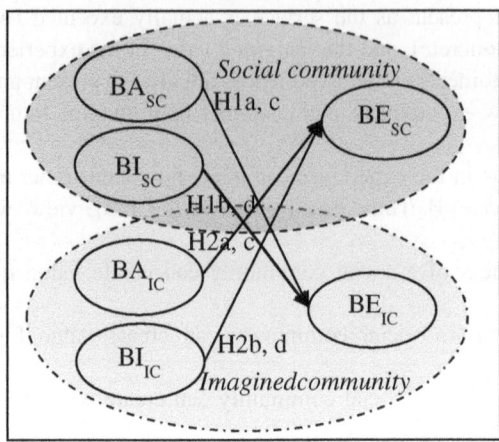

Fig. 1. A research model

pay more [28]. We apply measures from the branding literature but develop them further for the purposes of this study. For example, as our respondents do not pay for the service, we focus on sacrifices they are willing to make rather than on willingness to pay. The BE was measured with three questions in the questionnaire (Appendix). All the operational measures were expressed as attitudinal statements based on the 7-point Likert scale (strongly disagree ... strongly agree).

BA is traditionally considered as the customer's ability to recognize and recall the brand under different conditions [16, 28, 29]. Among communities, awareness becomes a collective phenomenon: when a brand is known, each individual knows that it is known [30]. Therefore, in our study BA refers to the respondents' view of the collective ability of community members to recognize and recall a community. BA is measured with three questions in the questionnaire.

BI is traditionally considered as 'perceptions about a brand as reflected by the brand associations held in consumer memory' [16]. Here, similarly to awareness, BI is seen from the collective viewpoint. In business services context, BI centers usually on such company attributes as experience and reputation; how the company takes care of its customers, how it operates, whether it offers high quality and how respected it is [28]. BI is measured with five questions in the questionnaire.

3 Methodology

3.1 Data Description and Estimation Method

Our empirical context is a solid mutual dependence and cooperation arrangement over driver education with the Finnish Defence Forces (FDF) and the Finnish road transport industry. Community A is the FDF transport division's military driving school (MDS). Young people interested in road transport may serve their six, nine or twelve months of military training (compulsory for men, optional for women) in the MDS. After successfully completing the service, recruits receive heavy goods and public service vehicle (bus or coach) licenses, as well as a letter of reference highly valued by civilian employers in the road transport industry. Almost all MDS recruits move on to employment in civilian transport companies, to be either truck or bus drivers, become entrepreneurs themselves or work for logistics service providers (LSPs). The sample consists of 367 recruits who participated in the MDS in the Karelia Brigade, a Readiness Formation in eastern Finland. The data was gathered through a questionnaire in 2008. 257 questionnaires were returned representing a response rate of 71.9 per cent.

Community B is the Finnish road transport industry. The vast majority of LSPs belong to an interest group called Finnish Transport and Logistics (SKAL), which is a member of the International Road Transport Union (IRU). As members of SKAL, LSPs participate in common education and social events. Most of the LSPs have served their military service in the MDS and currently operate as reservists for the military forces while updating their reservist skills on military refresher courses. The sample consists of people responsible for road transport services in 2,604 member companies of the SKAL association. The data was gathered through the internet-based Webropol online survey questionnaire in 2008. A reminder was sent to those who had not answered the questionnaire in time. The 428 returned questionnaires represent a response rate of 16.4 per cent. Non-response bias was studied by comparing different response waves [31, 32] using ANOVA. The first wave included those who responded after the original e-mail request (69.3 %) and the second wave of those who responded after the reminder (30.7 %). No statistically significant differences (using the criterion of $p > 0.05$) between the two groups were found; therefore, non-response bias is not a problem in this study. The estimations were made with the Lisrel software [33, 34].

3.2 Data Analysis and Results

The eight hypothesized relationships were tested from the data sets using confirmatory structural equation modeling (SEM). The analyses provided unacceptable models, thus we continued SEM using model generating SEM [35, 36]. We checked the modification indices of Lisrel software and respecified our models accordingly when theoretically justified.

This resulted in finding four statistically significant relationships; two similar relationships between social and imagined communities were found in both data sets (Fig. 2). Community A data reveals in Model A1 that the military driving schools' BA (MBA) affects positively the road transport industry's BE (professionals' BE, PBE); and in Model A2 that the road transport industry BI (PBI) affects positively the military driving school BE (MBE). Similarly, Community B data reveals in Model B1 that the road transport industry BA (PBA) affects positively the military driving school BE (MBE); and in Model B2 that the military driving school BI (MBI) affects positively the road transport industry BE (PBE). All relationships in the models are statistically significant and the factor loadings are good. The other hypothesized relationships were rejected.

In respecifying the models, one measure (PBE3) in the factor PBE in Model B2 needed to be dropped out. Additionally, four relationships between the error terms of the operational measures were found. These can all be explained by the similar nature of measures: in Model A2 the measures regarding how the industry takes care of its members (PBI1) and how it will perform (PBI2); in Model B1 if MDS is well-known (PBA1) or recognized (PBA2); and in Models A2 and B2 if the other community is considered respected (PBI5, MBI5) or respected in comparison to other similar communities (PBI4, MBI4).

In models A2, B1 and B2 the chi-square test shows an unacceptable fit of the model to the data (Table 1). As chi-square test may give unacceptable fit indices even though model is statistically acceptable with large sample size (>200), models can be tested and evaluated using other fit indices [37]. All other fit indices suggest accepting the models. In Model A1, RMSEA value less than 0.05 indicates a close fit of the model; and in Models A2, B1 and B2, RMSEA value about 0.08 or less indicates a reasonable error of approximation [38]. In all models NNFI, the most important fit indices with large sample size, is more than 0.90, SRMR is less than 0.08 [39] and NFI, CFI and GFI values are above 0.90 [40], which all indicate that all the models are statistically acceptable. Because all relationships are statistically significant and coefficients are relatively good, the both weak and strong conditions of convergent validity [41] are also fulfilled.

Table 1. Values of the models

Value	Community A				Community B			
	Model A1		Model A2		Model B1		Model B2	
Chi-sq (df)	10.98 (8)		29.40 (17)		29.35 (7)		30.80 (12)	
P-value	0.203		0.031		0.000		0.002	
RMSEA	0.038		0.053		0.083		0.058	
NFI	0.99		0.98		0.97		0.99	
NNFI	0.99		0.99		0.95		0.99	
CFI	1.00		0.99		0.97		0.99	
SRMR	0.028		0.025		0.033		0.020	
GFI	0.99		0.97		0.98		0.98	
Factor	MBA	PBE	PBI	MBE	PBA	MBE	MBI	PBE
CR	0.780	0.804	0.881	0.747	0.588	0.762	0.992	0.877
AVE	0.626	0.634	0.645	0.602	0.501	0.609	0.727	0.645

Each factor of each model was evaluated with construct reliabilities (CR) and average variance extracted (AVE) (Table 1). In Models A1, A2 and B2, all the CR values are more than 0.70 and the AVE values more than 0.50, which means that the models are statistically acceptable [42]. In Model B1, only the factor PBA provides an unacceptable CR value. Regarding the respecified models, adjusting them should not only be based on traditional test values like CR and AVE; also theoretical justifications should be acknowledged [43, 44]. As our modifications are theoretically justified, this particular CR value should not be considered as a reason to reject the model. To conclude, despite some justified exceptions, all four measurement models concur with each other concerning their operational measures and relationships, and as fit indices suggest acceptable fits we can judge our models statistically acceptable.

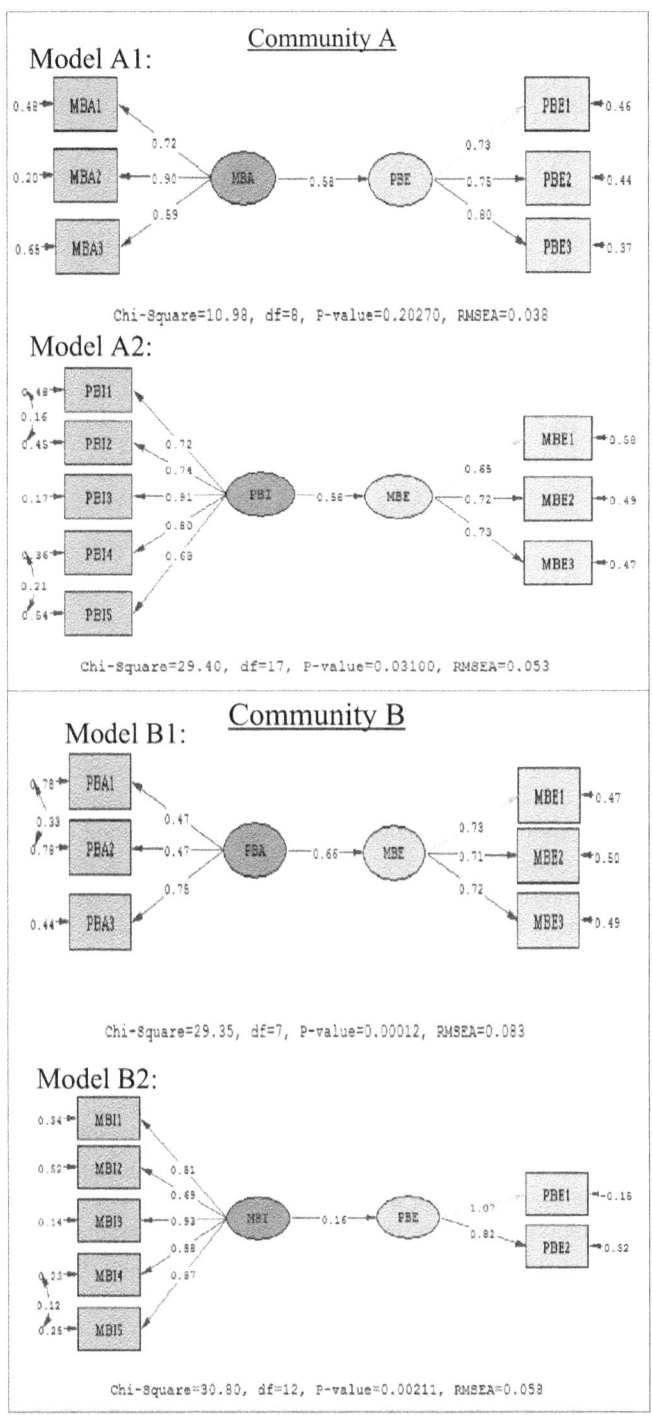

Fig. 2. Empirical models

We can conclude that the BI of the respondents' imagined community (BI_{IC}) affects the BE of their social community (BE_{SC}), and the BA of the social community (BA_{SC}) affects the BE of the imagine community (BE_{IC}) (Fig. 3).

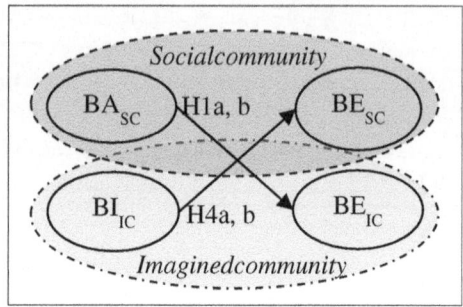

Fig. 3. Accepted hypotheses

4 Concluding Discussion

4.1 Theoretical Implications

Based on the results we can say that value can be cross-created between social and psychological communities. More specifically, individuals' think that their collective image of the other social community (which is their imagined community) offers value to their own social community; and when individuals collectively consider their own social community a well-known, recognized, or even leading brand, they think it offers value to the other, closely related social community - which is their imagined community. Thus, the contributions produced by the article are the introduction and verification of the concepts image-dominant logic and value cross-creation.

4.2 Managerial Implications

This kind of collective value cross-creation is taking place and being natural in every well-functioning and continuous service relationship where the end customer is not the one who pays for the service. For example, students' opinion of their school is largely formed based on others' opinions; and teachers are collectively proud of their students (the better the students, the prouder the teachers). It is highly likely that in these kinds of communities, individuals who perceive a sense of community with the other members, whether involving direct social interaction or not, are highly committed to continue the relationships and close co-operation for a long time even though the individual community members change in the course of time.

Although these ideas might be unfamiliar for marketers, in today's hypercompetitive and community-centered environment these are important factors which need to be taken into account. It becomes every manager's task to identify the most central communities around their companies, including not only the key stakeholder groups but also those who may feel a psychological sense of community toward a company but have not yet engaged themselves in exchange or social interactions of any kind. These are essential groups around a company to be taken into account, groups which build, maintain and share their collective views of the company, and while they may be presently invisible they can be extremely powerful especially in cases when something goes wrong; they may either save or literally destroy the company. Additionally, their influence over each other should be noticed: even though not visible, they may create value for each other - and also for a company.

4.3 Limitations and Further Studies

We understand that focusing on communities has restricted our view as we have not been able to utilize all the extant information on buyer-seller service relationships in value literature, which could have offered valuable further perspectives to our study. We also understand that using brand equity as a measure for value is not equivalent to the term value traditionally considered in value research. Additionally, justifying value cross-creation based on temporality can easily be questioned. Finally, we acknowledge that researchers who prefer confirmatory research may not be familiar with the use of SEM using model generating SEM.

We hope our study can operate as a research opening for further studies in many different levels (e.g. individual, community, groups of companies), from various viewpoints (e.g. company, customers, other stakeholders), and using a wide selection of methodologies. We would like to highlight three of these. First, we call for studies that examine how the image-dominant logic and value cross-creation can be conceptualized. Second, it would be interesting to further discover how value can be cross-created in buyer-seller relationships. And third, as it soon becomes obvious that understanding value cross-creation between only two communities or parties is not enough, this moves the discussion toward triads, or even networks, of communities. Therefore, examining value cross-creation in triads or networks would merit further attention.

Appendix 1: Latent Variables and Their Operational Measures (Further Developed from Davis, Golicic, and Marquardt [28])

Model/ factor	Operational measures in the questionnaire	Label
Community A: recruits as respondents		
A1/MBA	The name of the military driving school is well known among recruits	MBA1
	The military driving school is recognized as a competent provider of driver training	MBA2
	In comparison to other driving schools, the military driving school is the leading brand in the industry	MBA3

(*Continued*)

Model/factor	Operational measures in the questionnaire	Label
A1/PBE	I am willing to work irregularly in order to work in the transport industry	PBE1
	The transport industry brand is different from that of other industries	PBE2
	The name of the transport industry gives them an advantage over other industries	PBE3
A2/PBI	The transport industry is known as a work provider that takes good care of its workers	PBI1
	We can reliably predict how the transport industry will perform	PBI2
	In comparison to other industries, the transport industry is known to consistently deliver very high quality	PBI3
	In comparison to other industries, the transport industry is highly respected	PBI4
	The transport industry is highly respected	PBI5
A2/MBE	I am willing to serve a longer military service in order to co-operate with the military driving school	MBE1
	The military driving school's brand is different from that of other driving schools	MBE2
	The name of the military driving school gives them an advantage over other driving schools	MBE3
Community B: LSPs as respondents		
B1/PBA	The name of the military driving school is well known in our industry	PBA1
	The military driving school is recognized as a competent provider of driver training	PBA2
	In comparison to other driving schools, the military driving school is the leading brand in the industry	PBA3
B1/MBE	We are willing to give more time to our workers to serve a longer military service in order to co-operate with the military driving school	MBE1
	The military driving school's brand is different from that of other driving schools	MBE2
	The name of the military driving school gives them an advantage over other driving schools	MBE3
B2/MBI	The military driving school is known as a driver training provider that takes good care of its students	MBI1
	We can reliably predict how the military driving school will perform	MBI2
	In comparison to other driving schools, the military driving school is known to consistently deliver very high quality	MBI3
	In comparison to other driving schools, the military driving school is highly respected	MBI4

(Continued)

(Continued)

Model/factor	Operational measures in the questionnaire	Label
	The military driving school is highly respected	MBI5
B2/PBE	I am willing to work irregularly in order to work in the transport industry	PBE1
	The transport industry brand is different from that of other industries	PBE2
	The name of the transport industry gives them an advantage over other industries	PBE3

References

1. Vargo, S.L., Lusch, R.F.: Evolving to a new dominant logic for marketing. J. Mark. **68**(1), 1–17 (2004)
2. Heinonen, K., Strandvik, T., Mickelsson, K.-J., Edvardsson, B., Sundström, E., Andersson, P.: A customer-dominant logic of service. J. Serv. Manag. **21**(4), 531–548 (2010)
3. Heinonen, K., Strandvik, T., Voima, P.: Customer dominant value formation in service. Eur. Bus. Rev. **25**(2), 104–123 (2013)
4. Helkkula, A., Kelleher, C., Pihlström, M.: Characterizing value as an experience: implications for service researchers and managers. J. Serv. Res. **15**(1), 59–75 (2012)
5. Lepak, D.P., Smith, K.G., Taylor, M.S.: Value creation and value capture: a multilevel perspective. Acad. Manag. Rev. **32**(1), 180–194 (2007)
6. Anderson, B.: Imagined Communities. Verso, London (1983)
7. Carlson, B.D., Suter, T.A., Brown, T.J.: Social versus psychological brand community: The role of psychological sense of brand community. J. Bus. Res. **61**(4), 284–291 (2008)
8. Prahalad, C.K., Ramaswamy, V.: Co-creating unique value with customers. Strategy Leadersh. **32**(3), 4–9 (2004)
9. Sweeney, J.C., Soutar, G.N.: Consumer perceived value: the development of a multiple item scale. J. Retail. **77**(2), 203–220 (2001)
10. Boulding, K.E.: The Image: Knowledge in Life and Society. University of Michigan Press, Ann Arbor (1961)
11. Fyrberg, A., Jüriado, R.: What about interaction?: networks and brands as integrators within service-dominant logic. J. Serv. Manag. **20**(4), 420–432 (2009)
12. Merz, M.A., He, Y., Vargo, S.L.: The evolving brand logic: a service-dominant logic perspective. J. Acad. Mark. Sci. **37**, 328–344 (2009)
13. Payne, A.F., Storbacka, K., Frow, P., Knox, S.: Co-creating brands: diagnosing and designing the relationship experience. J. Bus. Res. **62**(3), 379–389 (2009)
14. Berry, L.L.: Cultivating service brand equity. J. Acad. Mark. Sci. **28**(1), 128–137 (2000)
15. Brodie, R.J., Glynn, M.S., Little, V.: The service brand and the service-dominant logic: missing fundamental premise or the need for stronger theory? Mark. Theor. **6**(3), 363–379 (2006)
16. Keller, L.: Conceptualizing, measuring, and managing customer-based brand equity. J. Mark. **57**, 1–22 (1993)
17. Peñaloza, L., Venkatesh, A.: Further evolving the new dominant logic of marketing: from services to the social construction of markets. Mark. Theor. **6**, 299–316 (2006)

18. Ballantyne, D., Aitken, R.: Branding in B2B markets: insights from the service-dominant logic of marketing. J. Bus. Ind. Mark. **22**(6), 363–371 (2007)
19. Keller, K.L.: Building and managing corporate brand equity. In: Schultz, M., Hatch, M.J., Holten Larsen, M. (eds.) The Expressive Organisation: Linking Identity, Reputation, and the Corporate Brand, pp. 115–137. Oxford University Press, Oxford (2000)
20. Schau, H.J., Muñiz, A.M., Arnould, E.J.: How brand community practices create value. J. Mark. **73**, 30–51 (2009)
21. McAlexander, J.H., Schouten, J.W., Koenig, F.: Building brand community. J. Mark. **66**, 38–54 (2002)
22. Muniz, A.M., O'Guinn, C.: Brand community. J. Consum. Res. **27**(4), 412–432 (2001)
23. Anderson, B.: Imagined Communities: Reflections on the Origin and Spread of Nationalism (New Edition). Verso, London (2006)
24. Kanno, Y., Norton, B.: Imagined communities and educational possibilities: introduction. J. Lang. Identity Educ. **2**(4), 241–249 (2003)
25. Norton, B.: Non-participation, imagined communities, and the language classroom. In: Breen, M. (ed.) Learner Contributions to Language Learning: New Directions in Research, pp. 159–171. Pearson Education, Harlow (2001)
26. Kanno, Y.: Negotiating Bilingual and Bicultural Identities: Japanese Returnees Betwixt Two Worlds. Lawrence Erlbaum Associates Inc., Mahwah (2003)
27. Dagenais, D.: Accessing imagined communities through multilingualism and immersion education. J. Lang. Identity Educ. **2**(4), 269–839 (2003)
28. Davis, D.F., Golicic, S.L., Marquardt, A.J.: Branding a B2B service: does a brand differentiate a logistics service provider? Ind. Mark. Manag. **37**(2), 218–227 (2008)
29. Yoo, B., Donthu, N.: Developing and validating a multidimensional consumer-based brand equity scale. J. Bus. Res. **52**(1), 1–14 (2001)
30. Kapferer, J.N.: The New Strategic Brand Management: Advanced Insights and Strategic Thinking, 5th edn. Kogan Page, London (2012)
31. Armstrong, J.S., Overton, T.S.: Estimating nonresponse bias in mail surveys. J. Mark. Res. **14**(3), 396–402 (1977)
32. Lambert, D.M., Harrington, T.C.: Measuring nonresponse bias in customer service mail surveys. J. Bus. Logist. **11**, 5–25 (1990)
33. Jöreskog, K.G., Sörbom, D., du Toit, S., du Toit, M.: LISREL 8: New Statistical Features. SSI Inc., Lincolnwood (2000)
34. Jöreskog, K.G., Sörbom, D.: LISREL 8: Structural Equation Modeling with the SIMPLIS Command Language. SSI Inc., Lincolnwood (1993)
35. Jöreskog, K.G.: Testing structural equations models. In: Bollen, K.A., Long, J.S. (eds.) Testing Structural Equation Models. Sage Publications Inc., Palm Spring (1993)
36. Kline, R.B.: Principles and Practices of Structural Equation Modeling. The Guilford Press, New York (2005)
37. Bollen, K.A., Long, J.S.: Testing Structural Equation Models. Sage Publications Inc., Palm Spring (1993)
38. Browne, M.W., Cudeck, R.: Alternative ways of assessing model fit. In: Bollen, K., Long, J. S. (eds.) Testing Structural Equation Models. Sage Publications Inc., Palm Spring (1993)
39. Hu, L., Bentler, P.M.: Cutoff criteria for fit indexes in covariance structure analysis: conventional criteria versus new alternatives. Struct. Equ. Model. **6**(1), 1–55 (1999)
40. Jaccard, J., Wan, C.K.: Lisrel Approaches to Interaction Effect in Multiple Regression. Sage Publications Inc., California (1996)
41. Steenkamp, J.B., van Trijp, H.: The use of LISREL in validating marketing constructs. Int. J. Res. Mark. **8**(1), 283–299 (1991)

42. Hair, J.F., Black, W.C., Babin, B.J., Anderson, R.E.: Multivariate Data Analysis: A Global Perspective. Prentice Hall, Upper Saddle River (2010)
43. Schumacher, R.E., Lomax, R.G.: A Beginner's Guide to Structural Equation Modeling. Lawrence Erlbaum Associates, Mahwah (1996)
44. Juntunen, J., Grant, D.B., Juga, J.: Short-run versus long-run trade-offs in outsourcing relationships: impacts on loyalty and switching propensity. Strateg. Outsourcing Int. J. **3**(3), 211–225 (2010)

E-Health and Value Co-creation: The Case of Electronic Medical Record in an Italian Academic Integrated Hospital

Sabrina Bonomi[1(✉)], Alessandro Zardini[2],
Cecilia Rossignoli[2], and Paola Renata Dameri[3]

[1] eCampus University, Isimbardi Street 10, 22060 Novedrate, CO, Italy
sabrina.bonomi@uniecampus.it
[2] Business Administration Department, University of Verona,
Via Dell'Artigliere 19, 37129 Verona, Italy
{Alessandro.Zardini,Cecilia.Rossignoli}@univr.it
[3] Department of Economics, University of Genova,
Via Vivaldi 5, 16126 Genoa, Italy
dameri@economia.unige.it

Abstract. The objective of the paper is to study the use of service science to create a systematic service innovation in the health environment. Starting from the basic abstraction of service science, which is considered as value co-creation when people, technology and value propositions are connected by internal and external service systems and shared information [1], the paper aims to explain the benefits of the electronic medical record (EMR) and its business and organizational impacts in an Italian Academic Integrated Hospital. The research method is based on a case study and on connected semi-structured interviews. The qualitative study shows the co-created value, i.e. the impacts of introduction and development (consolidation) of EMR on efficacy and efficiency of the organization, on data collection and processing, error reduction, sustainability of SSN (national health service) and especially the better quality of services to the citizens.

Keywords: Electronic medical record · Value co-creation · Service science for health · Hospital case study

1 Introduction

The main purpose of Service Science is to classify and explain how different types of service systems interact and evolve in order to co-create value through a continuous chain of interactions between service providers and consumers [2]. According to Hill [3], we can consider service as a change in one person's condition, as the result of the activity of some other economic entity, with the approval of the first person or economic organization. Service science can be applied in several sectors, among which e-Health, and it can create an open, collaborative environment in order to foster service innovation by means of information, trials, technological transfer of the research results aiming to develop sustainable service systems innovative solutions [4].

In service science, human factors, management-economic factors and engineering factors are involved in several interactions and in an interdisciplinary effort to co-create value [5, 6]. To make advances in service innovation it's necessary that the service system has information about the capabilities and the needs of its clients, its competitors and itself. Indeed, not all interactions between service systems co-create value and service science seeks to understand the reasons, looking at different behaviours [5].

The consumers' role is changed; they are connected, informed and active [7]. Customers receive resources from the provider and transform them into a valuable outcome, according to their preferences and needs [8] and interacting with them. Consequently, to create the basis for systematic service innovation, it is necessary to cultivate service science. [5, 9, 10].

In the last few years, the Public Administration started using the information and communication technologies (ICT) to produce and offer better services to its customers, that is the citizens. E-health, in particular, is in a continuous improvement process and it can reorganize processes and improve quality services, in order to develop the performance management system [11, 12]. Furthermore, E-health involves interactions between doctors and patients and highlights new challenges, opportunities and threats to all the organization. There are a lot of new technologies that are implemented and also a lot of information technologies that arise from them. There is already a strong service science foundation to build upon and many good ideas, strategies, tools and theories that could be widely applied to immediately benefit organizations [13]. A variety of resources, information technology solutions and network can be applied to health and health care to give the citizens different solutions to solve their problems with better services. Furthermore, information and communication technologies give instruments to doctors and their teams and the flow of information, which comes from consumers, becomes more reliable. The Electronic Health Record (EHR) is one of those instruments; it can be defined as a repository of patient's data in digital form that is stored and exchanged securely and in an accessible way by different levels of authorized users [14]. The adoption of EHR systems in healthcare has some advantages, which improve the quality of patients' care. Many studies [15, 16] highlighted and emphasized how such systems could enhance the quality of care and support its continuity [17]. In particular EHR is based on the Electronic medical record (EMR) [18, 19].[1]

The research questions are: which and how is the co-value created by EMR between hospital and patients? Which are the impacts created among hospital workers and staff by this new information technology?

2 Health Information System and Electronic Health Record

Enterprises introduce information systems and communication technologies (ICT) with the aim to supply information, to connect with customers, to supply instruments in productive areas, to create automation processes and rationalize business processes [20].

---

[1] It can also be called EHR - Eletronic Health Record [24] and EPR - Eletronical Patient Record [25]. In this paper EHR is meaning the dossier based on EMR as its first step.

The use of ICT is evolving and it is improving in every sector, including Public Administration; in the health environment the digitalization process has been in place for many years but its progress is slow, probably due to economic (e.g. costs for start-up and maintenance of information systems) and technical (for example workers training, knowledge transfer, new business roles…) barriers [21]. However, the digitalization process of hospitals and healthcare services has already reached excellent levels in some countries [22].

Health information systems can be classified as the set of elements and procedures whose digital output supports the decision-making processes for health care. They are able to re-organise and improve processes, input, output and quality services, aiming to increase hospital efficiency and provide services of a higher quality while reducing costs [23]. To have good results, it is necessary to invest in several resources, economic, organizational, human, collective, ontological, regulatory, security and infrastructural resources.

The Electronic Medical Record (EMR) is the principal instrument introduced in the public health administration [23]. It can be defined as «*an electronic medical data and reports about patients' conditions, images, physiological signals, checkup reports, medical treatment videos, and medical forms*» [19].

It will contain all health and social data in digital form about patients, thereby allowing significant savings both in terms of direct costs for production, conservation and re-production of their case history, and in terms of saving time in entering information. Therefore, a significant improvement in the decision process should be achieved [23]. The final user constitutes the focus of the information system, which adopts patient-centred logic for which the final infrastructure's aim comprises the distribution of the best possible efficient and qualitative service.

The EMR is one of the most important basic parts of the electronic health records (EHR), the dossier that allows hospital workers to unify any patient's clinical data, trial and diagnosis. It allows one to immediately know any information, independently from the hospital unit, which produced them.

The EHR system must achieve [26]:

- data processing and their integration to simplify their use by patients, doctors and any other health worker;
- support for clinical intervention and for patients, who can contribute with doctors aiming to improve information;
- simplify and decrease work in the health sector;
- reduce the loss of information, lower the amount of paper work;
- make simpler the supply chain of medicine and reduce errors in their orders.

Therefore, the EMR is based on an intense integration among all the health workers during the whole path. The EMR stimulates and improves relationship between patient and physicians but also between the latter and the workers of the other hospitals to obtain more efficiency, enhancing quality of care, evidence based, empowerment of consumers and patients, encouragement of a new relationship between doctors and patients [27]. These relationships, indeed, allow to more and better gather data and extract further information about the same patients and improve the quality of the care.

3 Electronic Medical Record and Value Co-creation

According to Vargo et al. [10] the co-creation of value within complex configurations of resources including people, information, and technology, is fundamentally derived from the integration and application of resources in a specific context. This is probably an ever-changing context. The introduction of EMR in a health structure has a lot of aims that can be achieved through mutual service. The health workers « *have to exchange relationships, improving the adaptability and survivability of all service systems engaged in exchange, by allowing integration of resources that are mutually beneficial* » as explained by Vargo et al. [10], speaking about service science. Indeed, the EMR gives health workers the possibility of having shared data and of exchanging them, makes coordination of different areas and patient's care easier, but it needs a good integration. In the health context, after the introduction of EMR, value is co-created by three key actors: physicians (all those that take care of the patient), hospital workers and patients themselves. These three actors, due to EMR use, have more synergic relationships and bring different information to EMR. It becomes a resource that allows value creation process; especially information transfer and sharing improves the quality of cares from which patients benefit, and improves the quality of work of health workers.

According to Shaw [28], a medical record should document a lot of patient's clinical data (health condition, examinations, results and so on) to give doctors some data that they can use to make clinically appropriate decisions; it should promote and facilitate collaboration and integration of health workers, of different wards or even of different health centres; it should create a database for scientific studies or clinical researches, for evaluation or control systems or other actions; it should make data input, data mining or data processing easier and should permit to track them.

Success or failure depends on several technical causes such as suitability of hardware, computer and vocational training, but it also depends on the organizational culture and on project leadership attitude. The different capabilities of information technologies and organizations should be integrated in context, to transfer their knowledge in a collaborative way, to create intangible assets aimed to create new and valued services and solutions to patients' problems and to create value out of that exchange. In the project improvement, a participative leadership is necessary [18] to motivate every stakeholder and to involve anyone in this co-value creation. Consequently the health information technology must be supported by health workers' specialization and especially by relationships among doctors and communications between doctors and patients. EMR puts citizens in the hearth of the health systems. They aren't anymore only the beneficiaries of the information that are included in EMR, but they are co-creators of it. In fact, they can add news and increase the information. Information that show from every relation among patients and any other component of health information system, should be integrated and structured to improve health care and so as to create co-value.

This topic has implications for advancing service science and it is necessary to try to measure the value-in-use and its improvement.

4 Case Study: An Italian Academic Integrated Hospital

4.1 Research Method

The research method used to answer to the research question is the case study. According to Yin, it is an empirical research that proposes to investigate a contemporary phenomenon in its real-life contest when the boundary between the phenomenon and the context is not sharp [29].

To do this research, it's necessary to define a protocol that unfolds in four steps: research design, data collection, data processing and data analysis, to achieve an outcome, conclusions and final report.

The case addressed in this paper began with an analysis of an academic integrated hospital (AIH) during the EMR analysis and implementation phase. Two main reasons led the authors to select AIH as their case study. First, the AIH case is particularly insightful for research into EMR adoption and use because it involves an E-health tool used by highly complex public healthcare providers. Further, the hospital has two different, highly structured organisational (university and healthcare) identities (spirits) that, while integrated, have specific, composite natures. Second, the authors were given direct access to the data [30].

The case study was conducted according to the methods and instructions suggested by Yin [29]. This entailed gathering data through semi-structured interviews, direct observance and document research. The interviews and the internal documentation were used as the testing sources. Privileged access to the relevant information enabled the authors to collect data from several sources, increasing the quality of the information obtained [31].

The case was analysed using the results of the ten semi-structured interviews (each of approximately 40 minutes duration) held with the AIH staff and designed to enable the respondents to answer freely, in their own words. Two researchers attended each interview. Data collection commenced in January 2014 and continued for approximately four months. The analysis and integration of the existing data began in June 2014.

4.2 Case Study

4.2.1 Scenario

The Academic Integrated Hospital is one of the most important hospital in Italy as patients' number. The health care centre has high qualifications in several research branches and in terms of medical assistance and education. The Academic Integrated Hospital is constituted by two hospital units, that guarantee medical assistance, recovery and emergency health services in the city for 24 h a day. Its First Aid service sees almost 500 people per day. More than 5,000 employees work in the Academic Integrated Hospital, including hospital and academic doctors, nurses, health workers, technical/professional employers and people assigned to the administrative area. At the first level there is a general manager for both territorial locations, supported by the board of Statutory Auditors, the Office of Address and the Organ Independent of Evaluation. At the second hierarchical level, there is an administrative director, whose job is to check the Department of Administration and Human Resources, the Department of Resources and Economic Instrumental and Technical Department; finally there is the Medical Director, who controls instead of the various departments at Business Integrated (Surgery, Oncology, Dentistry, General Medicine, Intensive Care, Maternity, etc.).

Every year, around 60,000 people are hospitalized in the Academic Integrated Hospital, of which around 10,000 arrive from other regions and more than 3,000 from foreign districts. Every day, almost 1,300 people are present for ordinary recovery and about 400 people access to the hospital for planned day hospital recovers.

4.2.2 Information Systems in AIH

The Information and Communication Technology process started in 2008 in a gradually way. One of the first steps of the process was tested in medicinal prescription, distribution and supplying process and thanks to a digital instrument.

The AIH has already introduced ICT in acceptance, in discharge and in transfer activities, into the laboratories of analysis procedures, in Radiology. It was introduced also in the data sharing and data communication on citizens, especially about discharged patients, to facilitate relationships between AIH and territorial health services units.

The Information and communication technology has the purpose of implement the EHR to improve management's efficiency and efficacy. To achieve this aim, the Academic Integrated Hospital is being equipped with a system for Electronic Medical Records through the digitalisation of the hospital processes into modules. It's undergoing EMR testing in several General Medicine wards (B, D and ex C).

This will later represent the focus for improving the processes of efficiency and efficacy management, and it will constitute the primary step for the future EHR.

5 Data Analysis and Discussion

The qualitative study chosen is the "survey" method; it is constituted by ten semi-structured anonymous interviews. Every questionnaire is composed by fourteen questions, the same for every interviewee; every interview was recorded, previous asking consent, and transcribed word by word. The interviewed people were five physicians, three nurses, one ward nurse and one practising doctor. In this first step we didn't interview patients, because we wanted to concentrate ourselves to understand and explore the EHR implementation in the hospital.

The data processing was made by a specific German software, Atlas.ti, which analysed the transcription of interviews, defining the frequency of some "codes"; the most numerous codes allow the comprehension of the relevant points of view of the interviewees. The main codes are collaboration and coordination (19 times), reducing errors (15 times), quality service improvement (11 times), simplification and reduction of bureaucracy (10 times) and knowledge dissemination (10 times).

All the interviewees agree that the EMR is useful. All people appreciate the improvement of service quality, the reduction of errors, the support of data sharing and other advantages.

For almost all the interviewees, an advantage comes from the clearer understanding of handwriting, because it reduces interpretative errors. Moreover, the EMR minimizes errors because the indications of different screen shots prevent the forgetting of some important information about patients' situation. Finally, every patient has a bracelet that identifies his illness and therapy, which can be read by a bar code; it reduces wrong dosage, confusions of patients and of therapy.

One practicing doctor said: *"we have good nurses, but with EMR we can minimize the risk of errors, of wrong or confused therapy"*. A nurse confirmed: *"the utility of EMR is to avoid wrong interpretation of handwriting, to minimize dosage errors and also improve the supply"*. And another said: *"nobody can forget to write the right dosage or leave out some information. We can't administrate the wrong medicine or make confusion between two patients"*.

Therefore, the EMR permits the collaboration and the consequent knowledge sharing between physicians and nursing staff, which can reduce the clerical errors and the homonym errors and can improve service quality.

The health workers, especially physicians and nurses, appreciate these collaboration and coordination that EMR stimulates and that can increase the service quality and patients' healthcare.

A physician said *"it facilitates data sharing and a collaborative approach and this is one of the most important characteristics of our job, that we can call 'team work'"*. And another physician said *"we can share data and information and compare opinions to find better solutions"*.

According to Shaw [28] the EMR allows knowledge sharing among physicians of different hospital departments to guarantee a better and accurate healthcare thanks to knowledge dissemination. One of the most important advantages appears in case of discharge; thanks to this computer program, physicians can coordinate the hospital recovery and the territorial health service after hospital release. The physicians can transfer all the information about the dismissed patient, explain his necessities to the new delegates of his health care and minimize bureaucracy time of the "protected release". A practicing doctor told us that the discharge time reduced from five to two workdays and information sharing creates a big value which benefits patients and health workers.

Another important advantage there is when patients have a complex health condition and need to be cured in several hospital departments. The EMR permits to know in few minutes all the patient's data, in particular examinations (i.e. hematic or radiological, etc.), also of previous hospital recovery history and letter of precedent release; the physicians can interact with nurses and the change of therapy can be rapid and they can be immediately shared. A doctor said that *"the collaboration and data sharing are improved; when something changes, everybody are informed and physicians and nurses can work simultaneously"*. An improvement, as a physician said, would be *"to have the same interaction with different hospitals, not only among different departments of the same hospital"*. The major value that it is co-created especially for elderly patients those are alone and those are not able to explain completely and with precision their health situation; by the EMR is possible to share information and to find the more adapted therapy.

The physicians and all the hospital workers, have also a lot of problems that come from the introduction of EMR, but they origin from technical causes, especially from inadequacy of software/hardware supports. The process is at the beginning (it started in January 2014) and technological supports can be surely improved, but this is not the aim of this paper.

The lack of appropriate and efficient supports is interesting in this research only for the reason why all those problems become a sensible reduction of the time that all health workers dedicate to patients and each other and that reduce the value creation. All people interviewed said that this is a negative impact because it reduces the time to stay with patients and the relationships get worse. A doctor said: "*at the moment, this procedure is a waste of time, but in the future we will make the most of it*"

Another doctor said that "*A big lack of this system is that it does not involve the final user, or not enough*". If everybody recognizes all the strengths that EMR has and the improvements that it can produce, it could be easy to correct its weakness if people are involved in the innovation process and they are collaborative.

An innovation, although it could be optimal and/or necessary, needs to be supported by information technology but especially it needs a high collaboration among health workers and between information system and them.

In this particular case, when a lot of times health workers are in emergency or they must decide something in a rapid way, the relationship with other colleagues to improve the new instrument and with patients who can explain some data, become fundamental.

6 Conclusions

The paper tries to understand which are the impacts created by the EMR among hospital workers and especially to understand if this ICT tool could be a source of value co-creation among physicians, between physicians and nurses and also between physician and patients, to give better aid to citizens.

According to Maglio and Spohrer [6], human, management-economic and engineering factors are involved in several interactions and in an interdisciplinary effort to co-create value. In our study we could see that the EMR is based on an intense integration among all the health workers during the whole path; all system is involved and the change is rife with all the organization to improve efficiency and productivity.

According to Scott et al. [18] and other many studies [14, 15, 17], the use of EMR permits to improve the quality of health care; in the case study analysed, we could verify that this is the opinion of all the interviewees too; all physicians and nurses said that after EMR introduction, they could give a better service to the patients and create a good working environment. Indeed, the EMR allows minimizing dosage errors, coming from bad interpretation of handwriting and reducing confuse of patients and therapy; finally, no one can forget to input information because the screen shots indicate the correct sequence.

The hospital workers can also be more collaborative, share information about patients and be quicker in data collection because of the significant reduction of bureaucracy and the knowledge dissemination; they can see all reports about previous patients' recoveries and their story, which are specially useful when patients are elderly or when they have a complex health condition and they need to be cured by different physicians in several hospital departments.

The data collected allow us to say that the introduction of EMR is useful and improve the quality of health service, but is necessary an interaction among hospital workers and between them and patients to co-create value. At the moment we interviewed only hospital workers and a future development of the research should be to understand the patients' opinions.

In this hospital, the process is at the beginning and there are still a lot of difficulties, not only for the inadequate instrumentation, but also for the organizational change that is required. According to Almuthiry et al. [17], the productivity and output contributions associated with computerization are up to 5 times greater over long periods, but the first results make us confident. A forward pass should be also a check system after some time, to confirm the expected value.

References

1. Maglio, P.P., Bailey, J., Gruhl, D.: Steps toward a science of service systems. Computer **40**, 71–77 (2007)
2. Spohrer, J.C., Maglio, P.P.: Toward a science of service systems. In: Spohrer, J.C., Maglio, P.P. (eds.) Handbook of Service Science, pp. 157–194. Springer, New York (2010)
3. Hill, T.P.: On goods and services. Rev. Income Wealth **23**(4), 315–338 (1977)
4. Bardhan, I.R., Demirkan, H., Kannan, P.K., Kauffman, R.J., Sougstad, R.: An interdisciplinary perspective on IT services management and service science. J. Manag. Inf. Syst. **26**(4), 13–64 (2010)
5. Maglio, P.P., Spohrer, J.: Fundamentals of service science. J. Acad. Mark. Sci. **36**(1), 18–20 (2008)
6. Maglio, P.P., Spohrer, J.: A service science perspective on business model innovation. Ind. Mark. Manage. **42**(5), 665–670 (2013)
7. Kryvinska, N., Kaczor, S., Strauss, C., Greguš, M.: Servitization - its raise through information and communication technologies. In: Snene, M., Leonard, M. (eds.) IESS 2014. LNBIP, vol. 169, pp. 72–81. Springer, Heidelberg (2014)
8. Fragidis, G., Konstantas, D., Paschaloudis, D.: A classification framework of value co-creation in electronic and mobile services. In: Snene, M., Leonard, M. (eds.) IESS 2014. LNBIP, vol. 169, pp. 40–55. Springer, Heidelberg (2014)
9. Chesbrough, H.: Toward a science of services. Harvard Bus. Rev. **83**(2), 16–17 (2005)
10. Vargo, S.L., Maglio, P.P., Akaka, M.A.: On value and value co-creation: a service systems and service logic perspective. Eur. Manag. J. **26**(3), 145–152 (2008)
11. Moullin, M., Mann, T.E., Ornstein, N.J., Mechanic, D., Rogut, L.B., Colby, D.C., Stewart Jr., C.T.: Delivering Excellence in Health and Social Care: Quality, Excellence and Performance Measurement. Open University Press, Philadelphia (2011)
12. Moggi, S., Suppa, A., Leardini, C., Campedelli B.: Managing performance in heathcare: the case of Verona Integrated University Hospital. In: Proceeding of the AIDEA 2013 Symposium, 23th-24th September 2013, Lecce (Italy), Cacucci ed., Bari, Italy
13. Bitner, M.J., Brown, S.W.: The evolution and discovery of services science in business schools. Commun. ACM **49**(7), 73–78 (2006)

14. Häyrinen, K., Saranto, K., Nykänen, P.: Definition, structure, content, use and impacts of electronic health records: a review of the research literature. Int. J. Med. Informatics **77**(5), 291–304 (2008)
15. Thakkar, M., Davis, D.C.: Risks, barriers, and benefits of EHR systems: a comparative study based on size of hospital. Perspectives in Health Information Management/AHIMA, American Health Information Management Association, vol. 3, access on the 12th September 2014. http://www.ncbi.nlm.nih.gov/pmc/articles/PMC2047303/
16. Flannery, K., Zandieh, S.O., Kuperman, G.J., Langsam, D.J., Hyman, D., Kaushal, R.: A qualitative analysis of an electronic health record (EHR) implementation in an academic ambulatory setting. Inform. Prim. Care **16**(4), 277–284 (2008)
17. Almutiry, O., Wills, G., Crowder, R.: Towards a framework for data quality in Electonic health records, In: IADIS International Conference, e-Society, Lisbon, Portugal (2013)
18. Scott, J.T., Rundall, T.G., Vogt, T.M., Hsu, J.: 'Kaiser Permanente's experience of implementing an electronic medical record: a qualitative study. Br. Med. J. **331**, 1313–1316 (2005)
19. Chang, I.C., Li, Y.C., Wu, T.Y., Yen, D.C.: Electronic medical record quality and its impact on user satisfaction: healthcare providers' point of view. Gov. Inf. Q. **29**(2), 235–242 (2012)
20. Antlová, K.: Motivation and barriers of ICT adoption in small and medium-sized enterprises. E + M Ekon. Manag. **12**(2), 140–155 (2009)
21. Kaye, R., Kokia, E., Shalev, V., Idar, D., Chinitz, D.: Barriers and success factors in health information technology: A practitioner's perspective. J. Manag. Mark. Healthc. **3**(2), 163–175 (2010)
22. Ludwick, D.A., Doucette, J.: Adopting electronic medical records in primary care: lessons learned from health information systems implementation experience in seven countries. Int. J. Med. Informatics **78**, 22–31 (2008)
23. Rossignoli, C., Zardini, A., Benettollo, P.: The process of digitalisation in radiology as a lever for organisational change: the case of the academic integrated hospital of verona. In: Phillips-Wren, G., Carlsson, S., Respício, A., Brézillon, P. (eds.) DSS 2.0 – Supporting Decision Making with New Technologies, vol. 261, pp. 24–35. IOS Press, London (2014)
24. Kalra, D., Ingram, D.: Electronic health records. In: Zieliński, K., et al. (eds.) Information technology solutions for healthcare, pp. 135–181. Springer, London (2006)
25. Pous, M.F., Camporese, M., Nobili, A., Frau, S., Del Zotti, F., Conforti, A., Zimol, R., Giustetto, G., Zermiani, G., Lombardo, G., Mezzalira, L.: Quality assessment of information about medications in primary care electronic patient record (EPR) systems. Inform. Prim. Care **18**(2), 109–116 (2010)
26. Ministero della salute (eng. trad. Ministry of Health), Il fascicolo sanitario elettronico: linee guida nazionali (eng. trad. 'the EMR: guidelines'), Ministry of Health, Italy (2012)
27. Eysenbach, G.: What is e-health? J. Med. Internet Res. **3**(2), 1–5 (2006)
28. Shaw, N.: The role of the professional association: a grounded theory study of electronic medical records usage in Ontario, Canada. Int. J. Inf. Manage. **34**(2), 200–209 (2014)
29. Yin, R.K.: Case Study Research: Design and Methods, 3rd edn. Sage Publications, Los Angeles (2009)
30. Eisenhardt, K., Graebner, M.: Theory building from cases: opportunities and challenges. Acad. Manag. **50**(1), 25–32 (2007)
31. Benbasat, I.: An analysis of research methodologies. In: Warren, F. (ed.) The Information Systems Research Challenge, pp. 47–85. Harward Business School Press, Boston (1984)

Service Convenience on Call Centers: Impacts on Repurchase

João F. Proença and Marisa Fernandes(✉)

School of Economics and Management, University of Porto, Porto, Portugal
jproenca@fep.up.pt, marisacostafernandes@gmail.com

Abstract. This study aimed to test the relationship between service convenience (time and effort expenditures), in a Call Center setting, and customers repurchase behaviour.

A database of 133 783 customers and 376 057 contacts were analyzed in what concerns three Call Center performance indicators, representative of customers' time and effort: First Call Resolution (FCR), Average Handling Time and Repeated Calls.

Time and effort expenditures on Call Centers were proved to be related to repurchase. Customers at early stages of their relationship with the service, low value customers and those participating on loyalty programs, were the most sensitive to time and effort expenditures on Call Centers. Understanding the impact of customers' time and effort on customers repurchase behaviour and knowing the customers less likely to wait and expend efforts, managers must seek to improve Call Centers performance, and select who are the customers to answer first.

Keywords: Service convenience · Call centers time · Effort · Repurchase behaviour

1 Introduction

This work focuses on the study of service convenience, which deals with customers' time and effort expenditures to purchase or use a service [1], in a Call Center setting.

Services will add value to consumers by reducing the time and effort they spend [2]. Thus, convenience may represent a distinctive competitive strategy and several studies have reported positive relations between perceived service convenience and consumer satisfaction [3–6].

Call Centers are fundamental to CRM strategies since they are responsible for 70 % of the contacts between the company and the customer [6] and customer overall satisfaction with Call Centers services seems to determine the customer satisfaction with the service itself [6, 7]. Call Centers are concerned about offering a convenient, fast and effortless service to customers and it is expected that understanding how Call Centers increase customer convenience, i.e., reduce time and effort, will increase customer satisfaction [3, 4] and loyalty [5].

Repurchase may mean repeating visits to the service and/or increasing the amount spent on the service [2]. This research considered repurchase behaviour as the repeated use of service, i.e., if the customer keeps the service active, in opposition to its deactivation.

This research aims to: (i) relate the concept of service convenience with Call Centers operations; (ii) determine how Call Centers performance may impact on service repurchase; (iii) explore the factors which can influence the relationship between Call Centers performance and service repurchase.

2 Literature Review

2.1 Convenience

Convenience concept appeared in the literature, for the first time, in Copeland's goods categories, identified as goods purchased at easily accessible stores [8], requiring minimal time and effort to acquire [8, 9]. Marketing has noticed a permanent rise in consumer preference for convenience and attribute it to socioeconomic changes [10–12]. Demanding time saving solutions [13], consumers opened doors to a convenience-oriented market, which must fulfil immediate needs or wishes, releasing time and effort [14]. Consumers' effort and time expenditures are the non-monetary costs that influence perceived convenience [12].

Convenience orientation deals with people preference for convenience goods and services [1, 15, 16], and convenience-oriented consumer are the one who seeks to "accomplish a task in the shortest time with the least expenditure of human energy" [17], p. 37.

Since individual consumer characteristics may affect the perceived importance of convenience [1, 18] several studies have attempted to establish the socioeconomic and demographic factors, which determine the consumers demand for convenient goods and services [14, 15, 19–23]. Segmenting convenience-oriented consumers, marketing could assign them convenience solutions [16].

3 Call Centers

3.1 Call Centers as Interaction Channels

The development and the decreasing costs of telecommunications and information technologies [24, 25] and the importance of CRM strategies have increased the need of Call Centers by companies [6, 25, 26]. They may be the core of successful CRM strategies [27, 28], representing an opportunity for high-volume, low-cost service [29, 30], which has resulted in the worldwide growth of Call Center numbers [7, 31]. Acting as an interaction channel and as an important source of customer-related information [32, 33, 56], they play a crucial role in the development of long-term relationships with customers [24, 25, 30, 34–36]. Call Centers allow customers to access services more immediately [37] meeting their convenience demand and working as a competitive advantage when compared to firms only physically available during limited hours [24].

Call Centers represent the main customer-facing channel for many firms [38, 39] Accordingly to [40] 92 % of customers have their opinion about a firm formed by their experience with Call Centers Thus, organizations need to manage customer contacts more effectively [41], which is likely to have important implications for companies' success [31].

3.2 Call Centers Metrics

Despite Call Centers exponential growth, little is known about customers' satisfaction [42–44], customers' expectations [32] or perceived customer quality [26, 43, 44] with Call Centers performance, which [45] combined in two types of indicators.

The first are qualitative, intangible metrics, which measure caller perceptions of the interaction with the Call Center agents [33, 36, 41]. Their competencies were proved to have impact on repurchase intentions [46].

The second are quantitative metrics, which focus mainly on operational indicators, such as waiting time, hold and average talk time, and are known as key performance indicators (KPIs) [47]. See [24, 45, 26] for common Call Centers KPIs. Operational Call Center indicators, however, proved to have little impact on customer satisfaction [24, 48, 49] and customers' perception about service quality [26] or expectations [50]. Other variables must determine customer satisfaction with Call Centers [26, 29, 51].

3.3 Call Centers Convenience

Operational, quantitative measures are representative of consumers' time and effort expenditures and literature has found clues of their impact on consumers' satisfaction.

Kolar [44] proposed that one of the criteria to achieve excellence in Call Centers quality is the reduction of customer sacrifice, such as time, efforts and psychological costs. The most important benefit of telephone interactions is speed (which saves time) and simplifying customers' life [44]. In fact, customers are concerned with speedy services and less tolerant with time based problems [51]. Bennington et al. [42] defend that, for customers, the main Call Center benefits are convenience, flexibility and customization. Consumers appreciate timely accessibility [7, 49, 52] any time, from anywhere, in any form, and for free [7], which is a determinant of customer satisfaction with Call Centers [34]. Nevertheless, there is no consensus about which Call Centers metrics impact on consumers overall satisfaction and not always research has found positive relations between all Call Center performance indicators and customer satisfaction [24, 26, 49].

4 The Research

4.1 Research Objectives

This study aimed to explore service convenience in a Call Center setting through three performance indicators, representative of customers' time and effort expenditures on their interactions with Call Centers: First Call Resolution (percentage of calls which were resolved on customer's first call and did not need further contacts), Average Handling Time (average time it takes to resolve a customer issue, since it is presented until it is closed) and Repeated Calls (percentage of times the customer had to call back for the same reason after it was given as resolved), and their relation with customers repurchase behaviour.

Furthermore, we intend to analyze the relationship between service convenience, and customers repurchase behaviour, in different groups, according to: (a) demographic factors (age and gender), (b) customer-service relationship length, (c) loyalty programs participation, and (d) customer value.

4.2 Hypothesis Development

Literature has shown positive relations between perceived service convenience and consumer repurchase intentions [17, 53–55] and service repurchase [2].

Consumers show preoccupations about time and effort expenditures on their interactions with Call Centers, namely in what concerns accessibility [7], timeliness [34], and Call Center agents' responsiveness on first contact [49]. First Call Resolution [24, 49] and timeliness in response, i.e., Average Handling Time [34] proved to be determinants of customers' satisfaction. As these metrics are representative of customers' time and effort to have their issues resolved, we expect they have impact on customers repurchase behaviour. So, the first groups of hypotheses are formulated:

H1 (a) There is a relationship between FCR and customers repurchase behaviour.
H1 (b) There is a relationship between Average Handling Time and customers repurchase behaviour.
H1 (c) There is a relationship between Repeated Calls and customers repurchase behaviour.

Research showed demographic factors which explain the demand for convenience [14, 15, 21, 22]. Age [21] was proved to be determinant of convenience oriented customers. Morganosky [22] stated that consumers below 30 years of age were more likely to buy convenience products. Therefore, the second group of hypotheses is formulated:

H2 (a) The relationship between FCR and repurchase behaviour is higher on younger customers.
H2 (b) The relationship between Average Handling Time and repurchase behaviour is higher on younger customers.
H2 (c) The relationship between Repeated Calls and repurchase behaviour is higher on younger customers.

Literature lacks research in what concerns gender convenience orientation. Some studies analyzed housewives and mothers convenience orientation, since female increasing employment may lead to perceptions of increasing time pressure [19, 22] and to demand for convenient products and services. But males were excluded from these researches. As men employment rates are higher than women's, so time pressure and convenience orientation are expected to be. Therefore, the third group of hypotheses is formulated:

H3 (a) The relationship between FCR and repurchase behaviour is higher on male customers.

H3 (b) The relationship between Average Handling Time and repurchase behaviour is higher on male customers.

H3 (c) The relationship between Repeated Calls and repurchase behaviour is higher on male customers.

Relational characteristics can work as switching barriers, creating competitive advantages to the companies [2]. Customer-service relationship length and participation on loyalty programs are both relational characteristics, which represent customers' interest in the building of relationships with a specific firm [2]. Both had a moderating role in the relationship between satisfaction and repurchase behaviour, in a context of contractual services [2]. Loyalty programs participation usually implies contractual relations, with penalties supported by the customer in case of abandonment, so an exit barrier, while customer-service relationship length seems to increase the customers willingness to expend time and effort in their relationship with the service [54]. The fourth and fifth groups of hypotheses are formulated:

H4 (a) The relationship between FCR and repurchase behaviour is higher on customers with a shorter relationship length with the service.

H4 (b) The relationship between Average Handling Time and repurchase behaviour is higher on customers with a shorter relationship length with the service.

H4 (c) The relationship between Repeated Calls and repurchase behaviour is higher on customers with a shorter relationship length with the service.

H5 (a) The relationship between FCR and repurchase behaviour is higher on customers not participating in loyalty programs.

H5 (b) The relationship between Average Handling Time and repurchase behaviour is higher on customers not participating in loyalty programs.

H5 (c) The relationship between Repeated Calls and repurchase behaviour is higher on customers not participating in loyalty programs.

Richer customers were expected to pay more for what meets their convenience needs [14, 56]. As income increases so does convenience preference [21]. Considering that healthier customers are those who spend more, they will be high value customers for the firm, and those who will be willing to pay for convenient services. We formulate the sixth group of hypotheses:

H6 (a) The relationship between FCR and repurchase behaviour is higher on high value customers.

H6 (b) The relationship between Average Handling Time and repurchase behaviour is higher on high value customers.

H6 (c) The relationship between Repeated Calls and repurchase behaviour is higher on high value customers.

4.3 Data Collection

Data were collected from a Portuguese Call Center database, in the telecommunications industry, which was selected because the telephony market where this Call Center operates is a highly competitive one [57].

We focused on customers who have contacted by phone the telecommunications company's Call Center during the first semester of 2012. The performance of the Call Center dealing with these interactions was analyzed concerning three metrics: First Call Resolution, Average Handling Time and Repeated calls, which were chosen because they are representative of customers' time and effort expenditures to have their questions resolved and were identified through exploratory interviews to four Call Center managers. Repurchase behaviour was measured three months after the contacts occurred. The database has a sample of 133 783 customers who all together did 376 057 contacts to the Call Center (an average of 2.8 calls per customer).

Five control variables were added to our model: customers' age and gender, customer-service relationship length (measured in months); the participation (or not) on loyalty programs; the customer value (measured through the average amount spent by the customer, during the first semester of 2012).

In order to measure the impact of the predictive indicators on repurchase behaviour, customers were divided into classes, see Table 1 for variables classes. Table 2 shows the descriptive statistics of the variables analyzed.

Table 1. Classes of variables. Source: authors

Variables	Class	Description
FCR (First Call Resolution)	Yes	Customers who had 100 % of their contacts resolved at their first contact
	NO	Customers who did not have their resolution at first contact, at least once
Average Handling Time	<1 h	Customers whose requests/complaints average handling time was up to 1 h
	1-24 h	Customers whose requests/complaints average handling time was between 1 and 24 h
	>24 h	Customers whose requests/complaints average handling time was more than 24 h
Repeated Calls	Yes	Customers who had to repeat the call at least once
	No	Customers who never had to repeat the call
Repurchase	Yes	Customers who had the service active at the end of third trimester of 2012
	No	Customers who did not have the service active at the end of third trimester of 2012
Age	Young	0–45 years
	Middle age	46–65 years
	Senior	>65 years

(*Continued*)

Table 1. *(Continued)*

Variables	Class	Description
Gender	Female	Female customers
	Male	Male customers
Customer/service relationship length	Beginner	Customers using the service up to 24 months
	Advanced	Customers using the service for more than 24 months
Participation on Loyalty Programs	Yes	Customers belonging to a loyalty program
	No	Customers not belonging to a loyalty program
Customer value	Low value	Customers spending, in average, the minimum amount of the rate plan (12,50EUR)
	Medium value	Customers spending, in average, between the minimum and twice the amount of the rate plan
	Senior value	Customers spending, in average, more than twice the amount of the rate plan

Table 2. Descriptive statistics of the variables analyzed. Source: authors.

FCR	%	Gender	%	Loyalty Programs	%
No	57,80%	Female	52,90%	No	56,10%
Yes	42,20%	Male	47,10%	Yes	43,80%
Total	100%	Total	100%	Total	100%

Average Handling Time	%	Customers Age	%	Customers value	%
1H	7,60%	Middle age	38,20%	High Value	16,27%
1H-24H	85,03%	Senior	47,60%	Low value	33,19%
>24H	7,20%	Young	14,20%	Medium value	50,54%
Total	100%	Total	100%	Total	100%

Repeated Calls	%	Relationship Length	%	Repurchase	%
No	46,90%	Advanced	66,50%	No	25,34%
Yes	53,10%	Beginner	33,50%	Yes	74,66%
Total	100%	Total	100%	Total	100%

4.4 Data Analysis

Database analysis was performed using a Chi Square test to assess if there is a relationship between variables. A p-value <.05 confirms the relationship between variables. Whenever we had a statistically significant p-value (<.05), we performed the Phi or Cramer's V coefficient, which analyzes the relative strength and direction of a statistically significant relationship between variables [58, 59]. Phi is only used on 2 × 2 contingency tables, if the table has more than two levels Cramer's V coefficient rescales Phi coefficient. According to [58] a Phi value of 0.10, 0.30, and 0.50 represent small, medium, and large effect sizes, respectively. However, what is a small versus a large Phi should be dependent on the area of investigation [58].

4.5 Results

Table 3 shows the Chi Square test outputs for the associations between FCR, Average Handling Time, Repeated Calls and Repurchase. P-value <.05 confirmed all the associations. These results show an association between variables, confirming the hypothesis **H1 (a)**, **H1 (b)** and **H1 (c)**.

Table 3. Chi Square test, p-value and Phi and Cramer's V results of FCR, Average Handling Time and Repeated Calls and repurchase. Source: authors

	Repurchase			
	Chi Square	p-value	Phi	Cramer's V
FCR	X^2=1022,079	p=.000	.087	
Average Handling Time	X^2=2349,599	p=.000		.133
Repeated Calls	X^2=490,606	P=.000	-.061	

The following Chi Square tests were performed adding a variable of control. When p-value is <.05, it confirms the association between variables. The strength of the association between the variables is then measured with Phi and Cramer's V coefficients, identifying the control variable for which the relationship is higher. When little difference was found, we rejected the hypothesis. If p-value was higher than .05, Phi and Cramer's V was not performed (Tables 4 and 5).

Table 4. Chi Square Outputs, p-values and Phi and Cramer's V coefficient, on the association between FCR and repurchase, Average Handling Time and repurchase and Repeat Calls and repurchase using gender, customer's age, relationship length with the service, participation on loyalty programs and customers' value as control variables. Source: authors.

			Repurchase		
			Chi Square	P-value	Phi and Cramer's V
Age	Young		X^2=7,592	.006	.055
	Middle age		X^2=14,252	.000	.046
	Senior		X^2=16,411	.000	.044
Gender	F		X^2=519,341	.000	.086
	M		X^2=488,980	.000	.088
Relationship length	Beginner	FCR	X^2=373,798	.000	.091
	Advanced		X^2=423,753	.000	.069
Loyalty programs	No		X^2=559,541	.000	.086
	Yes		X^2=503,186	.000	.093
Customer value	Low		X^2=789,159	.000	.135
	Medium		X^2=130,597	.000	.044
	High		X^2=14,591	.000	.026

(*Continued*)

Table 4. (Continued)

Age	Young		X²=49,099	.000	0,141
	Middle age		X²=126,277	.000	0,135
	Senior		X²=168,588	.000	0,141
Gender	F		X²=1267,036	.000	0,134
	M		X²=1091,477	.000	0,132
Relationship length	Beginner	Average Handling Time	X²=901,810	.000	0,142
	Advanced		X²=1398,408	.000	0,125
Loyalty programs	No		X²=1250,447	.000	0,129
	Yes		X²=1224,866	.000	0,145
Customer value	Low		X²=804,883	.000	0,135
	Medium		X²=946,932	.000	0,118
	High		X²=236,343	.000	0,104
Age	Young		0,382	.537	-
	Middle age		0,429	.512	-
	Senior		1,761	.185	-
Gender	F		240,561	.000	.058
	M		240,536	.000	.062
Relationship length	Beginner	Repeated Calls	165,174	.000	.061
	Advanced		146,761	.000	.041
Loyalty programs	No		253.675	.000	.066
	Yes		256.430	.000	.058
Customer value	Low		508.562	.000	.107
	Medium		17,843	.000	.016
	High		0,009	.924	-

Table 5. Results of the predicted hypotheses. Source: authors.

	Hypothesis	Result			Hypothesis	Result
H1	H1 a)	Supported		H4	H4 a)	Supported
	H1 b)	Supported			H4 b)	Supported
	H1 c)	Supported			H4 c)	Supported
H2	H2 a)	Supported		H5	H5 a)	Not supported
	H2 b)	Not supported			H5 b)	Not supported
	H2 c)	Not supported			H5 c)	Supported
H3	H3 a)	Not supported		H6	H6 b)	Not supported
	H3 b)	Not supported			H6 c)	Not supported
	H3 c)	Not supported			H6 c)	Not supported

5 Discussion

Our findings showed that First Call Resolution, Average Handling Time and Repeated Calls are the Call Centers indicators related to repurchase.

Demographic control variables, age and gender, did not show statistical significance in the relationships between the Call Center indicators and repurchase. Only young people proved to strengthen the relationship between one of the variables (FCR) and repurchase. But three control variables demonstrated a higher association with the variables: customers with shorter relationship length with the service; customers participating on loyalty programs and low value customers, since the relationship between the predicted variables were higher on these groups.

As we predicted, customers with a shorter relationship length with the service (beginners) were proved to be more sensitive to service convenience than customers with longer relationships (advanced). This may be happening due to the exit barriers and costs of changing into a competitor that advanced customers would face. Though we expected that customers not participating on loyalty programs would be more sensitive to convenience (they can easily change service provider), customers participating on loyalty programs proved to be more sensitive to time and effort expenditures on their interaction with Call Centers. We expected that higher value customers would be less willing to expend time and efforts on services, but we found out that low value customers are the ones more likely to abandon the service. High value customers have more barriers to change into competitors than low value customers, since they use the service more frequently than low value customers.

6 Conclusions and Implications

Our study brought new findings to service convenience literature. First, through the analysis of a database representative of customers' effective behaviour, we empirically validated the importance of service convenience on customers repurchase behaviour. Though literature has proved the impact of service convenience on customers satisfaction, loyalty or repurchase intentions before, it lacked studies on customers real behaviour, instead of behavioural intentions or perceptions, what strengthens our findings.

Second, for the first time, the convenience construct was related to Call Centers performance

Third, relating the concept of service convenience with Call Centers operations, we found clues of which Call Center performance indicators, in what concerns customers' time and effort expenditures, impact on repurchase behaviour.

Fourth, we explored and identified the contractual characteristics which distinguish convenience-oriented customers. Several studies had studied the demographic and socio-economic factors characterizing convenience-oriented customers, but only [2] stated that contractual characteristics may differentiate customers willing to spend time and effort on services.

Besides these new contributions to service convenience literature, we leave clues for Call Centers managers to operate. First, having found evidences that resolving customers issues the first time they call (First Call Resolution), the quickness of response (Average Handling Time) and preventing them to recall (Repeated Calls) are elements of the Call Centers performance impacting on customers' repurchase behaviour, we outlined the key indicators which Call Centers managers must manage and improve. Second, we helped to profile customers according to patterns of convenience demand, through contractual characteristics. Segmenting convenience-oriented customers and knowing who the groups less likely to wait are, managers may assign them higher answering priorities and convenience solutions, in order to assure the repurchase of the service. Our findings provided foundations for efficient planning and management strategies, based on patterns of convenience demand.

7 Limitations and Future Research

The telecommunications service we studied implies a contractual relationship with the service. A similar study may find different conclusions in services discontinuously used, whose exit barriers are little or inexistent.

Research should, also, look for convenience-orientated segments in what concerns: (i) the type of service. Future research must seek to understand in which services customers ask for more convenience and in which of them they are willing to spend time and effort; (ii) price. Some customers may be price-oriented and likely to expend time and effort if that means saving money, whereas others would prefer to pay more if it means a more convenient service; In other words, research should try to find out who convenience orientated customers.

References

1. Berry, L.L., Seiders, K., Grewal, D.: Understanding service convenience. J. Mark. **66**(3), 1–17 (2002)
2. Seiders, K., Voss, G.B., Grewal, D., Godfrey, A.L.: Do satisfied customers buy more? Examining moderating influences in a retailing context. J. Mark. **69**(4), 26–43 (2005)
3. Colwell, S.R., Aung, M., Kanetkar, V., Holden, A.L.: Toward a measure of service convenience: multiple-item scale development and empirical test. J. Serv. Mark. **22**(2), 160–169 (2008)
4. Thuy, P.N.: Using service convenience to reduce perceived cost. Mark. Intell. Plann. **29**(5), 473–487 (2011)
5. Chang, K.C., Chen, M.C., Hsu, C.L., Kuo, N.T.: The effect of service convenience on post-purchasing behaviours. Ind. Manage. Data Syst. **110**(8–9), 1420–1443 (2010)
6. Cheong, K., Kim, J., So, S.: A study of strategic call center management: relationship between key performance indicators and customer satisfaction. Eur. J. Soc. Sci. **6**(2), 268–276 (2008)
7. Anton, J.: The past, present and future of customer access centers. Int. J. Serv. Ind. Manage. **11**(2), 120–130 (2000)
8. Copeland, M.: Relation of consumers' buying habits to marketing methods. Harvard Bus. Rev. **1**(3), 282–289 (1923)
9. Holton, R.H.: The distinction between convenience goods, shopping goods, and specialty goods. J. Mark. **23**(1), 53–56 (1958)
10. Brown, L.G.: The strategic and tactical implications of convenience in consumer product marketing. J. Consum. Mark. **6**(3), 13–19 (1989)
11. Brown, L.G.: Convenience in services marketing. J. Serv. Mark. **4**(1), 53–59 (1990)
12. Seiders, K., Berry, L.L., Gresham, L.G.: Attention, retailers! How convenient is your convenience strategy? Sloan Manag. Rev. **41**(3), 79–89 (2000)

13. Berry, L.L.: The time-buying consumer. J. Retail. **55**(4), 58–69 (1979)
14. Anderson, W.T.: Identifying convenience-oriented consumer. J. Mark. Res. **8**(2), 179–183 (1971)
15. Anderson Jr., W.T.: Convenience orientation and consumption behaviour. J. Retail. **48**(3), 49–71 (1972)
16. Yale, L., Venkatesh, A.: Toward the construct of convenience in consumer research. Adv. Consum. Res. **13**(3), 403–408 (1986)
17. Seiders, K., Voss, G.B., Godfrey, A.L., Grewal, D.: SERVCON: development and validation of a multidimensional service convenience scale. J. Acad. Mark. Sci. **35**(1), 144–156 (2007)
18. Farquhar, J.D., Rowley, J.: Convenience: a services perspective. Mark. Theory **9**(4), 425–438 (2009)
19. Strober, M.H., Weinberg, C.B.: Working wives and major family expenditures. J. Consum. Res. **3**, 141–147 (1977)
20. Reilly, M.D.: Working wives and convenience consumption. J. Consum. Res. **8**(4), 407–418 (1982)
21. McEnally, M., Brown, L.: Do perceived time pressure, life cycle stage and demographic characteristics affect the demand for convenience? Eur. Adv. Consum. Res. **3**, 155–161 (1998)
22. Morganosky, M.A.: Cost-versus convenience-oriented consumers: demographic, lifestyle, and value perspectives. Psychol. Mark. **3**(1), 35–46 (1986)
23. Brown, L.G., McEnally, M.R.: Convenience: definition, structure and application. J. Mark. Manage. **2**(2), 47–56 (1993)
24. Feinberg, R.A., Kim, I.S., Hokama, L., De Ruyter, K., Keen, C.: Operational determinants of caller satisfaction in the call center. Int. J. Serv. Ind. Manage. **11**(2), 131–141 (2000)
25. Aksin, Z.N., Armony, M., Mehrotra, V.: The modern call center: a multi-disciplinary perspective on operations management research. Prod. Oper. Manage. **16**(6), 665–688 (2007)
26. Jaiswal, A.K.: Customer satisfaction and service quality measurement in Indian call centres. Manag. Serv. Qual. **18**(4), 405–416 (2008)
27. Michell, P.J.: Alighning customer call centres for 2001. Telemark. Call Centre Solutions **16**(10), 64–69 (1998)
28. Mattila, A.S., Mount, D.J.: The role of call centers in mollifying disgruntled guests. Cornell Hotel Restaurant Adm. Q. **44**(4), 75–80 (2003)
29. Robinson, G., Morley, C.: Call centre management: responsibilities and performance. Int. J. Serv. Ind. Manag. **17**(3), 284–300 (2006)
30. Abdullateef, A.O., Mokhtar, S.S.M., Yusoff, R.Z.: The mediating effects of first call resolution on call centers' performance. J. Database Mark. Custom. Strategy Manage. **18**(1), 16–30 (2011)
31. Dean, A.M.: The impact of the customer orientation of call center employees on customers' affective commitment and loyalty. J. Serv. Res. **10**(2), 161–173 (2007)
32. Burgers, A., De Ruyter, K., Keen, C., Streukens, S.: Customer expectation dimensions of voice-to-voice service encounters: a scale-development study. Int. J. Serv. Ind. Manage. **11**(2), 142–161 (2000)
33. Ruyter, K., Wetzels, M.G.: The impact of perceived listening behaviour in voice-to-voice service encounters. J. Serv. Res. **2**(3), 276–284 (2000)
34. Mattila, A.S., Mount, D.J.: The Impact of timeliness on complaint satisfaction in the context of call-centers. J. Hospitality Leisure Mark. **14**(3), 5–16 (2006)
35. Mount, D.J., Mattila, A.: The final opportunity: the effectiveness of a customer relations call center in recovering hotel guests. J. Hospitality Tourism Res. **24**(4), 514–525 (2000)

36. Mount, D.J., Mattila, A.: Last chance to listen: listening behaviours and their effect on call center satisfaction. J. Hospitality Tourism Res. **26**(2), 124–137 (2002)
37. Betts, A., Meadows, M., Walley, P.: Call centre capacity management. Int. J. Serv. Ind. Manage. **11**(2), 185–196 (2000)
38. Dean, A.M.: Rethinking customer expectations of service quality: are call centers different? J. Serv. Mark. **18**(1), 60–78 (2004)
39. Marr, B., Neely, A.: Managing and measuring for value: the case of call center performance. Cranfield School of Management; Fujitsu (2004)
40. Anton, J., Setting, T., Gunderson, C.: Offshore company callcenters: a concern to U.S. consumers. Technical report, Purdue University Center for Customer-Driven Quality (2004)
41. Gilmore, A., Moreland, L.: Call Centres: How can service quality be managed? Ir. Mark. Rev. **13**(1), 3–11 (2000)
42. Bennington, L., Cummane, J., Conn, P.: Customer satisfaction and call centers: an Australian study. Int. J. Serv. Ind. Manage. **11**(2), 162–173 (2000)
43. Miciak, A., Desmanais, M.: Benchmarking service quality performance at business-to-consumer call centres. J. Bus. Ind. Mark. **16**(5), 340–453 (2001)
44. Kolar, T.: Evaluating the performance of call centres frim consumers' perspective: marketing research industry example. Manage. J. Contemp. Manage. Issues **11**(2), 53–76 (2006)
45. Anton, J.: Call Center Management by the Numbers. Purdue University Press/Call Center Press, Annapolis (1997)
46. Pontes, M.C., O'brien Kelly, C.: The identification of inbound call center agents' competencies that are related to callers' repurchase intentions. J. Interact. Mark. **14**(3), 41–49 (2000)
47. Jouini, O., Koole, G., Roubos, A.: Performance indicators for call centers with impatient customers. IIE Trans. **45**(3), 341–354 (2013)
48. Feinberg, R.A., Hokama, L., Kadam, R., Kim, I.-S.: Operational determinants of caller satisfaction in the banking/financial services call center. Int. J. Bank Mark. **20**(4), 174–180 (2002)
49. Van Dun, Z., Bloemer, J., Henseler, J.: Perceived customer contact centre quality: conceptual foundation and scale development. Serv. Ind. J. **31**(8), 1347–1363 (2011)
50. Staples, W., Dalrymple, J., Bryar, R.: Assessing call centre quality using the SERVQUAL model. In: 7th International Conference on ISO (2002)
51. Dean, A.M.: Service Delivery and Operations Objectives: Listening to Call Centre Customers, Monash University. Department of Management. Faculty of Business and Economics (2004)
52. Lau, E.K.W., Chan, W.: An integrative framework capturing customer satisfaction and service quality in call centers. Rev. Bus. Res. **12**(3), 76–82 (2012)
53. Aagja, J.P., Mammen, T., Saraswat, A.: Validating service convenience scale and profiling customers: a study in the indian retail context. VIKALPA **36**(4), 25 (2011)
54. Chang, Y.-W., Polonsky, M.J.: The influence of multiple types of service convenience on behavioural intentions: the mediating role of consumer satisfaction in a Taiwanese leisure setting. Int. J. Hospitality Manage. **31**(1), 107–118 (2012)
55. Chang, M.-Y., Chen, K., Pang, C., Chen, C.-M., Yen, D.C.: A study on the effects of service convenience and service quality on maintenance revisit intentions. Comput. Stan. Interfaces **35**(2), 187–194 (2013)
56. Armistead, C., Kiely, J.: Creating strategies for managing evolving customer service. Manag. Serv. Qual. **13**(2), 164–170 (2003)
57. Aguir, S., Karaesmen, F., Akşin, O.Z., Chauvet, F.: The impact of retrials on call center performance. OR Spectr. **26**(3), 353–376 (2004)

58. Hinkle, D., Wiersma, W., Jurs, S.G.: Applied Statistics for the Behavioural Sciences, 5th edn. Houghton MifflinCompany, Boston (2003)
59. Pestana, M.H., Gageiro, J.N.: Análise de dados para ciências sociais: a complementaridade do SPSS, 2nd edn. Edições Silábo Lda, Lisboa (2000)

Tourism as a Life Experience:
A Service Science Approach

Jesús Alcoba[1(✉)], Susan Mostajo[2], Ricardo Clores[2], Rowell Paras[2], Grace Cella Mejia[2], and Romano Angelico Ebron[2]

[1] La Salle Campus Madrid, La Salle 10, 28023 Madrid, Spain
jesus@lasallecampus.es
[2] De La Salle University-Dasmariñas, Dasmariñas, Philippines
{stmostajo,raclores,rrparas,grmejia,
rtebron}@dlsud.edu.ph

Abstract. Service Science can be considered as the study of the interaction between human beings, technology and business. This paper describes the use of technology to analyse visitor's experiences in order to improve the tourism business sector. Despite what the mere accidental observation could show, tourism is one of the significant experiences for human beings. Moreover, it is one of the services with most potential for generating wealth. Service Science should be a key for companies and regions to properly design and manage tourist services. This paper describes a study with both sentiment and qualitative analysis carried out using the opinions of foreign tourists in the Philippines. The value of this work lies in providing recommendations on the basis of a systematic study. Thus, the potential of analyzing services through a scientific focus is shown.

Keywords: Tourism · Experience · Service science · Meaning · Narrative · Sentiment analysis

1 Introduction

An examination of the relevant literature finds limited studies that capture quality of experience using service science approach in tourism sector, a flourishing service industry and a potential driver of growth.

There has been a growing recognition that service science has directed the service sector, which is the largest sector of the economy in most advanced societies, to become more systematic about innovation. The service sector is turning into the largest sector in developing nations as well. This study, hence, examined the tourists' quality of experience in the Philippines, a developing country.

1.1 Service Science and the Importance of Meaning Construction

Service Science can be considered as the study of the interaction between human beings, technology and business. Regarding the first component, research has drawn science to the study of how the human mind perceives the environment and how it interprets and stores the events and concepts it processes. Furthermore, the relevance of meaning construction in the interaction between human beings and services has been already pointed out [1].

As research shows, the presence of meaning in life has a positive correlation with happiness and positive feelings, and a negative correlation with depression and negative feelings [2]. The search for meaning provides premium in the lives of human beings than the mere seeking for happiness.

At the biological level, the ability to predict is the main function of the cerebral cortex and the basis of intelligence [3]. This suggests that the brain is constantly making internal meaning making, predictions and connections to plan ahead. [4]. Arguably, memory is a constructive process where information is stored and retrieved to make simulations of the future [5]. As accurate prediction is a key for existence, human beings' search for meaning is related to survival. However, the main task of mental processes is the creation of meaning making instead of the simple generation of accurate predictions. Moreover, this suggests that there is a difference between logical and psychological meaning making of concepts [6].

Human beings cannot remember things as they happened. Studies on the reminiscence effect have proven that the period of years from which most events and activities are remembered is between 10 and 30, and that these events and activities are judged as the most important or the best. [7]. The construction of meaning, therefore, suggests that it is both biological and psychological processes that has bearing both to individual and public life.

1.2 Meaning, Narratives and Experiences

The elaborations carried out by the mind help to construct identity in the shape of an autobiographical narrative that needs to be meaningful for the person and the environment [8]. When a person interacts with an experience, a new opportunity for meaning construction appears. If there is an alignment between the experience and the former narrative of the person, or if that alignment can be developed, then meaning is constructed and the experience will be part of the affirmative identity of the person. If that alignment does not exist or cannot be developed, the experience will be part of the set of experiences the person has rejected, and thus will not be part of the person's identity. People will be likely to engage in experiences that naturally adapt to their parameters. This process resembles the idea widely spread by constructivist authors that every time the human mind finds a new concept there is an interaction between the matrix of previous knowledge and the incoming knowledge, producing an integrating effort usually called learning.

1.3 Services as Experiences

According to Hassenzahl and Tractinsky [9], experience is the consequence of the interaction among the user's inner states, the features of the designed system, and the context in which the interactions take place. Diller, Shedroff & Rhea [10] noted that experiences are the conscious feelings that something changes within the human being. Decidedly, experience occurs every day. Some experiences may be superficial while others are meaningful. Moreover, the experiences maybe random events such as family gatherings or work activities, but they can also be experiences deliberately designed to produce an effect, such as services. Thus, it is possible to model the interaction between customers and the services that can be considered deliberately designed experiences.

The new service is substantially related to the previous autobiography of the individual. Here, meaning is constructed and the service is accepted by the user as described using language and is finally integrated into an individual's life plot thus connecting to other related products and services. However, if the experience does not find a fixing point in the consumer's identity, quite probably it will be rejected.

In brief, the keys that establish the difference between successful and unsuccessful services are more complicated than the simple notion of quality assurance. This also suggests that the mere assumption of the emotional bond between people and the services they use should also be re-visited. People create life bonds with services searching for meaning in them. The active design and management of experiences is a central activity for companies in their effort to create value.

1.4 Tourism as a Life Experience

The narrative of interaction between experiences and services takes both central and peripheral roles. However, contrary to what perhaps a mere anecdotal observation could reveal, tourism is one of the relevant, if not vital experiences, in human life.

Indeed, for decades it has been noted that tourism means more than just the joy of leisure or the mere curiosity to know other realities. John B. Allcock's *Tourism as a sacred journey* [11] was a ground-breaking and inclusive work, in which previous studies by MacCannell (1976) and Horne (1984) were quoted to suggest that tourism appears as a secular substitute for organized religion and that the essential structure of tourist attractions, among which museums stand out as the most typical example, bases upon asymmetric power relations and the existence of authenticity.

A more recent study by Willson, Mcintosh and Zahra [12] shows that spirituality is the essence of human beings. This concerns the individual's search for the meaning of life related to self-fulfillment, transcendence and the making of connections between the individual and other entities. In their phenomenological study, they show that these three values can be found in specific touristic experiences.

It is relatively easy to see the importance that tourism has in the life of human beings when certain varieties are analysed, as in the case of frontier tourism, when a person embarks on adventures of extreme explorations, which sometimes recreate mythical journeys. In some cases, participants aim at recreating heroic journeys, such as going to the Antarctica to emulate polar explorer Ernest Shackleton, whom many frontier tourists consider almost a close friend [13]. In other cases, motivation implies rewriting the past, highlighting aspects of certain expeditions that had been forgotten or restoring the reputation of fallen heroes. Still others focus on facing challenges and overcoming them. Others focus on achieving prestige or a status, and the wish to live an authentic experience and assume an explorer's or an adventurer's role. However, none of these motivations has anything to do with simple passive rest or mere curiosity to know the world. Of growing attention are tourists that go to extreme places, such as the poles, the highest peaks, the most dangerous seas and the driest deserts in the world. Actually, this kind of tourism is becoming so common that critical voices claiming greater care of protected sites have begun to be heard [14].

Adventure tourism as put forward by Varley [15] suggests a different form where there is the elaboration of tourism's various new components. Firstly, the existence of the responsibility of tourists, and thus, the capacity to assume the consequences of one's own decisions. Secondly, the confrontation with risks and uncertainty, which implies the confrontation between one's own abilities and the environment. Thirdly, the experience of "transcendence" by crossing the frontier of the everyday life.

Another valuable example that illustrates the connection between tourism and central aspects of human life is film tourism, in which the main goal is to visit a site related to the film world. Bauchmann, Moore and Fisher [16] presented this type tourism experience in New Zealand in the cinematographic setting of *Lord of the Rings* where participants' wish was fulfilled to find them in a location they considered authentic as far as the film is concerned. These experiences are interpreted as expressions of the need to have a meaningful experience. Second, there is also that importance of being physically on the film location. The authors also noted the essential tourists' experience of meet other people as part of a community with similar interests. Interesting, authors pointed out, that the film tourists' experiences are similar pilgrimages.

Perhaps the most evident example of how tourism can constitute an essential experience in human life is found in those people who have made of travelling a way of life. In his research on this phenomenon, Cohen [17] shows that this way of understanding life is an extension of backpacking tourism, in which tourists eventually turn geographic mobility into their life's axis, whether as backpackers, crossing the ocean on a ship or travelling in their caravan. Cohen's ethnographic analysis of twenty-five life-style travelers that had been travelling for between three and seventeen years excludes any consideration of this way of seeing life as something anecdotic and trivial, and it exemplifies that the basic ingredients of tourism can provide full meaning to a person's whole life.

1.5 Tourism as an Impetus for Growth

Tourism has found its potential as an engine of growth of a country and has been tremendously progressing over the years. Despite the ambiguity of the world economy, global tourism industry has grown spectacularly from a mere 25 million in 1950 to a record of 1.087 billion in 2013 [18]. It is also considered as one of the world's largest industries, contributing trillions of dollars annually to global economy; creating jobs and wealth; and stimulating capital investment.

Despite sporadic shocks, international tourist arrivals grew by five percent in 2013 to 1.087 billion. In 2013, international tourism receipts reached USD 1.159 trillion worldwide, up from USD 1.078 trillion in 2012 as presented in 2014 by UNWTO. Furthermore, according to the World Travel and Tourism Council (WTTC), the direct contribution of travel and tourism to Gross Domestic Product (GDP) was USD 2, 155 billion (2.9 % of total GDP) while its total contribution to GDP was USD 6, 990.3 billion (9.5 % of GDP) in 2013 [19]. Travel and tourism generated 100, 894, 000 jobs directly in 2013 (3.4 % of total employment) while its total contribution to employment, including jobs indirectly supported by the industry was 8.9 percent of total employment (265, 855, 000 jobs). The industry has certainly wielded substantial economic benefits in exports and investment sector. Visitor exports generated USD 1, 295 billion (5.4 % of total exports in 2013) and tourism investment in 2013 was USD 754.6 billion or 4.4 percent of total investment.

In most developing countries endowed with significant tourist attractions, tourism has emerged as a new impetus for economic growth given its ability to generate foreign exchange and employment [20]. In the Philippines, international visitor arrivals jumped 9.56 percent to 4.68 million 2013, with an increase in average daily expenditures by 8.7 percent to USD 101.12. Moreover, total revenues gained from inbound visitors went up 15 % to an estimated USD 4.4 billion (PhP 186.15 billion) for 2013 [21]. The tourism industry employed 3.8 million Filipinos, or 10.2 % of national employment in 2011 [22]. As tourism continues to flourish in the Philippines, it has been tapped as a prime factor to uplift the economy.

1.6 Implications for the Design and Management of Touristic Experiences

Applying science to services can improve service design and delivery substantially. In this case, by highlighting the relevance of tourism for people. Human beings search for the construction of meaning drawn from the interaction with experiences provides coherent life narrative. The consistency of the life narrative in turn provides identity. If it is true that tourism experiences can actually posit as a central aspect of human life, then these types of experiences can actually transcend the mere quality assurance for tourists or the simple verification of emotional bond. Because in the same way that nobody goes to a restaurant just to feed themselves and that no vacation can just be seen as the addition between means of transport, a shelter and something to feed them with, it is easy to ascertain that people are almost always looking for something else in their touristic experiences. Tourism experiences can be connected to individual biographies and life narratives, even to the meaning they give to their existence.

For this reason, it is important to transcend the way in which the touristic service is usually studied, designed and delivered, coming closer to the deep understanding of what it means for participants. In this way, it is necessary to go beyond the concepts of quality assurance and customer service to immerse oneself in the design and management of customer experience, starting with the use of tools that truly reveal such meaning.

When the human brain models the world, language plays a key role since it contributes to cognitive development by providing the setting of analogies and relationships and representations that allow abstraction [23] and this is why the analysis of tourists' opinions when they describe their experiences must constitute one of the main approaches in this field.

The present work is precisely a contribution in this line, which intends to apply sentiment analysis tools [24, 25] to a significant series of tourists' opinions which describe their experiences in a specific geographic area in the world. The starting point of this approach is that only through the in-depth analysis of tourists' experience will the keys to its accurate design and management be revealed.

2 Methodology

This research sought to identify how the foreign tourists describe the quality of experience they had in the tourism facilities (TF) with the end goal of providing a research-based service and delivery design. It is mainly qualitative relying on the subjective experiences of foreign tourists in the Philippines.

The participating TF are from the Calabarzon Area (Cavite, Laguna, Batangas, Rizal and Quezon), Philippines, accredited by the Department of Tourism. The TFs include: Summit Ridge Hotel, Taal Vista Hotel, One Tagaytay Place, Island Cove Resort, Picnic Grove, Pagsanjan Falls, Enchanted Kingdom, Caliraya, Club Funta Fuego, The Farm at San Benito, Thunderbird Hotel-Tanay and Villa Escudero. All the TFs' on-line reviews from TripAdvisor.com and Agoda.com were gathered selecting only the reviews of foreign tourists from 2012 to 2014 with a total of seven hundred two (702) reviews. These reviews were sent to a sentiment analysis company for the processing of data (see acknowledgement at the end of the paper). This company uses a proprietary deep linguistic analysis platform powered by grammars, dictionaries and also business rules, specific for each case. Even if some amount of statistics is used, the key component of their engines is the linguistic analysis of each one of the sentences in the text. Based on these engines, sets of semantic services have been built, like entity and concept extraction, sentiment analysis or categorization. After the sentiment reviews were statistically treated, themes were formulated to set the tourists' sentiment topics. Based on a frequency count validated through SPSS statistics software, the top sentiment topics with the descriptive words associated by the tourists were identified, before proceeding to the qualitative analysis.

3 Results and Discussion

The sentiment analysis provided a series of data regarding the analyzed opinions:

1. An order number of the selected text string.
2. The text string that contains the opinion.
3. Sentiment topic: the concept about the opinion is given.
4. The words that express the opinion.
5. Sentiment score: intensity of the sentiment (ranging from −16,00 to 31,25).

A word frequency count was carried out through the whole text to detect the top ten commented concepts. Then another word frequency count was carried out to identify the top ten frequent words regarding those concepts. Table 1 summarizes the most commented topics, their frequency and the mean an standard deviation of all the text strings regarding them (all opinions: M = 1,13, STD = 2,28). As this table shows, the top ten concepts show a positive sentiment, so it can be said that the foreign tourists globally feel that the tourism experience in the selected places is good. The means and standard deviations show that the sentiment is quite similar across the different concepts.

Table 1. Most frequent concepts, frequency, sentiment analysis mean and standard deviation.

Most frequent concepts	Frequency	M	STD
Taal/volcano/lake/view/views	526	2,69	2,29
Room/rooms	360	1,14	1,9
Hotel	318	1,12	2,31
Staff	245	2,51	2,70
Food	190	1,30	2,29
Place/location	212	2,56	2,35
Service	111	2,15	2,05
Breakfast	108	1,16	1,83
Stay	103	2,38	2,22
Pool	72	0,96	2,01

The Taal Lake is a lagoon that surrounds the Taal Volcano. A significant percentage of the sentiment topics "view" and "views" were connected to it.
This concept was excluded from the analysis due to insufficient data.

3.1 Views

With a total of 526 mentions this sentiment topic group is the most important of all, the one in which the tourists focus their attention and ratings. Therefore, it is undoubtedly the epicenter of tourism in the area, and the opinions that tourists poured over it are of utmost importance. Some of the significant words used to refer to these attractions are "amazing", "breathtaking", "stunning" and "spectacular". The words undoubtedly speak of the potential of these places to arouse emotions. Other words they used to express appreciation of the views are "nice", "great" and "beautiful". The authors integrated Views/Taal Volcano and Place/Location together due to similarities of the type of TFs included in the study, wherein natural scenes can be commonly found, and the overlapping of tourists' idea of these variables.

These findings reveal that tourists are fascinated with natural attractions or places with appealing scenes because of the remarkable experience these places create. In a physiological perspective, the views (stimulus) processed through the limbic system of the brain perceived as "amazing", "breathtaking" and "stunning" generate pleasing emotions to the tourists. For such, the physiological impact of the views to the tourists also creates a favorable psycho-emotional experience.

Studies cited that people tend to prefer natural environments more than built environments because of the benefits in health and wellbeing an individual may acquire from engaging with a natural view such as restoration of physical and mental energy

[26–28]. While in a place or location from which a beautiful view of nature can be accessed, the individual tourist's feelings may consciously or unconsciously facilitate physical and mental restoration thereby produces pleasing and gratifying experience.

Attractions, whether natural or man-made, are of paramount importance to tourism industry because they have special appeal to visitors, and have major pull factors for tourists in their chosen destinations [29]. According to Swarbrooke [30], tourism would not exist if it were not for attractions. Furthermore, tourism attractions contribute significantly to the economy through increasing revenue and investment. Specifically, these attractions provide government direct income from government – owned attractions, taxes paid on bought items, and taxes paid by employees who are directly supported by the sector. These attractions also generate employment (both direct and indirect jobs) and foreign exchange earnings.

3.2 Service

Several sentiment topics were integrated under service such as rooms and staff of hotels. The service in the TFs were described positively by the tourists as "good", "great", "excellent", "impeccable", "friendly", "top", "efficient", "best" and "awesome"; and three counts of "poor" as negative description. Similarly, hotels were described as "nice", "great", "good", "clean", "friendly", "beautiful", "new", "comfortable", "big" and "excellent".

Service to a Filipino is an extension of the Self. This has been coined as *kapwa/* shared identity [31]. Quite often this concept is related to either the visible hospitality and/or generosity of the Filipino to guests. The idea does not mean that the Filipino does not draw inclusion versus exclusion among guests but such drawing of lines is so much flexible, even in work places. Thus, Filipinos extend extreme sensitivity to comments, desires and expectations of guests. This *kapwa* spirit is extended to the service of foods, rooms and/or staying areas as well as the intense focus of providing deep interpersonal relationships among guests. This study shows that this Filipino value was visibly felt and identified by tourists and was included in their meaningful experience.

3.3 Rooms

Running a frequency count, the top ten primary keywords across the text strings directly linked with the topic "room" are: "clean", "comfortable", "nice", "spacious", "big", "large", "good", "deluxe" and "great". It can be said that all of them are positive, that comfort and cleanliness are important, and it is also relevant that tourists pay attention to size of the room (three out of ten adjectives are related to that: spacious, big and large) The results show that when guests are paying for a room, they expect it to be clean, spacious and comfortable as should be.

Guests are expecting an accommodation that provides them excellent services, especially to meet the high standard quality of customer care [32]. Accommodation provides the base from which tourists can engage in the process of staying at a destination [33]. Primary accommodation covers basic lodging amenities: room with beds, furniture, bathrooms and air conditioning units. Other amenities include telephone units, television sets, internet connection, child care facilities, restaurants, and swimming pool to meet the demands of customers. These vary depending on the type or start-rating of hotel [34].

The accommodation sector is one of the most visible and tangible elements in the tourist's trip and experience, and is often sold as part of the product. Thus, quality standards and tourists' satisfaction levels with their holiday experiences are intrinsically linked to the accommodation sector. The consumer is consuming an experience where tourism, hospitality and accommodation are integrated [35].

Hotel cleanliness is part of an appreciated accommodation and is one of the most important factors in gaining customer loyalty. People tend to gravitate towards hotel options that are known to provide a clean environment. Moreover, hotel and accommodation focuses on service because excellent customer service combined with a proven product will lead to increased customer satisfaction and thus a higher service quality will be observed [36].

3.4 Staff

The frequency word count for "staff" detects these ten primary words as the main ones: friendly, helpful, attentive, courteous, polite, nice, great, professional, good and excellent. All of them are positive, and it can be relevant that the first two in frequency are "friendly and helpful", which could mean that the tourists feel that the staff are both kind and efficient.

Based on the result, tourists value the personality traits and skills of the staff in the tourism facilities visited. The primary words associated with the staff depict the idea that tourists give importance to staff services where personality traits such as being friendly, helpful, attentive, courteous, polite, nice and professional are demonstrated. In the study on service quality in hotel and influence of personality traits, it was concluded that there is a significant influence of personality traits such as "agreeableness and conscientiousness" on service quality as well as being respectful and courteous to customers [37]. Conceptually, Trait-and-Factor theory in Career Counseling stresses that individuals have unique patterns of ability or traits that can be measured and correlated with requirements of occupations because they are considered important in the successful performance of a job [38]. When an individual's competencies and traits are fitted in the job, the individual becomes effective and efficient resulting to job satisfaction. Consequently, the individual becomes more zealous in doing his job, thus provides quality service to customers. In return, customers are contented with the service provided to them leading to the creation of a pleasing experience.

Customer service is of critical significance for the tourism industry now more than ever before as customers (tourists) become more rational and spend more cautiously and are looking to increase value for money and are less forgiving of mediocre service [39]. High level of satisfaction results from excellent customer service. Thus, it is essentially important that customers are treated well and given the highest standards of service to ensure customer loyalty and improve business performance.

3.5 Food

The top ten primary words across the text strings directly related to the topic "food" are good, great, excellent, healthy, expensive, delicious, tasty, wonderful, pricey and fresh. The majority of these adjectives is positive, and reflects the interest of tourists on taste (tasty, delicious) and quality (healthy, fresh). Nevertheless, it can also be said that a few tourists perceive that the food is expensive. Likewise, breakfast was described positively as good, great, excellent, delicious, free, varied, satisfactory, huge and fresh, and negatively as bad. Food and breakfast were analyzed together because of their sameness as variables.

The other words (good, great, excellent and wonderful) in addition to tasty and delicious also refer to "taste" or words that the tourists used to describe the quality of the food. Although very few of them, tourists also value healthy foods.

The basic truth in the hospitality business cited in researches is that meeting the needs and expectations of guests is necessary for success [40]. Failure to meet the guests' expectations and needs means they will not return which may have negative impact on the business.

Previous studies on customer expectation and service-quality perception in the food-service industry have revealed certain important attributes, such as low price, food quality (food taste and nutrition properties), value for money, service, location, brand name, and image [41, 42]. More specifically, the fundamental factors that contribute to customer satisfaction in restaurants include the food (hygiene, balance and healthiness), physical provision (layout, furnishing, and cleanliness), the atmosphere (feeling and comfort), and the service receive (speed, friendliness, and care) during the meal experience [43]. Menu planning and development involves having a concept, knowing customers' wants and expectations, employing good staff and equipment, and correctly gauging profit margins. Many of those factors mentioned were observed by the foreign tourists in the visited TFs and have created a meaningful experience in their lives.

3.6 Stay

The sentiment topic "stay" can be considered as a summary of the rest of them as a general concept that the tourists use to comprise their whole experience. Again, all the adjectives are positive, being the most used: "comfortable", "great", "pleasant", "good", "nice", "enjoyable", "excellent", "relaxing", "wonderful", and "refreshing". This shows that the tourists' experience in their stay with the TFs in the Philippines had created favorable meaning in their lives. Nevertheless, their frequency is not high so this part of the analysis may not be relevant beyond the fact that the tourists evaluate it as positive.

4 Recommendations

Based on the results of the study, the following are hereby recommended:

4.1 Views

The tourism industry should promote and market natural views/attractions as tourist destinations. This research identifies that this is the most significant and meaningful experience as far as the foreign tourists are concerned. It is also necessary to work for the development, preservation, and maintenance of natural attractions and to promote eco-tourism in different localities. Additionally, in the absence of a natural attraction/view in a tourist destination, it is recommended that the tourism facility should be creative in providing a visually appealing atmosphere/environment in the area.

4.2 Rooms

The rooms and its amenities in the tourism facilities should be properly maintained, sanitized and kept in order to provide an ambiance of comfort. Likewise, the international standards on room size should be followed considering the physical built of different nationalities.

4.3 Staff

Tourism facilities are encouraged to develop and/or enhance the innate favorable traits and values, oftentimes identified in the Philippines as *kapwa*/shared identity, of their staff relevant in providing quality customer service. This research notes that the intense value (*kapwa*) of the Filipinos were observed, felt and picked up by foreign tourists. Thus, systematic and conscious-raising programs highlighting *kapwa* value are deemed necessary. Moreover, continuous training and monitoring of staff regarding customer relations/service should be enhanced. Likewise, devising creative ways to assess staff performance where customer feedback is prioritized to assure quality service should be given importance.

4.4 Food

Tourism facilities should provide more menu options and to review their pricing strategy. It is also recommended that tourism facilities should patronize locally produced products/ingredients and to offer the local cuisine in order for the tourists to appreciate the culture in the local area and because they are less expensive. In addition, healthy food options should also be part of the menu. It is encouraged, too, that tourism facilities should be sensitivity to the taste preferences and culture of tourists in providing menu options.

4.5 Stay

Tourism facilities should ensure provision of excellent quality service to customers at all times to create a meaningful stay in the place particularly on how staffs deliver their tasks, the kind of accommodation and food offered, and the view/ambiance in the area.

In summary, this research recommends a service tourism design that would create a psycho-physiologically meaningful touristic experience, capitalizing on the Philippines' natural attractions and the Filipino's deep sense of connection and interpersonal relationship. Moreover, the research suggests an enhanced community-based eco-tourism program that banks on the Filipinos' innate sense of *kapwa*/shared self-identity. If the community is involved in such an eco-tourism program, there is a "sense of ownership" that makes the local tourism stakeholders value the tourist attraction resulting into preservation, sustainability, and a safe and secured place to visit.

5 Conclusions

Foreign tourists in the Philippines are drawn to two meaningful experiences. First, the Philippines offers natural attractions which are visually appealing and gratifying because of its favorable psycho-emotional and physiological effect. Tourists also give premium to the cleanliness, size and comfort the room provides. Second, foreign tourists were able to observe, feel and ultimately experience the Filipino value for a deep sense of connection and interpersonal relationship that is called *kapwa*. This significant experience registers in tourists' appreciation of staff services where favorable personality traits like being friendly, helpful, attentive, courteous/polite, nice and professional are manifested. Tourists also associate the quality of food with its taste and its nutrition properties.

Service Science can be defined as the study of the interaction between human beings, technology and business. This paper has described the use of technology to analyse visitor's experiences in order to improve the tourism business sector. What the findings show is the subjective perception of the touristic experience. Based on these findings and on the above recommendations, the design and management of tourist services in the analyzed region can be more effective, since it begins in the views that tourists have written. This way of capturing the customer experience has a number of significant advantages over traditional quality assurance approach: first, the customer reviews have been written at the time the clients wanted. By contrast, the classical administration of questionnaires usually interrupts their natural activity to focus on them. Secondly, the opinions analyzed show the concepts that customers actually want to talk about, rather than narrowing their input to the few predefined types of a questionnaire. Lastly, customers use words that make meaning to them, expressing what they think and feel with all the subjectivity it implies. In short, these opinions represent the voice of the customer, which should be the point of origin and destination of the design and management of the tourist experience. More than that, the approach described here could be used for the study, design and delivery of other services, like education, entertainment, healthcare, cultural services and many others.

Acknowledgement. The authors of this paper would like to express their gratitude to Bitext for providing the sentiment analysis technology that made possible the data exploration.

References

1. Alcoba, J.: Beyond the paradox of service industrialization: approaches to design meaningful services. In: Wang, J. (ed.) Management Science, Logistics, and Operations Research. IGI Global, Hershey (2014)

2. Park, N., Park, M., Peterson, C.: When is the search for meaning related to life satisfaction? Appl. Psychol. Health and Well-being **2**(1), 1–13 (2010)
3. Hawkins, J., Blakeslee, S.: On intelligence. Times Books, Henry Holt and Company, New York (2004)
4. Raichle, M.E.: La Red Neuronal por Defecto. Investigacion y Ciencia, (Mayo), pp. 20–26 (2010)
5. Schacter, D.L., Addis, R.L.: The ghosts of past and future. Nature **445**(4), 27 (2007)
6. Ausubel, D.P., Novak, J.D., Hanesian, H.: Psicología Educativa. Un punto de vista cognoscitivo. Trillas, Mexico (2000)
7. Rubin, D.C., Rahhal, T.A.: Things learned in early adulthood are remembered best. Mem. Cogn. **26**(1), 3–19 (1998)
8. McAdams, D.P.: The psychology of life stories. Rev. General Psychol. **5**(2), 100–122 (2001)
9. Hassenzahl, M., Tractinsky, N.: User experience - a research agenda. Behav. Inf. Technol. **25**(2), 91–97 (2006)
10. Diller, S., Shedroff, N., Rhea, D.: Making Meaning: How Successful Businesses Deliver Meaningful Customer Experiences. New Riders, Berkeley (2008)
11. Allcock, J.B.: Tourism as a sacred journey. Loisir et Societé/Society and Leisure **11**(1), 33–48 (1988)
12. Willson, G.B., McIntosh, A.J., Zahra, A.L.: Tourism and spirituality: a phenomenological analysis. Ann. Tour. Res. **42**, 150–168 (2013)
13. Laing, J.H., Crouch, G.I.: Frontier tourism. Retracing Mythic Journeys. Ann. Tour. Res. **38**(4), 1516–1534 (2011)
14. Spennemann, D.H.R.: Extreme cultural tourism. From Antarctica to the Moon. Ann. Tour. Res. **34**(4), 898–918 (2007)
15. Varley, P.: Confecting adventure and playing with meaning: the adventure commodification continuum. J. Sport Tour. **11**(2), 173–194 (2008)
16. Buchmann, A., Moore, K., Fisher, D.: Experiencing film tourism. Authenticity and fellowship. Ann. Tour. Res. **37**(1), 229–248 (2010)
17. Cohen, S.A.: Lifestyle travellers. Backpacking as a way of life. Ann. Tour. Res. **38**(4), 1535–1555 (2011)
18. United Nations World Tourism Organization: UNWTO Tourism Highlights 2014 edition. Madrid, Spain (2014)
19. IPK International on Behalf of ITB Berlin: ITB World Travel Trends Report. Messe Berlin GmbH, Berlin, Germany, 9 (2013)
20. Kweka, J.: Tourism and the Economy of Tazmania: A CGE Analysis (2004)
21. Cheng, W.: PNoy: Tourist Spending in Philippines (2014)
22. Torres, T.P.: Tourism remains key pillar for sustained growth – NSCB. (2013)
23. Gentner, D.: Why we're so smart. In: Gentner, D., Goldin-Meadow, S. (eds.) Language in Mind: Advances in the Study of Language and Thought. MIT Press, Cambridge (2003)
24. Liu, B.: Sentiment analysis and subjectivity. In: Indurkhya, N., Damerau, F.J. (eds.) Handbook of Natural Language Processing. Chapman & Hall/CRC, London (2010)
25. Pang, B., Lee, L.: Opinion mining and sentiment analysis. Foundations and Trends in Information Retrieval **2**(1–2), 1–135 (2008)
26. Ikei, H., et al.: The physiological and psychological relaxing effects of viewing rose flowers in office workers. J. Physiol. Anthropol. **33**, 6 (2014). doi:10.1186/1880-6805-33-6, http://www.physiolanthropol.com
27. Kahn, P.H., Severson, R.L., Ruckert, J.H.: The human relation with nature and technological nature. Curr. Dir. Psychol. Sci. **18**(1) (2009). depts.washington.edu/hints/

28. Maller, C., et al.: Healthy nature healthy people: "contact with nature" as an upstream health promotion intervention for populations. Health Promot. Int. **21**(1) (2005). doi:10.1093/heapro/dai032, http://heapro.oxfordjournals.org
29. Luck, M., Robinson, P., Smith, S.L.: Tourism. CABI Publishing, Wallingford (2013)
30. Swarbrooke, J.: Sustainable Tourism Management. CABI Publishing, Wallingford (2002)
31. Enriquez, V.: From Colonial to Liberation Psychology: The Philippine Experience, pp. 53–57. University of the Philippines Press, Quezon City (1992)
32. Buswell, J., Williams, C.: Service Quality in Leisure and Tourism. CABI Publishing, UK (2003)
33. Page, S.: Tourism Management: Managing for Change. Butterworth-Heinemann, Oxford (2003)
34. Hotel Rise.: Hotel accommodation (2012). http://www.hotelrise.com/hotelaccommodation
35. Page, S., Connell, J.: Tourism, 3rd edn. Cengage Learning Asia Pte Ltd., Philippines (2012)
36. Bantilan, A.: User's satisfaction of information technology usage in the South Eastern University –CDM, MBA: unpublished thesis (2004)
37. Hovenga, E.: Service Quality in the hotel sector and the influence of personality traits (2010). http://dspace.ou.nl/bitstream/1820/3639/1/MWEHovengaaugustus2010
38. Zunker, V.: Career counseling: a holistic approach, 8th edn. Brooks/COLE Cengage Learning, Canada (2012)
39. Hudson, S., Hudson, L.: Customer Service for Hospitality and Tourism. Goodfellow Publisher Limited, Oxford (2013)
40. Chon, K., Maier, T.: Welcome to Hospitality - An Introduction, 3rd edn. Delmar/Cengage Learning, New York (2010)
41. Johns, N., Howard, A.: Customer expectations versus perceptions of service performance in the foodservice industry. Int. J. Serv. Ind. Manag. (1998). http://www.emeraldinsight.com/doi/abs/10.1108/09564239810223556
42. Tam W., Yung, N.: Managing customer for value in catering industry (fast food) in Hong Kong, MBA thesis, The Chinese University of Hong Kong (2003)
43. Johns, N., Pine, R.: Consumer behavior in food service industry: a review. Int. J. Hosp. Manag. **21**, 119–134 (2002)

Technological Trends in the Sport Field: Which Application Areas and Challenges?

Luisa Varriale[✉] and Domenico Tafuri

University of Naples "Parthenope", Naples, Italy
{luisa.varriale,domenico.tafuri}@uniparthenope.it

Abstract. This paper investigates the application of new technologies in the sport field. Technology, mainly information technology (IT) and internet, is deeply changing the overall picture of the sport sector. New technologies facilitate the knowledge transfer in the sporting event management process, such as the Olympic Games; at the same time, the innovative techniques can significantly affect the athletes' performance and the social integration of disabled persons. There is an explosion of technology applications in the sport field in different sub-organizational areas, but this phenomenon is still underrepresented in the literature. This paper aims to identify and evidence the main application areas and challenges faced by technology in the sport setting. This study, through a review of the literature, represents a research starting point that allows us to systematize and clarify the main contributions on this topic and to identify new research perspectives.

Keywords: Technology · Sport field · Performance improvement · Sport disability · Technological trends in sport

1 Introduction

Many processes, in which historically participants had to collaborate in person establishing physical interactions, have deeply changed thanks to the support of technology, and consequently virtual means have been adopted, such as e-commerce, ATMs automatic teller machines, online distance learning systems [1, 2], and so on [3]. During the last decades we observe an increasing use of the Internet especially for the services industry [4], e.g. educational, tourism and sport fields; people tend to use on line programs, above all e-learning and e-training programs because they can save time and money [5, 6]. Likewise, in the last years, characterizing by high levels of competiveness, innovativeness, and globalization, the global economy is deeply changed; in this scenario, in which human-computer interaction (HCI) contributes to transform significantly all the aspects of the human life through the adoption of information technology, specific fields, such as sport setting, that was not considered relevant in terms of economic impact, tend to play a crucial role becoming a very significant business, and are deeply changing thanks to the use of technology. Because of the increasing importance recognized to the sport field, scholars and practitioners tend to search for more effective and efficient tools to manage this business.

This paper through a review of the literature aims to investigate the main application areas with the related theoretical frameworks and the challenges of new technologies in the sport field. In particular, in the last years the introduction of internet or IT has contributed to promote the development of the sport field thanks to the search of strategies to improve athletes' performance or manage a broad range of information and data.

Technology can significantly affect sport in its facts thanks to computer-mediated-communication (CMC) and, in general, HCI. Although numerous technologies have been introduced in sport, in terms of software or digital programs to support the athletes' performance, or the transportation system for sporting event participants in a host community, this phenomenon is still underrepresented in the literature.

This paper aims to examine the implementation of new technologies within the sport industry showing advantages and challenges of these innovative instruments that significantly are changing this specific services sector. Hence, this study shows that the adoption of new technologies is an effective solution in many cases in the sport field because it is possible to overcome geographic and time boundaries (e.g. the media communication for the 2014 Football World Cup was characterized by extraordinary new ways to transfer data showing the football games anytime and anywhere with special effects), or also social barriers related to any forms of disability (e.g. many disabled people thanks to the technology can practice sport also at professional level).

This is a theoretical study conducted through a deep review of the literature aimed to categorize and clarify the main contributions on this topic and to identify new research perspectives. In fact, the deep review of the literature on the topic has been conducted considering some relevant aspects to categorize the existing contributions, such as the specific research area of the studies and the prevalent theoretical frameworks in order to identify the most technological trends in the field.

This paper is structured as follows: the Sect. 2 describes briefly the sport context and the role played by technology in the same field, observing the interesting increase of HCI in many application areas; the Sect. 3 analyzes the specific application areas of new technologies in the sport field and describe the main related challenges. In fact, we review the main contributions in the literature on the topic. Finally, the Sect. 4 shows some final considerations about the phenomenon investigated.

2 The Role of Technology in the Sport

In the prevalent literature, sport has been defined adopting different perspectives and considering various ways of interpreting. Some definitions have mostly emphasized physical and competitive elements inside sport issue, others have focused on its cultural determinants. Besides, in other cases there are generally references to the institutionalization of sporting forms and the increasing significance of rewards, largely financial, that overcome the personal satisfaction, identifying different and wider factors that contribute to define the contemporary sporting landscape. In this perspective, it starts the process of codification of sport with the need of an organizational structure that governs its development. For instance, North-Americans tend narrowly to associate sport concept with competitive game in which some relevant elements are applied, like time, space, formalized rules [7]. Further definitions tend to enrich the sport concept, providing a more comprehensive interpretation thanks to the incorporation of non-competitive elements, like recreation and health [8–11].

In the overall world it is very popular and well known the slogan "Sport for All", which contains a clear message with reference to individuals who are engaged in any physical activity, both in passive forms, such as passive mobilization or postural passive alignment, or in more highly active, like walking or playing competitive football [12]. Indeed, from the etymological point of view, the word sport derives from the term disport, which means to take own attention away from someone or something. This word sport is related to the more common habits of people to carry their attention from the stress and pressures of everyday life [13]. Even though the sport activity finds a deep motivation in the purpose to escape for entertainment and relax, today sport employs a wider concept, including both spectators and participants who can satisfy their needs and beliefs [14].

In the last decades, especially since 2005, the "International Year of Sport and Physical Education" as declared by the United Nations (UN), the use of sport is significantly widespread as a tool for facilitating social change; in fact, sport is usually associated to the promotion of social development, e.g. discouraging criminal behaviours or fostering the integration and rehabilitation of people with disabilities [15].

Moreover, over the past three decades, a very distinctive and expanding body of literature has focused on the sport topic, conceived expression of the characteristics of the physical and cultural phenomenon. In academic and practical studies sport is investigated also evidencing its relevant links to the societies. These numerous studies tend to cross traditional disciplinary boundaries, including historical works [16–19] or socio-political analyses [20–27]. Indeed, in the broad academic disciplines, such as social history and sociology, sport has been conceived as social and cultural constructions in the globalized era, replicating the characteristics of the societies from which they are situated [28–30] or succumbing to more homogenized traits because of the process of globalization [25].

Recently, Read and Bingham [31] have used the term sport "to describe a wide spectrum of culturally defined physical activities with considerable variation in the level and nature of organization and competition" [31, p. 5].

In addition, in the last years the meaning of sport has deeply changed enriching of new elements, even though it keeps the 'fun' element as a central characteristic, new and more complex factors have been included in the sport field, considering also the evolution of many specializing professional sporting forms in 'developed' societies.

This deep evolution of the sport field with its interpretations can be partially associated to the political and economic changes that have implied effects on the sports organizations. Thus, the wide debate concerning sport issue can significantly allows to conceive it as an agent with the capacity to change the environment, with social and cultural effects. Such debate is still opened and interesting with further developments.

In this perspective, one interesting theme widely discussed in the academic and practical sport literature is represented by the technology, more specifically, how the new technologies are deeply changing the overall picture of the sport field, allowing to define innovative research areas and developing very new mindsets in the field. IT and all the innovative technological tools find application in the sport field in different ways and with several implications.

In this evolving scenario, the role of technology is becoming more and more relevant helping to clarifying and simplifying complex situations, such as the sport event management process or the participation of disabled people to sport competitions, and it requires a specific set of skills and knowledge because of many challenges that individuals, companies, corporations and any other organizations are facing in the new era.

Starting from the concept of technology, Loland [32] has argued that this term is quite ambiguous assuming different expressions depending on the various philosophical perspectives of analysis. "Sport technology represents a certain type of means to realize human interests and goals in sport. Such technology ranges from body techniques, via traditional sport equipment used by athletes within competition, to performance-enhancing machines, substances, and methods used outside of the competitive setting" [32, p. 1]. Any discussions and critical analysis of sport technology in competitive sport might concern different interpretations of the main elements of these practices, such as athletic performance [32]. Three ideal-typical theories have been discussed also evidencing their implications by Loland [32], identifying the following frameworks: the non-theory (that is to find the way to achieve the goals through the sport), the thin theory (in this case sport is conceived as an arena for testing out the performance potential of the humans); the thick theory of athletic performance that requires equality of opportunity and recognizes sport as an arena for moral values and for human self-development and enrichment [32].

With reference always to the athletes' performance, some authors have analyzed the diverse information technologies used to provide relevant feedback to the athletes [33]. Indeed, in the sport field, we can observe different applications of technology-based feedback, among them systems, vision, audition, and proprioception are discussed [33].

Technology has deeply changed the content and nature of the sport events, especially the Olympics requiring more attention because of the need to perform in the best way [34]. Some scholars still have investigated how the technology can improve power output and its transferring to athletic performance [35]. Likewise, some interesting studies have paid their attention to the link between technology, disability and sport; in fact, technology can allow people with disability to face their challenges and mostly to facilitate their social integration through the sport practice [36, 37]. Technology has been largely and increasingly adopted in the sport competitive games, for instance, the Paralympic sport, in order to enhance the performance of athletes with disabilities [38]. Moreover, significant applications of technology have been discovered in the Olympics, for instance, in the Athens 2004 Olympic Games it was developed a specific project named PLATO (Process Logistics Advanced Technical Optimization), that was an innovative approach which, adopting innovative techniques from management science, systems engineering, and information technology, could change gradually the planning, design and operation of venues. The ATHOC (Athens 2004 Olympic Games Organizing Committee) received great benefits using the PLATO project due to the development of a systematic process for planning and designing venue operations; this was possible thanks to the use of knowledge modelling and resource management techniques and tools, generating a rich library of models that is easily and directly transferable to future Olympic organizing committees and other sport events [39].

Starting from these contributions in the literature, the role of technology in the sport field is highly recognized with its different applications and functions. In this wide range of applications and ways to consider the technology and its implications in the sport field we argue that it would be useful and interesting to clarify and systematize the existing studies on the phenomenon.

3 Which Technological Trends in the Sport Field?

In this study we conducted a wide review of the literature on the topic investigated, more specifically we considered only studies in the sport field clearly focused and related to the new technologies and any its forms of applications. The prevalent contributions in the literature were identified from a 26-year period (1989 to 2014).[1] More in details, we conducted a search on line adopting the key words "sport", "technology", "athletes", "communication", "IT", "sporting activities", "sport competition" in Google Scholar, one main freely accessible web search engine specialized in academic literature, and in the ISI Web of Knowledge, in the category of management, medicine, educational, and so forth. The key words were sought only in the published papers, not including books or book chapters; we considered through brief reading the abstract of each paper resulting in the search on line and went through the complete reading of the paper, after evidencing its relevance for our research goal.

We used the following three criteria for selecting papers. First, they must be published in journals in the range 1989-2014. Second, the selected papers have to be in English language and contain in their abstract at least the word sport or its derived terms and the other key words selected in the full text and terms directly or indirectly referred to all the key words (e.g. sporting or technical measurement or information systems, and so forth). Third, the articles have to deal with research issues rather than specialty topics, it means we selected papers from management, educational, medical, physical activity and all the issues available. We did not select articles only considering journals traditionally with high impact factor (e.g., Academy of Management Journal or Journal of Sport Management), we also have considered journals of relatively lower ranking (e.g., Journal of Sport History).

The reported studies (only papers published in English language on journals in different research areas) were analyzed to identify mainly the application areas of technology with all its manifestations (innovative techniques in sporting machines, technical innovations in sport infrastructures, information systems, and so on) related to the sport field. Indeed, the search has outlined significant elements showing an increasing attention by scholars on the issue, which has become stronger over the years. Most publications are available on two journals, Journal of Sport Adult Education and Journal of Beijing Sport University.

---

[1] First 6 months in 2014.

We can distinguish in the papers identified, responding to the search criteria, the following five application areas for the new technologies applied in the sport field:

- Sport Management (that concerns all studies aimed to investigate the following themes in the sport field: ethics, media and communication, infrastructures, gender diversity, sport infrastructures, innovation systems, sport programs and computer processing. All these issues have been analyzed with reference to the technology, hence, its specific impact on them);
- Sport Medicine (that includes studies focused on the link between technology and sport adopting a medical perspective, that is features as the impact of technology on the athletes' health, the innovative discovering of techniques to support individuals, also seniors, and so forth. The presence of the words medicine, medical, health, wellness allow to identify this application area);
- Sport Disability (that is referred to all the applications of new technologies for allowing people with disability to practice sport or in general physical activities, and also innovative instruments to acquire major autonomy);
- Sport Events (which consists of all the studies on sport events only if they represent innovative events thanks to the adoption of new and more interesting technologies to manage data and information or to realize spectacular ceremonies);
- Athletes' performance (this area regards all the technologies, like prosthesis or specific innovative equipments, that can really produce an high impact on the athletes' performance; in fact, some useful technological instruments find application to improve continuously the athletes' performance, searching for the best result).

The most theoretical frameworks applied in the investigated papers in our sample concern the Social-Cognitive Theory and the Transtheoretical Model with reference mainly to the athletes' performance research area, and the broader Social Marketing model that has been linked to physical activity programs and campaigns.

The papers resulting from the research were totally about 257, mostly in the Sport Management area with about 63 % on the total (165 papers vs. only 21 articles in the Athletes' performance area).

Since 2000 we observe a significant increase of the papers respecting the criteria search. This significant growth of articles on the topic can be partly explained considering the increasing attention to the sport field, recognized as relevant business, and also to the spread of new ways to "live" the sport and the great success reported by the Sydney 2000 Olympic Games, named "Green Games" for their great interest in respecting the earth equilibrium thanks also to the adoption of new technologies. The analysis conducted outlined two years with the highest number of articles responding of our search criteria: in 2006 and 2008 the prevalence of studies concerns the Sport Management area. In all the application areas identified, theoretical papers are mostly considered compared to empirical studies. The findings of the search also has outlined some challenges and critical aspects that still needed to be explored. Although the prevalent literature evidences and investigates the role played by the technology in the sport field; some critical themes have been identified, such as the implementation of the new Olympic technologies, the critical relationships between the adoption of new technologies to improve the performance and ethics issues, the impact of technology on coaching, traditionally known as "vis-à-vis" relationship, and so forth.

The search area mainly investigated, as evidenced, concerns "Sport Management", that considers many sub-themes very interesting, such as the impact of new technologies in the definition of the rules of the game (see e.g. the deep changes occurred in the regulatory system of the Football competitions) and in the traditional way to coach the athletes with the adoption of *ad hoc* sports management software (see e.g. the case of the German Football Team at the 2014 World Football Cup), the leisure and entertainment with the innovative channels for the communication (electronic mass media are able to show the sport competitions in real time), the ethical relevance of the issue [40–45].

One exemplary and interesting application area in the sport field is represented by the sport event, in fact we observe the presence of numerous papers on the topic. IT plays a key role in the sport event management process in facilitating and controlling information and data sharing, especially because of the unpredictability of economic, social, environmental and organizational effects linked to the event. Diversified and interesting applications of IT and control tools in many areas can be applied, such as transportation service, security, health care assistance, financial, socio-economic and cultural impact analysis, communication service, tourism, and so on.

An interesting application of Information and Communication Technology (ICT) in the 2002 Winter Olympic Games in Salt Lake City in the health care service for athletes, event participants, organizers, volunteers, and tourists. For example, an "information service system" was implemented to assist hospitals in the medical surveillance [46]. COMPASS2008 constitutes another information service system for planning all the planned, in fact, this software considers the mobile digital, multilingual and multimodal companion for participants and visitors of the 2008 Olympic Games in Beijing [47]. To manage all the data and information regarding sport events, in fact, the specific unit within each OCOG (Organizing Committee for the Olympic Games), the Olympic Knowledge Service (OKS), used the TOK (Transfer of Olympic Knowledge), a specific software (programme), that was established in the Sydney Olympic Games 2000 by the SOCOG to manage all the data and information regarding the event [48–50].

Another relevant area investigated regards the changes derived by the application of technology in the relation between disability and sport, in fact, thanks to the enrichment and development of innovative instruments (high quality standard prosthesis, software to monitor athletes with disabilities) people with disabilities can perform sport activities without high risks or any difficulties [51–54]. For instance the most famous case of athlete with disabilities is represented by Oscar Pistorius, that has activated a great discussion on the open question: is it an equal right or unfair advantage? [54]. This question is still debated. Otherwise, the adoption of new technologies with all its forms in the sport field affects significantly the traditional development of the sport activities, changing deeply the human interactions because of the increasing attention to the "technical part" of the sport, maybe not considering the main role played by the sport, that is to promote the social and cultural integration.

Many authors have paid their attention to the introduction of technologies to improve highly the athletes' performance, and in this case ethical issues are discussed too and also the relevance to know HCI appropriately [33, 55–57]. In this area the attention is also paid to the training process of the athletes, in fact Bettoli [58] has evidenced how information technology and computers can provide useful support in sport teaching situations, helping to simplify and increase the efficiency of working procedures, enhance professionalism and provide a platform for effective team work; while, Ross [59] analyzed computer programs useful to sports and recreation instruments, including important features, such as team capacity, league formation, scheduling conflicts, scheduling formats, master schedule, team schedules, reports, team rosters, standings, and optical scanning.

4 Final Considerations

Sport has now become a very important business for its growing economic and social impact and, it is also recognized a much interesting research field in many different disciplines such as medicine, management, economics, and so on. There exist also many technological, cultural and artistic approaches to sport.

The development and adoption of new technologies in any forms and tools have significantly changed relevant aspects of the traditional sport field. Technology can provide positive effects, such as to facilitate improvements in athletes' performance, thanks to the innovative understanding, monitoring and evaluation performance software, or to integrate people with disabilities, or to overcome geographic and cultural barriers thanks to the new mass media. Although all these recognized benefits derived from technology, its impact on the sport field is very relevant and sometimes alarming, because it contributes to change deeply the human interactions concerning the traditional sport competition. Otherwise, HCI changes significantly the development of human processes, especially in the sport field, e.g. the relationship between coach and athlete, or the way to perform and interact of athletes who, for instance, pay more attention to the public image for business, or the ethical and moral consequences of the use of technology.

Technological innovation often changes the nature of a sport, but this topic is still unsearched and underrepresented in the literature, either by scholars of sport or technology. The findings of our study can confirm that the interest in this topic is still limited, even though it is increasing in the last two decades and there are not specific theoretical frameworks developed to investigate how technology is deeply changing the overall sport field, for instance in terms of human relations theories.

This paper presents a brief review of the contributions in the literature on the sport related to technology. It is a theoretical study that presents many limitations, of course, for the methodology adopted and the need to deeply investigate the theme. In the future, thanks to this starting research point, it might be interesting to investigate the implications of new technologies in the traditional sport relationships, such as the coach-athlete relation or the assessment and measurement of athletes' performance. In many of these processes, new technologies can deeply change the way of their development with negative or positive effects. In the future development of this study, starting from the main research areas identified in the field, we might conduct a meta-analysis, to identify in a wide research design the main variables of the impact of technology on the sport field, also adopting and developing interesting theoretical frameworks and not easily describe the prevalent existing contributions. Interesting future research topics related to this starting study might be related to the following areas: the most effective way and tools to monitor and measure athletes' performance, adopting theoretical frameworks like resource based view (RBV) or social exchange theory; the development of software and programs aimed to plan any sport events and to perform the competitions with a deep data collecting and organizational memory of any relevant aspects; the impact of technology on the relationship between sport, health and medicine with particular attention to people with disability.

References

1. Spagnoletti, P., Za, S., North-Samardzic, A.: Fostering informal learning at the workplace through digital platforms and information infrastructures. In: Proceedings of 24th Australasian Conference on Information Systems (ACIS2013), Melbourne (2013)
2. Za, S., Spagnoletti, P., North-Samardzic, A.: Organisational learning as an emerging process: The generative role of digital tools in informal learning practices. Br. J. Educ. Technol. **45**(6), 1023–1035 (2014)
3. Overby, E.: Process virtualization theory and the impact of information technology. Academy of Management Best Conference Paper 2005 OCIS:G1 (2005)
4. Imperatori, B., De Marco, M.: E-Work and Labor Processes Transformation. In: Bondarouk, T., Ruel, H., Guiderdoni-Jourdain, K., Oiry, E. (Eds.) Handbook of Research on E-Transformation and Human Resources Management Technologies: Organizational Outcomes and Challenges, pp. 34–54. Information Science Reference, Hershey (2009)
5. Dobbs, K.: Too much Learning.com. Training, Feb 2000
6. Ricciardi, F., De Marco, M.: The Challenge of Service Oriented Performances for Chief Information Officers. In: Snene, M. (ed.) IESS 2012. LNBIP, vol. 103, pp. 258–270. Springer, Heidelberg (2012)
7. Mullin, B.J., Hardy, S., Sutton, W.A.: Sport Marketing. Human Kinetics, Champaign (1993)
8. Chu, D.: Dimensions of Sports Studies. Wiley, New York (1982)
9. Zeigler, E.F.: Ethics and Morality in Sports and Physical Education – An Experimental Approach. Stripe, Chicago (1984)
10. Goldstein, J.H.: Sports, Games, and Play: Social and Psychological Viewpoints. Lawrence Erlbaum, Hillsdale (1989)
11. Brooks, C.M.: Sports Marketing: Competitive Business Strategies For Sports. Prentice Hall, Englewood Cliffs (1994)
12. Palm, J.: Sport for all: Approaches from Utopia to Reality. Hofmann (1991)
13. Edwards, H.: Sociology of Sport. The Dorsey Press, Homewood (1973)
14. Hudson, S. (ed.): Sport and Adventure Tourism. Routledge, The Haworth Hospitality Press, Oxford (2003)
15. Levermore, R., Beacom, A. (eds.): Sport and International Development, pp. 26–54. Palgrave Macmillan, London (2009)
16. Gutmann, A.: From Ritual to Record. Columbia University Press, New York (1978)
17. Guttmann, A.: Games and Empires: Modern Sports and Cultural Imperialism. Columbia University Press, New York (1994)
18. Mandell, R.: Sport. A Cultural History. Columbia University Press, New York (1984)
19. Brailsford, D.: British Sport: A Social History. Lutterworth Press, Cambridge (1992)
20. Hargreaves, J.: Sport, power and culture: A social and historical analysis of popular sports in Britain. Polity Press, Cambridge (1986)

21. Hargreaves, J.: Globalisation theory, global sport, and nations and nationalism. In: Sugden, J., Tomlinson, A. (eds.) Power Games: A Critical Sociology of Sport, pp. 25–43. Routledge, London (2002)
22. Hargreaves, J.: Sporting females. Critical issues in the history and sociology of women's sports (1994)
23. Bairner, A.: Sport, Nationalism, and Globalization: European and North American Perspectives. Suny Press, Albany (2001)
24. Maguire, J.: Sport, identity politics, and globalization: diminishing contrasts and increasing varieties. Sociol. Sport J. **11**(4), 398–427 (1994)
25. Maguire, J.: Global Sport. Identities, Societies, Civilizations. Polity Press, Cambridge (1999)
26. Maguire, J.: Sport and globalization. In: Coakley, J., Dunning, E. (eds.) Handbook of Sports Studies, pp. 356–369. Sage, London (2000)
27. Cashmore, E.: Sport and Exercise Psychology: the Key Concepts. Routledge, London (2008)
28. Heinemann, K.: Sport in developing countries. In: Dunning, E.G., Maguire, J.A., Pearton, R.E. (eds.) The Sports Process: A Comparative and Developmental Approach, pp. 139–150. Human Kinetics, Champaign (1993)
29. Dunning, E.: Sport Matters: Sociological Studies of Sport, Violence, and Civilization. Psychology Press, London (1999)
30. Dunning, E., Malcolm, D. (eds.): Sport: Critical Concepts in Sociology. Taylor & Francis, London (2003)
31. Read, L., Bingham, J.: Preface UK sport. In: Levermore, R., Beacom, A. (eds.) Sport and International Development London, pp. 26–54. Palgrave Macmillan, London (2009)
32. Loland, S.: Technology in sport: three ideal-typical views and their implications. Eur. J. Sport Sci. **2**(1), 1–11 (2002)
33. Liebermann, D.G., Katz, L., Hughes, M.D., Bartlett, R.M., McClements, J., Franks, I.M.: Advances in the application of information technology to sport performance. J. Sports Sci. **20**(10), 755–769 (2002)
34. Roche, M.: Part 1 sports mega-events, modernity and capitalist economies: mega-events and modernity revisited: globalization and the case of the olympics. Sociol. Rev. **54**(s2), 25–40 (2006)
35. Cronin, J.B., Hansen, K.T.: Strength and power predictors of sports speed. J. Strength Condition. Res. **19**, 349–357 (2005)
36. Burker, T., De Paor, A., Coyle, E.: Disability and technology: engineering a more equitable ireland. IEEE Technol. Soc. Mag. **29**(1), 35–41 (2010)
37. Burkett, B., McNamee, M., Potthast, W.: Shifting boundaries in sports technology and disability: equal rights or unfair advantage in the case of Oscar Pistorius? Disabil. Soc. **26**(5), 643–654 (2011)
38. Burkett, B.: Technology in Paralympic sport: performance enhancement or essential for performance? Br. J. Sports Med. **44**(3), 215–220 (2010)
39. Beis, D.A., Loucopoulos, P., Pyrgiotis, Y., Zografos, K.G.: PLATO helps athens win gold: olympic games knowledge modeling for organizational change and resource management. Informs **36**(1), 26–42 (2006)
40. Rintala, J.: Sport and technology: human questions in a world of machines. J. Sport Soc. Issues **19**(1), 62–75 (1995)
41. Gelberg, J.N.: Technology and sport: the case of the ITF, spaghetti strings, and composite rackets. In: Proceedings and Newsletter-North American Society for Sport History (1996)
42. Marcus, B.H., Owen, N., Forsyth, L., Cavill, N.A., Fridinger, F.: Physical activity interventions using mass media, print media, and information technology. Am. J. Prev. Med. **15**, 362–378 (1998)

43. Wilson, B.: Believe the hype? The impact of the internet on sport-related subcultures. Tribal Play Subcultural Journeys Through Sport **4**, 135–152 (2008)
44. Gallardo-Guerrero, L., García-Tascón, M., Burillo-Naranjo, P.: New sports management software: A needs analysis by a panel of Spanish experts. Int. J. Inf. Manage. **28**(4), 235–245 (2008)
45. Coutts, A.J., Duffield, R.: Validity and reliability of GPS devices for measuring movement demands of team sports. J. Sci. Med. Sport **13**(1), 133–135 (2010)
46. Gundlapalli, A.V.: Hospital electronic medical record–based public health surveillance system deployed during the 2002 Winter Olympic Games. Am. J. Infect. Control **35**(3), 163–171 (2007)
47. Uszkoreit, H., Xu, F., Aslan, I., Steffen, J.: COMPASS2008: An Intelligent Multilin-gual and Multimodal Mobile Information Service System for Beijing Olympic Games, Proceedings of KI2006 Demo Collection, Germany (2006)
48. Toohey, K.: The sydney olympics: striving for legacies-overcoming short-term disappointments and long-term deficiencies. Int. J. Hist. Sport **25**(14), 1953–1971 (2008)
49. Bovy, P.: Olympic Games Transport Transfer of Knowledge, HITE/Ol.transp/Bovy-version XYZ. 1 22.4.2008, HITE-ATHENS, IOC Transport Advisor (2008)
50. Halbwirth, S., Toohey, K.: The olympic games and knowledge management: a case study of the sydney organising committee of the olympic games. Eur. Sport Manage. Q. **1**(2), 91–111 (2001)
51. Lane, A.: Relationships between perceptions of performance expectations and mood among distance runners: the moderating effect of depressed mood. J. Sci. Med. Sport **4**(1), 116–128 (2001)
52. Burkett, B.: Technology in Paralympic sport: performance enhancement or essential for performance? Br. J. Sports Med. **44**(3), 215–220 (2010)
53. Burkett, B.: Paralympic sports medicine—current evidence in winter sport: considerations in the development of equipment standards for Paralympics athletes. Clin. J. Sport Med. **22**(1), 46–50 (2012)
54. Burkett, B., McNamee, M., Potthast, W.: Shifting boundaries in sports technology and disability: equal rights or unfair advantage in the case of Oscar Pistorius? Disabil. Soc. **26**(5), 643–654 (2011)
55. Cronin, J., Sleivert, G.: Challenges in understanding the influence of maximal power training on improving athletic performance. Sports Med. **35**(3), 213–234 (2004)
56. Haake, S.J.: The impact of technology on sporting performance in Olympic sports. J. Sports Sci. **27**(13), 1421–1431 (2009)
57. Dwyer, D.B., Gabbett, T.J.: Global positioning system data analysis: Velocity ranges and a new definition of sprinting for field sport athletes. J. Strength Condition. Res. **26**(3), 818–824 (2012)
58. Bettoli, B.: Data processing: working procedures made easier: sport information technology and team work. Magglingen **54**(11), 18–19 (1997)
59. Ross, C.M.: Computer Technology and Its Impact on Recreation and Sport Programs (1998)

Shared Services: Exploring the New Frontier

Maddalena Sorrentino[1(✉)], Luca Giustiniano[2,3], Paolo Depaoli[4], and Marco De Marco[5]

[1] Università degli Studi di Milano, Milan, Italy
maddalena.sorrentino@unimi.it
[2] Department of Business and Management,
Luiss Guido Carli University, Rome, Italy
lgiusti@luiss.it
[3] Interdisciplinary Center for Organizational Architecture – ICOA,
Aarhus University, Aarhus, Denmark
[4] Luiss Guido Carli University-CeRSI, Rome, Italy
pdepaoli@luiss.it
[5] Uninettuno, Rome, Italy
marco.demarco@uninettunouniversity.net

Abstract. The big squeeze on public spending and the need to get Italy's small local councils fully on board the e-government agenda is forcing both the public and the private sector to think of new ways to source and deliver public services. The sharing of services is one solution that goes beyond the traditional insourcing/outsourcing model to cast the SSO in the primary role of Information and Communication Technology (ICT) provider. The paper illustrates a case study in which, after a few "false starts", an Italian company made the positive transition from PPP to public SSO, building relations of trust and a flexible offer that met the councils' need to retain their individuality. The general reflection that follows has the aim of further informing the debate on the redesign of organizational activities through service management, and supports the continuity of the basic organizational logics that inform the practices of the public SSO.

Keywords: Service science · Shared services · Shared service organization · ICT provision · Municipalities · Outsourcing · Public sector

1 Introduction

Italian local governments continue to scratch their heads over which Information and Communication Technology (ICT) sourcing strategies can best meet their needs, even though the public managers now have a wider spectrum of tools and modular solutions to choose from. Among Italy's various administrative entities, the local councils are the most adventurous in exploring the new solutions [1, 2] and some have even embraced the shared- services option that the corporate sector developed in the late 1980s [3].

The past 30 years have seen a multitude of ICT investments yet the current literature does not beat a clear path through the thickets of sourcing information systems, the implications on the firm's boundaries, and the related theoretical challenges [4].

A rich body of literature [5–7] has shown that in-house sourcing, shared services and outsourcing form a continuum of possible solutions in which the solutions are so mixed and multiple that even the definition of the organizational boundaries might be difficult [8].

"Shared services" (SSs) is an umbrella term [9, 10] that signifies the concentration of one or more processes spread across one or more organizations or across more divisions of the same organization [11]. A shared service organization (SSO) can therefore aggregate activities, functions, systems and personnel in one single hub of competences from which it manages these activities as the core part of its business model. Large corporations use the shared-services option mainly to achieve efficiency gains through the ongoing improvement of processes [3, 12]. Therefore, the adoption of the shared-services strategy and the involvement of specialized SSOs must fit into a more general organizational framework in order to increase supply chain integration and balance the expected economic performance and the related risks [13].

In the public sector, precise government mandates and independent choice are the two factors (antecedents) [4, 8] that lead the central and local administrations [12, 14, 15] to progressively adopt shared-services arrangements. The intrinsic features of information systems means that most of the SSs are directly or indirectly involved in information processes [16, 17, p. 261], not least because many public services rely on ICT for their delivery [18–20].

The qualitative study adopts an exploratory research approach to investigate the supply-side of the shared-services option and asks "What makes the SSO a new frontier in the way public services are delivered?" That may seem a rather trivial research question but few studies have focused on the nature of these organizations and the conceptualization of their founding principles to date (as confirmed by the recent review of Fielt and co-authors [21]). For example, the embeddedness and the centrality of information as a strategic asset in services means it is necessary to analyze also the coordination efforts required of the organizations concerned (the SSO and its customers) [22]. The nature of the information and the pervasiveness of information-based services in the host value chains can lead to lock-in and path dependency effects over time [4, 8]. The paper seeks to contribute to the current SSO debate by mapping an Italian PPP's initially bumpy but ultimately positive transition to public SSO.

The paper frames the theme addressed with a review of the relevant literature and then draws an overall picture of the status of e-government in Italy. After explaining the research approach taken by the authors, an overview of the research setting is provided as a necessary prelude to the case study, which analyzes the change of strategic direction taken by a public SSO that led it to reengineer and reposition the business [23]. The paper concludes with a general reflection on the underlying organizational logics that inform current practices.

2 Relevant Literature

The advances made in the field of shared services [2] have struck a march on academic inquiry, leaving many aspects of the public SSs phenomenon as yet unexplored. Moreover, most of the studies focus exclusively on the perspective of the decision maker, i.e., the buyer/recipient, and not on the SSO 'as an organizational entity in its own right' [21, p. 1018].

The research on SSs in local government agrees that shared services arrangements are highly promising solutions to enhance operational efficiency, assigning a key role to the cost-cutting potential [24–26], as well as to the immediate access to non-available expertise [10, 24, p. 87, 27]. Shared services also play a key enabling role in the re-design of internal processes [28, 29] and in increasing the resilience of the buyer's organization [21, 30]. Hence, like other sourcing strategies, the shared services option also has the potential to generate financial, strategic and organizational outcomes [4, 8].

As observed by Dollery and Akimov [14], most studies tend to adopt a pro-local shared service arrangements stance with no evidence to the contrary. Nevertheless, Tomkinson [30, pp. 34–37] notes that the general disadvantages include the implied limited control over resources, policies and practices between partner councils. Another recurrent theme is related to the burden of organizational change that is placed on the user/host organizations [30].

In the attempt to describe the main SSs business models some studies seek to anchor it to a more solid theoretical background [3, 15, 31]. Joha and Janssen [15] identified three typical SSs configurations in the public-sector context: (1) centralized, (2) federated, and (3) decentralized, linking each configuration to four distinct dimensions (and their respective variables): governance structure; strategic rationale; nature of the services; and customer orientation. Governance structure refers to the how of the organization of service delivery; strategic rationale addresses the object and purpose of the SSO; the nature of the services connotes the type of underlying business activities; and customer orientation refers to the intermediate or final users of the shared services. Slicing the cake in this way enables us to grasp the 'more granular and subtle' [15] reality of shared services and to use a multidimensional approach to investigate the complex nature of the SSO.

Ulbrich and Borman [28] observe that the appropriate level of standardization might vary amongst organizations due to the pressure exerted by several contingency factors, such as specific needs and expected quality of service. Hence, any imbalance in process standardization may undermine the effective functioning of the shared service centres. This contingent view of process standardization clashes with that of the mainstream view of SSs on two counts. First, it contradicts the school of thought that believes that only high levels of process optimization can improve the sharing of services. In the authors' own words, "process standardization might be counterproductive and negatively impact on a shared service center's ability to reach its original goals" [28, p. 2]. Second, there is another, often neglected variable, the time factor, which Ulbrich and Borman incorporated into their analysis. In particular, when process standardization becomes skewed, the SSO has the option of taking one of four logical trajectories: centralized, outsourced, collaborative or decentralized. A reversal of those trajectories indicates an SSO's "freedom of action to not transition toward one of the four adapted service delivery modes" [28, p. 3]. Ulbrich and Borman suggest some managerial strategies to prevent the decline of an SSO and to counter-balance the negative effects of transiting from one trajectory to another. Given that the major challenges faced by the 'modern' ICT provider are operational stability, security and flexibility (i.e., scalability) [32], the service-oriented perspective adopted by Brocke,

Uebernickel and Brenner [33] can provide significant insights into how the SSOs can perform the job of 'mass customizers'. In fact, like in other fields, the effective use of modularity could be applied to an intangible service agreement via different operational types of *modularity* [33, pp. 3, 4]: (a) *commitment swapping*, where customers can choose between the different services packages (i.e., Gold, Silver); (b) *option*, the possibility to expand the scope of the service offered; (c) *sectional*, in which the agreements cover only partial modules (parts) of services; and (d) *commitment sharing*, when service agreements are designed along identical commitments (reuse of services in different agreements). Alternatively, the customer could intervene and interact with the provider in one or more of the service delivery phases of *design, contracting, usage*. Further, depending on the SS provider's strategy and adherence to the defined commitments, it can take on multiple roles [5, 6, 33] as *Assemblers, Individualizers, Modifiers, Engineers*. These four roles must be considered just as archetypical. The authors developed a service model that suggests, first, strictly separating the run and the change of the business; second, 'modularizing self-contained commitments; and third, productizing options, variants and changes' [33, p. 10].

All the cited contributions see shared services as a dynamic field that responds to the needs of an increasingly service-oriented economy in which the ICT provider's strategy of standardization (aimed at achieving economies of scale and scope) must allow for adapting the content of the service portfolio to the user's needs. The academic debate has only just started to gain a better understanding of the factors at work. The new aspects of the SSs operating model are still a fledgling object of study in the current literature, which leaves pretty much unexplored the SSO 'as an organizational entity in its own right' [21, p. 1018]. The aim of the paper is to take an initial step forward to redress that asymmetry.

3 Italian Councils and the Quest to 'Go Digital'

The approaches taken by Italy's 8000 + local governments to satisfy the demand of a connected society for digital municipal services vary considerably. This is because, in sharp contrast to the fact that almost all the local councils have the same organizational structure, legal status and reporting requirements, the same fairly basic level of computerization and that they all deliver a similar range of services, the law leaves them free to choose how to best implement and manage their ICT strategies.

This has created a municipal landscape in which the overall level of computerization is not only fragmented and discontinuous, but fluctuates significantly from one local area to another. And, while most of the larger councils seem to have found the resources to set up an in-house ICT office – 80 out of 100 councils with 60000+ inhabitants, according to ISTAT – those councils with 5000 inhabitants or less have had a much tougher time of it, with the indicator shrinking to a mere six out of 100 (ISTAT 2013).

A lack of financial and professional resources to fully invest in technological innovation and thus meet digitization needs is the main reason why the smaller councils are forced to outsource their ICT requirements to service providers in the private sector, which, in turn, has opened the door to *colonization*. In other words, the intimate knowledge of the local government's digital administration system and processes gained by the ICT service providers – know-how that far exceeds that of the large system integrators tasked with developing the central government's e-government projects – not only has sown the seeds of client path-dependency and lock-in, but also places the ICT providers in an advantageous position from which to exert significant influence, which, naturally, they do their best to defend [30, 31, 34, 35].

These incumbents thus have ended up steering the small councils' innovation policies (for instance, e-government), using the rhetoric of "those who know best" to exploit their position of dominance over the user [30, p. 90, 36].

4 Research Approach

The exploratory approach adopted by the paper is underpinned by the fact that effective theory-building and theory-testing is built on "good descriptions of what happens or what has happened on the ground" [31] and by the need to bridge the gaps in the current literature on SSO as an organizational entity in its own right [21].

The main source of evidence for our study is the case of Consorzio.IT (CIT), a public-owned SSO based in Lombardy, Northern Italy. Lombardy is the most developed and populous region in Italy, home to about 10 million people (or 16.2 % of the national population), and is served by a total of 1546 councils, of which 1091, or 70.57 %, have 5000 or fewer residents, while the number of inter-municipal arrangements applied across the most diverse sectors adds up to approximately 500 [36–39].

CIT, which started out in the early 2000s as a Private-Public Partnership (PPP), is, today, the wholly owned subsidiary of a multi-utility company founded by 47 municipalities and the Province of Cremona that delivers ICT services and support to the same 47, mostly small Lombard councils.

The authors' selection of CIT as the case study for this research effort was thanks to the access freely given by the company to the records and data needed to map its longitudinal history and evolutionary pattern. Of particular interest was the fact that CIT's journey led it to abandon the in-house business model initially adopted, completely reengineer its range of services and reposition the company. The following pages present the key aspects of the case, i.e., those that the authors deem most relevant and useful for the study's exploratory purpose and to respond to the research question posed earlier.

The field research, conducted in the period from June 2012 to July 2013, saw the authors hold semi-structured interviews (40–60 min each) with CIT staff to collect the necessary data. The interviews, guided by the literature review, addressed four main areas: activity, organization, environmental context, operations. The CIT respondents were the CEO, two top managers, the commercial director, and a second-level helpdesk line employee. Two researchers transcribed the interviews. Follow-up symmetric phone interviews were held in July 2013 and the entire set of interviews was further enriched with the information provided voluntarily by six mayors of CIT client councils. More recently, the authors critically analyzed and discussed the ensuing store of information.

5 The Case Study

In 2004, the central government's decision to allocate funding of €15 million to get neighbouring small councils fully on board Italy's e-gov agenda led to the founding of CIT and its mission to deliver ICT services to the Province of Cremona's smaller councils (those with 5000 or less residents). The government then enacted a special law to introduce the 'local area services centre' (in Italian, Centro Servizi Territoriali or 'CST') strictly for the use of neighbouring councils to help them prepare for online public engagement. Consequently, some of the regional governments, including Lombardy, opened special funding lines to facilitate the councils' acquisition and implementation of ICT infrastructure, hardware and software, and ICT aggregation [37].

However, the desire to expand the user base nurtured by the two private ICT firms that initially took minority stakes in CIT clashed with its full-outsourcing mission. Hence, the two private shareholders cashed in their shares and CIT obtained regional government funding to purchase the hardware needed to set up a CST data centre and a low-cost connectivity wireless network for the exclusive use of the councils. Nevertheless, despite these efforts, two years later not one council had retired their information system and migrated to CIT, leading to its decision to reposition the business. CIT's General Manager, a former corporate TLC executive, hired a new Commercial Director whose marketing-oriented approach matched his own. Both managers had to accept that standardizing the services to meet the needs of all the municipalities, and thus enable CIT to become a fully-fledged 'outsourced service centre', was an impossible feat [26, p. 5]. As a result, CIT embraced modularity in an arena where operational stability and flexibility seemed to be the most important source of competitiveness [33].

To get to grips with *"the biggest problems"*, the new commercial director paid personal calls on the officers and councillors of the neighbouring municipalities only to discover that *commitments swapping* and *option modularity* [33] were de facto pushed by the local councils. Indeed, *"80 % of requests for help concerned operational issues that often had nothing to do with connectivity or the performance of the software applications installed at the councils."* Moreover, there were some instances of *unrestrictedness* to the selection of services acquired [30]. In fact, it was only by speaking with the "respective mayors" that the company learned about the *"oft-voiced need to implement widespread training, an issue that had never been raised before, which led CIT to start organizing basic training courses for the council staff."* According to Brocke, Uebernickel and Brenner [33], unrestricted conditions "allow more efficient designing of new services agreements" [33, p. 3]. Therefore, *"the next step was to convince the councils to use us as outsourcers for those technical activities that, kept in-house, generated no particular benefits. We then proposed a brand new range of services to complete and integrate the applications portfolio"* (Commercial Director, CIT).

The next challenge faced by CIT was to earn the trust of the ICT suppliers appointed by the councils, which *"initially saw us as a threat to their business, so we had to assure them that our position was non-partisan and that it was our policy to never pressure customers into anything. Now the ICT suppliers see us as an ally of sorts, and not only have we become their sole spokesperson [...], but some have even reported growth in revenue since we started working together*" (Commercial Director, CIT).

Therefore, by bringing its module- and bridge-building capabilities into the game, CIT took on the role of *engineer* [33], serving both the client councils and their existing ICT suppliers.

6 The CIT Business Model

Taking our cue from the work of Joha and Janssen [15, pp. 33, 34], we can split CIT's SSO business model into four interrelated dimensions: (1) governance structure; (2) strategic rationale; (3) nature of the services; and (4) customer orientation.

Governance Structure. Incorporated in Italy, CIT is a limited liability company with share capital of Euro 100,000 wholly owned by SCRP SpA, a public utility group based in the Crema area of Lombardy that is the indirect expression of its multi-utility council partners. CIT has the same CEO as parent company SCRP, its offices and technological resources at SCRP's head office and employs a staff of six tasked with the following functions: Commercial (1), first-level help desk (2), second-level help desk (2), and Cartographic services (1).

The company uses a Customer Relationship Management (CRM) system to manage its assistance activities. In particular, a first-level call centre provides telephonic and online assistance, while the perceived quality of services is monitored using the customer satisfaction survey method.

Although CIT fuelled Euro 1.2 million in FY2012 revenue, its annual profit for each of the past five financial years was fairly low. "*That is because*" explained the CEO "*our goal is simply to calibrate two needs, that is, to keep a good managerial balance and to minimize the costs for the client councils.*"

Strategic Rationale. CIT was founded thanks to central and regional government funding with the objective of leveraging economies of scale to optimize the delivery and effectiveness of the standard package of core ICT services, initially using the CST model of data centre consolidation. However, this was in direct conflict with the strategic rationale of the private partners to grow the business by giving preferred access to a captive client base, hence, the private-sector minority shareholders exited the share capital and CIT repositioned as an SSO, responsible for coordinating the specific requirements of the client municipalities.

That the municipalities most pressing need was to ensure their core information system users an appropriate level of operational support became immediately clear to CIT, leading it to reengineer its structure around this service and to launch the help-desk, which soon became a resource critical to the functioning of the client councils. CIT's later decisions also were guided by this rationale, i.e., to identify potential niches and to find the best solutions (for example, the unbundling of ICT activities) to respond to the client's specific needs. Over time, it is these sourcing-related decisions that map the sourcing path of an organization [39].

Nature of the Services. While the needs of CIT's target clients translate into a standard services portfolio, the individual sourcing choices differ significantly. CIT's core business is split into two distinct lines: (i) assistance, i.e., online help desk, legislative/regulatory assistance, software applications assistance, and (ii) ICT services, i.e., the centralization of software applications, connectivity, e-mail management, website design, hosting and maintenance, software application program development, back-up and disaster recovery, management of video-surveillance systems, and software asset management. CIT has since expanded the original services portfolio of 2007 and the ICT demand of the individual councils has become modular and articulated. This has created a market in which several suppliers provide a range of solutions and services, including CIT, which provides online assistance in the event the partner councils encounter connectivity problems.

Customer Orientation. CIT favours the multi-sourcing logic that leaves the client councils free to assess which of CIT's services best satisfy their specific requirements – for example, its servers run the information systems of four different software providers – and, as each client council's requirements change over the course of time, so do the contents of the service agreements.

CIT's corporate approach means that it offers an advisory service to those clients who are uncertain about whether to take the "make it in-house" or the 'buy it on the market' route. In fact, CIT owns both a centrally hosted environment and a virtual infrastructure (some 20 machines) located at the data centre of a Cremona public TLC services company. As a result, CIT is the hub-and-spoke of a network of business relations based on trust: both external, i.e., from and to the user councils; and internal, i.e., from and to the sub-contractors. In fact, CIT seamlessly matches the councils' demand for technological innovation to the potential capabilities of the market players, using third parties to keep both organizational structure and fixed costs lean.

7 Discussion

The case study reveals a situation in which the full-outsourcing strategy of a PPP was cast aside in favour of a selected range of services aggregated under the umbrella of a public SSO. That transition can be explained by the reverse trajectories identified by Ulbrich and Borman [26], which demonstrate how the implementation phases of sourcing decisions can redesign the scope of the organizational activities [4]. Further, the case shows how a strategic change of direction can reshape the organizational dynamics and lead to positive outcomes. Indeed, although the shared services strategy veered off the initial design path, that shift enabled the public SSO to not only achieve its cost-saving mission, but also to generate strategic and organizational benefits [8]. We will now use the CIT case to critically discuss the configurations, the trajectories and the dynamic settings described in the literature review.

The change in the nature of the services as defined by Joha and Janssen [15] shows how the original goal of CIT to provide a limited range of ICT resources based on the service agreement model was expanded to include complementary and frequently requested services, such as operational helpdesk and staff training.

CIT is a special-purpose vehicle that can be defined as a supra-corporate model [29] that delivers services to all its partners according to a precise strategy of concentration of activities and services. Despite its small size, CIT possesses all three of the publicness criteria identified by Andrews, Boyne and Walker [40]: ownership, funding, and control. While the company's ownership is crystal clear, more in-depth analysis was required to shed light on funding and control. CIT's hybrid nature is attested by several factors: (i) it is an established main player in a competitive market of peers; (ii) it self-finances its operations with the income generated by services; and (iii) it drives innovation by anticipating customer needs. The physical proximity of the interlocking directorates of the SSO and the parent company is fair evidence also of public funding and public control.

The dynamics of CIT's forward and reverse organizational trajectories chime fully with the situation described by Ulbrich and Borman [28]. In fact, the present configuration of the SSO is the result of a kind of heuristic process that involved a series of decisions to remedy the unexpected effects of earlier decisions. Nevertheless, we are not talking of the linear or continuous progression envisaged by the theoretical models. Rather, CIT embarked on several trajectories *simultaneously*, according to the level of process consolidation required by each client council. In this sense, CIT demonstrates that antecedents (drivers), processes (of implementation) and expected outcomes of sourcing strategies can be connected by several links [8], and that the organizational trajectories follow the diversity of such links.

The CIT case informs that (i) it is not easy to set-up an SSO, above all, in the presence of risk-adverse customers (the small councils); (ii) it is exposed to complex, uncertain and equivocal environments; (iii) the new SS provider has to overcome challenges that range from cultural (e.g. digital divide, familiarity with different standards) to infrastructural (e.g. legacy systems, installed bases), and, (iv) it has to find a way to deal with incumbent suppliers that are reluctant to collaborate and go on the defensive because they feel threatened by the new arrival [35].

The strategic key adopted by CIT to break through the environmental barriers was relational, i.e., it was based on building relations of trust across the board. Indeed, the comments of the mayors interviewed confirmed that the public SSO's business approach (e.g., flexible offer, assessment of internal skills and resources) was to build and maintain rock solid relationships [41–44].

The shared services portfolio of CIT differs profoundly from those of the more usual consolidation ventures, such as the CSTs, which target the needs of service providers that have a vested interest in getting all clients on the same platform and using solutions or to choose from a catalogue of standard options. CIT bucked that trend, opting instead to identify the real and potential needs of the users, thus enabling it to develop a shared services offer 'customized for individual customer sets' [25]. In short, CIT 'retains the individuality of councils' [30, p. 33].

From the resource-based viewpoint, CIT's intimate knowledge of client digital administration processes is a crucial competitive asset. In fact, such distinctive knowledge (e.g. gathered in one pioneer council) can be strategically used to increase the level of customization, to cross-implement solutions in other councils or for other potential clients (e.g. other public administrations). This has enabled CIT to sow the seeds of customer path dependency, to enhance switching costs and to create psychological commitment [34], which are all pillars of its sustainable competitive advantage.

And so to the paper's research question "What makes the SSO a new frontier in the way public services are delivered?", which perhaps is a subtle dig at the mainstream literature's tendency to focus solely on the more superficial or structural aspects of SSO arrangements or the SSO portfolio. Clearly, we cannot use the CIT case as a universal source of organization design solutions, but neither should we underestimate the important role its flexible, coordinating and trust-building approach has played in originating effective service delivery [43, 44].

In addition, as evidenced by the CIT case, the legal form has no bearing on the firm's boundaries [4, 8], which are blurred into a grey area in which the client-supplier relationship is fluid and in constant evolution. In fact, the SSO uses its knowledge to drive innovation, exerting its influence over the client councils and challenging the technological environment [41, 42]. In other words, in seeking to augment its exercisable control over external service receivers, CIT has charted a new frontier.

8 Conclusions

This paper builds on the evidence that the SSO is an unconventional combination of control, coordination mechanisms and permeable organizational boundaries and, hence, a new frontier. In fact, CIT has not only succeeded in staking its place in the market, it is also a case of *virtuous localism* [19, 20], confirming that even a pocket-sized SSO can lever the knowledge gained and build relations of trust.

The study confirms the useful contribution of service science as a basis for designing consumer-oriented service propositions in the ICT services sector. According to this perspective, ICT services should not be seen as a unit of output but as a process of value co-creation for and with another party with a relational focus.

The study spurs the debate on the SSO by exploring those aspects that can help to deepen our understanding of its sustainability. The effectiveness of CIT is, in fact, the result of specific contingencies that may not apply in other cases, in particular, the public SSO has (i) won the challenges posed by an environment made up of many small councils with limited bargaining power; (ii) created value through technological investments in existing management systems and managerial resources; (iii) used its internal capabilities to generate switching costs; (iv) aligned with the multi-sourcing strategies of its clients; and (v) formulated an affordable price policy based on the services actually delivered, rather than on exploiting a position of advantage position in a captive market.

The conclusion drawn from the study is that we are looking at a positive example of a service dominant approach, indeed, a new frontier that meets the needs of its local communities with an offer of flexible organizational solutions.

References

1. IRPA: Il capitalismo municipale. IRPA, Roma (2012)
2. Warner, M., Hebdon, R.: Local government restructuring: privatization and its alternatives. J. Policy Anal. Manag. **20**(2), 315–336 (2001)
3. Walsh, P., McGregor-Lowndes, M., Newton, C.J.: Shared services: lessons from the public and private sectors for the nonprofit sector. Aust. J. Public Adm. **67**(2), 200–212 (2008)
4. Giustiniano, L., Marchegiani, L., Peruffo, E., Pirolo L.: Understanding outsourcing of information systems. In: Tsiakis, T., Kargidis, T., Katsaros, P. (eds.) Approaches and Processes for Managing the Economics of Information Systems, pp. 199–220. IGI Global, Hershey, PA (2014)
5. Lacity, M.C., Khan, S.A., Willcocks, L.P.: A review of the IT outsourcing literature: insights for practice. J. Strateg. Inf. Syst. **18**(3), 130–146 (2009)
6. Lacity, M.C., Khan, S., Yan, A., Willcocks, L.P.: A review of the IT outsourcing empirical literature and future research directions. J. Inf. Technol. **25**(4), 395–433 (2010)
7. Schwarz, A., Jayatilaka, B., Hirschheim, R., Goles, T.: A conjoint approach to understanding IT application services outsourcing. J. AIS **10**(10), 748–781 (2009)
8. Marchegiani, L., Giustiniano, L., Peruffo, E., Pirolo, L.: Revitalising the outsourcing discourse within the boundaries of firms debate. Bus. Syst. Rev. **1**(1), 157–177 (2012)
9. Local Government Association: Shared Services (2013). http://www.local.gov.uk/web/guest/productivity/-/journal_content/56/10171/3510759/ARTICLE-TEMPLATE. Accessed 11 May 2013
10. Joha, A., Janssen, M.: Factors influencing the shaping of shared services business models: balancing customization and standardization. Strateg. Outsourcing Int. J. **7**(1), 47–65 (2014)
11. Gospel, H., Sako, M.: The unbundling of corporate functions: the evolution of shared services and outsourcing in human resources. Ind. Corp. Change **19**(5), 1367–1396 (2010)
12. Accenture: Driving high performance in government: maximizing the value of public-sector shared services The Government Executive Series (2005)
13. Nenni, M.E., Giustiniano, L.: Increasing integration across the supply chain through an approach to match performance and risk. Am. J. Appl. Sci. **10**(9), 1009–1017 (2013)
14. Dollery, B.E., Akimov, A.: Are shared services a panacea for Australian local government? A critical note on Australian and international empirical evidence. Int. Rev. Public Adm. **12**(2), 89–102 (2008)
15. Joha, A., Janssen, M.: Types of shared services business models in public administration. In: 12th Annual International DGO Conference, pp. 26–35. ACM, College Park (2011)
16. Ghia, A.: Capturing value through IT consolidation and shared services. McKinsey on Government (Autumn), pp. 18–23 (2011)
17. Hui, P.P., Fonstad, N.O., Beath, C.M.: Technology service inter-organizational relationships. In: Cropper, S., Ebers, M., Huxham, C., Smith Ring, P. (eds.) The Oxford Handbook of Inter-Organizational Relations, pp. 256–280. OUP, Oxford (2008)
18. Borman, M., Janssen, M.: Critical success factors for shared services: results from two case studies. Paper presented at the 45th HICSS, Maui, Hawaii, USA (2012)
19. Ricciardi, F., Rossignoli, C., De Marco, M.: Participatory networks for place safety and livability: organisational success factors. Int. J. Netw. Virtual Organ. **13**(1), 42–65 (2013)
20. Dameri, R.P., Perego, A.: Translate IS governance framework into practice: the role of IT service management and IS performance evaluation. In: Proceedings of the 4th European Conference on Information Management and Evaluation, Lisbon, Portugal 9–10 Sept 2010, p. 53. Academic Conferences Ltd. (2010)

21. Fielt, E., Bandara, W., Suraya, M., Gable, G.: Exploring shared services from an IS perspective: a literature review and research agenda. Commun. AIS **34**, 1001–1040 (2014)
22. McIvor, R., McCracken, M., McHugh, M.: Creating outsourced shared services arrangements: lessons from the public sector. Eur. Manag. J. **29**(6), 448–461 (2011)
23. Levina, N., Su, N.: Global multisourcing strategy: the emergence of a supplier portfolio in services offshoring. Decis. Sci. **39**(3), 541–570 (2008)
24. Alford, J., O'Flynn, J.: Rethinking Public Service Delivery. Palgrave Macmillan, Basingstoke (2012)
25. Pollitt, C., Bouckaert, G.: Public management reform. In: A Comparative Analysis: New Public Management, Governance, and the Neo-Weberian State, 3rd edn. OUP, Oxford (2011)
26. Sako, M.: Outsourcing vs shared services. Commun. ACM **53**(7), 27–29 (2010)
27. Scannell, M., Bannister, F.: Shared services in Irish local government. In: Scholl, H.J., Janssen, M., Wimmer, M.A., Moe, C.E., Flak, L.S. (eds.) EGOV 2012. LNCS, vol. 7443, pp. 114–125. Springer, Heidelberg (2012)
28. Ulbrich, F., Borman, M.: Preventing the gradual decline of shared service centers. Paper presented at the AMCIS 2012, Seattle, Washington, 9–12 August 2012
29. Bovaird, T.: Developing new forms of partnership with the 'market' in the procurement of public services. Public Adm. **84**(1), 81–102 (2006)
30. Tomkinson, R.: Shared Services in Local Government: Improving Service Delivery. Gower, Aldershot (2007)
31. Huxham, C., Vangen, S.: Doing things collaboratively: realizing the advantage or succumbing to inertia? Org. Dyn. **33**(2), 190–201 (2004)
32. Uebernickel, F., Brenner, W.: The Challenges of modern IT. In: Abolhassan, F. (ed.) The Road to a Modern IT Factory, pp. 11–32. Springer, Heidelberg (2014)
33. Brocke, H., Uebernickel, F., Brenner, W.: Mass customizing IT service agreements: towards individualized on-demand services. In: ECIS 2010 Proceedings, Paper 101, pp. 1–12 (2010). http://aisel.aisnet.org/ecis2010/101
34. Niehaves, B., Krause, A.: Shared service strategies in local government – a multiple case study exploration. Transform. Gov. **4**(3), 266–279 (2010)
35. Polites, G.L., Karahanna, E.: Shakled to the status quo: the inhibiting effects of incumbent system habit. MIS Q. **36**(1), 21–42 (2012)
36. Ancitel: Le ICT nei comuni italiani. Ancitel, Roma (2010)
37. IReR: Lo stato delle forme associative tra enti locali in Lombardia. Consiglio Regionale della Lombardia, Milano (2009)
38. Sorrentino, M., Simonetta, M.: Assessing local partnerships: an organisational perspective. Transform. Gov. People Process Policy **5**(3), 207–224 (2011)
39. Mola, L., Carugati, A.: Escaping 'localisms' in IT sourcing: tracing changes in institutional logics in an Italian firm. Eur. J. Inf. Syst. **21**, 388–403 (2010)
40. Andrews, R., Boyne, G.A., Walker, R.M.: Dimensions of publicness and organizational performance: a review of the evidence. J. Public Adm. Res. Theor. **21**, i301–i319 (2011)
41. Zardini, A., Rossignoli, C., Mola, L., De Marco, M.: Developing municipal e-government in Italy: the city of Alfa case. In: Snene, M., Leonard, M. (eds.) IESS 2014. LNBIP, vol. 169, pp. 124–137. Springer, Heidelberg (2014)
42. Casalino, N., Buonocore, F., Rossignoli, C., Ricciardi, F.: Transparency, openness and knowledge sharing for rebuilding and strengthening government institutions. In: Proceedings of the IASTED International Conference on Web-Based Education, pp. 866–871 (2013)

43. Giustiniano, L., Bolici, F.: Organizational trust in a networked world: analysis of the interplay between social factors and information and communication technology. J. Inf. Commun. Ethics Soc. **10**(3), 187–202 (2012)
44. Bolici, F., Giustiniano, L.: Design science and eTrust: designing organizational artifacts as nexus of social and technical interactions. In: Spagnoletti, P. (ed.) Organizational Change and Information Systems, pp. 177–190. Springer, Heidelberg (2013)

Towards a Conceptual Framework for Classifying Visualisations of Data from Urban Mobility Services

Thiago Sobral[✉], Teresa Galvão Dias, and José Luís Borges

FEUP – Faculdade de Engenharia da Universidade do Porto,
Rua Dr. Roberto Frias, 4200-465 Porto, Portugal
{thiago,tgalvao,jlborges}@fe.up.pt

Abstract. Urban mobility services generate massive amounts of raw data that are usually not explored in depth by the entities that own them. Visualisation techniques could improve knowledge extraction and decision-making, as well as support the reengineering of those services. Some studies in Information Visualisation provide a domain-independent classification for visualisations based on their own characteristics and the data they support, although independent of their context of use. We propose a classification for visualisations of urban mobility data according to their context of use and their characteristics. Our first results are encouraging and are supported by a user-centred design process carried with urban mobility experts, in which we developed and evaluated a set of visualisation prototypes. The conclusions form a first effort towards a conceptual framework proposal for classifying visualisations of this domain, and are expected to guide researchers and practitioners searching for adequate ways to visually represent their data.

Keywords: Information visualisation · Urban mobility services · Big data · Intelligent transport systems · User-centred design

1 Introduction

Mobility levels increased notoriously in urban areas over the last decades, driven by economic and political changes. It is forecast that 6.3 billion people will live in urban areas by 2050, which sum up to 70 % of the world population [1]. Factors such as lifestyle, longer life expectancy and migration have direct impact on urban mobility behaviour and urban infrastructure demands, including public transport. Authorities and transport entities should identify mobility trends periodically, analyse and (re) shape their operations based on those changes. These attitudes can lead to an increase on citizens' perception of service quality, competitive advantage to transport services through reengineering and innovation opportunities on urban mobility.

Intelligent Transport Systems (ITS) have been one of the approaches for improving transport, integrating Information and Communication Technologies (ICT) into transport infrastructure. ITS allow retrieving data such as travel behaviour, ticketing and traffic flows, which is made possible by telematics, electronic ticketing, travel information systems and traffic sensors. Through the lens of Big Data, those data sources are powerful for understanding the dynamics of urban mobility in cities.

Likewise, the continuous evolution of Information Visualisation brings new techniques for representing data from large datasets, and has been applied to diverse areas. The variety of techniques and tools allows the continuous development of creative and scalable ways of visualising data. Nonetheless, the richness of technological features does not necessarily waive understanding the domain of application and the users who will take benefit from visualisations.

Notwithstanding that Information Visualisation is considered 'user-centric', current research is still scarce in providing examples of thorough approaches that involve users actively during the design process. Most studies found on literature do not seem to emphasise evaluation with potential users or do not perform evaluations at all. This puts to question how adequate those techniques actually are, from the users' perspective, as they cannot benefit from flawed, context-inadequate visualisations.

Also, authorities and transport services typically do not explore the data they own at its full extent, missing a potential opportunity to understand the dynamics of a city, which could impact activities such as service quality evaluation and decision-making.

The aforementioned scenario motivates this research, which consists on a first effort for classifying visualisations of data from urban mobility services. This classification considers data characteristics and the context of use on the routines of urban mobility experts. We developed a set of visualisation prototypes by running a thorough user-centred process with continuous evaluation with those experts. We consider that our classification proposal moves towards the development of a conceptual framework for classifying visualisations for the urban mobility domain.

The contributions found herein are expected to assist researchers and practitioners in finding visualisation techniques that properly fit their data and context of use. Moreover, they are expected to highlight the need of involving target users in order to reinforce the adequacy of visualisations.

2 Theoretical Background

2.1 Information Visualisation

Information Visualisation is a recent yet wide multi-disciplinary field that has been gaining attention from researchers and practitioners. It comprises fields such as Computer Science, Human-Computer Interaction, Design and Cognitive Psychology.

One of the first definitions of Information Visualisation regards it as "the use of computer-supported interactive visual representations of abstract data to amplify cognition" [2]. Despite the diversity of applications inside itself, it is a consensus that visualisation techniques can help informing and improving analysis and decision-making. Furthermore, some authors emphasize that Information Visualisation does not rely solely on computer graphics, but it is the connection to data that is crucial [3].

Visualisation techniques and tools abound, but it is still possible to identify lack of engagement of researchers with the users that will benefit from them. In fact, visualisation tools are useless if users cannot effectively interact with them, thus naturally compromising the processes of knowledge extraction and decision-making.

A study by Ellis and Dix – one of the few on evaluation for Information Visualisation so far – supports this statement: after analysing 65 papers describing new visualisations, it finds that only 12 of them engaged users on evaluation processes [4]. The effectiveness of the evaluation is also questioned, given that a small amount of studies that implemented evaluation as part of the development process are somewhat problematic. Also, the inherent nature of visualisation makes evaluation a complicated process. Again, the authors indicate factors that contribute to making evaluation in Information Visualisation a hard process:

1. *Variety of datasets:* despite some earlier efforts in creating a standard for datasets, datasets are heterogeneous. This fact might harden the evaluation process, as it might limit the availability and quality of data to be visualised.
2. *Indeterminacy of tasks:* the tasks to be performed during the evaluation process are usually more structured, which differs from the ones to be performed in "real life" that are more exploratory; these ones are harder to replicate in an experiment.
3. *Participants in context:* depending on the complexity of the application context, participants need to have a clear understanding of the problem that the visualisations are trying to solve. Some authors suggest that it is possible to obtain better information by involving domain or usability experts, even though it is typically harder to have access to those people [5, 6].

2.2 User-Centred Design

The term User-Centred Design was introduced by Norman and Draper [7] and has been widely acknowledged by researchers and practitioners. Moreover, other equivalent terms exist, such as Usability Engineering and Human Centred-Design. Despite the variety of equivalent terms and their acceptability, there is a lack of agreement upon a common definition of UCD. Several definitions were proposed throughout time. This lack of agreement has generated efforts in order to propose a definition and a set of guiding principles for the UCD process [8]. Still, most of those principles are based on usability principles found in earlier literature [9]:

- *Early focus on users and tasks:* designers must understand the users that will take benefit from a system.
- *Empirical measurement:* users should manipulate simulations and prototypes, and their performance and reactions should be observed, recorded and analysed.
- *Iterative design:* there is a need of having a design cycle, driven by the problems that are found during empirical measurement.

3 Related Work

The involvement of users during the design process of visualisations is well acknowledged by researchers. Studies on visualisation have mostly been technology-driven. Now, it is possible to identify a shift towards user-centred approaches in diverse contexts such as epidemiology, hydrography and crime-spotting visualisations [10–12].

Urban mobility data is typically collected from systems such as Global Positioning System (GPS) or telematics systems such as Automatic Vehicle Location (AVL) and Automatic Passenger Count (APC). There are uncountable examples of visualisations of this kind available online. Some of them resemble more of interesting technological experiments than systematic approaches with actual intentions of collaborating with knowledge extraction. It is also possible to find advances in the development of visualisations that use data from ITS [13–16].

Some studies provide a general, context-independent classification for visualisations based on their own characteristics [17, 18]. We consider that providing a context-specific classification framework could benefit researchers and practitioners when deciding which visualisations would best fit their needs, depending on the type of data they own and the activities to be supported. To the best of our knowledge, there are still no approaches on this direction for the urban mobility domain.

4 Research Materials and Methodology

Our methodology consisted of two phases: the analysis of urban mobility datasets and a user-centred process for developing visualisations. The analysis of urban mobility datasets consisted of two activities: (1) exploration of datasets, which identified the data primitives they contained and the inherent issues that arise when manipulating raw data; (2) a formal data characterisation, in order to understand how data should be regarded within each visualisation. Finally, the UCD process took advantage of the results of the first phase for the development of visualisation prototypes and continuous evaluation with experts. The outcomes from both phases were used for providing a classification for our prototypes.

We collected three datasets from different sources. The first contained users' requests from Move-me,[1] a mobile application that provides real-time information about public transport in Portugal [19]. The second contained bus-ticketing data from Sociedade de Transportes Coletivos do Porto S.A. (STCP). The latter contained readings from traffic counter sensors for a set of streets from Porto. Data primitives were conceptually tied to a date, time and location. Depending on the data primitive, it was necessary to translate the conceptual locations (e.g. "Airport") into geographical coordinates, which is commonly regarded as geocoding. Finally, raw data were further ported to a Database Management System (DBMS).

4.1 Analysis of Datasets

Exploration of Datasets. The exploration phase analysed the contents of each dataset, in order to identify which data primitives they contained, their data type and format. The heterogeneity of datasets creates technological constraints that should be identified prior to the design stage, so as to prevent drawbacks. Most of these constraints were

---

[1] Website: http://move-me.mobi.

related to the format of data primitives (e.g. special characters at a string, XML data), which required intervention prior to parsing them to a DBMS. Four questions guided this exploration:

- What is the nature of each dataset?
- What is the meaning of each entry (row) in each dataset?
- Which attributes (columns) are relevant as inputs for our visualisations?
- Do the relevant attributes require prior adaptation before using them as inputs for our visualisations?

Data Characterisation. In order to provide a formal characterisation of data, this research considered the pyramid framework proposed by Mennis et al., which defines three perspectives for data: location (where is it?), time (when is it?) and theme (what is it made of?) [17, 20]. These perspectives form the data component, which can be regarded as un-interpreted observational data. The derived knowledge from those perspectives forms the knowledge component, regarded as a semantic object: a conceptual entity.

4.2 The User-Centred Design Process for Developing Visualisations

We adapted the UCD methodology proposed by Lian Chee et al. to fit our purposes [21]. This choice enforces the commitment of involving potential users throughout all phases and acknowledges rapid prototyping in order to foster feedback and to overcome time constraints. Prototyping could be performed anytime, even if not all specifications or requirements were gathered.

The aforementioned adaptation included a preliminary phase that consisted in selecting 10 experts in urban mobility interested in participating in this UCD process. They belong to transport companies, government authorities, a company specialised in transport planning solutions and university. Implementation and Debugging phases did not happen, as the objective did not consist in developing a complete system for data visualisation. Prototyping and evaluation were the core of this research.

We conducted semi-structured interviews with experts for evaluating visualisations and retrieving feedback and ideas. Most of the sessions with experts took place at their working environments. We also wanted that experts could actually interact with visualisations by zooming, querying details on demand or filtering data according to pre-defined parameters. This naturally implied the risk of investing significant time in prototyping complex visualisations that could be of no practical use by urban mobility experts if they were not satisfied with them.

We initially classified visualisations into two frames or reference: geographic and abstract (non map-based). Geographic visualisations were built with Google Maps and Earth API[2]; Abstract visualisations were built with HTML5 and D3[3].

---

[2] Website: https://developers.google.com/.
[3] Website: http://d3js.org.

5 Analysis of Datasets

Move-me Dataset. Move-me is a mobile application that intends to improve the quality and access of information about public transport (Fig. 1). It is capable of providing the location of the companies' fleet in real time. The current available types of information are:

- *Next departures:* provides the next bus/train/metro departures for a specific stop selected by the user.
- *Route finder:* for a given origin and destination selected by the user, it provides a sequence of bus/train/metro routes that should be taken.
- *Near stops:* provides the nearby stops based on the location provided by the user (assisted by the user's mobile phone GPS).

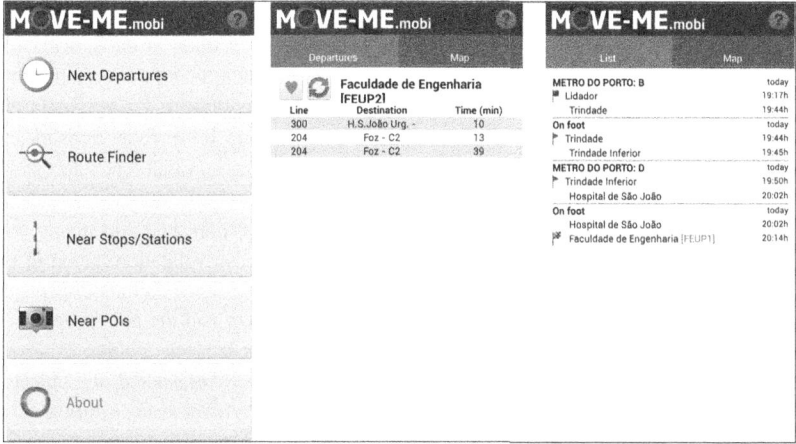

Fig. 1. Move-me interface (main screen, next departures and route planner)

STCP Dataset. The electronic bus ticketing system used by STCP consists of contactless travel cards named Andante and validating machines installed on all buses. An Andante card has a unique serial number. Whenever a passenger boards a bus, he/she must validate the ticket by moving it closer to the validating machine.

Traffic Counter Sensors Dataset. The Porto City Hall installed traffic counter sensors in streets in order to keep track of the number of vehicles for further analysis and studies. The sensor sends the count to a central computer periodically. By the end of the day, the software responsible for receiving the sensor counts gathers the data into a plain text file.

The pyramid framework allowed us to formalise data characterisation for those datasets (see Table 1), from which we derived the conceptual object.

The exploration of datasets and data characterisation also allowed identifying that the data primitives from the three different datasets share structural characteristics in

Table 1. Data characterisation for the various datasets

Dataset	Aspect	Description
Move-me dataset	Theme	Information request about the public transport network
	Location	*Near Stops service*: consists of all possible coordinates in Porto, thus suggesting a continuous spatial domain *Next Departures service*: consists of a discrete spatial domain $[s_1,...s_n]$ of all bus/metro/train stops in Porto *Route Planner service*: consists of origin-destination pair, which are labelled with an address or stop name. Again, this suggests a continuous location domain
	Time	The instant when the request was made. For simplicity, we assume that the request time and travel intention time are equal
	Object	Travel intention within the public transport network, which can be summarised as (1) *an intention to use the nearest public transport available within an area* (Near Stops); (2) *an intention to be informed about the next departures from a given location in the network* (Next departures); (3) *an intention to know the different ways of traveling between two points of Porto* (Route plan)
STCP Dataset	Theme	Ticket validations on the STCP bus route network
	Location	Discrete spatial domain $[s_1,...s_n]$ of all STCP bus stops in Porto
	Time	The time perspective can be branched into two components, given that each validation is tied to two time perspectives: the *time when the passenger validated the Andante card* and the *time in which the bus trip started (from the terminus point)*
	Object	If the first time perspective is considered, the object can be interpreted as a *single travel event within the transportation network*. The second time perspective allows interpreting an object as *all travel events that happened on a certain bus trip*
Traffic Counter Sensors Dataset	Theme	Count of vehicles detected by a sensor
	Location	Consists of a discrete set $[l_1,...l_n]$ of locations for each sensor. Each sensor belongs to a pre-defined city zone.
	Time	One of the possible 288 5-min intervals for each day (24 h)
	Object	Traffic flow on a specific street during a 5-minute interval

terms of *spatial domain* and *weight* (see Table 2). It follows that they could, at first, be compatible with the same visualisations, at a technical level. However, this would not imply they are adequate to represent that data from the experts' point of view, thus requiring further evaluation. A visualisation might not suit two different data types if there are substantial differences at the conceptual (theme) level.

We define *spatial domain* as the set of possible locations that a data unit can be associated with. For example, a data unit from a Move-me request for near stops can be tied to any geographic location, as this information is directly retrieved through GPS. By establishing an analogy with mathematical numeric intervals, we can infer that the spatial domain for this data unit is essentially *continuous*, considering the precision of GPS systems.

On the other hand, for example, a data unit from a Move-me request for next departures is tied to a discrete set of stops that are previously determined by transport authorities, where each stop is tied to a unique geographic location. This allows us to infer that the spatial domain for this data unity is *discrete*.

Finally, a data unit can be associated with a spatial domain consisting of origin and destination points, as well as intermediate passing points, which resemble the concept of a graph. This naturally implies the concept of direction. We classify this type of spatial domain as a *vector*.

We define *weight* as the magnitude (a scalar quantity) of a geographic location, i.e. a stop or passengers' location. For example, the concept of weight can be used to suggest that locations with higher magnitude have increased demand.

Table 2. Classification of structural similarities between data primitives

Spatial domain	Discrete
	Continuous
	Vector
Weight	Weighted
	Non-weighted

6 Results

The outcomes from the analysis of datasets and the user-centred design process led to 10 visualisation prototypes, from which we selected 5 for presenting in this paper. The remaining are available in [22].

Clustered Markers. This visualisation groups data units into clusters according to the zoom level that is applied. The goal was to reduce visual clutter and to provide a colour coding based on a heat scale. When zooming into an area, clusters unfold into smaller clusters. We coupled the prototype with data from Move-me's Near Stops service, which belongs to a continuous spatial domain. Each cluster consists of a collection of requests for nearby stops made by citizens for a set of locations. Areas with hotter colours suggest higher flows of potential passengers at that area looking for a stop to start their trip within the transport network. Figure 2 shows a high demand around Casa da Música, with 183 requests for near stops at surrounding locations during a specific weekday.

Experts considered that Clustered Markers are adequate for representing and analysing trends at lower zoom levels (city neighbourhoods). Also, they stated that the clustering characteristic would only fit data from *travel intentions* that belong to a *continuous spatial domain*. The fact of having unfolding clusters at higher zoom levels turns unsuitable to analyse trends in specific streets. Experts emphasised the significance of this visualisation for supporting operational and strategic decisions.

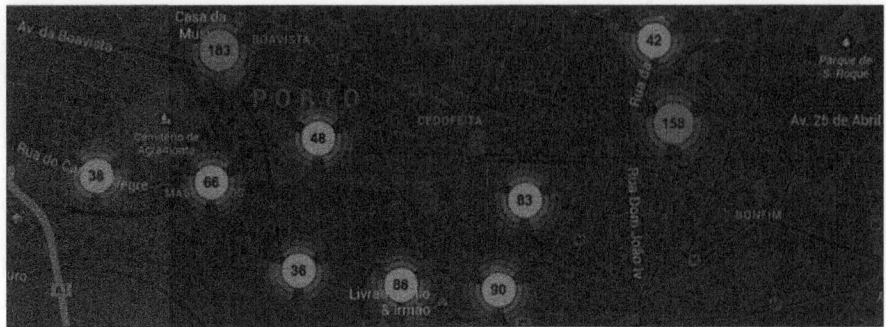

Fig. 2. Clustered markers focusing on downtown city zone

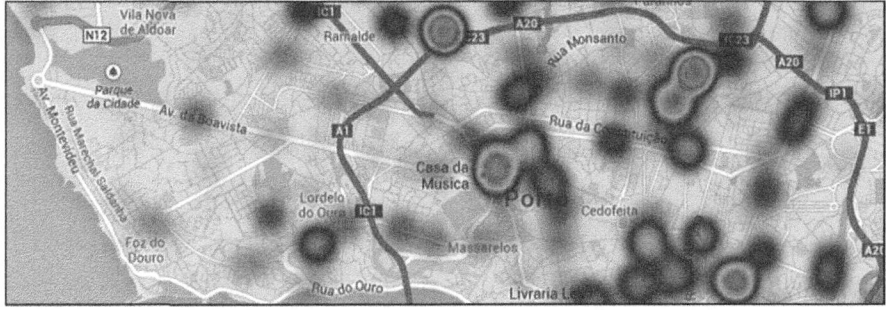

Fig. 3. Heat map for near stops requests for a given day in Porto

Heat Maps. In this visualisation, hotter colours indicate areas with higher concentration of (potential) passengers. In Fig. 3, we used data from Move-me's Near Stops service.

If data consists of a small discrete set of sparse locations, as in the case of data from Next Departures service, heat maps might not be equally effective, except in cases of unusual occurrences as shown in Fig. 4, during St. John's Night in Porto.

Fig. 4. Heat map for next departures requests on St. John's Night 2013 in Porto downtown

Heat maps were considered a powerful and straightforward way of analysing density of weighted or non-weighted spatiotemporal data, both at the level of the entire city (lower zoom levels) and at the level of a specific zone (higher zoom levels). However, experts stated that heat maps are more effective if data belongs to a continuous or non-sparse discrete spatial domain, as in the case of Move-me's Near Stops service and traffic sensors data respectively. Experts believe that this visualisation might be significant for strategic analysis given its easy readability.

Sized Circles. This visualisation tackles the limitation of heat maps for data with a discrete spatial domain, as reported by experts. Each data unit is represented as a circle with a radius that depends on a certain parameter, here referred as weight. In this example, the coordinates of a stop determine a circle's centre. The weight is the total number of information requests for next departures made by users through Move-me. Hence, larger circles suggest stops with higher demand. Circles are colour-coded and represent different transport providers. Figure 5 depicts Porto during St. John's Night.

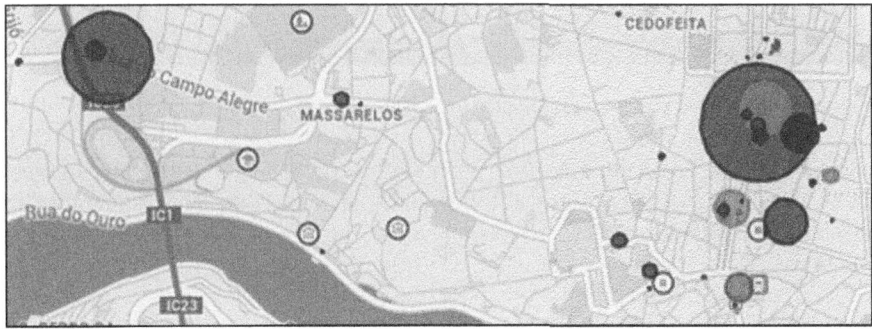

Fig. 5. Sized circles for Next Departure requests at St. John's Night 2013

In Fig. 6, Sized Circles are used to visualise the historical evolution of the Annual Average Daily Traffic (AADT) for a set of traffic counter sensors installed in Porto, in the period between 2010 and 2013. The visualisation draws circles centred at each sensor's location. A circle's radius is defined by the absolute AADT variation in relation to the previous year, represented as $r = |AADT_{year} - AADT_{year-1}|$. The algebraic sign of variation is depicted as colour. Positive AADT variations (increase in traffic flow in relation to the previous year) are represented in red. Negative variations are represented in blue. The label for each circle indicates the sensor tag and ID. Sized circles were considered suitable for analysing weighted data within a discrete spatial domain regardless of sparseness. The depiction of magnitude as size was considered adequate for analysis at strategic levels. When combined with other visualisation techniques that provide detailed information, such as the line plot, it was found that it turns into a suitable tool for analysis at operational levels.

Radial Heat Charts. This visualisation aggregates data on a cyclic pattern, such as ticket validations and travel intentions from a specific stop, and might better support

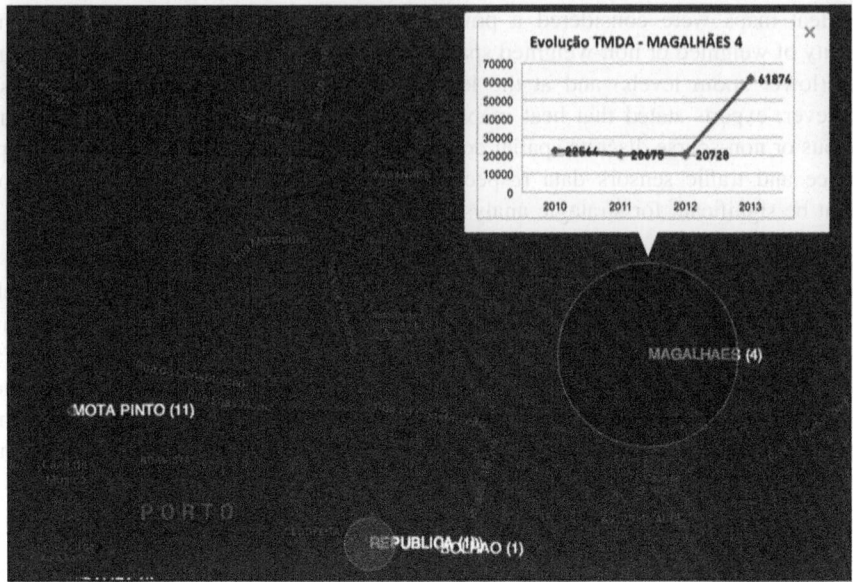

Fig. 6. Sized Circles and line plot for AADT data of a traffic counter sensor

pattern detection. The natural reading order (left to right) might cause false interpretations when using visualisations that follow linear layouts. Users tend to minimise eye movements; if graphic artefacts are spatially close, the sampling cost could be reduced [23, 24].

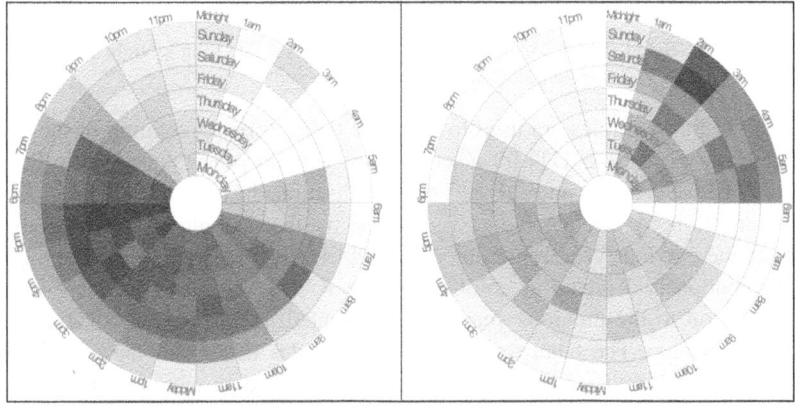

Fig. 7. Radial heat chart of ticketing data for two bus stops

Figure 7 represents bus-ticketing data for two bus stops. Each ring represents a day of the week, and each circular sector represents a day hour. It is noticeable that the station on the left has higher demand during work hours, whereas the one on the right has higher demand during late night hours, especially on Saturdays between 1-2 a.m.

Experts considered radial heat chart a powerful visualisation for ticketing data that could help analysing seasonality in stops, and it might play a crucial role when supporting decisions involving changes in bus lines. However, this visualisation might not be equally meaningful when considering travel intentions, as experts believe this type of data might not be sufficient for week-to-week analysis.

Radial Layout. This visualisation depicts travel intentions (route plans) between origin-destination pairs. Instead of representing stops according to their geographic location, they are organised into chords proportional to the number of requests that involve them. Chords represent travel intentions between two stops. Here, their weights vary according to the number of requests made through Move-me. Colours are randomly assigned to stops, and a chord's colour is mapped to the colour of the destination stop. Figure 8 shows all travel intentions for Metro do Porto network on November 2010. A filtering hides segments that did not have significant amount of travel intentions.

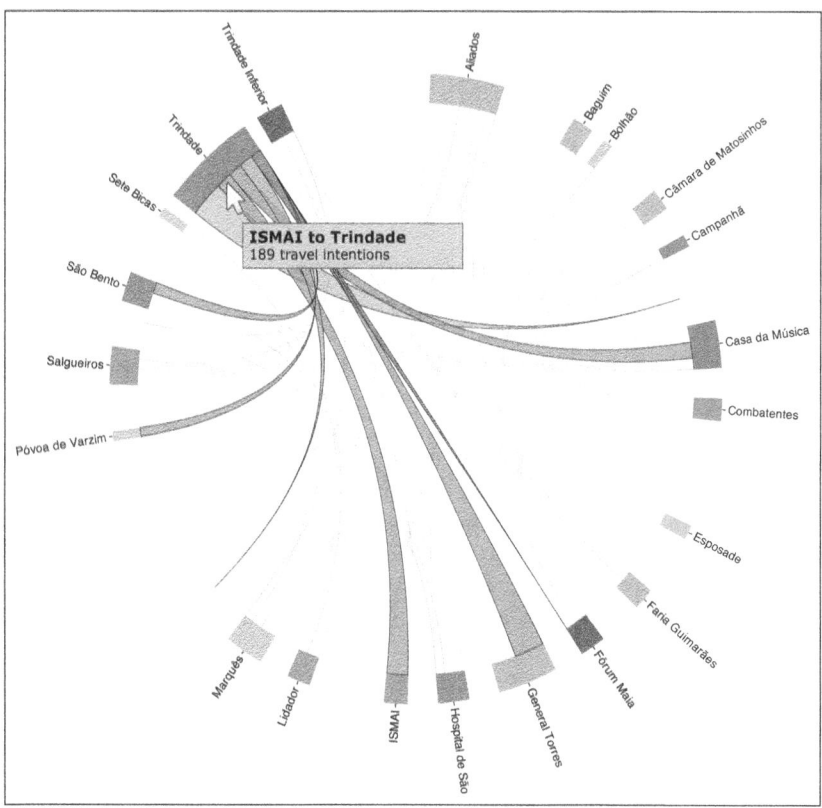

Fig. 8. Radial Layout with focus on a specific chord

Table 3. Classification of visualisation techniques

Visualisation	Frame of reference		Type of urban mobility data			Spatial domain			Weight		Context of use	
	Geographic	Abstract	Travel intentions	Travel events	Traffic flows	Discrete	Continuous	Vector	Weighted	Non-weighted	Strategic	Operational
Clustered markers	●		●			●				●		●
Heat map	●		●	●	●	●	●		●	●	●	
Sized circles	●		●	●	●	●			●		●	●
Radial heat chart		●		●		●			●		●	●
Radial layout		●	●	●				●	●			●

Experts considered this visualisation a powerful tool for representing data belonging to a *vector spatial domain,* both from *travel intentions* or *events*. It was also considered a complex visualisation, which could be of better use for operational levels rather than strategic levels of transport related services and government authorities. They highlighted that it was a creative and functional way of representing data that is strongly connected to geographic visualisations, and usually thought as the only way to depict those data.

7 Conclusions and Evolution Perspectives

The analysis of datasets and the UCD process led to the classification of the visualisation techniques according to the *type of urban mobility data* that adequately fit them, *frame of reference, spatial domain, weight* and *context of use* (see Table 3).

Having such classification at hand, we believe that the problem of finding the adequate visualisation for representing a specific type of urban mobility data for a certain context of use is facilitated significantly, such as analysis of trends in urban mobility throughout time (e.g. detecting lines or stops that could be decommissioned/created; detecting the increase/decay in traffic flow on specific locations throughout time); collaboration with urban researches (e.g. identifying areas or lines/stops that may be more valuable for marketing purposes or traffic signaling); support decisions in traffic/route deviations.

From the data perspective, most of the proposed visualisations focus on the "stop" level of the transportation network, meaning that they have stops as the core element for analysis. Other perspectives such as "line" and "vehicle" level are also fundamental and should be regarded in the future, as they pose additional complexity and new challenges for finding adequate ways for visually representing data. Although we consider the distinction between strategic and operational contexts meaningful, a more thorough understanding about these terms is needed. This could be achieved by carrying a deeper context of use analysis during the UCD process.

References

1. United Nations: World Urbanization Prospects - The 2011 Revision. United Nations (2012)
2. Shneiderman, B., Mackinlay, J.D., Card, S.K. (eds.): Readings in Information Visualization: Using Vision to Think. Morgan Kaufmann Publishers Inc., San Francisco (1999)
3. Ward, M., Grinstein, G., Keim, D.: Interactive Data Visualization: Foundations, Techniques, and Applications. A. K. Peters, Ltd., Natick (2010)
4. Ellis, G., Dix, A.: An explorative analysis of user evaluation studies in information visualisation. In: Proceedings of the 2006 AVI Workshop, pp. 1–7. ACM, Venice (2006)
5. Christopher, R.K., Healey, C.G., Interrante, V., Laidlaw, D.H., Ware, C.: Thoughts on user studies: why, how, and when. IEEE Comput. Graph. Appl. **23**, 2003 (2003)
6. Tory, M., Moller, T.: Evaluating visualizations: do expert reviews work? IEEE Comput. Graph. Appl. **25**, 8–11 (2005)
7. Norman, D.A., Draper, S.W.: User Centered System Design; New Perspectives on Human-Computer Interaction. L. Erlbaum Associates Inc, Hillsdale (1986)
8. Gulliksen, J., Göransson, B., Boivie, I., Persson, J., Blomkvist, S., Cajander, Å.: Key principles for user-centred systems design. In: Seffah, A., Gulliksen, J., Desmarais, M. (eds.) Human-Centered Software Engineering — Integrating Usability in the Software Development Lifecycle, vol. 8, pp. 17–36. Springer, Netherlands (2005)
9. Gould, J.D., Lewis, C.: Designing for usability: key principles and what designers think. Commun. ACM **28**, 300–311 (1985)
10. Slocum, T.A., Cliburn, D.C., Feddema, J.J., Miller, J.R.: Evaluating the usability of a tool for visualizing the uncertainty of the future global water balance. Cartography Geogr. Inf. Sci. **30**, 299–317 (2003)
11. Robinson, A.C., Chen, J., Lengerich, E.J., Meyer, H.G., Maceachren, A.M.: Combining usability techniques to design geovisualization tools for epidemiology. Inf. Sci. **32**, 243–255 (2005)
12. Roth, R.E., Ross, K.S., Finch, B.G., Luo, W., MacEachren, A.M.: A user-centered approach for designing and developing spatiotemporal crime analysis tools, Zurich, Switzerland (2010)
13. Polisciuc, E., Alves, A., Bento, C., Machado, P.: Visualizing urban mobility. In: Special Interest Group on Computer Graphics and Interactive Techniques Conference, p. 115 (2013)
14. Du, F., Brulé, J., Enns, P., Manjunatha, V., Segev, Y.: MetroViz: Visual Analysis of Public Transportation Data (2013)
15. Sagl, G., Loidl, M., Beinat, E.: A visual analytics approach for extracting spatio-temporal urban mobility information from mobile network traffic. ISPRS Int. J. Geo-Inf. **1**, 256–271 (2012)
16. Hong Thi, N., Chi Kim Thi, D., Tha Thi, B., Phuoc Vinh, T.: Visualization of spatio-temporal data of bus trips. In: 2012 International Conference on Control, Automation and Information Sciences (ICCAIS), pp. 392–397 (2012)
17. Aigner, W., Miksch, S., Schumann, H., Tominski, C.: Visualization of Time-Oriented Data. Springer, London (2011)
18. Wehrend, S., Lewis, C.: A problem-oriented classification of visualization techniques. In: Proceedings of the First IEEE Conference on Visualization, Visualization 1990, pp. 139–143, 469 (1990)
19. Cunha, J.F., Galvão, T.: State of the art and future perspectives for smart support services for public transport. In: Borangiu, T., Trentesaux, D., Thomas, A. (eds.) Service Orientation in Holonic and Multi-agent Manufacturing. SCI, vol. 544, pp. 225–234. Springer, Heidelberg (2014)

20. Mennis, J.L., Peuquet, D.J., Qian, L.: A conceptual framework for incorporating cognitive principles into geographical database representation. Int. J. Geogr. Inf. Sci. **14**, 501–520 (2000)
21. Lian Chee, K., Slingsby, A., Dykes, J., Tin Seong, K.: Developing and applying a user-centered model for the design and implementation of information visualization tools. In: 2011 15th International Conference on Information Visualisation (IV), pp. 90–95 (2011)
22. Sobral, T.: Developing Visualisations for Urban Mobility Data: A User-Centred Approach. Master Thesis. Faculty of Engineering of the University of Porto (2014)
23. Keim, D.A., Mansmann, F., Schneidewind, J., Schreck, T.: Monitoring network traffic with radial traffic analyzer. In: 2006 IEEE Symposium on Visual Analytics Science and Technology, pp. 123–128 (2006)
24. Ware, C.: Information Visualization: Perception for Design. Morgan Kaufmann Inc., San Francisco (2004)

Agent Based Simulation of Trust Dynamics in Dependence Networks

Stefano Za[1,2,3,4](✉), Francesca Marzo[1,2,3,4], Marco De Marco[1,2,3,4], and Maurizio Cavallari[1,2,3,4]

[1] eCampus University, Novedrate, CO, Italy
stefano.za@uniecampus.it
[2] LUISS Guido Carli University, Rome, Italy
fmarzo@luiss.it
[3] Uninettuno University, Rome, Italy
marco.demarco@uninettunounversity.net
[4] Dipartimento S.E.Gest.A., Università Cattolica del Sacro Cuore,
Via Necchi 5, Milan, Italy
maurizio.cavallari@unicatt.it

Abstract. Online communities can be seen as service systems, in which actors interact providing, requesting or sharing resources for [co-]creating value. On the basis of the resources needed/owned for achieving a goal it is possible to draw several dependence links among the actors (agents), creating a dependence network. On the other hand, since trust is the key coordinating mechanism in community based organizations, by analyzing the dynamics of trust in dependence networks is possible to better understand the behavior of this kind of service system, viewed as a complex social systems. In this paper we develop an architecture of cognitive agents and of the environment in which they act and interact. This architecture will be the basis for implementing a platform for agent based simulation that serves as a tool for investigating the dynamics of information sharing, collaboration, and collective action within different service systems.

Keywords: Social networks · Communities · Dependence networks · Cognitive agents · Multi-agent simulation

1 Introduction

Service systems are defined as dynamic, value co-creation configurations of resources (people, technology, organizations, and shared information) [1]. In literature it is possible to find several ways in which the components of a service systems are expressed [2]. In this paper we adopt the definition provided by Kim and Nam [2] looking at the components of a service system defined as "value activity network, resource integrator network, and capability network", where:

- Value Activity Network (VAN) represents the set of customers' and suppliers' activities; the goal of their interactions is to provide a set of solutions to customers for solving their problems.

- Resource Integrator Network (RIN) has as primary role to provide and organize resources for each participants, in order to support the value creation activities; it represents several actors with their roles in the value creation process, such as customers, service providers, customer communities, suppliers.
- Capability Network (CN) consists of the capabilities and resources (physical and not) that could exist inside or outside the resource integrator network but needed to enable the value creation process.

On the basis of these assumption, an online community (focus of our study) can be seen as a service system, in which: (i) the VAN is formed by all the actors' interactions happened in the online community; (ii) the RIN is represented by the actors and their roles as customers, suppliers or both (on the basis of the position in the value chain), and (iii) the CN consists of a variety of resources such as tools (operand resources) and skills and knowledge (operant resources) which are owned by service providers and/or customers.

The availability of Information Infrastructures such as Internet and more recent social network sites has provided the ground for the emergence of many forms of online communities [3]. In such environments individuals can interact both within and across organizational boundaries with different purposes such as for instance working in global distributed teams [4], developing open source software [5], participating in political decisions [6, 7], crowdsourcing [8], exchanging resources with community members [9].

The main sources for investigating governance structures that characterize this virtual world refer to the work of Shirky [10] and the work of Demil and Lecocq [11]. The latter work deals with a specific activity: the development of open source software as a particular form of peer production process whose governance structure has been called bazaar. Bazaars are characterized by self-organizing, rather than by authority, as in the case of the hierarchy, or by prices, as in the case of the market. According with Shirky, virtual world is populated not only by collaboration forms (i.e. bazaars), but also by information sharing forms and collective action forms. While trust has been recognized as the key coordinating mechanism in community based institutions [12], the micro-foundations of trust in online communities still need further investigation for better understanding social networks' behavior [13].

Drawing on complex adaptive systems theory, we recognize that social phenomena emerge from the bottom-up interactions among learning agents in a given environment [14]. This view has recently gained much attention in different fields of management and organization studies [15–18] and integrate contributions from cybernetics, cognitive sciences, decision and organization sciences [19, 20]. With these assumptions information sharing, collaboration, and collective action are seen as new governance forms emerging in online networked environments for handling the complexity of social exchanges. Like other institutions, such as markets, hierarchies, clans and fiefs, these are transactional structures of data-processing agents that are contingent to the type of complexity that must be handled [21].

In this paper we present an agent based model for simulating the dynamics of interacting agents whose behavior is determined by their learning capability and by a set of environmental rules. The model is grounded on the theory of trust and dependence networks [22–24] and provides a tool for studying emergent properties/phenomena within social networks. Following previous works that introduce formal models of trust and dependence networks, we propose an architecture of cognitive agents and of the environment in which they act and interact. This architecture will be the basis for implementing a platform for agent based simulation that serves as a tool for investigating the dynamics of information sharing, collaboration, and collective action within social networks.

The paper is structured as follows. We first introduce the theoretical framework on which the model is grounded. Then we describe the architecture of cognitive agents and the environment. Finally we discuss about implications and research directions.

2 Trust and Dependence Networks

As pointed out by Castelfranchi et al. [22] dependency and trust are concepts strictly related with each other. From a cognitive point of view, trust is a complex object built on tasks, goals etc. and based on beliefs of different kinds (evaluations, expectations etc.), including dependence beliefs [25]. Therefore trust networks are basically connected with what is called dependence network.

The cognitive theory of dependence developed by Conte and Castelfranchi [26] includes two type of dependences: (1) the objective dependence, which says who needs who for what in a given society and (2) the believed dependence, which says who is believed to be needed by whom.

The model of dependence network proposed by Conte and Sichman [27] in order to supply a tool for improving coordination in multi-agent systems and used to build a simulation must then be integrated. By assuming that there exists an objective reality not necessarily known by agents as it is, we propose an updated model of dependence networks based on the evolution described in more recent works [24]. Therefore, the three basic notions of the first model, i.e. external description, dependence relationship and dependence situation, must be extended. In particular, while we build external descriptions and dependence relationships following the instruction presented in the previous model of dependence network we consider some additional features of dependence situations in order to classify them. Together with the nature (given by dependence relations) and the locality (considered by Conte and Sichman [28]), we add the distance between the locally believed dependence and the real dependence. In other terms, we extend the model by explicitly considering subjective and objective points of view in order to test how their distance influences agents behaviors in the networks. The cognitive model we used as theoretical framework takes into account both an objective dependence network, built on the real dependence relation between agents in the network, and multiple believed dependence networks (as many as the number of agents in the network) [29].

Furthermore, we introduce in the model the concept of trust, as a first step to start investigating what the dynamics of this complex object are. The importance of trust is in fact crucial to allow exchanges to happen: although agents can depend on each other and, then, need each other to reach their own goals, delegation is a choice that can be activated only when there is a trust relationship between agents (that become namely truster and trustee).

We can consider the model as made up by an environment exogenously given, characterized by different dependence relations, and a set of goal oriented agents autonomous in making decision but dependent by other agents to reach their own goal. Each agent has a level of trust towards the others that can be updated while interactions go on. On the basis of their locally believed dependence network (BDN), agents can proceed by trial and error in order to reach the goal (updating their own beliefs about the network in a process that can lead to reduce the divergence between it and the real environment and by developing trust relationships between each other). As for this first attempt, in order to make it as simple as possible, we tested only a single type of dependence relationships among the set defined in [27], namely the mutual one, which means that agents depend on some of the others in the network to reach a common goal. The idea is to test interactions more and more complex once the simulator described in the next section is built and operative.

3 The Architecture for Simulation

Each agent in the environment has her own representation of the reality on the basis of her beliefs. She knows well the actions and resources available to her, and she starts pursuing some goals, by combining actions and resources and/or asking some of them to other agents in the environment. In this way, she interacts with other agents either to perform an exchange of resources or to involve other agents in performing a specific action. The interaction is based on agent's own BDN, and it can be equal or different from the dependence network that really hold in the social environment agent acts in. After every interaction the agent can update her believed dependence network on the basis of the information exchanged. The interaction among agents happens every slot of time defined as rule of the environment (called round).

In this work, the agent decides to take into account the information stored in the working memory for updating her BDN, on the basis of the level of trust put on the respondent agent. The level of trust perceived by an agent about another one is based on the behavior of the latter. In the paragraph related to the agent's behavior we introduce a mechanism adopted by an agent to evaluate the level of trust put on the others. For now it is only related to the trustworthiness concept.

3.1 Agent Mind and Environment Configuration

Each agent has two kind of memories for storing several information, namely the Long Term Memory (LTM) and the Working Memory (WM). The former contains all information needed by agents to act (goals, actions, plans, resources, etc.), whereas the latter is used to know what an agent will do in the next round and also to store the information produced by the interactions in the environment. This last kind of information may also be useful to update in the LTM the Believed Dependence Network by the agent. In particular the LTM contains:

- a set of goals $G = \{g_1,...,g_n\}$;
- a set of plans $P = \{p_1,...,p_n\}$ where each p_i is the collection of actions to reach the goal g_i (each plan can be updated at runtime if needed);

- a set of possible actions Act = $\{a_1,\ldots,a_m\}$ where one or more resources are associated to each action
- a set of resources R = $\{r_1,\ldots,r_n\}$ owned by the agent
- a network dependence of the society built on the basis of agent's beliefs
- a set of rules (Rules for Updating - RU) with which the information present in the Working Memory can be considered reliable and useful for updating the believed dependence network and the RU themselves.

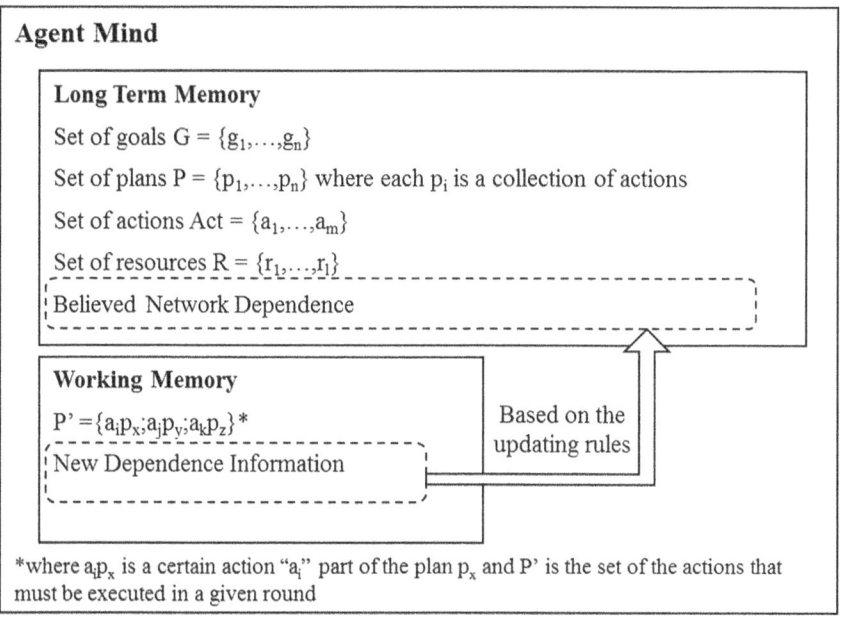

Fig. 1. The agent's mind

As regards the WM, it contains the step of the plan to execute, the stored information received (obtained during the interaction), and other practical information (e.g. the number of rounds awaiting for a certain response) (Fig. 1).

The acting of agents is driven not only by the information stored in their own LTM but also by the information or constraints inherited from the environment. The environment settings contains:

- the real dependence network (it can be unknown to all the agents)
- the set of priority rules for executing some actions (not necessarily they involve all possible actions, i.e. some actions are executable independently from others)
- the set of possible resources needed for executing an action (i.e. some actions require using certain resources)
- the information about the latency between one round and the next one (an arbitrary technical requirement, on which agent's consideration about others' answers must be calibrated).

3.2 A Simple Scenario

As a first step of our research, we consider a simplified scenario with the following assumptions:

- The Goal is the same for each agent: consuming resources following a given sequence; each agent can start from a different position in this sequence depending on the resources she has; she reaches the goal if the sequence is complete. Given the goal G = {R1, R2, R3, R4} if agent Ax has the set of resources R = {R3, R5, R3, R2, R4}, she combines her resources for reaching the longest sequence she can: R2, R3, and R4; then she must start looking for R1; once obtained R1 by another agent, she reaches the goal G (in this example it could be in five rounds, should she have received R1 in one interaction);
- The actions for each agent can be: Act = {consume a resource; ask for a resource to a given agent; give a resource to a given agent; ask for a resource through a broadcasting request}; for now we consider the only possibility for an agent to give the requested resource, when that resource is not needed by the owner (in which case it will be pre-allocated to be consumed by the latter in next rounds);
- Each agent can execute only one action in a given round;
- The number of resources owned by agents either is the same or it is higher than the number of resources for achieving the goal;
- The unique set of given priority rules is related to the sequence of resources to consume;
- Each agent has her own believed dependence network (on which she base her interactions);
- There is a unique updating rule: the new information collected in a certain round can update the believed dependence network on the basis of the subjective level of trust towards the respondent agent involved in the exchange, and it will be used in the next round.

3.3 The Agent Behavior

In this first work, we assume that Agents cannot mislead, giving wrong information (i.e. asking for a not needed resource, or not answering to a request). In future works we are planning to consider also misleading situations in order to simulate also either mutual and reciprocal trust relationships. In our simulation architecture, each agent can answer to a request more or less quickly on the basis of two parameters: the dependence level (DL) with the requester, and the number (N) of requests already performed by the same agent for the same resource.

Starting from the definition of dependence relationships in [28], the levels of dependence for two agents, Ax on Ay, are defined below from the lower to the higher.

- Total Independence (TI): Ax does not depend on Ay, and every agent from which Ax depends does not depend on Ay.
- Indirect Dependence (ID): Ax does not depend on Ay, and some agents from which Ax depends, also depend on Ay.

- Direct Dependence (DD): Ax depends on Ay and, every agent from which Ax depends, does not depend on Ay.
- Total Dependence (TD): Ax depends on Ay and, some agents from which Ax depends, also depend on Ay.

In the environment, a coefficient for measuring the degree of dependence is associated to each level. Furthermore it is also possible to introduce a gap between the coefficient of totally independence and the other one, emphasising the clear difference between the dependence relationships (strong or soft) and the complete independence (for example a possible set of value for each level can be: TI = 1, ID = 3, DD = 4 and TD = 5). Finally, the null value (0) is not considered as a coefficient for avoiding to block some requests forever.

Every time an agent receives a request (directly or in broadcast), she multiplies the coefficient of the dependence level (related to the requester) for the number of requests asked to her by the same agent for the same resource. The result of this multiplication is defined as "weight of the request" (W). In the environment it is possible to define a minimum level of W that forces agent's response.

With this architecture setting, agent's answer, and then the resource exchange, is performed more or less quickly on the basis of the believed dependence network (BDN) configuration. Moreover, during the simulation run, the BDN update can modify the perceived dependence relationships, changing previous behaviour of the same agent.

After every resource exchange, each agent stores those information on her own working memory and uses them for updating the BDN on the basis of trust levels about the respondent agent.

In this simulation architecture, the trust level (TL) is strongly related to the number of rounds (RN = Rounds Number) consumed for having a response: given agents Ax and Ay, Ax (truster) has a high trust level on Ay (trustee) as much faster is the Ay's response to the Ax's requests. Even though in this manner the trust level is mainly related to the trustworthiness concept (one of the aspects used to build the trust perception [25]), it is anyway close to what happens in the real cases in which trust is often related to the reliability for performing some tasks [25]. Moreover, if the trustee behaves in the same manner with a given requester, the requester (truster) increases also the level of trust towards her.

The value of TL is between 0 and 1, and initially it is set to 0 (zero) by each agent for all the agents in the BDN. The calculation of TL is described below and it is performed by an agent Ax for every known agents in her BDN when the simulation runs.

- When Ax asks a resource to another agent Ay, she counts the number of requests performed before obtaining that resource from Ay, calculating the RN.
- When Ax receives the resource from Ay, she sets her value of TL for Ay as $1/(RN-1)$ if the previous TL is already equal to $1/RN$ and $RN > 1$ (with $RN = 1$ we have already the maximum level of trust), otherwise $TL = 1/RN$.

For the broadcast requests, the calculation is quite similar: Ax counts the number of requests before obtaining a certain resource and uses it for assigning a TL to the respondent agent. With this definition, an agent Ax considers as a positive element both the decrease of RN and the constant value of TL evaluated in two consecutive exchanges.

Finally, an agent updates her BDN using information arisen by the resource exchanges in which the response is performed by an agent with a certain level of trust. This level can be fixed to a value between 0 and 1 as parameter for the simulation run.

4 Discussion and Conclusion

In this paper we presented a first and simplified version of an agent based model developed to study emerging behaviors of social networks, in which actors (agent) could play either the request (customers) and the provider (supplier) role. Following previous works that introduce formal models of trust and dependence networks, we developed an architecture of cognitive agents and of the environment in which they act and interact. This architecture will be the basis for implementing a platform for agent-based simulation that serves as a tool for investigating the dynamics of information sharing, collaboration, and collective action within online communities, seen as service systems. Thanks to this insight into social networks dynamics, then, we will be able to rich useful findings both in identifying regularities that characterize different service systems and in defining features for each specific system. Hence, it could be adopted for designing a digital platform to support a collaborative service environment [30].

Computational simulations are gaining an increasing attention for studying the behavior of complex social systems [19, 31–33]. Previous simulation models have mainly addressed the emergent states in virtual teams [34, 35]. Further works can extend the applicability of this research approach to community environments governed by trust mechanisms.

References

1. Maglio, P.P., Spohrer, J.: Fundamentals of service science. J. Acad. Mark. Sci. **36**, 18–20 (2007)
2. Kim, Y.J., Nam, K.: Service systems and service innovation: toward the theory of service systems. In: AMCIS 2009 Proceedings (2009)
3. Resca, A., Za, S., Spagnoletti, P.: Digital platforms as sources for organizational and strategic transformation: a case study of the midblue project. J. Theor. Appl. Electron. Commer. Res. **8**, 71–84 (2013)
4. Mattarelli, E., Bertolotti, F., Prencipe, A., Gupta, A.: Perceived modularity: A case study of a globally distributed team. In: Thirty Third International Conference on Information Systems, Orlando, 15–18 December 2012, pp. 1–14 (2012)
5. Spagnoletti, P., Federici, T.: Exploring the interplay between FLOSS adoption and organizational innovation. Commun. Assoc. Inf. Syst. **29**, 279–298 (2011)
6. Resca, A.: Constructing and implementing e-participation tools in the Emilia Romagna Region: assemblages and sense making. J. Balk. Near Est Stud. **13**, 67–92 (2011)

7. Ricciardi, F., Lombardi, P.: Widening the Disciplinary Scope of eParticipation. Reflections after a Research on Tourism and Cultural Heritage. In: Tambouris, E., Macintosh, A., Glassey, O. (eds.) ePart 2010. LNCS, vol. 6229, pp. 140–150. Springer, Heidelberg (2010)
8. Afuah, A., Tucci, C.: Crowdsourcing as a solution to distant search. Acad. Manag. Rev. **37**, 355–375 (2012)
9. Spagnoletti, P., Resca, A.: A Design theory for IT supporting online communities. In: Proceedings of the 45th Hawaii International Conference on System Sciences, pp. 4082–4091 (2012)
10. Shirky, C.: Here Comes Everybody: The Power of Organizing Without Organizations. Penguin Press, New York (2008)
11. Demil, B., Lecocq, X.: Neither market nor hierarchy nor network: the emergence of bazaar governance. Organ. Stud. **27**, 1447–1466 (2006)
12. Adler, P.S.: Market, hierarchy, and trust: the knowledge economy and the future of capitalism. Organ. Sci. **12**, 215–234 (2001)
13. Ricciardi, F., Rossignoli, C., Marco, D.M.: Participatory networks for place safety and livability: organisational success factors. Int. J. Netw. Virtual Organ. **13**, 42–65 (2013)
14. Holland, J.: Emergence: From Chaos to Order. Basic Books, New York (1998)
15. Lewin, A.Y.: Application of complexity theory to organization science. Organ. Sci. **10**, 215 (1999)
16. Allen, P.M., Varga, L.: A co-evolutionary complex systems perspective on information systems. J. Inf. Technol. **21**, 229–238 (2006)
17. Amaral, L.A.N., Uzzi, B.: Complex systems–a new paradigm for the integrative study of management, physical, and technological systems. Manage. Sci. **53**, 1033–1035 (2007)
18. Anderson, P.: Complexity theory and organization science. Organ. Sci. **10**, 216–232 (1999)
19. Simon, H.: The Sciences of the Artificial. MIT Press, Cambridge (1996)
20. Ricciardi, F.: Epistemology of information systems: time for something new? Positivism, interpretivism, and beyond. In: D'Atri, A., Saccà, D. (eds.) Information Systems: People, Organizations, Institutions, and Technologies, pp. 267–275. Physica-Verlag HD, Heidelberg (2010)
21. Boisot, M., Child, J.: Organizations as adaptive systems in complex environments: the case of China. Organ. Sci. **10**, 237–252 (1999)
22. Castelfranchi, C., Falcone, R., Marzo, F.: Being Trusted in a Social Network: Trust as Relational Capital. In: Stølen, K., Winsborough, W.H., Martinelli, F., Massacci, F. (eds.) iTrust 2006. LNCS, vol. 3986, pp. 19–32. Springer, Heidelberg (2006)
23. Marzo, F., Castelfranchi, C.: Trust as individual asset in a network: a cognitive analysis. In: Spagnoletti, P. (ed.) Organization Change and Information Systems. LNISO, vol. 2, pp. 167–175. Springer, Heidelberg (2013)
24. Conte, R., Sichman, J.S.: Dependence graphs: dependence within and between groups. Comput. Math. Organ. Theor. **8**, 87–112 (2002)
25. Castelfranchi, C., Falcone, R.: Trust Theory: A Socio-Cognitive and Computational Model. John Wiley & Sons Ltd., Chichester (2010)
26. Conte, R., Castelfranchi, C.: Simulating multi-agent interdependencies. a two-way approach to the micro-macro. In: Mueller, U., Troitzsch, K. (eds.) Microsimulation and the Social Science. Lecture Notes in Economics. Springer, Heidelberg (1996)
27. Conte, R., Sichman, J.S.: DEPNET: how to benefit from social dependence. J. Math. Sociol. **20**, 161–177 (1995)
28. Sichman, J., Conte, R.: Multi-agent dependence by dependence graphs. In: Proceedings of the First International Joint Conference on Autonomous Agents and Multiagent Systems: Part 1 (AAMAS 2002), pp. 483–490. ACM Press, New York (2002)

29. Marzo, F., Za, S., Spagnoletti, P.: Modeling dependence networks for agent based simulation of online and offline communities. In: Demazeau, Y., Ishida, T., Corchado, J.M., Bajo, J. (eds.) PAAMS 2013. LNCS, vol. 7879, pp. 192–203. Springer, Heidelberg (2013)
30. Spagnoletti, P., Za, S.: A design theory for e-Service environments: the interoperability challenge. In: Snene, M. (ed.) IESS 2012. LNBIP, vol. 103, pp. 201–211. Springer, Heidelberg (2012)
31. Davis, J.P., Eisenhardt, K.M., Bingham, C.B.: Developing theory through simulation methods. Acad. Manag. Rev. **32**, 480–499 (2007)
32. Za, S., Spagnoletti, P.: Knowledge creation processes in Information Systems and Management: lessons from simulation studies. In: Spagnoletti, P. (ed.) Organization Change and Information Systems. LNISO, vol. 2, pp. 191–204. Springer, Heidelberg (2013)
33. Spagnoletti, P., Za, S., Winter, R.: Exploring foundations for using simulations in IS research. In: Thirty Fourth International Conference on Information Systems, Milan (2013)
34. Rao, H., Chaudhury, A., Chakka, M.: Modeling team processes: Issues and a specific example. Inf. Syst. Res. **3**, 255–285 (1995)
35. Curşeu, P.L.: Emergent states in virtual teams: a complex adaptive systems perspective. J. Inf. Technol. **21**, 249–261 (2006)

Towards an IT-Based Coordination Platform for the German Emergency Medical Service System

Melanie Reuter-Oppermann[✉], Johannes Kunze von Bischhoffshausen, and Peter Hottum

Karlsruhe Service Research Institute (KSRI),
Karlsruhe Institute of Technology (KIT), Englerstraße 11,
76128 Karlsruhe, Germany
{Melanie.Reuter,Johannes.Kunze,Peter.Hottum}@kit.edu

Abstract. The German healthcare service system is facing a number of challenges in the years to come, prominent among these a decreasing number of hospitals and practices dealing with an increasing number of treatments and patient transportation tasks. In this paper, we introduce the idea of building a decision support tool to improve scheduling of patient transportation in the German Emergency Medical Service (EMS) system to reduce waiting times and costs, as well as increasing reliability. We outline a service platform on which the decision support tool could be realized and integrated with existing systems in EMS coordination centers. The paper thus introduces a promising approach for one of the main challenges of the German EMS system and builds the basis for further research on transport scheduling and healthcare services.

Keywords: IT-based platform · Patient transport · German EMS system · Healthcare logistics services

1 Introduction

The ageing population is one of the main challenges the German healthcare service system has to face in the upcoming years. While in 2000, 16.44 % of the German population was 65 years or older, it was already 20.63 % in 2010, and the number is expected to grow even faster in the future [23]. On the other hand, the number of hospitals has decreased by 7.94 % from 2,242 to 2,064 over the same time period [4]. Similar effects could be observed for outpatient health care facilities run by physicians: While in 2002 there were 96,169 practices, in 2011 there were only 85,759 available for patients [21] – a relative decrease by 10.82 %. This trend is also reflected in the development towards small, specialized hospitals, the percentage of which has been growing [4]. This means that patients will have to travel longer distances in order to receive medical attention at fewer, more distributed, and more specialized treatment facilities, increasing also the demand for patient transportation. Already between 2000 and 2010, the number of patient transports has increased by 35.1 %, from 3.935.884 to 5.317.425 [20].

In Germany, Emergency Medical Service (EMS) systems are not only responsible for emergency rescues, but also for patient transports (usually to or from a hospital as well as between hospitals). This applies when the attendance of an emergency medical technician (EMT) is required, while the condition of a patient is not life-threatening. In general, transports are executed by special patient transport ambulances. If necessary, emergency rescue ambulances can also be used, although this means higher costs for the healthcare system. With about 40–80 % of the transportation demands known at least the day before - varying depending on the region - the remaining tasks are requested spontaneously.

With patients traveling longer distances and more frequently, we conjecture patient transports to be an ideal starting point to analyze efficiency and cost saving potentials in a focused area of the health care system. What is more, patient transports represent a comparably 'safe' application for optimization and planning endeavors, due to their typically non-critical nature. At present, transports are usually not planned in advance and the individual coordination centers are responsible for allocating ambulances manually on demand. This causes dispatchers in the coordination centers to be unavailable for handling critical situations, which in the worst case might lead to longer reaction times for emergency rescues. A partially automated and IT supported scheduling of transportation tasks is envisioned to reduce this risk, as well as to reduce transaction costs and to increase efficiency, thereby lowering costs and improving service quality for all parties involved in the patient transport system. This includes coordination centers, patients, hospitals, doctors, and insurance companies. Based on our cooperation with a coordination center and its corresponding zone of influence (called EMS region) in the South of Germany, the implementation of such an IT system is discussed and its evaluation is outlined.

Recognizing a growing use of emergency ambulances for transportation tasks due to extensive waiting times, the German Red Cross's regional association of Baden-Württemberg has demanded in a position paper from March 2012 to define a maximum waiting time of 40 min for patient transports in Baden-Württemberg [8]. This strengthens the impression that the current situation (the scheduling of transports) needs to be improved.

Therefore, the main motivation for this research is to increase the efficiency of the Emergency Medical Service system by scheduling transports in order to reduce costs, i.e., waiting times and traveled distances.

The aim of our work is to develop an IT-based coordination platform for the Emergency Medical Service system in Germany. We will first build a Decision Support System for the scheduling of patient transport services within an EMS region as these transports are not time critical and comparatively easy to handle. As stated by Arnott and Pervan [1], Decision Support Systems (DSS) is the area of the information systems (IS) discipline that focuses on developing and deploying IT-based systems to support and improve (managerial) decision making. In our case, these decisions are mainly about the assignment of transportation tasks to resources and the corresponding routing of the vehicles. In this paper we want to sketch a tool implementing the required functionality for transport scheduling and discuss further research needed. The tool described will be built around an online heuristic, which is particularly well suited for handling short-term demand. This is important for the optimization problem, since not all tasks are known with sufficient lead-time to allow purely offline planning. Additionally, when a request arrives, a statement whether the task can be fulfilled within the required time window must be made immediately.

Our working hypothesis is that by using an appropriate IT supported system, the planning of patient transports within an EMS region can be improved with regard to efficiency, punctuality of transports, and, most importantly, costs. The aim is to build this tool using existing infrastructure and interfaces, and to implement it as an add-on to currently used dispatching software, thereby minimizing costs and effort for both implementation and user acceptance. An additional advantage of this approach is enhanced scalability and transferability, increasing the chances of the tool gaining acceptance in practice.

The scope of this paper is to explain the need for and the design of the envisioned decision support tool to handle patient transports. In addition, the focus is on the service aspects of the German EMS system including the discussion of different roles and the co-creation of value. The underlying optimization methods for the envisioned decision support tool will be studied in future work.

The paper is structured as follows. In the next section a problem description is given and existing literature is briefly discussed. Subsequently, the realization of the envisioned transportation system is presented. The paper finishes with a summary and an outlook on issues for future research.

2 Problem Description and Literature Review

Modern service science theory states that a service system consists of several partners who generate value together. The concept of service systems is for example discussed by Spohrer et al. [18]. As for many other service systems also for EMS co-creation of value of provider and customers is essential. This concept of value co-creation is for example presented by Vargo and Lusch [22]. Unfortunately, the determination of the customer and his role is not always completely obvious. Therefore, the different roles of participants and their potential to contribute in the EMS system need to be discussed first. In case of an emergency rescue, the patient is in general the customer, as he is medically treated by an emergency doctor or a paramedic. But very often he is not the one who is calling for an ambulance, but relatives or passersby do call. The same is true for patient transports. Rarely the patient himself asks for a transport, but hospitals or general practitioners call the EMS dispatcher and order the transport of the patient to, from or between hospitals. They all – hospitals, general practitioners, emergency medical assistants driving the ambulance and the patients – want the transports to be on time. While for the patient this is often due to convenience, for hospitals and EMS providers waiting times can mean additional unnecessary costs.

Other important partners of the Emergency Medical Service system are the insurance companies as they are the ones paying for the services. Of course, their main interest is to save costs. But as they probably have to pay for all the (medical) treatments and services of a patient, they have an even broader view. It might be beneficial in terms of costs to install another ambulance that can decrease the time needed to arrive at a patient. For diseases like Stroke or Cardiac Arrest the time until the treatment starts is crucial. If treatment can start earlier this might safe costs for long-term care and therefore costs for the insurance company. At the same time, also the patient benefits if he recovers. That is, it can be stated that healthcare service systems including EMS are very complex. Therefore, assuring the quality of healthcare service systems is important. Hottum et al. [11] for example present an approach for systematically measuring the service quality and productivity in healthcare.

Concerning the value co-creation different aspects exist that can have an impact on the service delivery and quality. First of all, it is important that the right and complete information is given when an emergency is reported or a transportation task is ordered. Only if a patient is cooperative the emergency and transportation services can be fulfilled. In case of a transportation task, the patient must be "available" in time. Either the patient has to make sure that he is ready when the ambulance arrives or the hospital needs to take care for that, depending on where the patient is picked up. If the patient is dropped off at a hospital, then they should also be able to take over the patient when he arrives.

Concerning the development and usage of decision support systems, two areas are of main interest for his work, namely healthcare and vehicle routing/transportation planning. In their third review on DSS Eom and Kim [9] state that these two application areas are well presented in literature. For healthcare, most publications are about clinical DSS. In the book published by Berner [3], for example, different applications are presented. In addition, decision support systems are built for (large scale) emergencies and the training for it. Yoon et al. [24] describe a training prototype DSS for emergency response and transportation. For example Ruiz et al. [16] develop a decision support system for a vehicle routing problem. They propose an integer programming formulation and an implicit enumeration algorithm for solving it and present screenshots of the implemented tool. Further approaches are published by Tarantilis and Kiranoudis [19] and Mendoza et al. [12]. Scheduling the patient transportation in the Austrian EMS system, which in many aspects is comparable to the German one, is studied for example by Ritzinger et al. [15], Schilde et al. [17] and Parragh et al. [13]. They present mathematical models and provide different formulation and solution approaches that can serve as a basis for this research. The problem of transporting patients within large hospitals as it is analyzed in Beaudry et al. [2], using data from German hospitals, is also comparable to the studied EMS transportation problem. Nevertheless, due to legal regulations and the practical implementation of the EMS system in Germany, a thorough review and probably an adaption of the proposed methods is necessary.

To the best of our knowledge, the problem of scheduling patient transports has always been modeled as a so-called Dial-a-Ride Problem (DARP) in the existing literature. DARP is a form of Vehicle Routing Problem (VRP). Vehicle routes and schedules for n users which satisfy pickup and delivery requests between origins and destinations are to be designed and m minimum cost vehicle routes capable of serving as many users as possible are to be determined, under a set of constraints. It has been stated that the most common example of such a routing problem arises in the form of door-to-door transportation for elderly or disabled people as for example by Cordeau and Laporte [6]. The static DARP in general is quite well studied; see for example [7] or [14].

At present, there is hardly any methodologically grounded or formalized scheduling of patient transports in Germany. This means that in particular, automated scheduling does not take place. Most of the IT systems used by coordination centers implement a central list of transportation tasks to be fulfilled and a list of vehicles, showing their current status with regard to operability and availability. Dispatchers can then manually assign tasks to vehicles using drag and drop mechanisms.

At the moment, as dispatchers do not have a fixed schedule for the transports in a coordination center's region, they cannot provide customers (hospitals, doctors, patients, and relatives) with real-time information, for example on expected arrival times. Therefore, these parties are usually not informed when an ambulance is running late. As this is understandably unsatisfying, customers tend to order an ambulance earlier than it is needed to avoid these waiting times. Of course, this can in turn result in costly waiting times for the EMS provider, if the ambulance is on time. By implementing a tool for scheduling patient transports, and by therefore being able to communicate a certain arriving time, we should be able to motivate customers to order transports for the actual time needed, since they could then rely on the times stated by the EMS provider. In addition, the tool would facilitate an active exchange of information in both directions - both to inform patients about changes in arrival times via the Internet or via text messages (SMS), or to deliver changed transportation requests back to the coordination centers.

Transportation tasks that were fulfilled are usually saved in the dispatching software's log. Unfortunately, these software programs usually do not offer an automated data analysis. The transport data has to be extracted manually to an Excel-file, for example, and can then be analyzed using other (statistics) software. Due to a lack of experience as well as resources, this is in general not done in practice. Therefore, the duration of transports, especially loading times (as well as expected waiting times) are often unknown and are not examined further.

To assess the current situation and to be able to compare it to results determined by the software, the following key performance indicators can be used:

1. Time /delay:
    a. Late arrival when dropping off the patient in a hospital/practice as this can destroy the treatment plans and can cause high costs.
    b. Waiting time for the patient when the ambulance arrives late for pick-up; this is unsatisfactory for the patient and as we deal with ill patients this might be disadvantageous for the patient's health.
    c. Waiting time for the EMTs at pick-up if the patient is not ready as this waiting time is paid as "normal" working time of the EMTs. In addition, the ambulance is unnecessarily occupied during that time and not able to serve another request.
2. Trips:
    a. Number of empty trips when transporting patients between regions.
    b. Trips and types of trips (lying, sitting or walking patients; overweight patients; infectious patients) per ambulance staff as a balancing of workload should be assured.
    c. Length of the trips in km as ambulances have to be inspected and exchanged due to the overall traveled distance.

3 Transportation Planning System

3.1 Use Cases

The main goal is not only to find a superior heuristic for scheduling the transportation tasks, but also to create a tool for directly supporting dispatchers' decision making while trying to avoid unnecessary additional efforts. The envisioned tool therefore needs to interact with patients, hospital staff, EMTs and insurers in the context of the following use cases, which are depicted in Fig. 1.

The use case *Plan Transportation* should contain the following steps:

1. The dispatcher should be able to determine routes for the available ambulances serving the transportation requests and propose allocations of vehicles to transportation tasks.
2. The dispatcher should be able to schedule the pick-up and delivery times and determine whether the task can be fulfilled within the expected time window.
3. The system should leverage historical routing data, scheduling data, and actual transportation data in order to increase the precision for predictions of transport times, interceptions, etc.

The use case *Request Transportation* relates to the request of a patient transportation. A transportation request can be initiated by hospital staff and patients (usually phone calls) and entered by dispatchers. This use case is extended by the use case *Request Urgent Transportation*. If for example a doctor calls and requests for a patient to be transported to the hospital and the dispatcher is not sure whether it is possible in time or not, the doctor can declare the patient to be an emergency case and then an emergency rescue vehicle must take over. This is a lot more expensive and usually, emergency rescue resources (ambulances as well as personnel) are scarce and valuable. Therefore, whenever possible, it should be avoided for transportation tasks to become emergencies.

An EMT interacts with the system in the use case *Request Transportation Schedule*. The schedule contains the routes and patient transportation tasks, which should be fulfilled by the EMTs. This schedule can be updated in real time. In order to allow the

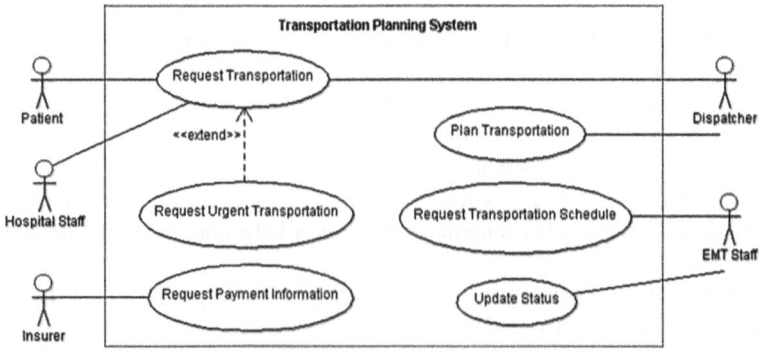

Fig. 1. Use case diagram of patient transportation service system

system to track the current status of the ambulances during the transportations, the use case *Update Status* allows EMTs to inform the system about their progress, possible delays, etc.

As transportation data is not just a valuable source of insight for dispatchers, insurers may access transportation data of their patients in the use case *Request Payment Information*. This increases transparency between all involved parties, namely patients, EMTs, and insurance companies.

3.2 Non-functional Requirements

An important requirement for the use cases is that the planning tool responds in real time (within seconds) and that the solution of the implemented procedures only deviates a few percent from the optimal solution. Considering the tasks that are already known, routes are determined in the morning (or the evening) before starting the transports. During the day, when new tasks become known, they are inserted into the routes or routes are rescheduled if necessary. Furthermore, the proposed approach should be integrated into existing dispatching software.

3.3 Implementation

As an example for a dispatching software, the product "Cobra" developed by ISE GmbH Aachen is chosen, since it is widely used for example in Baden-Württemberg, Hesse, Rhineland-Palatinate and North Rhine-Westphalia. Therefore, there is the possibility of a further roll-out of the tool after the pilot study. Another important feature of this dispatching software is that interfaces for accessing needed data are available and that in addition it is possible to design user interfaces adjusted for the specific needs of a dispatching center. The architecture of the software is shown in Fig. 2. The left side illustrates the existing architecture, while the right side illustrates how the work presented in this article is integrated. The existing dispatching software contains the components Databases, Cobra-Server and Cobra-Client. In the databases, the following data are available:

1. Available ambulances (in case of real-time planning the current status and locations of the ambulances must be transmitted to be able to keep track of the schedules).
2. Transportation tasks, including origin and destination locations (either addresses or geo-codes) and one critical time (either for pick-up or drop-off).

Cobra-Server and *Cobra-Client* is the existing software, which however does not provide any considerable decision support. Therefore, the components are extended in order to improve patient transportation planning.

The kernel of the system is the *OR Heuristic* that can schedule tasks in real-time and can therefore indicate whether a transportation demand can be fulfilled within the requested time window. For each vehicle, a route is built consisting of the tasks that are scheduled for the specific vehicle. The length of a route is limited by the duration of the shift of the EMTs associated to the vehicle.

In order to determine the arrival times and route lengths, the driving times between the different locations are needed. Thanks to the latest developments in this field, exact driving times can be computed at hardly any cost (i.e. computation time). For example, the Open Source Routing Machine (OSRM) developed by researchers from the Karlsruhe Institute of Technology (KIT), Germany, can be used for the proposed tool. OSRM is a C++ implementation of a routing engine that determines shortest paths in a road network. It uses specialized routing algorithms and the free road network data of OpenStreetMap project. OSRM is able to compute any shortest path within a few milliseconds. Therefore, there is no need to produce distance matrices beforehand, which could otherwise compromise the flexibility of the tool.

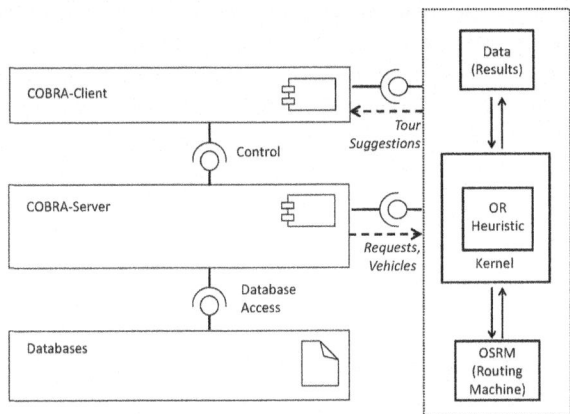

Fig. 2. Architecture of transportation planning service system (based on [10])

4 Evaluation

We executed a first brief data analysis for the cooperating EMS region. We found out that they fulfilled up to 100 transportation tasks per day in 2012. This means that sometimes 70–80 transports were known in advance. Most of the transports were demanded on weekdays, only very few transports took place during weekends. In total, the more than 20,000 patients were transports in 2012. For 2013 the data looks similar with a slight increase in the overall number of transports.

We identified more than 300 villages and districts for the pickup and drop off locations. The duration of a trip was often between 30 and 120 min. Transports from or to farther locations could take 180 min and more. This data will be quite helpful when building the system and tuning the approaches.

In a next step, we will work on different optimization methods (exact as well as heuristic approaches) and compare the results. We will also start with a DARP formulation. The objective minimizes the weighted sum over the different types of waiting times. In addition, an extension that ensures a work load balancing is considered. We did a first basic study of a simple DARP for the patient transportation problem that needed <10 h to solve instances of the considered problem sizes. Therefore, an application in practice is realistic when a schedule can be determined over night, but for rescheduling and including short-term demand fast heuristics will be needed. For example, an insertion heuristic is easy to implement and to adapt to the problem specifics, but for example metaheuristics like tabu search can be another possibility. In addition, sophisticated approaches based on the savings algorithm [5], for example, exist that can also be used to solve the patient transportation problem. Using the optimal solutions determined by solving the DARP formulation, the heuristics can be evaluated. The approaches and results will be presented in future work.

We will do a trial run, i.e., a case study with the coordination center, to collect data for determining the concrete optimization potential for a decision support system and to test the methods, as well as the platform itself. We will then track all requests (including the demanded time point or time intervals) – even those that cannot be fulfilled – all changes to the requests and the status (and if possible the locations) of all vehicles whenever a task is assigned by a dispatcher, or when a call arrives demanding an immediate transport. The schedule that has been produced by the dispatchers in practice can be extracted from the system directly. The data collected by the tool can be transformed into a set of scenarios and taken as input for the optimization. As mentioned above, different Operations Research heuristics will then be applied to the data set and be compared based on the defined optimization criteria. Exact methods will be used to create a base line for reference, assuming that all the information was known at the beginning of the planning task, to determine the quality of the heuristics.

5 Summary and Future Research

In this paper, we have introduced the idea of building a decision support tool to improve scheduling of patient transportation in the German Emergency Medical Service system. This approach aims to improve the current situation for all involved parties, reducing waiting times and costs, and increasing reliability. The proposed decision support tool relies on Operations Research methods to model the scheduling of transportation tasks as a Dial-a-Ride Problem. We have outlined the basic features of the decision support tool, of the optimization approaches to solve the underlying planning problem, and of the IT components that will support dispatchers in coordination centers by integrating the tool into their existing systems. We have started to investigate the applicability of heuristics to address the problem of transport scheduling. Further work is needed, both on this Operations Research aspect of the proposed tool, as well as on technical implementation and acceptance issues, such as the use of the decision support tool within a coordination center. The intended case studies together with rescue coordination centers as described in the last section will be the most important next step and we expect the results to be very insightful both for researchers and for the people working in the coordination centers.

Concerning the planning methods, a combination of emergency rescue and patient transport will be investigated, which is especially promising in case of shared ambulances. A decision support tool would then advice which ambulance to assign for a particular kind of service request and also where to locate ambulances after having finished a task, or generally during the day. Here, incorporating a GIS into the system might be very helpful. Unfortunately, nowadays only very few ambulances in Germany have a GPS installed. Therefore, they cannot be tracked and there would be hardly any benefit of adding a GIS to the system then. Nevertheless, the potential as well as needed adaptations should be investigated in order to be prepared when GPS systems are finally installed.

In some of the European neighboring countries like Austria or the Netherlands, patient transports are handled similarly as in Germany. This could be taken into account when building the system to increase the potential key market.

As mentioned above, it would be really beneficial for the whole system if information on the current status and on short notice changes can be transferred (semi-) automatically between the coordination center, the hospitals and the patients. The tool described could serve as a platform to facilitate this communication. Eventually, having several rescue coordination centers run the decision support tool, the aim is to build a platform for the coordination of patient transport services that not only considers tasks within one EMS region, but that is able to connect these regions (within a federal state). A key achievement of this approach is envisioned to be the avoidance of empty trips of the vehicles after completing a transportation task, while limiting the data transferred on the platform to the necessary minimum. Realizing these improvements relies on overcoming a number of integration and acceptance challenges. In particular, differences between dispatching systems and software in the coordination centers, issues of data protection, and user acceptance will be addressed in creating the platform solution.

References

1. Arnott, D., Pervan, G.: Eight key issues for the decision support systems discipline. Decis. Support Syst. **44**, 657–672 (2008)
2. Beaudry, A., Laporte, G., Melo, T., Nickel, S.: Dynamic transportation of patients in hospitals. OR Spectr. **32**, 77–107 (2010)
3. Berner, E.S.: Clinical Decision Support Systems. Springer Science+Business Media, LLC, New York (2007)
4. Bölt, U., Graf, T.: 20 Jahre Krankenhausstatistik, Statistisches Bundesamt, Wirtschaft und Statistik (2012)
5. Clarke, G., Wright, J.W.: Scheduling of vehicles from a central depot to a number of delivery points. Oper. Res. **12**(4), 568–581 (1964)
6. Cordeau, J.-F., Laporte, G.: The dial-a-ride problem: models and algorithms. Ann. Oper. Res. **153**, 29–46 (2007)
7. Cordeau, J.-F., Laporte, G.: A tabu search heuristic for the static multi-vehicle dial-a-ride problem. Transp. Res. Part B: Methodol. **37**, 579–594 (2003)
8. DRK Position Paper 2012. Die Zukunft des Rettungsdienstes in Baden-Württemberg (2012)
9. Eom, S., Kim, E.: A survey of decision support system applications (1995–2001). J. Oper. Res. Soc. **57**, 1264–1278 (2006)
10. Gies, T.: Methoden zur Aktualisierung einer Client- / Server-Software im laufenden Betrieb, seminar thesis, FH Aachen (2013)
11. Hottum, P., Schaff, M., Müller-Gorchs, M., Howahl, F., Görlitz, R.: Capturing and measuring quality and productivity in healthcare service systems, In: Proceedings of the 21st International RESER Conference (2011)

12. Mendoza, J.E., Medaglia, A.L., Velasco, N.: An evolutionary-based decision support system for vehicle routing: the case of a public utility. Decis. Support Syst. **46**, 730–742 (2009)
13. Parragh, S., Cordeau, J.-F., Doerner, K., Hartl, R.: Models and algorithms for the heterogeneous dial-a-ride problem with driver-related constraints. OR Spectr. **34**, 593–633 (2012)
14. Parragh, S.: Ambulance routing problems with rich constraints and multiple objectives. Dissertation, Fakultät für Wirtschaftswissenschaften. Universität Wien, Vienna (2009)
15. Ritzinger, U., Puchinger, J., Hartl, R.F.: Real-world patient transportation. In: ODYSSEUS 2012 5th International Workshop on Freight Transportation and Logistics (2012)
16. Ruiz, R., Maroto, C., Alcaraz, J.: A decision support system for a real vehicle routing problem. Eur. J. Oper. Res. **153**, 593–606 (2004)
17. Schilde, M., Doerner, K.F., Hartl, R.F.: Metaheuristics for the dynamic stochastic dial-a-ride problem with expected return transports. Comput. Oper. Res. **38**, 1719–1730 (2011)
18. Spohrer, J., Maglio, P.P., Bailey, J., Gruhl, D.: Steps toward a science of service systems. IEEE Comput. Soc. **40**, 71–77 (2007)
19. Tarantilis, C.D., Kiranoudis, C.T.: Using a spatial decision support system for solving the vehicle routing problem. Inf. Manag. **39**, 359–375 (2002)
20. The Federal Health Monitoring System (2011). http://www.gbe-bund.de/. Accessed Jan 2013
21. The Federal Health Monitoring System (2012). http://www.gbe-bund.de/. Accessed Jan 2013
22. Vargo, S.L., Lusch, R.F.: Evolving to a new dominant logic for marketing. J. Mark. **68**(1), 1–17 (2004)
23. World Health Organization (2012). http://data.euro.who.int/hfadb/. Accessed Aug 2014
24. Yoon, S.W., Velasquez, J.D., Partridge, B.K., Nof, S.Y.: Transportation security decision support system for emergency response: a training prototype. Decis. Support Syst. **46**, 139–148 (2008)

Education on Service Science Management and Engineering: A Comparative Analysis

Esperanza Marcos[1], Valeria de Castro[1(✉)], María Luz Martín Peña[2], Eloísa Díaz Garrido[2], Marcos Lopez-Sanz[1], and Juan Manuel Vara[1]

[1] School of Computer Science, Rey Juan Carlos University,
28933 Móstoles, Spain
{esperanza.marcos,valeria.decastro,marcos.lopez,
juanmanuel.vara}@urjc.es
[2] Faculty of Social Science and Law, Rey Juan Carlos University,
28032 Madrid, Spain
{luz.martin,eloisa.diaz}@urjc.es

Abstract. Approximately 60 % of the world's workforce is currently employed by either public or private branches of the Service Sector and this value rises to 80 % in developed countries. There is also a tendency towards constant growth in the Service Sector at an international level, with people working in a broad spectrum of areas such as tourism, commerce, logistics, finance, insurance and community, social and personal services. However, and in spite of the fact that society increasingly needs more professionals who are oriented towards this sector, there are hardly any specific training plans for service professionals. This paper presents a comparative analysis about training programs in Service Science Management and Engineering (SSME). This comparative analysis was made during the definition and creation of a new curriculum for training of professionals in SSME which will be taught at the Rey Juan Carlos University, in Madrid, Spain, from the next academic year onwards. The degree is briefly described in this paper and analyzed in the comparative analysis.

Keywords: Service Science Management and Engineering · Curriculum · Discipline · Comparison

1 Introduction

The Service Sector, defined as that which does not produce material goods, but rather provides the population with services that are necessary to satisfy its needs [1], is currently dominating the world economy, and provides about 63 % of the workforce with employment. These data vary between values of over 80 % in countries such as Hong Kong, Saudi Arabia, the United States or the United Kingdom and values below 40 % in countries such as Cameroon, Cambodia, Pakistan or India. Between 50 % and 80 % of the workforces in the majority of developed countries are employed in the Service Sector [2].

The evolution of employment in Europe for different sectors shows that Agriculture and Industry sectors decrease while the Service Sector grows year by year [3]. In 2013,

Spain, where the present curricula is beginning to be implemented, had a 75 % of employees working in the Service Sector [4].

However, and in spite of the fact that society increasingly needs more professionals who are oriented towards this sector, there are hardly any specific training plans for service professionals. But, what is a service professional? What type of training should a professional in a sector that is clearly on the increase have?

The Service Sector requires personnel who are qualified in service systems, i.e., dynamic configurations of people, technologies, organizations and shared information that create and deliver value to customers, providers and other stakeholders [5]. We are thus referring to professionals who understand and can deal with the complete lifecycle of service systems, from the conception of new services, innovation, design and production to marketing and commercialization, etc.

The relatively new field denominated as Service Science, Management and Engineering (SSME) aims to integrate disciplines regarding the business management, technology and engineering, and social sciences in order to encourage innovation in how organisations create value for customers and stakeholders that could not be achieved through such disciplines working in isolation [5, 6].

The educational sphere has also begun to take steps as regards SSME [7]. White papers have, for example, appeared in both Spain and at an international level, with the intention of taking the first step as regards creating study plans for the training of professionals in this field [8, 9, 10]. Jim Spoher, one of the precursors of Service Science has, together with other authors, stressed the ten reasons why universities have a lot to say in the SSME sphere [11]. One of these is that universities already impart concepts related to service innovation, although in 'silos', or isolated disciplines such as economics, marketing, operations, computer sciences, systems engineering, etc., thus affirming that SSME can assist universities to move from teaching in silos to transdisciplinary teaching, adapted to the real needs of a service economy. As previously stated, service professionals must have a combination of skills that originate from various disciplines such as business, technology and social sciences. Various authors therefore discuss the training of T-shaped professionals, who will be excellent problem solvers in their own discipline but will also be capable of interacting with and understanding specialists from a wide range of disciplines and functional areas [5].

Although the majority of the training initiatives in SSME are Master's degree programmes, some universities have also committed to creating Bachelor's degree programmes. In this paper we present a comparative analysis of existing Bachelor's degree programs on SSME. As a basis for the comparison we considered first the three large areas related to SSME: business management, technology and engineering, and social science. Then we identified and analyzed the disciplines included on each particular degree and the weight that each of them had in each specific program.

The comparative analysis presented in this paper was made during the process of creation of a new curriculum for training of professionals in SSME. The proposed curriculum, a Bachelor' degree, is the result of a project that has been going on for more than three years at the Rey Juan Carlos University (RJCU) in close collaboration with two significant and complementary companies from the service sector: IBM (as a computing service provider) and EULEN (as as a supplier of security services, cleaning services, etc.). The project has been reviewed and endorsed by various organisms such as the ERISS, the SRII, the IBM Almaden Research Centre, etc. The present curriculum is briefly described in this paper and analyzed in the comparative analysis.

The present work is structured as follows. Section 2 presents the required knowledge and skills for the emerging field of SSME, and describes the principal disciplines related to it. Section 3 shows a summary of the SSME degree proposed by the RJCU. Section 4 presents a comparative study of the Bachelor's degrees on SSME. Finally, Sect. 5 shows main conclusions and open lines of work.

2 Knowledge and Skills for a SSME Professional

In one of the first works on the area of SSME: *"Service Science: a New Academic Discipline?"*, IBM stated that Service Science could bring together ongoing work in the more established fields of computer science, operations research, industrial engineering, mathematics, management sciences, decision sciences, social sciences and legal sciences to create new skills and markets that offers services that help transforming, optimizing and managing business-support functions in organizations [10].

In 2007, the Cambridge Service Science, Management and Engineering Symposium [5] similarly stressed the importance of uniting the knowledge from computer science, operations research, industrial engineering, business strategy, management sciences, and social and legal sciences, with the objective of training professionals who will help to improve organizations' success through service innovation.

In agreement with the previous proposals [7, 8], we can state that they all coincide as regards indicating that a professional in SSME should have three fundamental types of skills: *business and management skills*, *information systems engineering skills* (also denominate as *Technological skills*), and *socio-organisational skills*. The knowledge related to these skills is currently taught at universities on different Bachelor's and Master's degree courses that can be grouped into three areas, as is shown in Fig. 1: *Business and processes*, *Engineering and technology*, and *People and culture* [7].

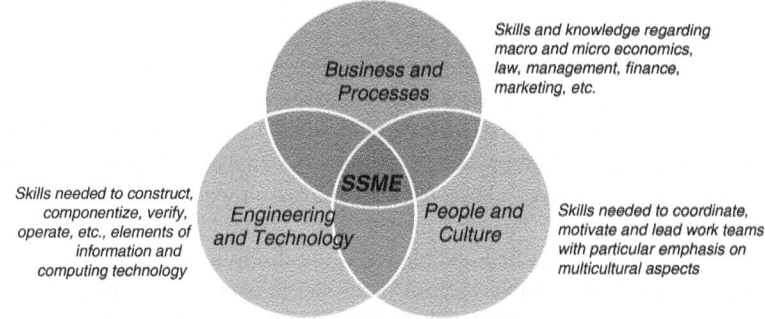

Fig. 1. Relationship between SSME professionals' knowledge and skill areas

In the last years many universities at a worldwide level have begun to create study plans with which to cover training in SSME according with the tree previous areas [7]. Although the majority of the currently existing initiatives are Master's degree programs, various Bachelor's degree programs are also being taught.

Education on Service Science Management and Engineering: A Comparative Analysis 267

Taking into account the proposals of various experts in SSME [5, 7, 12], along with the analysis of different Bachelor's and Master's degree curricula that are currently being taught at an international level, we have identified a set of main subjects that should be taught in training programs on SSME. We have grouped these subjects into three large blocks, which we have denominated as disciplines, with the objective of establishing groups of subjects with themes that are related to each other. Figure 2 shows the relationship between these disciplines and the three large areas of which SSME is composed.

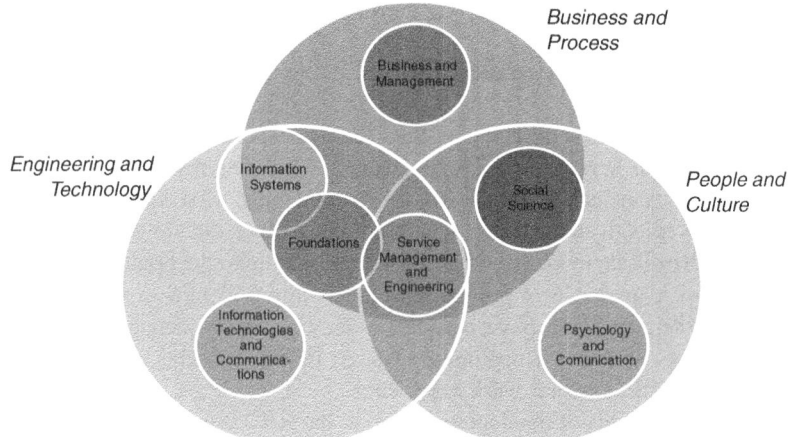

Fig. 2. Relationships among disciplines according to areas in SSME

In **Foundations** we involves a basic knowledge of mathematics and statistics, along with the basic concepts for a service professional such as systems theory, history of services, and the legal and ethical aspects that are basic to any profession. This knowledge is related to the three areas of SSME knowledge, although it could be said that they are principally related to the areas of *Engineering and Technology* and *Businesss and Processes*.

Business and Management involves knowledge related to business, management, human resources and marketing. This block of subjects is directly connected to the area of *Business and Processes*.

The discipline **Social Science** involve knowledge from the areas of economics and sociology. This knowledge is related to the areas of both *Business and Processes* and *People and Culture*.

Information Systems involves knowledge from Information Systems, Data Bases and Business Information Systems. These subjects include knowledge from the traditional areas of *Engineering and Technology* and *Business and Processes*.

As a different discipline, we include **Information Technology and Communications (ITC)**. It involves knowledge related to technical and engineering skills from the areas related to Computer Science, such as architecture, hardware, programming, networks, operative systems, etc. They are subjects from the Engineering and Technology area.

Service Management and Engineering involves knowledge related to the management of services in organisations, such as service engineering, service management, quality of services, service process management, etc. This type of knowledge, which is fundamental from the point of view of services, is related to all three large areas of SSME.

Finally, the discipline of **Psychology and communication** involves knowledge from psychology and communication which are related to social skills along with communication skills, emotional intelligence, team management, leadership, etc. These subjects are encompassed within the SSME area denominated as People and Culture.

3 The URJC SSME Curriculum

In this section we briefly present the Rey Juan Carlos University' proposal for a Bachelor's degree in Service Science, Management and Engineering.

In Spain, any curriculum that leads to the obtaining of a bachelor's degree is formed of 240 credits. It should contain a minimum of 60 credits for basic education, of which at least 36 will be linked to subjects that are specific to the branch of knowledge. If external work experience is programmed, then this will have a maximum of 60 credits. The dissertation will have between 6 and 30 credits, and the academic recognition of credits will have a maximum of 6. At RJCU, 6 credits are assigned to the dissertation and 24 to external work experience.

Table 1 shows details of the degree created at the RJCU. As it is shown in Table 1, each of the aforementioned disciplines is composed of modules, and the modules are composed of subjects. Each subject may contain one or more topics that will allow the student to acquire a set of both general and specific competencies.

4 Comparison of Bachelor' Degrees on SSME

The disciplines presented in Sect. 2, which unite knowledge that is considered to be central to the training of SSME professionals, are also present in the majority of Bachelor's and Master's degrees taught at a European and international level (see in appendix some current programs on SSME).

The basis of analyses used in this comparison will be the 7 areas that are included in the three large areas of which SSME is composed: foundations (F), business management (BM), social science (SS), psychology and communications (PC), information technology and communications (ICT), information systems (IS) and service management and engineering (SME).

In order to compare the existing degree on SSME we considered that was important to analyse the disciplines included and the weight that each of them had in each specific programme. We have done this by classifying all the subjects taught according to the seven previously defined disciplines and then calculating the weight of each discipline in the degree according to the number of credits assigned to the subjects of which they are composed with regard to the total number of credits assigned to the degree. Table 2 shows these results.

Table 1. RJCU SSME Curriculum

Disciplines	Modules	Subjects	N°Cred. - Course/Semester
Foundation	Modern Languages	• Modern Languages	6 - 2/Annual
	Mathematics and Logic	• Mathematics for Computation and Services	6 - 1°/1°
		• Logic	3 - 1°/2°
	Statistics and Operation Research	• Statistics	6 - 2°/1°
		• Operation Research	3 - 2°/2°
	History	• History and Fundamentals of Services	6 - 1°/1°
	Systems Theory	• Systems Theory	3 - 1°/1°
	Legal issues	• Ethical, Legal and Professional Aspects	3 - 1°/2°
		• Private Law	6 - 2°/1°
Business and Management	Business and Management	• Business Organisation	6 - 1°/2°
		• Business Communication	6 - 2°/2°
		• Service Marketing	6 - 3°/2°
		• Service Operation Management	3 - 3°/1°
		• Strategic Management of Businesses and Service-Oriented Business Consultancy	3 - 4°/1°
		• Business Initiative	3 - 4°/2°
		• Human Resources	3 - 4°/2°
Social Science	Economy	• Service Science Economy	6 - 2°/2°
		• Financial Economy and Accounting	3 - 3°/2°
		• Microeconomy	3 - 3°/1
	Sociology	• Service Sociology	6 - 1°/1°
Psychology and communication	Psychology	• Emotional Intelligence	3 - 1°/2°
		• Leadership and Group Work	3 - 3°/1°
	Communication	• Communication Skills	6 - 2°/1°
Information Technologies and Communications	Information Technologies and Communications	• Introduction to Programming	6 - 1°/1°
		• Computer Architecture	3 - 1°/1°
		• Service Development	6 - 1°/2°
		• Operation Systems and Networks	6 - 1°/2°
		• Service Design and Maintenance	3 - 2°/1°
		• Software Engineering	3 - 2°/2°
		• Mobile and Ubiquitous Services	3 - 3°/2°
		• Human-Computer Interaction and Multimedia	6 - 3°/2°
Information Systems	Information Systems	• Data Bases	6 - 2°/1°
		• Information Systems	3 - 2°/2°
		• Information Systems Architecture	6 - 2°/2
		• Business Intelligence and Analysis	3 - 3°/2°
		• Technologies for the Management of Large Volumes of Data	6 - 3°/1°
		• Business Information Systems	6 - 3°/1°
		• Business Architectures	3 - 4°/1°
Service Management and Engineering	Service Management and Engineering	• Service Engineering	6 - 3°/1°
		• Project Management	3 - 3°/1°
		• Service Management	6 - 3°/2°
		• Business Process Engineering	3 - 3°/2°
		• Optional: Service Applications	12 - 4°/1°,2°

Table 2. Comparison of Degrees in SSME

Degree	Cred.	Representation weight of each discipline in the Degree							
		F	BM	SS	PC	ICT	IS	SME	Total
Degree in Information Technologies and Services. Universidad Autónoma de Barcelona (Spain)	240	14 %	10 %	3 %	–	43 %	11 %	19 %	100 %
IT Service Science major: Bachelor of Computer and Information Sciences. Auckland University of Technology (New Zealand)	360	4 %	4 %	–	4 %	46 %	29 %	13 %	100 %
Bachelor of Science in IT Service Management. University of Applied Sciences Schmalkalden (Alemania)	180	11 %	17 %	4 %	–	32 %	21 %	15 %	100 %
Degree in IT Service Management. Missouri State University (USA)	125	22 %	27 %	16 %	6 %	15 %	8 %	6 %	100 %
Baccalauréat Universitaire en Systèmes d'Information et Science des Services. Universidad de Ginebra (Suiza)	180	2 %	20 %	-	4 %	22 %	25 %	27 %	100 %
Bachelor of Science in Business with a concentration in Service Sector. University of Phoenix (USA)	120	21 %	18 %	21 %	3 %	3 %	6 %	28 %	100 %
Service Science, Management and Engineering Degree. Rey Juan Carlos University (Spain)	240	22 %	15 %	9 %	6 %	17 %	16 %	15 %	100 %

One important difference that may be observed in the degrees in SSME that are currently being taught is the influence of those areas most closely related to SSME, such as *Engineering and Technology* and *Business Management*. The profiles of those degrees that are most closely related to Information Technologies, which are usually taught at Computer Science schools, are clearly different to those more closely related to Business Management, which are taught at Business schools.

Although both types of degrees focus on the concept of service, the former clearly tend towards the idea of IT service, with more content regarding information technologies, while the latter focus more on the idea of service operations and on the

Education on Service Science Management and Engineering: A Comparative Analysis   271

management of services as a business activity. Those degrees that are less influenced by information technologies appear to be closer to the idea of an SSME degree in which new knowledge arises as a result of the synergy of various disciplines, which include computing, business studies, marketing, sociology, psychology, etc.

Of the degrees analysed, we can name three whose contents are closer to the area of **Information Technology** and which are taught at Computer Science schools (the first three rows of Table 2). These are:

- *Degree in Information Technologies and Services* at the Escola Universitària d'Informàtica "Tomàs Cerdà" at the Universidad Autónoma de Barcelona (Spain) [13].
- *IT Service Science major: Bachelor of Computer and Information Sciences* at the School of Computing and Mathematical Sciences at Auckland University of Technology (New Zealand) [14].
- *Bachelor of Science in IT Service Management* at the Faculty of Computer Science at the University of Applied Sciences Schmalkalden (Germany) [15].

Figure 3 shows in a graph the distribution of percentages of knowledge per discipline for these tree SSME degrees. The analysis of such distribution shows that the degrees contain approximately 50 % of subjects from the area of Information and Communications Technologies.

It should be borne in mind that if we also contemplate other information systems subjects that are closely related to Computer Science, such as data bases or enterprises systems, these values rise much more, reaching almost 70 % in the case of the Auckland University of Technology, and more than 50 % in that of the University of Applied Sciences Schmalkalden.

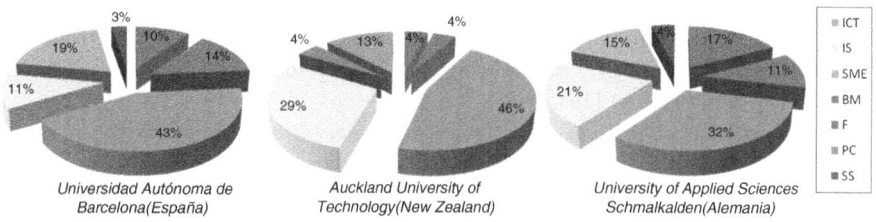

Fig. 3. Distribution of percentages of knowledge per discipline in SSME degrees closer to the area of Information Technology

There are also three degrees that are most influenced by the area of **Business Management** and which are taught at Social or Business schools. These are:

- *Degree in IT Service Management* at the College of Business Administration at Missouri State University (USA) [16].
- *Baccalauréat Universitaire en Systèmes d'Information et Science des Services* at the Faculty of Social and Economic Sciences at the University of Genève (Switzerland) [17].

- *Bachelor of Science in Business with a concentration on the Service Sector* at the Business at the University of Phoenix (USA) [18].

As is shown in the Fig. 4, the percentages in these degrees are better distributed among the different disciplines analysed. The degrees at both the Missouri State University and the University of Phoenix contain a high percentage of disciplines related to Business Management and Social Science, but these do not exceed 50 % of the total contents of the degree.

The University of Phoenix has a particularly high percentage of Service Management and Engineering since it is highly focused on studying specific service sectors. The University of Geneva has more content as regards information technologies and information systems, but it does not exceed 50 % of the total content of the degree.

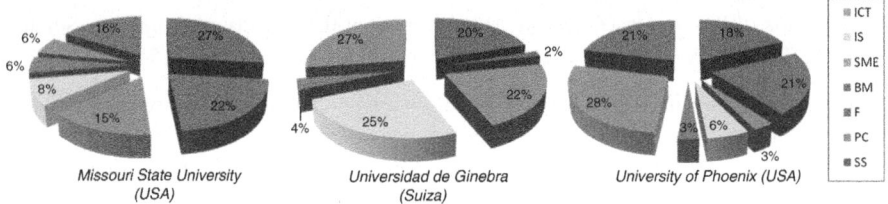

Fig. 4. Distribution of percentages of knowledge per discipline in SSME degrees closer to the area of Business Management

It should also be noted that, although we have not included them in this study, there are other degrees that are oriented towards the third area related to SSME: **People and Culture**. Of these we could mention the next:

- *B.S. Degree in Service Management* at the College of Human Development and College of Technology, Engineering & Management at the University of Wisconsin-Stout (USA) [19].
- *Bachelor of Science in Human Services with a concentration in Management* at the College of Social Sciences at the University of Phoenix (USA) [20].

Both degrees are oriented towards the social and human aspects of SSME in conjunction with business management, although the area of technologies and engineering is not dealt with in any way whatsoever.

Figure 5 shows the distribution of the percentages that represent each discipline in the **SSME degree proposed by the RJCU**. It is important to notice that in the case of the RJCU there has been a special interest in creating a study plan that will allow students to attain a transdisciplinary SSME profile that is unlike the traditional computer science profile with a specialization in Services or a business management profile. This is reflected in the balanced distribution of the percentages for the areas in the RJCU degree.

A more detailed analysis of the URJC SSME shows the distribution of subjects (see Fig. 6), which correspond to each of the SSME disciplines identified previously, throughout the four years of the degree. As can be seen in Fig. 6, in agreement with [11],

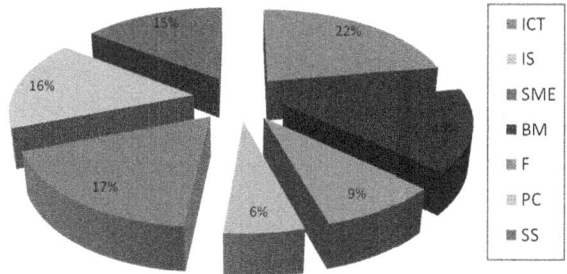

Fig. 5. Distribution of percentages of knowledge per discipline in the URJC SSME degree

we have defined a teaching model in which areas are gradually developed in increasingly greater depth.

As the graphs show, both the first and second years contain a high percentage of subjects that correspond to fundamentals. The subjects of Service Management and Engineering are fundamentally taught in the third and fourth year. Although the area of Service Management and Engineering may visually appear to be greater in the fourth year, the number of credits show that fewer credits are taught. This is because the fourth year includes credits for work experience, the dissertation and the recognition of credits that have not been classified in a specific module since it is understood that these credits imply an application of the knowledge obtained in all of them.

One important characteristic of this distribution that should be highlighted is that up until the third year, skills and knowledge from the three areas defined by SSME

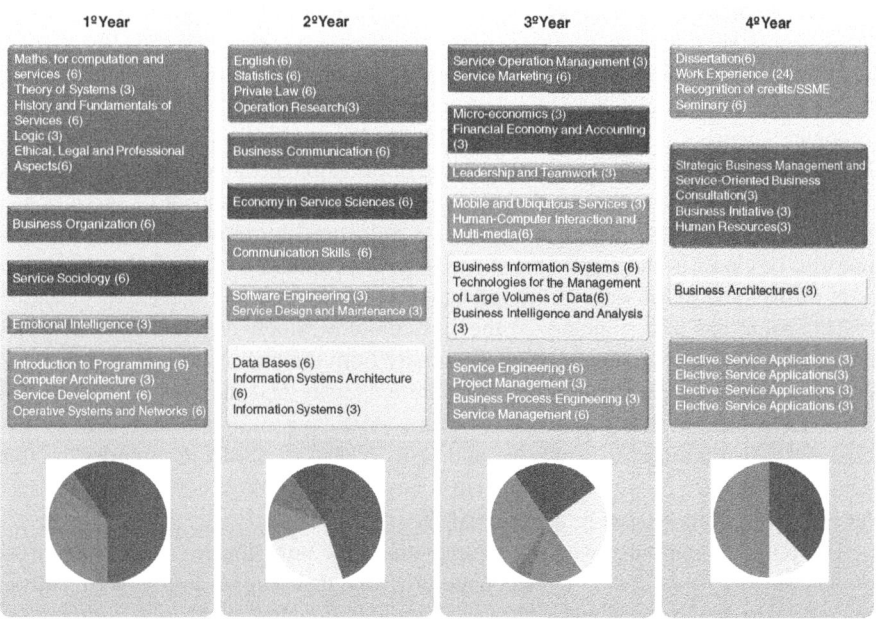

Fig. 6. Distribution of subjects per term and module in the RJCU SSME Curriculum

(business and process, engineering and technologies, and, people and culture) are developed in each academic year.

Thus, for example, with regard to the skills from the area of people and culture, it will be observed that in the first year 9 credits are taught for the subjects of emotional intelligence and service sociology, in the second year 6 credits are taught for communication skills, and in the third year 3 more credits are taught for leadership and teamwork. Although there is no specific subject regarding these skills in the fourth year it should be stressed, as explained previously, that in the final year credits are developed for subjects such as work experience and the dissertation, during which social and personal skills are definitively put into practice.

5 Conclusions and Future Work

Service Sector requires qualified personnel in service systems. It refers to professionals who understand and can deal with the complete lifecycle of service systems, from the conception of new services, innovation, design and production to marketing and commercialization, etc. The Service Science Management and Engineering (SSME) is an emerging and transdisciplinary field that integrates aspects of business management, along with information technologies and engineering, and social sciences.

Since the appearance of the first works related to SSME, many universities at a worldwide level have begun to create study plans with which to cover training in this area. Although the majority of the currently existing initiatives are Master's degree programs, various Bachelor's degree programs are also being taught. This paper present a comparative analysis of Bachelor's degree in SSME at international level.

After our analysis we observe one important difference in the degrees in SSME that comes from the influence of those areas most closely related to SSME, such as Engineering and Technology and Business Management. The profiles of those degrees that are most closely related to Information Technologies, which are usually taught at Computer Science schools. The former clearly tend towards the idea of service from an IT point of view, with more content regarding information technologies, while the latter focus more on the idea of service operations and on the management of services as a business activity. Those degrees that are less influenced by information technologies appear to be closer to the idea of an SSME degree in which new knowledge arises as a result of the synergy of various disciplines.

This paper has also summarized the curriculum of a new degree in SSME which will be taught at the Rey Juan Carlos University from the next course. The degree has been designed by experts in SSME from the university and the Service Sector. The URJC SSME degree shows a distinctive characteristic regarding to other degrees, that is balanced distribution of knowledge and skills related to SSME throughout the four years of the degree, as well as the balanced distribution of the credits taught for each one of the disciplines more related to SSME.

The RJCU is currently working to implement the new degree. As a future work we plan to work by following the students' progress, their employability, the results of the companies in the sector, etc., all of which will undoubtedly lead to new reviews of the degree program.

Acknowledgements. This work was partially funded by the MASAI project (TIN2011-22617) financed by the Spanish Ministry of Economy and Competitiveness and SICOMORo-CM project (S2013/ICE-3006) funded by the Regional Government of Madrid.

We would also like to thank all the participants in this project: experts from IBM Spain (Victor Camargo, Soledad Linniers, Elisa Guijarro, Jesús Freire) and EULEN (Ricardo Gabarro), external advisors, external reviewers at ISSIP (Jim Spohrer, IBM Innovation Champion and Director of the IBM University Programs World Wide), SRII (Pere Botella, Full professor at Services & Information Systems Engineering Department at the Universitat Politècnica de Catalunya), ERISS (Mike Papazogou, executive director at the University of Tilburg) and IBM-Almaden (Jorge Sanz, currently Chief Innovation Officer, Retail Banking Industry, IBM), and reviewers at the ANECA Commission. The collaboration of all of them has been the key to achieving good results.

We would particularly like to mention Pedro Lázaro (IBM Spain), one of the principal driving forces behind SSME in Spain and especially as regards this project, and who we unfortunately lost along the way.

Appendix: Current SSME Undergraduate and Graduate Programs

Undergraduate Programmes		
Denomination	School/Centre at which taught	University
Degree in IT Service Management	College of Business Administration	Missouri State University (USA)
B.S. Degree in Service Management	College of Human Development and College of Technology, Engineering & Management	University of Wisconsin-Stout (USA)
Baccalauréat Universitaire en Systèmes d'Information et Science des Services"	Facultad de Ciencias Económicas y Sociales	Universidad de Genève (Switzerland)
Bachelor of Science in Human Services with a concentration in Management	College of Social Sciences	University of Phoenix (USA)
Bachelor of Science in Business with a concentration in Service Sector	School of Business	University of Phoenix (USA)
Degree in Information Technologies and Services	Escola Universitària d'Informàtica "Tomàs Cerdà"	Universidad Autónoma de Barcelona (Spain)

(*Continued*)

(Continued)

Undergraduate Programmes		
Denomination	School/Centre at which taught	University
IT Service Science major: Bachelor of Computer and Information Sciences	School of Computing and Mathematical Sciences	Auckland University of Technology (New Zealand)
Bachelor of Science in IT Service Management	Faculty of Computer Science	University of Applied Sciences Schmalkalden (Germany)
Graduated Programs		
Master's Programme in IT Service Management	Northampton Business School	University of Northampton (UK)
International Master in Service Engineering	European Research Institute in Service Science (ERISS), School of Economics and Management	University of Tilburg (The Netherland), University of Stuttgart (Germany), University of Crete (Greece)
Master in Services Engineering and Management	Department of Industrial Engineering and Management	Universidad de Oporto (Portugal)
Master in Service Design and Engineering	EIT ICT Labs Master School	University of Trento (Italia), TU Eindhoven (The Nederland), Aalto University (Finland) and ELTE Budapest (Hungry)
Master's Programme in Service Design and Engineering	The Department of Computer Science and Engineering, School of Science	Aalto University (Finland)
Services Management concentrating on the MBA program	College of Management	North Caroline State University (USA)
Service Engineering and Management	Faculty of Automatic Control and Computers	University Polytechnic of Bucharest (Rumania)
Master's degree in Service Science, Management, and Engineering	Faculty of Informatics	Masaryk University (Czech Republic)

References

1. Riddle, D.I.: Service Led Growth: The Role of the Service Sector in World Development. Greenwood Pub Group, Westport (1987)
2. World Bank data. http://www.worldbank.org/

3. European Union Office of Statistics. http://epp.eurostat.ec.europa.eu/
4. Spanish National Institute of Statistics. http://www.ine.es/inebaseDYN/epa30308/epa_inicio.htm
5. Bishop, K., Bolan, G., Bowen, D., Cromack, C., Evans, S., Fisk, R.P., Ganz, W., Gregory, M., Johnston, R., Lemmink, J., Lovelock, C., Lyons, M., Macaulay, L., McFarlane, D., Menor, L., Neely, A., Ren, G., Sampson, S., Spohrer, J., Stiles, P., Street, S., Tasker, P., Throssell, J. and Vargo, S.: Succeeding through service innovation: a service perspective for education, research, business and government, White paper based on Cambridge Service Science, Management and Engineering Symposium. University of Cambridge & IBM, Cambridge (2007)
6. Glushko, R.J.: Designing a service science discipline with discipline. IBM Syst. J. **47**(1), 15–27 (2008)
7. Hefley, B., Murphy, W.: Service Science, Management and Engineering: Education for the 21st Century. Springer, New York (2008)
8. Lázaro, P., Galán, I., Suárez, B., Domínguez, A.: The service science: a challenge for the Spanish university system, White paper, Studies and Analysis Program of the Ministry of Education. Project EA2008-0307 (2007)
9. Martínez, A., Lázaro, P.: Services science: a new innovation approach for services providers. Universia Bus. Revi. 3rd Quarter (2007)
10. IBM Research: Services Sciences: a new academic discipline?, Report on the Architecture of On Demand Business Summit, Yorktown Heights, NY (2004). http://www.almaden.ibm.com/asr/SSME/facsummit.pdfIBMResearch
11. Spohrer, J., Fodell, D., Murphy, W.: Ten reasons service science matters to universities. J. Educause Rev. November/December (2012)
12. Kieliszewski, C.: Educating the new service professional: what are the essentials of a service curriculum? In: Workshop on Service Science, Management and Engineering (SSME) Education: Looking Ahead Co-Located with ICSOC 2008 Workshops, University of Technology, Sidney, Australia (2008)
13. Degree in Information Technologies and Services. http://informatica.eug.es/es/estudios/grados/grado-de-informatica-y-servicios-2
14. IT Service Science major: Bachelor of Computer and Information Sciences. http://www.aut.ac.nz/study-at-aut/study-areas/computer-mathematical-sciences/undergraduate-degrees/bachelor-of-computer-and-information-sciences-it-service-science
15. Bachelor of Science in IT Service Management. http://www.fh-schmalkalden.de/Module+bis+SS2013-p-11020.html
16. Degree in IT Service Management. http://cis.missouristate.edu/ITServiceManagement/
17. Baccalauréat Universitaire en Systèmes d'Information et Science des Services. http://cis.missouristate.edu/ITServiceManagement/
18. Bachelor of Science in Business with a concentration on the Service Sector at the Business. http://www.phoenix.edu/programs/degree-programs/business-and-management/bachelors/bsb-svc.html
19. B.S. Degree in Service Management. http://www.uwstout.edu/programs/bssm/
20. Bachelor of Science in Human Services with a concentration in Management. http://www.phoenix.edu/programs/degree-programs/humanservices/bachelors/bshs-m.html#tab=overview

Business School Innovation Through a Service Science Approach: Organizational and Performance Measurement Issues

Valter Cantino[1], Alain Devalle[1], Silvia Gandini[1],
Francesca Ricciardi[2(✉)], and Alessandro Zerbetto[1]

[1] University of Turin, Turin, Italy
{valter.cantino,alain.devalle,silvia.gandini,
alessandro.zerbetto}@unito.it
[2] University of Verona, Verona, Italy
francesca.ricciardi@univr.it

Abstract. In many cases, there is a serious gap between the needs of real-world organizations and the skills that business school graduates actually develop during their studies. In order to close this gap, innovative pedagogic solutions can be implemented in business schools, such as hands-on, work-group information systems courses; but such changes may imply serious budget and organizational problems, also because of the inertial nature of university institutions. Service science is emerging as a very promising approach to tackle the challenges implied in such practice-oriented, demand-driven innovation of educational services. In this paper, we apply a service science approach to propose a bottom-up re-design of the educational service system in a representative case: the School of Management and Economics of the university of Turin, Italy. We identify the network of stakeholders and propose a model in which students, graduates and firms interested in hiring specialized personnel play an active role in co-creating the value delivered by the university educational services. Finally, we outline the main performance measurement and organizational issues implied by this project.

Keywords: Service science · Service innovation · Service system · University · Business schools · ERP education · Information systems education

1 Introduction

The traditional business model of universities is being challenged in the emerging global scenario [26]. New and often very competitive alternatives for third level education are more and more available, both locally and in foreign countries, while the phenomenon of massive open online courses (MOOC) is booming.

Meanwhile, the demand is changing: in the traditional model, students go to university in their 20 s; whilst in the next future, as innovation continuously wipes out some jobs and changes others, many older people will need to replenish their human capital throughout their lives.

Many universities are highly inertial institutions, where innovation and change are very slow and difficult; but the pace of technological, societal and economic changes has dramatically accelerated, and so there is a growing gap between the quickly evolving educational needs and the old-fashioned educational services that most traditional universities actually provide.

The idea that university education is a doorway to well-paying jobs is then more and more perceived as a myth, while on the other hand the costs of getting a degree are constantly rising in many countries: it is not surprising that, for more and more people, a traditional degree is not value for money.

These factors are disrupting the traditional customer base of universities, especially those middle-tier institutions which used to be the only and obvious choice for aspiring graduates in their territories. Many of these institutions are witnessing decline in enrollments, morale and social prestige [17].

In this paper, we focus on economics universities, and especially on first-level business-oriented curricula, such as the BBA (Bachelor of Business Administration).

We deem that the gap between educational needs and educational service performance risks to become irreversible in many of these majors. In fact, due to the specific historical evolution of business schools [8], this academic environment often penalizes practice-oriented research and teaching, differently from what happens in other fields such as medicine or engineering.

Recent surveys, which will be more thoroughly described in the Literature Review section, show that the typical business school curricula do not provide students with the technical skills that businesses actually request to entry-level graduate employees. Moreover, other surveys demonstrate that business schools tend to give a poor contribution also to the so-called soft skills of graduates, such as the capability to adapt, to interact, to solve problems, to holistically understand the business environment they are confronted with. Students are often provided with separated silos of theoretical knowledge, such as marketing, accounting or business law, but the university does not help them in merging the inputs and getting an overall picture of how a real-world business works. Today, many undergraduates and graduates seek to take initiatives on their own in order to complement their education with highly specialized skills that give them actual competitive advantage in the labor market. Some of the organizations providing such complementary educational services are already evolving into possible competitors of traditional universities, since they are perceived as much more dynamic and cost-effective [8].

The service science approach suggests to leverage the network of stakeholders in order to build a shared view on the expected performance of a certain service, and to consistently design a new service system and a roadmap for innovating services based on stakeholder cooperation. Organizational inertia and resistance to change are taken into account to make the strategic choices between radical or incremental service innovation and periodically adjust the program [18, 25]. Third-level (business) education can be seen as a very stimulating issue for service science studies and projects. The first, pioneering papers on this subject are being published in these years; we will synthetically present them in the Literature Review section.

In this paper, we will apply the service science approach to a representative case: the School of Management and Economics of the University of Turin, Italy.

This school has witnessed a decline in enrollment and customer satisfaction in the last decade, and is then representative of the situation we described above. On the other hand, this school can leverage a 14-years' experience in developing and implementing hands-on information systems courses: thanks to this experience, an embryonic network between the university and some businesses interested in hiring specialized graduates has been developed, and can be extended to achieve a systematic cooperation between stakeholders for improved educational performance. This is consistent with an emergent stream of studies identifying the inclusion of integrated information systems, such as ERPs (Enterprise Resource Planning), into existing curricula as a key driver for educational innovation. We will build upon such resources to design a new service system for the business school under study, and we will discuss possible generalizations from this case, along with further research steps. In particular, we will highlight the main implications of the proposed service system innovation, in terms of service performance measurement and organizational issues.

2 Literature Review

Leoni and Mazzoni [16] conduct an in-depth statistical analysis of the gap between the competencies that Italian business graduates should master to effectively compete in the labor market, and those they actually receive from the university. They find alarming mismatches, both as for technical competencies, and as for soft skills. These findings are confirmed by Fabbris [12].

Also Navarro's [19] web-based survey of the MBA core curricula of top-ranked U.S. business schools finds a lack of emphasis on required multidisciplinary integration and experiential components, and a lack of attention on key themes such as information technology and soft skills. As De Villiers [10] claims, developing the students' problem-solving and social capabilities is the best way to prepare graduates for their unpredictable futures. Kavanagh and Drennan [15], on the other hand, identify business awareness and knowledge of the real world as the key soft skills that university accounting programs fail to develop in students.

A very interesting survey from David and David [8] thoroughly analyzes the skills, competencies, licenses and certifications required to graduates applying for entry level jobs. As many as 140 skills and competencies are extracted through text analysis from 200 job descriptions for entry level jobs in the U.S.. Most of these 140 skills consist in, or imply, (certified) IT skills, ranging from MS Project to SPSS, from Word Press to MS Dynamics CRM, from SAS Business Intelligence to SAP. Then, the authors compare the required competencies with those provided by a sample of U.S. business schools, and they find that there is a severe disparity between the skills required and the academic tracks that are feeders for such positions. The authors conclude that the situation encourages students and prospect students to search for complementary, or alternative, educational service providers, in order to get the competencies they actually need.

Of course, many strategies and pedagogical innovations have been suggested in order to tackle such an educational gap. Among these, we concentrate on the literature reflecting on the possible role of ERP-based pedagogy. Given its nature of widely comprehensive, integrated Information System, an ERP "can provide a framework through which learning communities can be developed to inject change into the educational environment. ERP enables integration of curriculums through developing connecting points and providing a nervous system for integration" [14]. Some authors, then, suggest to include hands-on ERP courses, not only to provide students with practice–oriented competencies that may be requested in their future job, but also to help them build the process-based interdisciplinary attitudes that are necessary in most business settings today [6, 7].

Some studies demonstrate that hands-on experience is particularly useful if associated to stimulating, design-oriented group work [21].

On the other hand, the implementation of hands-on, work-group ERP experience in business schools may imply serious financial and organizational problems [14].

Service science is emerging as a very promising approach to tackle such a challenge. The literature on service science often refers to educational services as very suitable for this approach [25]. A most cited paper, which is an important reference point for our work, is Maglio et al. [17]. In this case, the authors concentrate on U.S. computer science curricula, whose prestige is threatened by offshore IT outsourcing, and suggest a three-steps process to innovate educational services, based on service science.

3 Case Presentation and Research Method

At present, the University of Turin includes three different business schools for aspiring graduates at the bachelor's level: the School of Management and Economics (SME), the School of Business Administration (SAA) and the School of Economics and Statistics (CLEST - Cognetti De Martiis).

Like many other business schools based on a traditional curriculum, the School of Management and Economics of the University of Turin is witnessing a decline in the so-called external effectiveness of the educational service. The surveys published by AlmaLaurea (the national institution studying Italian universities) collect many data, including the perceived effectiveness of university studies. As a proxy of service performance, we may consider the share of graduates of the School of Management and Economics of the University of Turin who were in employment one year after graduation, and evaluated their university degree as "effective or very effective" for their jobs. This share was 55.6 % in 2003, but dropped to 24.8 % in 2013. Such a decline cannot be simply attributed to the economic crisis triggered by the financial collapse of 2008, because more than half of the decline had already occurred before 2009 (share in year 2009: 39.1 %).[1]

In this paper, we present this business school as a representative case to be studied through the service science lens.

---

[1] Data available (in Italian) at: http://www.almalaurea.it/universita/occupazione. Data on year 2003 refer to the 4-year curriculum which was in force until 1999 (then involving graduates interviewed in 2003), whilst data on years 2009 and 2013 refer to the new 3-year first-level degree.

In order to collect information, we utilized some of the typical data gathering techniques of case study research: document analysis, interviews, participant and non-participant observation.

Our work results in both a retrospective analysis and a design-oriented model of a new service system.

4 Research Outcomes

4.1 Retrospective Analysis - ERP Education Experience at the University of Turin, 2000–2013

In 2000, the School of Management and Economics of Turin launched a series of practice-oriented Information Systems courses within the BBA curriculum. These courses involved more than 1000 students each year. The costs of hardware, teachers' training and textbook production were covered thanks to EU funding. Also crucial was the cooperation with a leading ERP software firm, which provided free software license for educational purposes. These courses were focused on accounting issues mainly: the attempts to encourage a wider inter-disciplinary approach were unsuccessful. In the following years, the Master of Information System was launched, including more specific practice-oriented classes, directly conducted by professional from consulting firms.

Meanwhile, at the SAA Business School the Master of Information Technology and Business Process Management (ITBPM) was also launched, based on a tighter collaboration between the University and some external stakeholders interested in hiring specialized personnel. A custom-designed model was adopted: classes were created upon request after specific agreements with firms planning to hire new personnel with particular skills. Students were admitted to the master program after a selection directly conducted by the partnering firms. Students that successfully completed the course were almost always hired by the partnering firms, which also refunded the master program costs.

After 2008, due to the crisis, firms became less willing to fund these master programs. Then, the public administration was involved as a new stakeholder: the Piedmont Region now refunds the costs, but the partnering firms, in exchange, must hire as apprentice the students who successfully complete the master classes.

Interviews and feedback from students, alumni and involved companies show that this model has a great potential. This potential could be fully exploited only by expanding and systematically managing the network of stakeholders. The custom-designed master courses just stem from the personal initiative of some faculty members: thus, classes are few, and built upon the limited network of already extant personal relationship with external stakeholders.

Conversely, hands-on ERP classes at the BBA level were closed for both organizational and financial problems. The new rules establish that faculty members must teach the core subjects of their BBA school only, and unfortunately the Information Systems subjects are excluded from the official BBA curriculum. Only external lecturers could be hired to teach in these classes, but the EU funding is over and no further resources are available at the moment. Moreover, the costs of very large classrooms with hundreds of (rapidly outdated) computers are not sustainable any more for such specific purposes.

In a nutshell, the ERP large scale courses at the BBA level failed, whilst the custom-designed model of Information Systems courses at the master degree level proved successful, but remains under-exploited.

4.2 Explorative Design-Oriented Research: A New Service System Model

In 2013, a new pedagogical project has been set up, based on the experiences described above.

In order to build a design-oriented model to innovate educational services, we built upon the following three-step guideline based on service science, provided by Maglio et al. [17]:

1. identify the stakeholders and interact with them to learn about the boundaries of the service system and about problems and opportunities the stakeholders see;
2. create a draft formal model of the service system;
3. extrapolate the year-over-year evolution of the system and the activities of the stakeholders.

Following this guideline, we re-examined the interviews, documents and feedback data produced during the 14 years' experience of Information Systems courses described in Sect. 4.1. Moreover, we conducted further interviews to key stakeholders; we contacted firms offering hands-on courses in topics such as ERP, CRM (Customer Relationship Management), SCM (Supply Chain Management), etc.; and we examined and tested the new cloud platform of a leading ERP firm, that allows students to do most of their hands-on exercises autonomously, also on their own laptops.

We then identified the following and complementary needs of, and opportunities for, the potential stakeholders of the new service system:

- students would like their University to act as a coach, helping them to dynamically integrate their knowledge and relationships, to became aware of labor market expectations, to design their own future competences and certifications. On the other hand, students are growingly provided with their own hardware tools and capable to interact through the Internet;
- both employed people and those who lost their jobs are often willing to replenish their skills and competences;
- companies and business associations are interested in collaborating with the university, in order to co-design educational and training activities for both entry-level and senior employees;
- faculty members are often interested in the long-term research projects that could possibly stem from a well-developed network of relationships with partnering firms: in fact, firms involved in the pedagogical initiatives are perceived as more probably willing to share data, ideas and further contacts;

- professionals and firms specialized in information systems training (ERP, CRM etc.) are interested in giving courses/lessons within university programs, also for prestige reasons;
- IT companies, such as SAP etc., are interested in enhancing the number of certified experts of their software applications on the labor market;
- public bodies (State, regions, UE) need to show taxpayers and controllers that public investments in the educational system result in really enhanced employability and competitiveness.

In light of these considerations, we designed a new service system in which the business school acts as the focal actor of the stakeholders' network, able to optimize all the relationships in order to create value. The new model, as the previous, is based on two different strategies for graduate and under-graduate courses.

Graduate courses are thought to be suitable also for vocational training or lifelong education. The custom-designed model described in Sect. 4.1 is maintained: partnering firms and business associations are expected to collaborate in defining contents and goals of each specific course, and to hire the successful students. Funding is provided by the partnering firms and/or public bodies. The teaching staff is going to include people from software training institutes or consulting firms (to develop technical and specialized skills); people from the business world (to develop students' business awareness); and faculty members (to integrate knowledge, discuss implications and encourage the development of soft skills).

We plan to develop systematic agreements between the university and some leading software firms, in order to provide successful students with official international certifications. The network of stakeholders needs to be systematically enlarged, developed and cared for, so that a much wider customer base is exploitable. These master programs, once their potential is more fully developed (which will take at least 1 or 2 years) are expected to yield the financial, relational and knowledge resources that will allow to launch innovative courses at the undergraduate level, too.

Undergraduate courses will indeed be conceived differently from those organized in the years 2000–2006. In fact, that model is not sustainable any more. Moreover, a highly specialized mass training on a single software, although very important, like SAP, is not sufficient to close the educational gap described in Sects. 1 and 2.

We then plan to launch a course of "Information Systems and Business Processes", based on the cloud educational platforms already available from many leading software firms. This solution will allow students to develop technical skills about business software through e-learning courses and online exams, but also to improve knowledge about business processes. Classroom activities will be based instead on the analysis of some real-world cases and representative job descriptions, in order to improve problem solving and service-based attitudes, and, ultimately, to increase students' capability to co-design their own careers.

The development of this service system will allow access to valuable information for further research, through high-quality, long-term relationships with stakeholders. Our project is aimed to stimulate collaboration between faculty members of different disciplines, to activate relevant and interdisciplinary research pipelines, and ultimately to leverage the educational partnerships in order to create research partnerships.

We think that the implementation of this system calls for further work, especially in the areas of performance measurement and organization science. The next paragraph is dedicated to synthetically outline the issues that our work implies in these two areas.

5 Implications and Further Research

5.1 Performance Measurement Issues

The service science approach and, more generally, a system view on business has been often linked to improved performance, especially in terms of long-term, sustainable and enduring competitiveness [1]. On the other hand, the literature on how service performance should be measured is still scarce; this opens up important new agendas for scholars.

Thus, in order to implement our service system model, we need to discuss and carefully define the measurement criteria and the system of indicators that will allow to monitor and report on the change process in the business school's service system, drafted in the paragraph above.

The main issues we identified to pursue this goal follow.

- Universities, and especially large State universities, can be seen as providers of public interest services, because of their complex, relevant societal impact. As such, the measurement of organizational performance is complex and multidimensional: as public sector scholars claim, this relates to the number of dimensions of performance, and the number of stakeholders Boyne [3]. A recent review of many different criteria and methods to measure university performance is included in Fabbris [12].
- The evaluation process should build upon the key concepts of service science (strongly focusing on the value created by the interactions between stakeholders) to avoid mechanistic or simplistic approaches to performance measurement. For complex services involving also public interest, in fact, too mechanistic and control-oriented approaches to performance measurement are associated to perverse and dysfunctional consequences [20]. Since subjective performance evaluation is often more suitable to support prospector strategies in turbulent environments, an integrated performance measurement system, including both subjective and objective criteria, is probably the most effective to measure complex and intangible aspects, such as stakeholder satisfaction and stakeholder contribution [5].
- The literature on Intellectual Capital [11] may provide very useful tools to define some important measurement criteria in our case. An emerging stream of studies concentrates on intellectual capital in universities, but these studies usually focus on measuring the internal intellectual capital (of professors, employees etc.) [22, 24], whilst we propose that measuring also the intellectual capital of students and graduates may be crucial. In fact, intellectual capital (and human capital especially) measures value-creating skills and attitudes mainly [5], thus may very usefully complement university grades, which usually measure students' knowledge. Moreover, another important dimension of intellectual capital, i.e. social capital, focuses on the actual and potential value of social relationships, and is then a particularly suitable construct in order to assess a service system.

- More specifically, the concepts of "service performance gap" [2] and "human capital gap" [4] provide particularly useful tools to our goals.

5.2 Organizational Issues

Bitner et al. [2] provide useful guidelines to identify the organizational innovations needed in order to successfully implement a new service system.

The authors focus on how service delivery gaps can be closed, and identify three complementary strategies, each implying organizational action. We translated these three strategies into our case as follows:

- *Aligning the firm's human resource strategies around delivering service excellence.* This means to hire, develop, reward and retain human resources (professors, employees, etc.) willing and capable to contribute to the new educational service system described above. This is a particularly difficult organizational challenge in our case, since the hiring, promotion and tenure criteria of universities are strongly institutionalized and reward mainly highly theoretical and specialized research published on top journals. Moreover, the structure of business school departments may be an issue, since it is often based on functional disciplines, which encourages the insular focus of scholarship and teaching [9].
- *Defining customers' roles and help them to understand and perform effectively.* In our service system model, we have at least two categories of customers paying for the university's services: students and firms. Helping such customers to play their roles in the system implies a sort of Copernican revolution, since it implies that students should be helped to go beyond the mere role of studying, and firms should be helped to continuously and clearly communicate the skill sets they require and the opportunities that exist, both now and in the future. At the same time, this demand-pull strategy can be leveraged to make students more aware of which academic programs and courses are most likely to provide them with the required skills. "Businesses can also have a significant influence on the structure of postgraduate programs, even to the point at which programs can be custom-designed to meet individual organizational needs. In working with academics to develop these new programs, both sides can gain from the experience, and the results can extend into the more formal degree programs offered by academic institutions" [9].
- *Integrating technology effectively and appropriately to aid service performance.* Technology is often essential to facilitate effective interactions and to support stakeholders in playing their respective roles. In particular, technology can enhance the capability of customers to contribute to value creation, and in some cases makes it possible for some services to be produced almost entirely by the customers (in this case, students and firms), minimizing efforts and costs for the service system's focal organization (in this case, the university). For this reason, it is essential that the implementation of our service system is supported by a smart, web-based information system, which may be the object of scholarly research and publication, and may be developed with the help of the software firms involved in the pedagogic projects.

6 Conclusions

Most of the technical skills required to business school graduates are related to the software solutions commonly used in the world of practice, including not only business operations systems such as ERP, SCM or CRM, but also analytical and executive information systems such as Business Intelligence, Big Data or Decision Support Systems [13, 23]. The required technical competences, on the other hand, must be integrated with soft skills, which usually include problem-solving attitudes, cooperative capabilities, and an integrated view of real-world business.

In this paper, we suggested that Information Systems courses may be designed innovatively within business schools, in order to provide students with not only valuable technical certifications, but also enhanced soft skills and improved capabilities to adapt their curricula throughout life.

The case of the School of Management and Economics of the University of Turin shows that cloud technologies, web 2.0 solutions and social networks can allow sustainable pedagogic solutions for hands-on, work-group information systems education. We utilized a service science approach to build a new service system model for the university, in which both students and the organizations interested in hiring specialized graduates are seen as customers and value co-creators. We analyzed the challenges implied in this service system innovation, and we identified some key performance measurement and organizational issues. We hope that our contribution opens up interesting and inter-disciplinary research agendas.

References

1. Barile, S., Polese, F.: Smart service systems and viable service systems: applying systems theory to service science. Serv. Sci. **2**(1–2), 21–40 (2010)
2. Bitner, M.J., Zeithaml, V.A., Gremler, D.D.: Technology's impact on the gaps model of service quality. In: Maglio, P.P., Kieliszewski, J.A., Spohrer, J.C. (eds.) Handbook of Service Science, pp. 197–218. Springer, New York (2010)
3. Boyne, G.A. (ed.): Public Service Performance: Perspectives on Measurement and Management. Cambridge University Press, Cambridge (2006)
4. Cabrilo, S., Nesic, L.G., Mitrovic, S.: Study on human capital gaps for effective innovation strategies in the knowledge era. J. Intellect. Cap. **15**(3), 411–429 (2014)
5. Chenhall, R.H., Langfield-Smith, K.: Multiple perspectives of performance measures. Eur. Manage. J. **25**(4), 266–282 (2007)
6. Dameri, R.P., Marchi, L.: Accounting management and information systems. In: D'Atri, A., et al. (eds.) Management of the Interconnected World. Springer, Heidelberg (2010)
7. Dameri, R.P., Garelli, R., Ricciardi, F.: The didactic challenge of accounting information systems and ERPs for business schools: a proposal for the Italian Universities. In: Mancini, D., Vaassen, E.H.J., Dameri, R.P. (eds.) Accounting Information Systems for Decision Making, pp. 337–349. Springer, Heidelberg (2013)
8. David, F.R., David, M. E., David, F.R.: What are business schools doing for business today? Bus. Horizons **54**(1), 51–62 (2011)
9. Davis, M.M., Berdrow, I.: Service science: catalyst for change in business school curricula. IBM Syst. J. **47**(1), 29–39 (2008)

10. De Villiers, R.: The incorporation of soft skills into accounting curricola: preparing accounting graduates for their unpredictable futures. Meditari Accountancy Res. **18**(2), 1–22 (2010)
11. Edvinsson, L., Malone, M.S.: Intellectual Capital: Realizing Your Company's True Value by Finding Its Hidden Brainpower (1997)
12. Fabbris, L. (ed.): Effectiveness of University Education in Italy. Physica-Verlag, Heidelberg (2007)
13. Ferrari, A., Rossignoli, C., Zardini, A.: Enabling Factors for SaaS Business Intelligence Adoption: A Theoretical Framework Proposal. In Information Technology and Innovation Trends in Organizations, pp. 355–361. Physica-Verlag HD (2011)
14. Joseph, G., George, A.: ERP, learning communities, and curriculum integration. J. Inf. Syst. Educ. **13**(1), 51–58 (2002)
15. Kavanagh, M.H., Drennan, L.: What skills and attributes does an accounting graduate need? Evidence from student perceptions and employer expectations. Acc. Financ. **48**(2), 279–300 (2008)
16. Leoni, R., Mazzoni, N.: Competenze richieste dal mercato e competenze possedute dai laureati. In: Leoni, R. (a cura di) Competenze acquisite, competenze richieste e competenze espresse. Franco Angeli, Milano (2006)
17. Maglio, P.P., Srinivasan, S., Kreulen, J.T., Spohrer, J.: Service systems, service scientists, SSME, and innovation. Commun. ACM **49**(7), 81–85 (2006)
18. Maglio, P.P., Spohrer, J.: Fundamentals of service science. J. Acad. Mark. Sci. **36**(1), 18–20 (2008)
19. Navarro, P.: The MBA core curricola of top-ranked US business schools: a study in failure? Acad. Manage. Learn. Educ. **7**(1), 108–123 (2008)
20. Pidd, M.: Perversity in public service performance measurement. Int. J. Prod. Perform. Manage. **54**(5/6), 482–493 (2005)
21. Ragan, J.M.: An implementation strategy for developing interdisciplinary professional skills within the accounting curriculum. Rev. Bus. Inf. Syst. (RBIS) **11**(4), 27–36 (2011)
22. Ramírez, Y., Gordillo, S.: Recognition and measurement of intellectual capital in Spanish universities. J. Intellect. Cap. **15**(1), 173–188 (2014)
23. Ricciardi, F., De Marco, M.: The challenge of service oriented performances for chief information officers. In: Snene, M. (ed.) Exploring Service Science, Ginevra, 15–17 February, pp. 258–270. Springer, Berlin (2012)
24. Siboni, B., Nardo, M.T., Sangiorgi, D.: Italian state university contemporary performance plans: an intellectual capital focus? J. Intellect. Cap. **14**(3), 414–430 (2013)
25. Vargo, S.L., Maglio, P.P., Akaka, M.A.: On value and value co-creation: A service systems and service logic perspective. Eur. Manage. J. **26**(3), 145–152 (2008)
26. Wildavsky, B.: The Great Brain Race: How Global Universities are Reshaping the World. Princeton University Press, Princeton (2012)

Disclosing Paths for Multi-channel Service Research: A Contemporaneous Phenomenon and Guidelines for Future Investigations

João Reis[1(✉)], Marlene Amorim[1], and Nuno Melão[2,3]

[1] Department of Economics, Management and Industrial Engineering,
Aveiro University, Aveiro, Portugal
{reis.joao,mamorim}@ua.pt
[2] Department of Management, School of Technology and Management of Viseu,
Polytechnic Institute of Viseu, Viseu, Portugal
nmelao@estgv.ipv.pt
[3] CEGE, Catholic University of Portugal (Porto), Lisbon, Portugal

Abstract. The present paper reports on the findings of a systematic literature review on multi-channel services. In doing so, it uses an affinity diagram to show the results of a content analysis regarding the issues addressed by the existing literature in the field. This enables to understand areas of interest in the contemporary subject of research, find gaps in the literature and, lastly, to uncover guidelines for future research. The results suggest that future investigations should focus on the integration of traditional and virtual services, on quality issues and customer behaviour towards the use of multi-channel services. Previous research also suggests that multi-channel services are largely unaddressed, regarding issues as back-office processes, within the scope of operations management. Subsequently, since multi-channel services are multidisciplinary in nature, these guidelines represent a fruitful opportunity for future research to involve other disciplines.

Keywords: Service integration · Multi-channel services · Systematic literature review

1 Introduction

Following the first decade of the 21st century, it has become obvious that multi-channel service delivery is changing. This change was first described by Froehle and Roth [1], arguing that customers used to interact directly with service employees (face-to-face), but, more recently, it is complemented with new technologies (face-to-screen). In face-to-screen settings, the role of technology can either be the mediation of contact with a service employee or performing automated service delivery without human intervention [2]. A second perspective, presented by Sousa and Voss [3], distinguishes virtual and physical channels of service delivery. A virtual channel consists of a means of communication using "advanced telecommunications, information, and multimedia technologies" and physical channels consist of means of communications with the customer employing a physical (brick-and-mortar) infrastructure [3, 4]. As Robert Yin [5] mentioned before, a contemporaneous phenomenon, whose boundaries are unclear, makes it technically difficult to define. Concomitantly, the understanding of this phenomenon is largely connected on how the *multi-channel service* term is defined. While there is a definition that has gathered some scholar approval, i.e. service composed of components (physic and/or virtual), delivered through two or more channels [3], the field of multi-channel service still did not reach a consensus regarding the meaning of its core concept [6], as it can be seen from Table 1. The difficulty of defining the term "multi-channel service" led us to search the literature for a more comprehensive element, known as "multi-channel service system", associated to distinct aspects of multi-channel system.

The term *multi-channel service system* was initially described as the "use of more than one channel to manage customer integration across all channels" [7]. From Table 1, it seems clear that different authors use different terms and several settings to refer to the same thing: the "multi-channel services" term. Based on the definitions, our intention is to define the minimal set of features associated with the term, as well as the set of elements of a multi-channel service system. In an attempt to understand the phenomenon we reduce the term to its essential elements derived from the multi-channel service definition. The challenge of defining the multi-channel service concept can be tackled after the definitions have been reduced to their basic elements. A multi-channel service i.e. "service, composed by its elementary components (physical and/or virtual), delivered consistently to customers through the interaction of two or more organizational channels". In fact, physical distribution channels (such as a branch or retail outlet), telephone, automatic teller machines (ATMs), Internet, enable today service firms and their customers to interact with each other [1, 14]. In particular, the Internet is fast becoming a feasible alternative to the traditional face-to-face channel [1] as it is integrated into multi-channel servicing system [15, 16]. The opportunities offered by the Internet and the infatuation it aroused among customers led service firms to adopt a multi-channel distribution by combining both traditional physical channels and virtual channels such as the Internet and telephone [14]. A good example is the financial sector, which has a long history of developing new ways to interact with customers and has, therefore, been employing multi-channel strategies for a long time [17, 18].

In sum, the emergence of hybrid distribution systems such as multi-channel services rapidly changed the world and became a standard business model [19, 20]. The proliferation of multi-channel services has created a challenge for firms insofar as how to manage these new environments effectively and created opportunities for academics to produce insights that can help address this challenge [10].

Subsequently, to close this section, we present the research question, in order to understand the areas of interest in the contemporary subject of research, find gaps in the literature and to disclose guidelines for future research.

- RQ: What are the research domains associated to the multi-channel services?

This research question will allow achieving the main purpose of the investigation, and disseminate the leading contemporary domains that are associated to multi-channel services.

Table 1. Definition for multi-channel service system

Year	Author	Terms	Multichannel services system definition
2002	Stone et al. [7]	Multi-channel management	The use of more than one channel or medium to manage customers in a way that is consistent and coordinated across all the channels or media in use
2004	Payne and Flow [8]	Multichannel services	These main channel categories can be represented as a continuum of forms of customer contact ranging from the physical (such as a face to face encounter with a company sales representative) to the virtual (such as an e-commerce or G3 phone transaction)
2004	Wallace et al. [9]	Multiple channels	Offering multiple complementary channels provides a greater and deeper mix of customer service, thereby enhancing the seller's overall value preposition
2006	Neslin et al. [10]	Multi-channel management	The design, deployment, coordination and evaluation of channels through which firms and customers interact, with the goal of enhancing customer value through effective customer acquisition, retention, and development
2006	Sousa and Voss [3]	Multichannel services	Services composed of components (physic and/or virtual), delivered through two or more channels
2008	Agatz et al. [11]	Multi-channeling	Different channels differ in their abilities to perform various service outputs
2009	Cassab and MacLachlan [12]	Multi-channel service	Multi-channel services are the use of alternative modes of contact by customers to interact with and obtain service from an organization
2011	Chiu et al. [13]	Multichannel environment	Consumers can move easily among different channels. They engage in cross-channel free riding when they use one retailer's channel to obtain information or evaluate products and then switch to another retailer's channel to complete the purchase

2 Methodology

To conduct research about a given subject, it is crucial to find answers, contextualized in terms of a larger research problem. This necessarily involves reviewing the literature of that subject to indicate what has been researched in the area and to demonstrate a need for future research [21]. This study discusses the findings of a systematic literature review (SLR) on multi-channel services. In doing so, it uses an affinity diagram to show the results of a content analysis regarding the issues addressed by the existing literature in the field. This strategy will permit to find guidelines for future research.

2.1 Systematic Literature Review

The adoption of the SLR method is due to the fact that multi-channel services is a relatively new area of study [22], but also because it is an explicit and reproducible method for identifying, evaluating and synthesizing the existent body of completed and recorded work produced by researchers [23].

However, this method is limited, in that it does not cover the whole body of knowledge related to a specific phenomenon, as it is restricted to a selected number of keywords [24]. Thus, it is acknowledged that some relevant articles could be missing; the results are based on the application of filters, which may exclude broad cited articles or, in the individual perception of readers, articles that should be interesting to integrate the study *per se*. Furthermore, to present a literature review of almost 120 articles, in such a few pages, it is a difficult task for any author, but is also motivating and requires a good capacity for synthesis. Despite these difficulties, a SLR allows for searching through a vast pool of research [24, 25] – in this case, a broad range of journals over a period of 25 years.

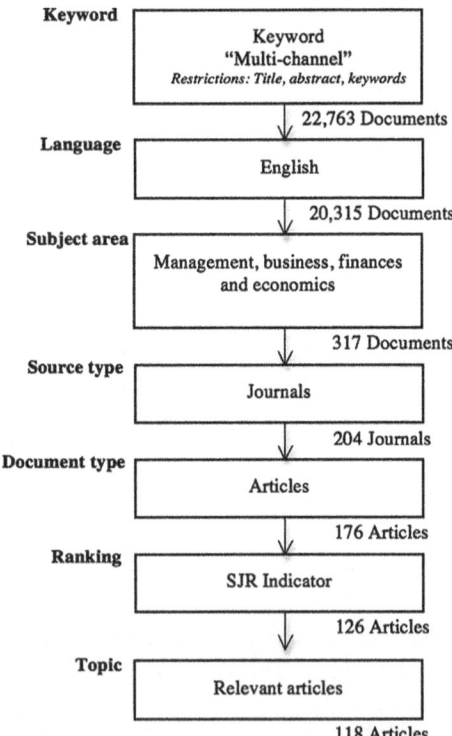

Fig. 1. Methodological approach [6]

This paper precedes the results of a conference proceeding [6] and a summary of the search process is presented below, shown in Fig. 1.

This paper is based on a search made in March 2014, using the Scopus database with the keyword "multi-channel" in the title, abstract and keywords, which found a total of 22,763 documents. The review process was based on the application of successive filters to exclude irrelevant papers and ensure viable results (Fig. 1). In this figure, readers can see that only articles written in English language were deemed relevant. To ensure the adequacy and quality of findings, the authors only considered articles in the management area within the quartiles Q1 and Q2 of the SCImago Journal & Country Rank (scimagojr.com).

In comparison with the previous one, the current paper presents new contributions, since it identifies dimensions and gaps in the literature of multi-channel services, and suggests guidelines for future research.

2.2 Affinity Diagram

The affinity diagram is a useful tool to structure a large amount of information. After reducing and filtering 22,763 documents to 118 articles it was necessary to understand their similarities. An affinity diagram was used to show the results of a content analysis [26] regarding the issues addressed by the existing literature in the field.

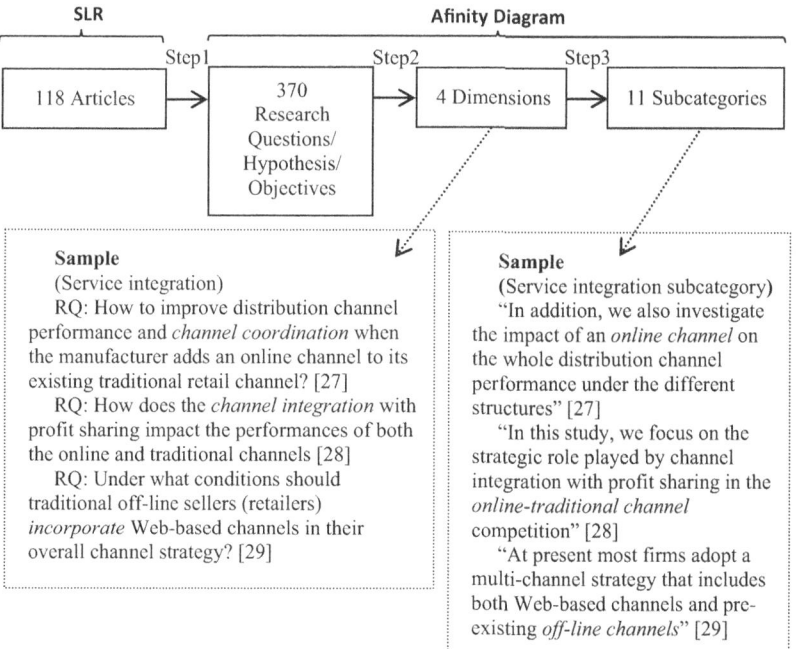

Fig. 2. Data analysis procedures

Figure 2 resumes the data analysis procedures. First, the research questions of all 118 articles were listed, including hypothesis and objectives; the result was a total of 370 questions, objectives or hypothesis to analyse. Second, to find the dimensions, those research questions were grouped by their similarities and affinities, as shown in the sample on Fig. 2. In this case, all research questions, concerning service integration, use words as "channel integration" or "channel coordination". Third, a similar process was performed to retain and subcategorize the selected dimensions. In this case, we analysed the most mentioned words of each article that are interrelated with "service integration", an example is "online channels" and "offline channels". In sum, most of the articles are related to issues such as customer behaviour, service integration, quality issues and financial services (Fig. 3).

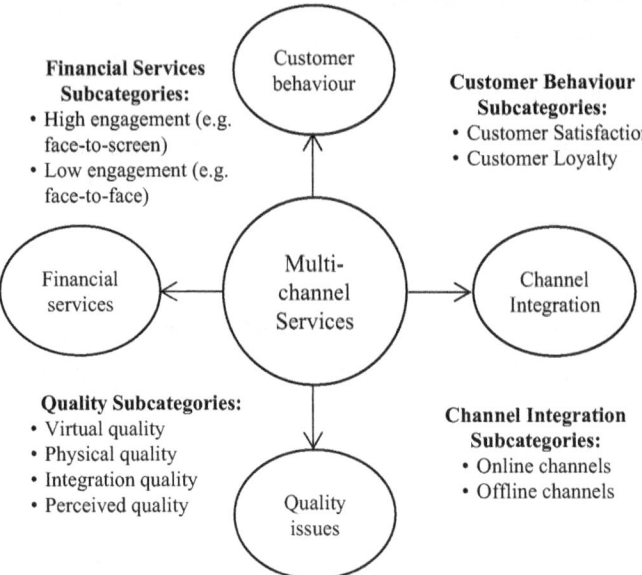

Fig. 3. Affinity diagram of multi-channel service theme

The next stage was to settle each of the topics and find the existing research gaps in each group in order to identify guidelines for future research to practitioners and academics. The affinity diagram approach may help discover hidden linkages between articles from a multidisciplinary range of documents.

3 Discussion

Several dimensions have emerged, the most cited concern customer behaviour, service integration, multi-channel quality and financial services. Each one poses different research opportunities. Due to space limitations, we only present brief discussion of the literature within each dimension.

3.1 Customer Behaviour

According to existent literature, consumer's perceived multi-channel service quality, channel-switching difficulties and satisfaction mediate the effect of channel characteristics on their behaviour intentions [12]. Therefore, multi-channel characteristics will influence multi-channel quality and channel switching difficulties. Although there is an abundance of literature about the determinants of customer loyalty in either the brick-and-mortar or online contexts, there is limited research in multiple channel contexts, especially in the service industry [30]. Furthermore, offline channel fulfilment appears to be at least as important as website performance in a front-office context [2] and [30]. Some authors have also suggested that further research could investigate the influence of quality of the multi-channel service interface, information consistency and the ability of consumers to use multiple modes of contact efficiently [12, 20]. Indeed, the absence of consistency in providing a service across multiple channels can frustrate consumers when they have pretentions to purchase a service or a product [30, 31]. Therefore, a question can be posed for future investigation: What are motivating customers to pursuit multi-channel services?

3.2 Service Integration

Despite the growth of multi-channel services, little empirical research has offered insights into cross-channel issues, such as understanding how consumer's integrate the service with experiences via physical store and offline marketing communications, with website characteristics [32]. Moreover, the synergy between online and offline operations generated through the integration of channels has been argued to enrich customers' experiences with a service and cultivate customer loyalty in both channels [32, 33]. To improve the level of channel integration and avoid channel overlap [15] managers should understand these particular aspects in order to avoid channel conflicts [34] or address a possible cannibalization of a channel towards another [35–37]. In integration strategies, the channels are seen as complementary components of a multi-channel system that aim to provide a high level of convenience to customers [38]. Therefore, a question can be posed for future investigation: How is the integration of traditional and virtual services accomplished?

3.3 Quality Issues

A preliminary insight of multi-channel services usually comes from the service marketing literature. Particularly, the concept of service quality has been extensively studied in the last two decades, since the publication of the seminal work of Grönroos [39] and the development of the SERVQUAL instrument [12, 40]. In a multi-channel setting, however, other investigators have studied the multi-channel service quality [3]. This study proposes that in a multichannel setting, multi-channel service quality comprises three components: virtual (e.g., Web site), physical (people-delivered, including logistics), and integration quality (seamless service experience across channels). But, a question remains: what is the perceived quality of a multi-channel service? Grönroos [39] states that the perceived quality of a service stems from the direct relationship between the expectations those customers have regarding the quality of a service, and the experience they have with the organization when the service is provided. Parasuraman et al. [40] and Berry et al. [41] refers, as Grönroos [42], that perceived quality of a service is made by comparing customer expectations and the performance of an organization. Another definition is presented by Zeithaml [43], which states that perceived service quality is the consumer's judgment about a service's overall excellence or superiority, similar to those previously reported. In a multi-channel context, customers' perceived service quality of each channel depends not merely on the service that one channel provides, but also on the service other channels provide [35]. Multi-channel users perceive the quality of every channel and then integrate them into an overall perceived service quality [30]. It would be useful to investigate why the main part of the studies on quality have focused on marketing issues. As Zeithaml [43] points out the relationship between quality perceptions and customer attitude has long been a focus of marketing literature. Eventually, it will be interesting to drive quality studies to other areas of knowledge (e.g. operation management). Therefore, an interesting question can be also posed for future investigation: How is service quality applied to multi-channel services?

3.4 Financial Services

The first self-service technologies emerged in the financial sector in the 1970s [44], when banks installed the first automated teller machines (ATMs) [45], and continued changing during the past decade with the proliferation of mobile communications technologies [46]. Hence, the importance of these services for multi-channel context. In analysing the results of the SLR, we found that financial services is a category with wide variation in terms of product purchase and management, customer involvement levels and perceived risk, all of which may influence consumer choice and multi-channel behaviour [16]. Recent studies [16] mention that while there is little involvement in financial services (e.g. routine procedures) consumers usually use the face-to-screen service, however, for more complex services, where there is high engagement (e.g. loan requirement), consumers prefer face-to-face services. The presented information shows that financial services are a good example of the engagement in multi-channel services; this study area is fertile for fieldwork and several places can be used for that propose (e.g. banks, insurance companies). Therefore, some questions can be posed for future investigation: To what extent does the financial services have influenced the developments of multichannel services?

It should be interesting to pursue the questions listed in Table 2 with empirical work (e.g. case study research). If the questions are well adapted to the phenomenon it can lead to fruitful results and mitigate some difficulties already identified. A case study could be also a great tool to reveal some answers, as it can study the phenomenon in its natural setting and, additionally, can also lead itself to early exploratory investigations where the variables are still unknown and the phenomenon is not at all understood [47, 48].

A previous study [6] reports that these questions are dedicated to the analysis of consumer interactions with front-office services, thus, other disciplines, as operation management, have a limited engagement with the literature. The listed questions, in Table 2, are not surprisingly as readers can find, however, the main suggestion goes towards moving the discussion of these issues to topics such as the back-office processes, an area still largely undressed in the literature.

Table 2. Questions and suggestions for multi-channel service

Multi-channel services topic	Questions	Suggestions
Customer behaviour	What are motivating customers to pursue multi-channel services?	Extend these topics to a new comprehensive approach concerning the operation management area. Usually these topics are analysed from a marketing perspective
Service integration	How is the integration of traditional and virtual services accomplished?	
Quality issues	How is service quality applied to multi-channel services?	
Financial services	To what extent does the financial services have influenced the developments of multichannel services?	

4 Conclusions

The results of the analysis show that there are two main findings. First, there are four major areas related to the investigation of multi-channel services. Concerning the first area, customer behaviour, there is an abundance of literature about the determinants of customer loyalty, in either the brick-and-mortar or online contexts, but the multiple channel context and especially the offline processes remain unaddressed. On other hand, and despite the growth of multi-channel services, little empirical research has offered insights into cross-channel issues, such as the understanding on how consumer's integrate the service with experiences face-to-face and face-to-screen. A preliminary insight of multi-channel services usually comes from the service marketing literature. Particularly, the concept of service quality has been extensively studied in the last two decades. However, few studies have a multi-channel scope and there are other areas besides marketing that are being neglected (e.g. operations management). The lack of studies may jeopardize the quality of multi-channel services, particularly, with regard to the integration quality. Regarding these concerns, it is important to mention that there is scope for further research, especially in the area of financial services, more specifically, to perform fieldworks in banks or insurance companies. Second, this research also highlights the need for further research regarding the issues of back-office processes, which have been surprisingly overlooked by the academic community. Bridging these gaps may provide useful knowledge for practitioners and would deepen the academic understanding.

Several methodological limitations can be mentioned. Due to space limitations it is not possible to list all the 118 references. References can be provided on request, by contacting the first author. The findings from this study have been limited due to the methodological constraints that resulted from the research design and the data-set [26]. The Scopus citation index is constantly being updated with new peer-reviewed international literature and our sample consists of journal articles, based on the assumption that these amount to the frontier of research [26], although, there may be other publications that are not included in this database and, thus, in this study [24]. Nevertheless, the review has undeniable value as it synthesizes scientific knowledge of the conceptualizations and outcomes of multi-channel services research [24]. This paper is also a part of a work in progress since a SLR is an overview of primary studies that contains an explicit statement of objectives, materials, and methods [49].

The results suggest that future investigations should focus on the integration of traditional and virtual services, on quality issues and customer behaviour towards the use of multi-channel services. Thus, the main guidelines for future investigations relate the need to approach certain issues in multi-channel services from an operations management perspective. Reis *et al.* [6] remark that it is imperative the need to direct studies into a prospective analysis of back-office processes, contrary to what has been done so far. This paper alerts scholars to the need to conduct new researches, suggesting direct attention to the issues presented in this paper, which are usually placed in the marketing area, but we believe that can also be applicable to the sphere of operations management. Since multi-channel services are multidisciplinary in nature, the benefits are clear; these guidelines represent a fertile opportunity for future research since it calls the engagement of other disciplines (e.g. operation management) besides marketing, which can lead to new contributions for management.

References

1. Froehle, C., Roth, A.: New measurement scales for evaluating perceptions of the technology-mediated customer service experience. J. Oper. Manag. **22**, 1–21 (2004)
2. Semeijn, J., Riel, A., Birgelen, M., Streukens, S.: E-services and offline fulfilment: how e-loyalty is created. Manag. Serv. Qual. **15**, 182–194 (2005)
3. Sousa, R., Voss, A.: Service quality in multichannel services employing virtual channels. J. Serv. Res. **8**, 356–371 (2006)
4. Sousa, R., Amorim, M.: A framework for the design of multichannel services. Project for the Foundation for Science and Technology; under grant number PTDC/GES/68139/2006 (2009)
5. Yin, R.: Studying phenomenon and context across sites. Am. Behav. Sci. **26**, 84–100 (1982)
6. Reis, J., Amorim, M., Melão, N.: Research opportunities in multi-channel services: a systematic review. In: Proceedings of the 21st EurOMA Conference, Palermo-Italy (2014)
7. Stone, M., Hobbs, M., Khaleeli, M.: Multichannel customer management: the benefits and challenges. J. Database Mark. **10**, 39–52 (2002)
8. Payne, A., Frow, P.: The role of multichannel integration in customer relationship management. Ind. Mark. Manag. **33**, 527–538 (2004)
9. Wallace, D., Giese, J., Johnson, J.: Customer retailer loyalty in the context of multiple channel strategies. J. Retail. **80**, 249–263 (2004)
10. Neslin, S.A., Grewal, D., Shankar, V., Teerling, M.L., Thomas, J.S., Verhoef, P.D.: Challenges and opportunities in multichannel customer management. J Serv. Res. **9**, 95–112 (2006)

11. Agatz, N., Fleishchmann, M., Nunen, J.: E-fulfillment and multi-channel distribution – a review. Eur. J. Oper. Res. **187**, 339–356 (2008)
12. Cassab, H., MacLachlan, D.: A consumer-based view of multi-channel service. J. Serv. Manag. **20**, 52–75 (2009)
13. Chiu, H., Hsieh, Y., Roan, J., Tseng, K., Hsieh, J.: The challenge for multichannel services: cross-channel free-riding behaviour. Electron. Commer. Res. Appl. **10**, 268–277 (2011)
14. Seck, A., Philippe, J.: Service encounter in multi-channel distribution context: virtual and face-to-face interactions and consumer satisfaction. Serv. Ind. J. **33**, 565–579 (2013)
15. Birgelen, M., Jong, A., Ruyter, K.: Multi-channel service retailing: The effects of channel performance satisfaction on behavioural intentions. J. Retail. **82**, 367–377 (2006)
16. Cortiñas, M., Chacarro, R., Villanueva, M.: Understanding multichannel banking customers. J. Bus. Res. **63**, 1215–1221 (2010)
17. Easingwood, C., Storey, C.: The value of multi-channel distribution systems in the financial services sector. Serv. Ind. J. **16**, 223–241 (1996)
18. Pikkarainen, T., Pikkarainen, K., Karjaluoto, H., Pahnila, S.: Consumer acceptance of online banking: an extension of the technology acceptance model. Internet Res. Electron. Netw. Appl. Policy **14**, 224–235 (2004)
19. Moriarty, R., Moran, U.: Managing hybrid marketing systems. Harvard Bus. Rev. **68**, 146–155 (1990)
20. Webb, K., Hogan, J.: Hybrid channel conflict: causes and effects on channel performance. J. Bus. Ind. Mark. **17**, 338–356 (2002)
21. Given, L.: The SAGE Encyclopaedia of Qualitative Research Methods, vol. 1&2. Sage, Thousand Oaks (2008)
22. Thorpe, R., Holt, R.: The Sage Dictionary of Qualitative Management Research. Sage, London (2008)
23. Fink, A.: Conducting Research Literature Reviews: From Paper to the Internet, 2nd edn. Sage, Thousand Oaks (2005)
24. Mustak, M., Jaakkola, E., Halinen, A.: Customer participation and value creation: a systematic review and research implications. Manag. Serv. Qual. **23**, 341–359 (2013)
25. Wang, C., Chugh, H.: Entrepreneurial learning: past research and future challenges. Int. J. Manag. Rev. **16**, 24–61 (2014)
26. Coombes, P., Nicholson, J.: Business models and their relationship with marketing: a systematic literature review. Ind. Mark. Manag. **42**, 656–664 (2013)
27. Tang, F., Xing, X.: Will the growth of multi-channel retailing diminish the pricing efficiency of the web? J. Retail. **77**, 319–333 (2001)
28. Yan, R., Wang, J., Zhou, B.: Channel integration and profit sharing in the dynamics of multi-channel firms. J. Retail. Consum. Serv. **17**, 430–440 (2010)
29. King, R., Sen, R., Xia, M.: Impact of web-based e-Commerce on channel strategy in retailing. Int. J. Electron. Commer. **8**, 103–130 (2004)
30. Hsieh, I., Roan, J., Pant, A., Hsieh, J., Chen, W., Lee, M., Chiu, H.: All for one but does one strategy work for all? Building consumer loyalty in multi-channel distribution. Manag. Serv. Qual. **22**, 310–335 (2012)
31. Rangaswamy, A., Bruggen, G.: Opportunities and challenges in multichannel marketing. J. Interact. Mark. **19**, 5–12 (2005)
32. Carlson, J., Cass, A.: Managing web site performance taking account of the contingency role of branding in multi-channel retailing. J. Consum. Mark. **28**, 524–531 (2011)
33. Kwon, W., Lennon, S.: Reciprocal effects between multi-channel retailers' offline and online brand images. J. Retail. **85**, 376–390 (2009)
34. Sharma, A., Mehrotra, A.: Choosing an optimal channel mix in multichannel environments. Ind. Mark. Manag. **36**, 21–28 (2007)

35. Montoya-Weiss, M., Voss, G., Grewal, D.: Determinants of online channel use and overall satisfaction with a relational, multichannel service provider. J. Acad. Mark. Sci. **31**, 448–458 (2003)
36. Steinfield, C.: Does Online and Offline Channel Integration Work in Practice? Paper presented at the Workshop on E-Commerce Impacts Revisited, DIW, Berlin (2004)
37. Kollmann, T., Kuckertz, A., Kayser, I.: Cannibalization or synergy? Consumers' channel selection in online-offline channel systems. J. Retail. Consum. Serv. **19**, 186–194 (2012)
38. Muller-Lankenau, C., Wehmeyer, K., Klein, S.: Strategic channel alignment: an analysis of the configuration of physical and virtual marketing channels. Springer, New York (2006)
39. Grönroos, C.: A service quality model and its marketing implications. Eur. J. Mark. **18**, 36–44 (1984)
40. Parasuraman, A., Zeithaml, V., Berry, L.: SERVQUAL: a multiple-item scale for measuring consumer perceptions of service quality. J. Retail. **64**, 12–40 (1988)
41. Berry, L., Zeithaml, V., Parasuraman, A.: Five imperatives for improving service quality. Sloan Manag. Rev. **31**, 29–38 (1990)
42. Grönroos, C.: Service quality: The six criteria of good perceived service. Rev. Bus. **9**, 10–13 (1988)
43. Zeithaml, V.: Consumer perceptions of price, quality, and value: a means-end model and synthesis of evidence. J. Mark. **52**, 2–22 (1988)
44. Railton, J.: Automated teller machines. Comput. Law Secur. Rev. **1**, 1–12 (1985)
45. Dabholkar, P.: Consumer evaluations of new technology-based self-service options: an investigation of alternative models of service quality. Int. J. Res. Mark. **13**, 29–51 (1996)
46. Hoehle, H., Scornavacca, E., Huff, S.: Three decades of research on consumer adoption and utilization of electronic banking channels: a literature analysis. Decis. Support Syst. **54**, 122–132 (2012)
47. Benbasat, I., Goldstein, D., Mead, M.: The case research strategy in studies of information systems. MIS Q. **3**, 369–386 (1987)
48. Meredith, J.: Building operations management theory through case and field research. J. Oper. Manag. **15**, 441–454 (1998)
49. Greenhalgh, T.: How to read a paper: papers that summarize other papers (systematic reviews and meta-analyses). Br. Med. J. **315**, 672–675 (1997)

Interrelations of Success Factors for Selling Product-Service Systems from a Solution Sales Perspective

Heiko Felber[1] and Johannes Kunze von Bischhoffshausen[2(✉)]

[1] Karlsruhe Institute of Technology, Englerstr. 11, 76131 Karlsruhe, Germany
f.heiko@gmail.com
[2] Karlsruhe Institute of Technology, Karlsruhe Service Research Institute, Englerstr. 11, 76131 Karlsruhe, Germany
johannes.kunze@kit.edu

Abstract. Many Business-to-Business (B2B) companies are shifting their focus from transactional selling to engaging in long-lasting relationships with their customers. This impacts how companies sell their products and services. Instead of selling isolated products and services in single transactions, companies bundle and individualize their products and service to address individual customer needs. These bundles are called product-service systems (PSS) or solutions. This work reflects the current body of knowledge on selling PSS based on a literature review and provides new insights based on a qualitative study conducted with three multinational B2B companies providing PSS. Our findings propose that companies struggle to profit from PSS with a variety of different reasons. Implications on PSS itself are not quantified easily due to high variability of accounting practice regarding PSS and their service components. Furthermore, according to our interview results, for achieving long-term success with PSS three factors and their interrelations are critically important. First, PSS must fit into the targeted market strategy. Second, PSS and the market strategy must be consequently implemented within the organizational structure and the conduct of day-to-day business. Third, PSS providers have to deal with complexity which PSS comprise.

Keywords: B2B · Product-Service Systems (PSS) · Sales force management · Sales organization · Service selling · Solution sales · Service science

1 Introduction

During the past decades, more and more Business-to-Business (B2B) companies approached their customers in a different way: instead of focusing on individual selling transactions, companies strive to co-create value by selling individual solutions and engaging in long-term relationships with their customers [1]. Instead of selling isolated product and maximizing short-term revenue, companies strive to fulfill the individual needs of their customers by combining, integrating and individualizing products and services according to the needs of the customer. This requires B2B providers to integrate internal and external resources to create their value proposition to their customer accounts.

This transformation is perceived as a means to improve the competitive position, particularly in mature markets characterized by fierce competition and limited growth.

However, 75 percent of the companies that attempt to offer solutions fail to return the cost of their investment [2]. Little research has been conducted on how the sales force is being impacted by this shift and how the sales force contributes to the success of this transformation. In particular, we identified a research gap regarding comprehended markets and general implications on major companies within different stages of implementing Product-Service Systems (PSS) and solutions as sales offerings. To address this gap, we focused on three main (research) questions:

1. Where and why are PSS sales processes becoming more complex?
2. What are the main issues of PSS sales management and how are the solved?
3. What are the implications of selling PSS on requirements and skills of sales representatives and the organizational structure?

For investigating these research questions, we conducted explorative interviews on interrelations of success factors for selling product-service systems. The interview guideline was derived from a review of literature on product-service systems and related concepts, solution selling, and personal selling sales management in general.

Our findings are in line with [2] that companies are often struggling to generate additional profit from selling PSS. This struggle can surface regarding financial statements or in utilization and allocation of resources. There are a lot of external and internal reasons for this struggle which vary from the development stage of implementing PSS. Implications on PSS itself are not quantified easily due to high variability of accounting practice regarding PSS and their service components. According to our interview results, for achieving long-term success with PSS, some factors and their interrelations are crucial. First, PSS must fit into the targeted market strategy. Second, PSS and the market strategy must be consequently implemented within the organizational structure and the conduct of day-to-day business. Third, PSS providers have to deal with complexity which PSS comprise. And overall the logic for selling PSS has to be adapted by the whole company and its employees.

A review of fundamental literature on the impact of the shift towards product-service systems and solutions on the sales force is conducted in Sect. 2. Our interview methodology and findings are presented in Sect. 3. Section 4 discusses the results and their managerial implications. In the last section, we conclude this work and propose future research directions.

2 The New Role of the Sales Force

This section elaborates on the relationship between personal selling and the shift towards individualizing and integrating products and services and its academic paradigms.

Personal selling and sales management is indisputably impacted by this shift, which has been the topic of some research which is presented in the following.

2.1 Personal Selling and Sales Management

Personal selling is crucial for the sale of many goods in several industries, especially for B2B Companies. 10 % of the total workforce in the United States works in Sales [3] and 800 billion US dollars were spent in 2006 on sales forces in the United States [4], which is three times the amount spend on advertising activities. Subsequently, personal selling and sales management emerged as major subtopics in current literature on B2B marketing and related fields. Although sales force management drew interest from marketing researchers in the past years, still "the volume of research on sales force topics in the leading marketing journals has not matched its importance in the marketing mix" [4]. In the traditional marketing mix, personal selling takes place in promotion as illustrated in Fig. 1.

Fig. 1. Personal selling in the marketing mix, adapted from Cron and DeCarlo [3]

Salespeople play a key role in the development of the relationship between the B2B provider and the customer [5], as they are the primary link between both firms [6]. Indeed, Biong and Selnes [6] state that salespeople have a high influence on the account's perception of provider reliability, the perceived value of the provider's services, and finally the buyer's likelihood to continue the relationship. Furthermore, previous empirical research suggests that future sales opportunities of complex service offerings depend mostly on the relationship quality between sales representatives and accounts [5].

2.2 A Paradigmatic Shift Towards Individualizing, Integrating Products and Services

Scholars from marketing and related disciplines provided several theoretical foundations for this paradigmatic shift, specifically the Service-Dominant Logic and Product-Service-Systems. According to the Service-Dominant Logic [7], services are the fundamental unit of exchange. By providing a service, the provider company applies its resources, skills and knowledge. This also implies that "the normative marketing goal should be individualization" [8, p. 5] rather than selling standardized products, which is often the case in transactional selling.

Another related academic paradigm are product-service systems. In this context, Vandermerwe [9] coined the term servitization as offering services and solutions through products or at least in association with them (cf. [10]). This view on servitization is based on the value proposition for the customer and is independent of possible organizational transformation requirements. British academics such as Neely and Baines propose servitization as "innovation of an organizations capabilities and processes to shift from selling products to selling integrated products and services that deliver value in use" [11].

Definitions for systems selling are not unanimous in academia but mostly mutually understood. Page and Siemplenski [12] proposed systems selling as the provision of products and services as integrated systems that provide solutions to customer's operational needs. This definition for systems selling has all the components and the means to describe the selling of Product-Service Systems (PSS).

The practical application and usage of servitization terminology is gaining access into companies' strategies. For example Siemens AG uses servitization as strategic development from product vendor to vendor of hybrid product-service combinations. Grönroos [13] proposed the similar term servicizing as turning all elements in a customer relationship, regardless of their type and nature, into value-supporting inputs into the customers' process. His proposition for servicizing requires analysis of all customer contacts and all resources and activities in those contacts and all interactions with the customer and the effects they have on the customer process they influence. Rothenberg [14] uses the term servicizing to describe the focus shift of suppliers' business models from selling products to providing services. Her approach emphasizes material reduction and the substitution of products through services in order to gain more sustainable and profitable market advantages. She also indicates that services can create efficiency and value to support product sales. Although her approach seems to be more elaborate, the more common term servitization is also sufficient to cover the necessary market strategy changes and organizational implications.

A concept widely known in the practitioner literature is solution selling. Johansson et al. [2] propose solutions as a set of products and services, technically and commercially integrated to address the specific needs of a customer firm. This concept is strongly related to some PSS definitions as "an integrated combination of products and services" [15] and the terms PSS and solution can therefore be used interchangeable. A comparison of those terms and their similarities is presented by Velamuri et al. [16].

2.3 The New Role of the Sales Organization as Co-creators of Value

Selling solutions radically changes the selling approach. Selling solutions increases the importance of long-term relationship rather than focusing on individual transactions [1]. Furthermore, successful solution selling companies sell in teams, consisting of different sales roles with specific responsibilities and skills [2]. This difference is illustrated in Fig. 2.

The shift towards relational co-creation of value significantly impacts the role of the client rep: "The role of a salesperson in the emerging era will be more than that of a general manager. Salespersons will be responsible for marshaling internal and external

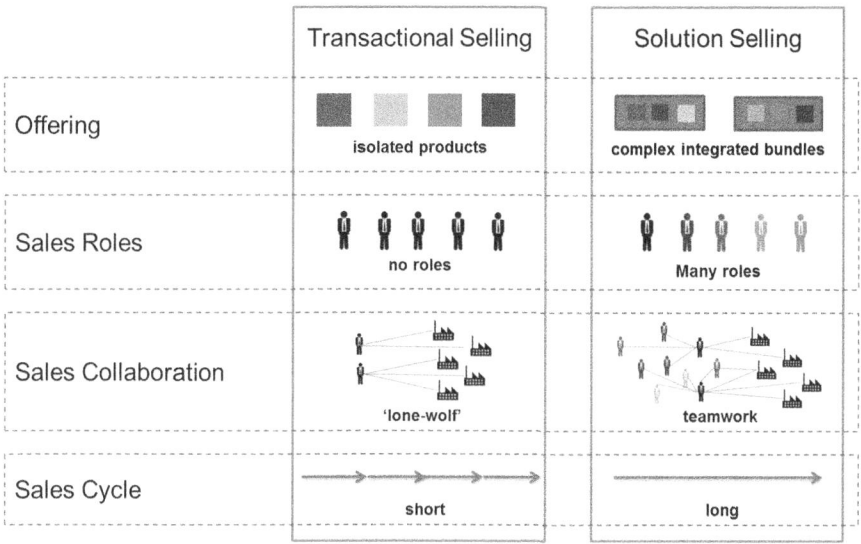

Fig. 2. Difference between transactional selling and solution selling

resources to satisfy customer needs and wants" [5]. A similar role description for sales reps has been proposed in the context of selling complex services: "Salespeople involved in the marketing of complex services often perform the role of relationship managers" [19].

Literature on servitization agrees on this change: "adding the service element makes the sale more complex; and complex sales take longer to explain to customers, longer to negotiate, and therefore longer to sell." [16, p. 4].

This implicates a wider range of tasks for solution sales reps than their traditional counterparts in the marketing mix.

Finally, current literature states that these days successful client reps develop a different relationship with their accounts. Instead of being a reactive problem solver, successful client reps are proactive partners to their accounts, maintaining and leveraging relationships with several account stakeholders [20].

3 Interrelations of Success Factors from a Sales Perspective

This section shows the identified success factors and their interrelations to each other as well as to the complexity of the underlying PSS. It shows also the design of the study with a description of the interviewed companies and a brief digest regarding the answers of the interviews.

3.1 Study Design

In 2013, personal interviews with sales managers and sales representatives were conducted, using a semi-structured qualitative questionnaire. The eight interviewees from three multinational B2B companies worked in sales on different management levels (from top management to account management). The companies itself operate on a multinational scale and offer Product-Service Systems (PSS). To build deductive hypotheses the companies are chosen according to different stages of organizational development regarding their implementation of PSS.

Company 1 achieves multiple billions US Dollar of revenue with medical systems and 5,000 - 10.000 personnel worldwide. The organizational structure and PSS development is not yet fully adapted as intended.

Company 2 achieves multiple millions US Dollar of revenue with software and integrated business solutions and up to 500 personnel. The organizational structure is built from the start to underline the PSS offers which are main focus of the company.

Company 3 achieves multiple billions US Dollar of revenue with hardware, software and integrated business solutions and more than 100,000 personnel worldwide. It has already finished the organizational implementation of PSS as a major part of its offerings.

The questionnaire is designed to guide through a semi-structured personal interview as suggested from Gläser and Laudel [21] and Mayer [22] and it has been tested in front of an audience with different professional backgrounds. It contains 18 main questions (see Table 1) as well as further annotations and follow-up questions to achieve the same detail depth throughout all interviews. Main questions are asked as given. Depending on the interviewers understanding either the term PSS or solution is used throughout the interviews. Follow-up questions are asked either as open or closed question, depending on the targeted answering depth. All interviews started with a scheduled duration of one hour, which could be extended to one and a half hour if necessary. To avoid a language barrier within the interviews and due to the native language of the interviewees, the interview and the analysis of the results are conducted in German. The results are comprehended in English to address the included relevance for the international service community. Especially topics regarding market characteristics and strategies, described from the interviewee, include international references.

Each interview started with an introduction of the participants and a brief description of the studies purpose. This includes an explanation of the usage of terminology and its mutual understanding. Finally the main questions and their follow-up questions are asked and answered. The interview ended with a brief comprehension of the discussed contents. At this time, all interviewees received the results of the study.

For analyzing and comprehending the given answers, the approach from Gläser and Laudel [22] is chosen because of its intuitive logic to deal with long textual answers. If an interviewee used pictorial language, the answers are interpreted with best of knowledge to comprehend the core meaning. Obvious biases of the interviewee are taken carefully into consideration while analyzing the answers and in case of doubt the answer is excluded from the analysis.

3.2 Overview of Success Factors

The identified success factors can be categorized according to their main sphere. There is consensus within the interviewees that there has to be some external fit or strategy fit, so that the provider's market strategy fit market conditions.

Table 1. Overview of interview results

Main Question	Amount of answers	Answered by company #	Selected analysis focus of the question	Brief content digest (consensus or ambiguity)
1 What solutions does your company offer?				
	8	1,2,3	PSS offering	Offered PSS vary from basic to full PSS
2 What is the personnel structure (roles) and process (activities) of the first customer contact to the conclusion of contract?				
	8	1,2,3	Organization structure	Consensus: matrix organization
3 How do you assign sales personnel to their tasks?				
	8	1,2,3	Assignment (task and customer)	Consensus: manual assignment
4 What is the proportion of the solutions in your company?				
	7	1,2,3	Revenue proportion of sales	PSS: 30 % to 70 %
5 Who within your company is the driver for solutions?				
	7	1,2,3	Companies internal PSS support	All (companies with full PSS), from top (companies with basic PSS)
6 What components are part of the targets of your sales personnel?				
	8	1,2,3	Salary goals	Signing goals (instead of revenue) for PSS or service components
7 What are the tasks within your solutions sales management?				
	8	1,2,3	Sales management tasks	PSS project pre-selection, ressource planing
8 How are these tasks implemented technically?				
	7	1,2,3	Usage of IT-tools	Consensus: CRM-software and communication hard- and software
9 What sales abilities and skills are important for selling solutions?				
	7	1,2,3	Skill requirements for selling PSS	Methodological skills become more important than in pure product sales
10 How would you describe the success of the solutions?				
	7	1,2,3	Assessment of PSS success	Neutral – very good
11 What other issues / examples can you think of that are different between solution selling and product selling?				
	6	1,3	Other issues which became more important	Complexity handling, customer satisfaction and utilization
12 Would you describe the basic product (within the solution) as complex?				
	8	1,2,3	Complexity of underlying product base	Complex (if standard software), project dependent (all others)
13 Would you describe the solutions as complex?				
	7	1,2,3	Complexity of whole PSS composition	No (basic PSS), yes (full PSS)
14 Would you describe the solution sales organization as complex?				
	7	1,2,3	Complexity of PSS sales organization	No (if it is designed to provide basic PSS), partially yes (full PSS)
15 Would you describe the solution sales management as complex?				
	7	1,2,3	Complexity of PSS sales management	Consensus: PSS sales management is complex
16 How do you set the prices for the solutions?				
	6	1,3	Pricing of PSS	Usually based on internal costs and customer budget, seldom on value
17 How do you conclude a contract with your solution customer?				
	5	3	Conclusion of PSS contracts	High variety (standard and individual contracts)
18 How long have you been with your company / in your current position?				
	8	1,2,3	Years of interviewees employment	Average = 12 years, minimum = 7 years

According to the interviewees, most PSS sales are high quality offerings and usually go along with unique selling propositions. They are also less exposed to price pressure than pure product sales.

As Treacy and Wiersema [23] pointed out, companies' can leave competition behind, pushing boundaries either on operational excellence, customer intimacy or product leadership while meeting industry standards in the other two. Offering PSS challenges this distinction. To achieve product leadership with PSS, companies' seem to require also excelling in customer intimacy to customize the service component. Apparently this is valid for high quality PSS and not for basic PSS (like maintenance). Additionally, interviewees pointed out that competition which operate as cost leaders have significant problems to sell high quality PSS.

Therefore companies' strategy requires being formulated and implemented accordingly to the characteristics of the PSS and not the other way around.

Most interviewees accord also upon that there has to be an internal fit, so that organizational structure supports PSS sales activities which are dependent on the complexity of the PSS or its components.

PSS inherently contain multiple components. Besides basic PSS, PSS usually have a certain degree of complexity. As complexity parameters are mentioned: number of components in one PSS, number of possible component combination into one PSS, and the underlying component complexity itself.

To sell complex PSS, the interviewed companies use two kinds of sale representatives, specialists and generalists. Specialists excel in detailed knowledge regarding on component while generalists excel in knowing all different kinds of PSS and their combination possibilities. They are staffed dependent on sales volume and requirements of one targeted customer.

All interviewed companies are able to provide the whole PSS bundle to their customers along their value chain and prefer the matrix organization to do so. The matrix organization comprehends all departments and the one side is input oriented (e.g. PSS component oriented) while the other side is output oriented (e.g. solution application and usage of PSS oriented).

Another success factor mentioned by the interviewees is that the inherent complexity of PSS is being covered in day-to-day sales activities.

When the PSS sales activities become too complex to handle spontaneously and individually by each sales representative, most interviewed companies thrive to standardize components of PSS and the processes to provide PSS.

Some interviewees are able to pinpoint several time-eaters like internal communication between internal project personnel or administrative processes (e.g. contracting, invoicing, audit by the customer).They thrive to ensure professional and sufficient communication of project personnel on the customer side and within their own company.

Another success factor seems to be the integration and training of personnel base according to the project requirements. Most requirements needed to provide PSS are too specific, so they cannot be obtained within the classical education system. Therefore PSS providers have to develop, educate and train these required knowledge and skills by themselves.

3.3 Interrelations and Complexity

To succeed with the provision of PSS the interviewed companies describe similar central characteristics according to the success factors from the chapter above. As main emphasis they point to three different levels: market characteristics, organizational characteristics and sales personal characteristics.

First, the market characteristics which comprise the structure of the underlying market, competition and service proposal.

Offer-driven markets are superior in achieving high margins. In demand-driven markets vendors can also achieve high margins through establishing tangible USPs or use information about customers, competitors or PSS which the customers do not have (usage of non-transparencies).

Provider specialists which focus only on single PSS or only on single components of PSS are supporting transparency in PSS offerings and apply price pressure to general offerings. General PSS provider focus on out-of-one-hand solutions. PSS vendors with a general market approach have to consider offerings from specialists, especially if those are able to provide comparable quality output to less costs than the generalist is able to.

If the service component does not include a unique selling proposition (USP), than the service offering and possible the PSS offering as well is substitutable. This leads to more competition and pressure upon the margin, especially if there are many competitors specializing on the service component of the PSS. Possible counter strategies are dependent on the availability and controllability of the product component - at least one USP has to be controlled.

Second, the organizational characteristics which include parameters on various levels, the underlying business model and the strategy fit.

The most chosen organizational structure is the matrix organization with one side focusing on technology input (PSS components) and the other side on provision related output (solution offerings).

If the vendor has a major organization size of its own he can integrate a special division team to identify sales leads on a general basis. The necessity to do so derives from the degree of division of labor to support the sales activities.

There are two characteristics which lead to the requirement to adapt to local parameters. First, different governmental regulations may lead to different business opportunities. Second, competition can force local or regional irregularities which can also lead to different business opportunities. Both characteristics may lead most likely in different prices and maybe in different PSS characteristics as well. Either way, the vendor has an own interest to ensure that their own PSS and its components will not pirate their business in other regions. This also implies if different local sales teams of the vendor concur on the same contract which may be implemented in more than one region.

Efforts to keep the sales cost down lead not only to higher internal cost transparency but also to more fairness according to the input involved and abilities to influence them. For example, whilst previously the installation costs did not have any direct mapping, they are now accounted to the sales division. This cost transparency is also needed for pre-selection of PSS projects.

Due to different revenue stream characteristics of services the salary targets of sales representatives have to be different. Usually the product component is paid in full after delivery but the service revenue occurs over time (month and years). Therefore sales representatives are getting signing targets besides product revenue targets. They cannot be measured in one target figure because the margins of product revenue and service signings are usually different.

Usual goal is to sell the PSS in one piece. In some cases this is not always possible. For example, if the customer is from the public sector and has its own regulation for requesting proposals, the service components could be explicitly excluded from the proposal and the contract. This often happens especial if the product components relate to the buildings budget.

PSS offerings have to fit into the customer perception of the vendor company. They have to show an understandable and believable strategy how PSS complement the product strategy. For example, PSS offerings from vendors who focus on product leadership tend to have difficulties, if the customers do not believe in the high quality delivery.

The more complex PSS components are, the more implemented is a comprehensive overall support from all the personnel. In early implementation stages, PSS are integrated on the top management level within the company's directive. Within further development stages PSS become more integrated in the day-to-day business of the provider and the support comes from all the personnel.

Similar to product manufacturing where the transportation costs have to be considered against full production on one location, there can also be observed a concentration of personnel related to the service component. This regards explicitly competence bundling on one office location compared to a high number of offices spread to different locations.

Third, the sales personnel characteristics, which comprehend trait requirements and resource utilization.

Sales representatives need the ability to fast comprehend and discuss complex and contextual issues. Implications are that the company has to train all sales representatives in the same tools so they speak the same methodological language and if needed train special abilities which are not available on the personnel market.

Especial with complex PSS, sales representatives do often not know all the details of the PSS characteristics. This implicates that the vendor implements a system with sales representatives who know general characteristics (goal: knowing all possible PSS combinations) and other with a higher focus on details (goal: knowing all possible details of some components). Also the personnel have to be trained regularly according to the complementary knowledge.

One main task of the sales manager is the utilization of his respective resources. The personnel are assigned manually to the tasks according to their ability and availability. Main implication is that both characteristics have to be transparent (e.g. skill matrix). Another implication according to the size of the company is that in small companies there is less potential for derivation of the usual team settings. Although in companies with thousands of personnel the teams can be built in also thousands of constellations. It is most common to not derive much from successful teams and personal contacts to the team members. Usual one member of the customer account put the PSS team together. Most common characteristic (besides ability and availability) for this is, if the team member and the customer worked successfully in the past and the internal team fit (social component).

The sales team is assigned on different characteristics. Most common is the regional root of the sales personnel to minimize driving distances. This characteristic appears sometimes as secondary but is usual the purporting characteristic. For example, if the assignment is based upon if the sales representatives has worked already successfully with the customer, the underlying characteristic is the availability and the first setting assignment of the sales representatives which is indicated to include regional considerations.

4 Discussion and Implications for Research and Management

As qualitative conducted study, the results give indication for further research approaches. From a service science and marketing perspective it is most interesting to verify quantitatively the identified success factors of PSS and the dependent parameters which have to be controlled as far as possible. The underlying study comprehends companies operating in different markets and assumes that the market characteristics have impact on implementation details only, but not in general how to implement PSS. Further research, to verify or deny this assumption, requires a large scale research and contacts to the same top management level as used for the interviews. This possible follow-up research could also look into the matrix organization as preferred organizational structure for major international PSS providers and at which organizational size smaller providers should also assume matrix organizations. Another possible research approach is, if smaller PSS providers use hierarchical organizational structures and on which development stage of implementing PSS they are. It might be that in some constellations hierarchical organizations are superior to matrix organizations for providing PSS successfully.

From our perspective, the most interesting implication for PSS provider is how to use PSS to create value for the customer and profit for the provider. The more all parameters are aligned the more successful the PSS implementation and value creation can be. All interviewed companies seem to struggle or at least have to invest resources and financials to profit from PSS. Whilst the development stages of implementing PSS cover the more formal success factors, the market and customer insight seems to be equally important for financial success of PSS. The interviewed companies struggle to create an environment to successfully use value based pricing and obtain a higher margin as a result. In new markets such environments occur naturally but in mature markets they are rather scarce. How these circumstances can be economically created and protected is equally interesting from a management and an academia perspective.

On a practical level the identification of required skills, how to train and how to allocate them into successfully operating teams seems to be an organizational success factor which is mostly dependent on personnel qualifications on the involved management levels (e.g. human resources, sales management). Within the interviewed companies there is no specific technical or automatically system to support these process steps, but possibly required to further creating value and reducing inefficiencies.

5 Conclusion

In this work, we investigated the interrelations of success factors for selling product-service systems through a solution-oriented sales force. Therefore, we first conducted a literature review on the impact of the shift towards product-service systems and solutions on the sales force. As discussed, several academic and practical paradigms embody the shift towards individualization and integrating bundles of products and services in B2B scenarios. Our interview findings suggest that providers struggle to profit from PSS, which is in line with the body of knowledge in literature. Furthermore, success of PSS requires a fit to targeted market strategy, a rigor implementation of the marketing strategy in the organizational structure and operational boundaries and the capability to deal with increased complexity.

The limitation of the presented study regarding the design and execution of the interviews are deliberate and agreeable. This applies specifically to the amount of interviewees and amount of interviewed companies as well as the extent of the study.

In delimitation to the focus and the results of this thesis, further research can be conducted as deductive research or deepen this thesis' emphasis.

This work lays the foundation for our future research. It is a starting point for designing quantitative studies and verify quantitatively the identified success factors of PSS and the dependent parameters.

References

1. Tuli, K.R., Kohli, A.K., Bharadwaj, S.G.: Rethinking customer solutions: from product bundles to relational processes. J. Mark. **71**, 1–17 (2007)
2. Johansson, J.E., Krishnamurthy, C., Schlissberg, H.E.: Solving the solutions problem. McKinsey Q. **3**, 116–125 (2003)
3. Cron, W.L., DeCarlo, T.E.: Dalrymple's Sales Management. Wiley, New York (2008)
4. Mantrala, M.K., Albers, S., Caldieraro, F., Jensen, O., Joseph, K., Krafft, M., Narasimhan, C., Gopalakrishna, S., Zoltners, A., Lal, R., Lodish, L.: Sales force modeling: state of the field and research agenda. Mark. Lett. **21**, 255–272 (2010)
5. Sheth, J.N., Sharma, A.: The impact of the product to service shift in industrial markets and the evolution of the sales organization. Ind. Mark. Manage. **37**, 260–269 (2008)
6. Biong, H., Selnes, F.: The strategic role of the salesperson in established buyer-seller relationships the strategic role of the salesperson in established buyer-seller relationships. J. Bus.-to-Bus. Mark. **3**(3), 39–78 (1997)
7. Vargo, S., Lusch, R.: Service-dominant logic: continuing the evolution. J. Acad. Mark. Sci. **36**, 1–10 (2007)
8. Vargo, S.L., Lusch, R.F.: The four service marketing myths remnants of a goods-based, manufacturing model. J. Serv. Res. **6**(4), 324–335 (2004)
9. Vandermerwe, S.R.: Servitization of business: adding value by adding services. Eur. Manag. J. **6**(4), 314–324 (1988)
10. Neely, A.: Exploring the financial consequences of the servitization of manufacturing. Oper. Manage. Res. **1**(2), 1–50 (2008)
11. Baines, T.S., Lightfoot, H.W., Evans, S., Neely, A., Greenough, R., Peppard, J., Wilson, H.: State-of-the-art in product-service systems. Proc. Inst. Mech. Eng. Part B: J. Eng. Manuf. **221**(10), 1543–1552 (2007)

12. Page, A., Siemplenski, M.: Product systems marketing. Ind. Mark. Manage. **12**(2), 89–99 (1983)
13. Grönroos, C.: Service Management and Marketing: Customer Management in Service Competition. Wiley, Chichester (2007)
14. Rothenberg, S.: Sustainability through servicizing. MIT Sloan Manage. Rev. 48(2) (2012)
15. Baines, T.S., et al.: State-of-the-art in product service-systems. J. Eng. Manuf. Part B **221**, 1543–1552 (2007)
16. Ryals, L., Rackham, N.: Sales Implications of Servitization - The Implications of the Servitization Trend for Selling. White Paper, Cranfield School of Management (2012)
17. Velamuri, V.K., Neyer, A.K., Möslein, K.M.: Hybrid value creation: a systematic review of an evolving research area. Journal für Betriebswirtschaft **61**(1), 3–35 (2011)
18. Krishnamurthy, C., Johansson, J., Schlissberg, H.: Solution selling: is the painworth the gain? White Paper (2003)
19. Crosby, L., Evans, K., Cowles, D.: Relationship quality in services selling: an interpersonal influence perspective. J. Mark. **54**, 68–81 (1990)
20. Adamson, B., Dixon, M., Toman, N.: The end of solution sales. Harv. Bus. Rev. **4**, 61–68 (2012)
21. Gläser, J., Laudel, G.: Experteninterviews und qualitative Inhaltsanalyse (2010)
22. Mayer, H.: Interview und schriftliche Befragung - Entwicklung, Durchführung und Auswertung (2001)
23. Treacy, M., Wiersema, F.: Customer intimacy and other value disciplines. Harv. Bus. Rev. **71**, 84–93 (1993)

How to Encourage the Use of Public Transport? A Multiservice Approach Based on Mobile Technologies

Marta Campos Ferreira[✉] and Teresa Galvão Dias

Universidade do Porto – Faculdade de Engenharia,
Rua Dr. Roberto Frias, 4200-465 Porto, Portugal
{mferreira, tgalvao}@fe.up.pt

Abstract. It is crucial to promote the use of cleaner transport modes, and new technologies are key to achieve this goal. Most mobile-based solutions are focused on services related with the journey itself (mobile ticketing, real-time traffic information and trip planners). Adopting a holistic point of view, and considering every trip has a purpose (work, school, shopping and entertainment), a new service approach is considered. This paper presents a multiservice approach that links city services and public transport to encourage the use of sustainable transport modes. This multiservice approach is based on mobile technologies, which are a unique channel of interaction between service providers and customers. The conceptual model of this approach is materialized in a concrete example. This multiservice approach may represent a step towards a sustainable mobility, while improving the image and efficiency of Public Transport Operators (PTOs), boosting local businesses loyalty and sales and bringing convenience, better service quality and monetary savings to customers.

Keywords: Multiservice approach · Mobile technologies · Public transport · City services · Sustainable mobility

1 Introduction

In order to perform their daily activities people need to travel, and there are several means of transport available. European Commission is concerned about promoting a sustainable mobility through the use of cleaner and more efficient means of transport such as the public transport [1]. To achieve that goal, public transport must become more attractive by offering better service quality, accessibility and reliability. European Commission also believes that new technologies are the key to increase the use of cleaner transport means in the cities. New technologies also allow PTOs to reduce operational costs of ticketing, improve fare collection efficiency, and enhance their knowledge about customer's behaviour, choices and preferences.

Several mobile-based service solutions have been studied and developed in order to simplify the way of travelling and using public transport. Most of them are focused on the development of services related with the trip itself, such as mobile ticketing, real-time traffic information and timetables, and interactive journey planners. However, the transport system must be looked holistically and in context. Every trip has a purpose:

work, school, recreation, social, and this requires a new service approach: a multiservice approach. This idea was deeply discussed during focus group sessions with public transport users and non-users and was presented to Public Transport Operators (PTOs) from the city of Porto and to companies connected to local businesses of the city.

This multiservice approach was then materialized in a concrete example: a mobile ticketing application integrated with other service providers, through a vouchers market. The application would enable users not only to buy and validate travel tickets but also to acquire discounts and offers at restaurants, boutiques, gyms and other service providers with points earned with the purchase of travel tickets.

The proposed multiservice approach will contribute to modernize the image of PTOs, improve quality of service, attract new customers and retain the existing ones, and increase the use of public transport services. It will also boost local businesses, due to increased awareness, loyalty and sales. Customers benefit from convenience, availability, better services, and increased savings.

The main contributions of this paper include the definition of a conceptual model of a multiservice approach and the materialization of such concept into a real example. This multiservice approach represents a step towards a sustainable and seamless mobility.

The outline of the paper is as follows: first the related work is described, and then the multiservice approach is presented, followed by an application scenario that materializes the concept. Finally the conclusions and future work are presented.

2 Related Work

Public transport plays an important role in decreasing traffic congestion, reducing carbon emissions, and promoting a sustainable mobility. Despite the significant benefits of using public transport means, many commuters are reluctant to make the switch. New technologies are key to improve the public transport service, reduce the barriers of travelling with sustainable transport means and thus increase the use of public transport. Although there are several technological solutions that can be used to improve public transport service offerings, such as dynamic displays, interactive bus stops, vehicle Global Positioning System (GPS) sensors, and touchscreen transit maps, they are very expensive and new solutions are being developed to support other interfaces, like mobile devices. Mobile solutions are often cheaper to deploy and can support additional personalized functionalities, such as customized information and alerts.

In fact, the use of mobile technology on public transport has become extremely common. This is even more evident in bus and train trips [2]. Mobile technology provides travellers with access to voice and text communications, information and entertainment en route, enabling time spent waiting for buses or travelling on trains to be used more pleasantly and productively than before. Users who perceive public transport as providing an opportunity to multitasking may be more likely to choose public transport over driving [3].

PTOs are aware of this reality and are introducing this new channel on their service delivery process. Since September 2014, the major public bus operator in the city of Porto (STCP) provides free internet access to their customers inside the bus. The free

Wi-Fi internet is available in 400 buses, almost all the company's fleet, and it became the first public transport road operator in Europe to provide Wi-Fi coverage inside their buses [4].

Mobile ticketing systems are also an example of such initiatives. The concept of mobile ticketing systems applied to the public transport sector can be defined as the purchase and validation of travel tickets through the use of mobile devices, such as smartphones or tablets. Mobile ticketing has several advantages when compared to traditional ticketing systems. They provide passengers remote and ubiquitous access to payment services, queue avoidance, simplicity and availability [5]. They also allow PTOs to reduce operational costs of ticketing systems, improve fare collection efficiency, and enhance their knowledge about customer's behaviour, choices and preferences [6].

Ferreira et al. [7] propose a mobile ticketing solution based on customers mobile devices, which only need internet access to purchase and validate travel tickets. This solution doesn't require any investment in equipment from PTOs and brings convenience and easy-of-use to customers [8]. Others [9] propose mobile ticketing models based on GPS and Wi-Fi. In this case, the customer only needs to check-in when starting a trip and check-out at the end. The customer is located by the service provider during his trip at defined intervals. At the end of the journey, the system determines the performed route within the public transport network and calculates the price, which is then debited from the customers' account. This system is really intuitive since it does not require having any particular knowledge about tariffs or ticketing machines.

Real-time traffic information is another research topic that has being advocated as increasing satisfaction among current customers and increasing the use of public transport, especially among new or infrequent passengers and for off-peak hours. Traveller information systems may enhance the usability of public transport, decrease waiting time, increase feelings of safety and increase overall satisfaction with public transport [10].

Researchers have been proposing models of real-time traffic information based on mobile devices. Tiramisu is a public transport information system where commuters share GPS traces and submit problem reports. Tiramisu processes incoming traces and generates real-time arrival time predictions for buses. This solution produces real-time traffic information based on crowd-sourcing and the service is co-created between citizens and PTOs [11]. OneBusAway is another solution focused on providing real-time arrival information for Seattle-area bus passengers. This solution is based on information provided by the regional transit agency and is available for passengers through their mobile devices [10].

Further mobile solutions, like Move-Me [12, 13], not only provides real-time multimodal public transport information, but also provides interactive maps and a journey planner tool. Passengers may search on their mobile devices for near public transport stops around them, points-of-interest and plan a journey by choosing the origin and destination stops. Further researchers [14] propose an integrated architecture that covers mobile trip planning, intelligent mobile ticketing and community solutions during the trip. Such integrated solutions meet user needs in terms of flexibility and convenience.

Despite these solutions bring convenience to passengers and improve their travelling experience, all of them are based on services related to transport. In this paper, is our intention to include a holistic view of the transport system and we propose a multiservice approach that includes services other than mobility related. Research studies in this area are scarce, however [15] identified potential commercial partnerships that could exploit, in that case, the characteristics of smartcards. The researchers used data from Montreal, Canada, to identify the business establishments that tend to concentrate near metro stations. Nevertheless, this study does not dwell on what kind and how these partnerships can be established. The proposed multiservice approach is presented in the next section.

3 Proposal of a Multiservice Approach

Mobile technologies constitute an opportunity to simplify the way of travelling and using public transport. Most studies have focused on the development of mobile-based services related with the trip itself, such as mobile ticketing, real-time traffic information and timetables and interactive trip planners.

We wanted to go further on our research and think about new and complementary ideas to foster the use of public transport. To achieve this goal we created a facebook group to discuss these ideas, organized meetings and focus group sessions with potential and regular customers, PTOs and companies connected to local businesses of cities. Some of the participants had already participated in a real pilot of a mobile ticketing system deployed in the city of Porto [16]. When choosing the sample, it was our intention to gather people that already use public transport on a daily basis, some familiarized with mobile payments and others do not, and people who do not use public transport.

When asked about what would propel them to use public transport more often, several suggestions emerged. Some suggested that companies should give a travel subsidy to their employees in the form of a pre-loaded value on their travel card or mobile ticketing application. Others suggested the creation of an application where users could evaluate the security of a given stop in real time, providing important information to other users and even to security agents. And others suggested the creation of an application that presents ecological information to the user during the course of the trip through the concept of gamification.

Nevertheless, the most discussed and supported idea by the users was to establish partnerships with other service providers like museums, restaurants and cinemas, and reward the use of public transport. For instance, large families could benefit from discounts if they perform entertainment activities together and use the public transport as the mean to commute. Tourists could benefit from integrated solutions that combine touristic attractions and events with public transport services at discounted prices. These combined solutions have already demonstrated their importance in fostering the use of public transport and optimizing the use of the infrastructures [17, 18].

This idea was presented to the major PTOs in the city of Porto and other companies connected with local businesses. PTOs were totally in favour of such idea. Nowadays, there are few initiatives that link public transport to other service providers; they work separately towards individual objectives. PTOs could envision several benefits from these partnerships: increased loyalty, increased use of public transport, better image and marketing results. This idea was also presented to companies that are connected to local businesses, which recognized an opportunity to increase local commerce, loyalty and awareness of brands.

This multiservice approach consists of creating partnerships among city services and public transport. These partnerships may include discounts, combined packages, reduced prices, deals, marketing campaigns and others. New technologies are essential to make these initiatives more effective and targeted. For example, services made available through personal mobile devices allow companies to interact directly with their customers and customize the offer. Service providers acquire knowledge about their customers, through their mobility profiles and spending habits, and are able to target their offerings to a specific audience. It is also important to measure the effectiveness and efficiency of the campaign to improve future service offerings. Currently, if PTOs want to partnership with other service providers it is difficult to direct marketing and communication efforts and is even more difficult to measure the impact of the initiative.

This multiservice approach is represented in Fig. 1 through a conceptual model. Mobility is just the mean to achieve something. Every trip has a purpose: work, school, child care, shopping, recreation and entertainment activities [19]. So, the public transport services link passengers to their daily activities. The objective is to encourage people to use cleaner transport modes during their daily commute. This can be achieved through different ways, but here we present a holistic approach, where different city services (cinemas, restaurants, museums, hairdressers, gyms) partnership with PTOs to target service offerings to a specific segment. Through new technologies this initiatives can be easily measured in terms of awareness, engagement, sales and loyalty, which is essential to improve future initiatives. The conceptual model of the multiservice approach can be divided in four steps: (1) analyse mobility profiles and interests; (2) target and deliver service offerings; (3) measure the efficiency and effectiveness of the campaign; and (4) improve future service offerings.

1. *Analyse mobility profiles and interests*

    According to a survey of 5.000 people from 8 different countries, 84 % stated they couldn't go a single day without their mobile device in hand. Also, people never get too far away from their mobile devices, even in sleep (75 % of 25-to-29-years-old said they took their phones to bed) [20].

    When providing ticketing services through the mobile device PTOs know exactly where travellers' journeys start and end. Mobile journey planners also help PTOs to know passengers' travelling intentions, and systems based on crowd-sourcing and exchanging messages between travellers provide information about traffic, vehicle conditions and emotional feelings. All of these data sources are important for PTOs and authorities to define transport policies, routes, tariffs, and improve the quality of service.

    However, all of this information is only related with the journey experience itself and little is known about the activities performed. Our multiservice approach allows overcoming this limitation. Customer information may be explicitly elicited through questionnaires or registration forms, or implicitly elicited through a service system that records every choice the customer makes. In the case of this multiservice approach, covering services other than mobility related, allows the identification of personal interests and consumption profiles of users. The mobility and consumption profiles must be then analysed, using, for instance, data mining techniques to provide inputs to the following phase.

2. *Target and deliver service offerings*
   After the analysis of the travelling profiles and consumption habits it is possible to establish some patterns and identify groups or clusters of customers who have similar behaviours or who made similar choices. Then, to target a service offering to a particular segment it is necessary to use algorithms developed for that purpose. Personalization plays here an important role, since it increases perceived quality, customer satisfaction and ultimately customer loyalty toward a service provider [21].

   Additional mobile devices features allow going further in the personalization since they usually have location sensors, which can be used to contextualize the user in terms of activity and location. This can be used to send location-based service offers to a personal mobile device, like notifications or discounts for nearby restaurants or boutiques.

3. *Measure the efficiency and effectiveness of the campaign*
   More important than sending personalized service offerings to customers, is to measure if whether those offers are being effective or not. Service providers must have a way to measure if they are increasing brand awareness, driving foot traffic and influencing purchases.

   The multiservice approach allows calculating deeper ROI (return-on-investment) and sales metrics. For instance, it is possible to determine brand awareness by calculating the click through rate (for example, ads click on, coupons downloaded), understand if customers are inside or near a store through location providers and analyse purchases (for example, number of coupons redeemed).

4. *Improve future service offerings*
   It is important to analyse the indicators and realize what is going well or badly to improve future service offerings. Also customers may provide explicit feedback when they fill out a customer satisfaction questionnaire or complain by email. So, it is crucial to capture and learn from both kinds of customer feedback in order to adapt future initiatives. It is also important to be aware that preferences and interests may change over time, in an evolutionary way or discontinuously, due to a specific life event like having kids or losing a job. These changes are also important to be captured to refine the model.

   Concluding, this multiservice approach will allow contributing to the improvement of the public transport service levels, enhance their image and increase the use of sustainable transport means. It will also increase the number of customers and sales of local businesses. In the next section we materialize this multiservice approach in a concrete example.

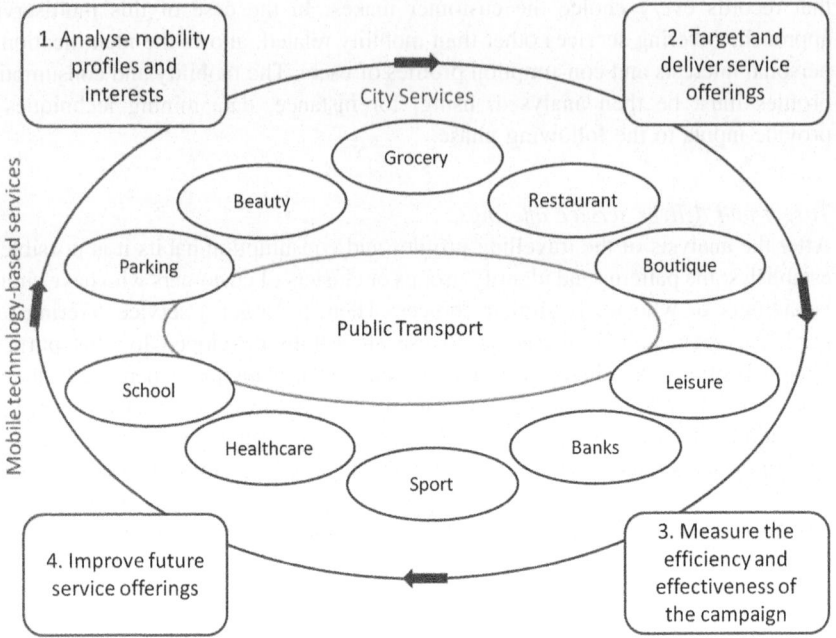

Fig. 1. Conceptual model of the multiservice approach

4 Illustrative Example of a Multiservice Approach

The multiservice approach can be materialized in several practical examples and business models. In this section we explore an example that only represents a proof of concept of the multiservice approach. The main objective was to develop a mobile service that would cover the different perspectives and interests from the main stakeholders (users, PTOs and local businesses).

The mobile service developed was materialized in a functional prototype of a mobile ticketing application for public transport for Android devices, which was integrated with other service providers. The application enables users not only to buy and validate travel tickets but also to access to a vouchers market. Every time a user buys a travel ticket he earns points in a proportional amount to the total amount spent. These points can then be redeemed, in the vouchers market, for discounts and offers at restaurants, boutiques, bookstores and other service providers that are part of the ecosystem. The campaigns are inserted by each service provider through a backoffice system.

In this section we will focus on the features of the vouchers market, since it is the practical demonstration of the multiservice approach described above. Further details about the ticketing system can be reviewed in [16]. Thus, bellow, we present the architecture of the system, the mobile application and the web backoffice and the main evaluation results.

4.1 Architecture

The system architecture (see Fig. 2) comprises two main areas: business area, composed by the web backoffice and the client area, which consists on the Android mobile application. Outside of these two areas, there is a webservice responsible for accessing the central database and for tying the whole system.

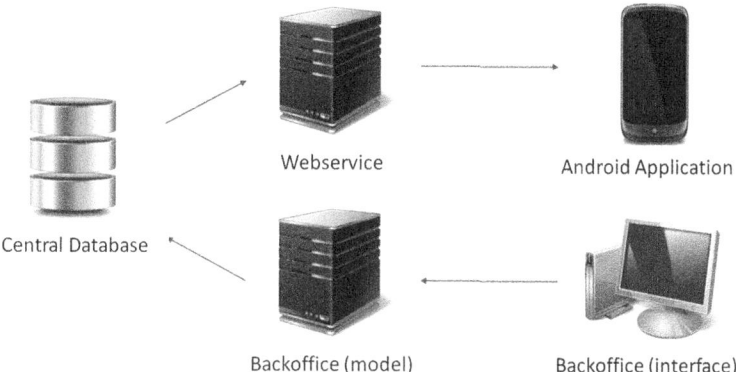

Fig. 2. Overview of the system architecture

The web backoffice acts as an interface for the service providers (including PTOs) to create and manage their own campaigns, by accessing a browser. This component allows signing up for an account, creating and editing a promotion, validate vouchers and check statistics about current and past campaigns (number of clicks, number of vouchers sold, number of validations, type of customer).

The mobile application allows customers to interact directly with the services. This interaction is achieved through the use of a mobile phone, tablet, or any other mobile device running the Android operating system. This component allows redeeming points for vouchers, checking vouchers balance, search for promotions, check vouchers already used and access to location based notifications.

The webservice, accessible through an API, is responsible for managing the data inside the database, only available locally, and it is crucial for the Android application to work.

4.2 Mobile Application and Web Backoffice

Each customer when starting to use the application needs to register and provide some personal details like gender, age, address, and interests (books, cinema, sports, music). This information is important not only for the ticketing system, but also for the vouchers market, in order to target the campaigns. The first campaigns to be shown to the customer are those that meet their personal characteristics and their consumption history. The campaigns are inserted by each service provider through a backoffice system (see Fig. 3).

The customer can choose one of the promotions that are shown to him (see Fig. 5) or he can search for a specific promotion by filling some fields of the search menu (name, category, location and/or number of points). Then the customer redeems his points to get access to the voucher, which generates a random code. When the customer goes to the service provider (e.g. a restaurant) to use his voucher, he only needs to show the code that was generated to the merchant. The merchant inserts the code on his web backoffice to validate it (see Fig. 4). The system verifies if the code matches the customer and validates it successfully (see Fig. 6).

Another feature of the system is the notifications activated by the location of the customer. Considering that the customer possesses a voucher for a given promotion still not used, in case he gets closer than a threshold distance, an alert is displayed in the notification area of the mobile device.

Finally, service providers may access to statistics about their current and past campaigns. They can check the number of clicks, number of vouchers downloaded, number of voucher used at the point of sale (trough the unique code) and type of customer. This is important to analyse the impact of the campaign and to prepare future initiatives.

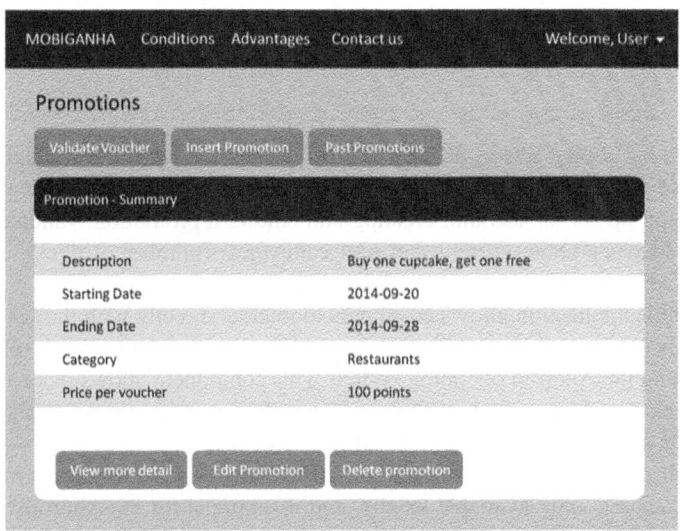

Fig. 3. Web backoffice interface

4.3 Evaluation

The main objective of the evaluation phase was to validate the concept that was developed with users, PTOs and local businesses.

Regarding the users evaluation, the application was tested in a controlled environment by fifteen users, randomly sampled in the campus of the University of Porto in both strata among 20–45-year-old citizens. The test was divided into three parts: (1) questionnaire for sample characterization; (2) user test with eight tasks regarding the mobile application and four tasks regarding the web back office (tasks correspond to

How to Encourage the Use of Public Transport? 323

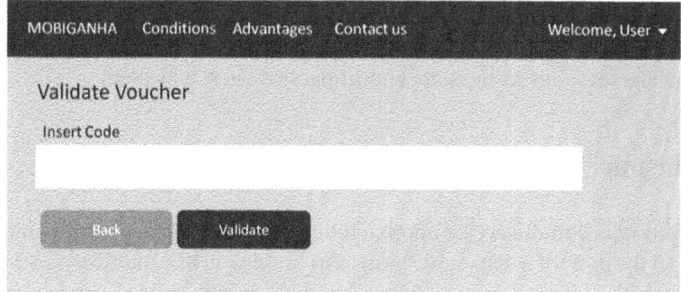

Fig. 4. Voucher validation form

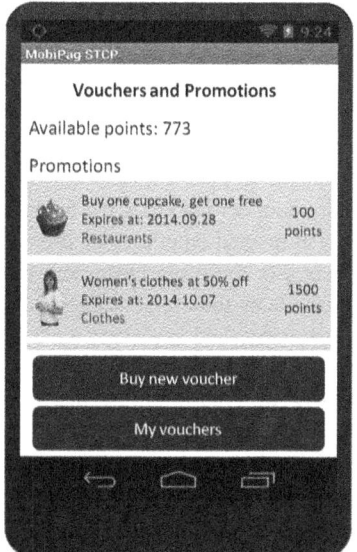 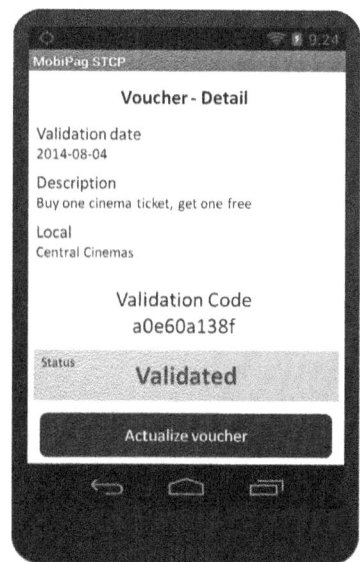

Fig. 5. Main menu of the vouchers market   **Fig. 6.** Details of a validated voucher

actions performed on the prototype); (3) questionnaire with nine unstructured about the user satisfaction with the application and the concept itself. Each test, including the questionnaire, lasted about thirty minutes. The participants were videotaped and voice recorded.

Users considered almost all tasks easy or very easy to perform, except when they were asked to check the points' balance, which was not on the menu they were expecting. They also suggested several improvements such as providing more feedback to user using dialog boxes, possibility of offering or trading vouchers and tickets with other users and a dynamic points attribution system instead a static one.

The solution was also presented to PTOs of the city of Porto. They enjoyed the concept and could foresee several advantages. They proposed the inclusion of reminders or notifications suggesting the purchase of relevant vouchers for the user.

Regarding the local businesses, they valued the idea and suggested the introduction of more statistics and metrics related to the promotions system. These indicators are key to their business and to measure the impact of such a system.

5 Conclusions and Future Work

This paper presents a multiservice approach that links city services and public transport to encourage the use of sustainable transport modes. This multiservice approach is based on mobile technologies, which are a unique channel of interaction between service providers and customers. In the middle of the conceptual model of the multiservice approach are the public transport services, which represent the common link with the other city services (restaurants, boutiques, groceries, banks). This conceptual model is also composed by four steps: (1) analyse mobility profiles and interests; (2) target and deliver services offerings; (3) measure the efficiency and effectiveness of the campaign; and (4) improve future service offerings.

This multiservice approach was materialized in a concrete example. It was developed a mobile ticketing application for public transport for Android devices, which was then integrated with other service providers. The application enables users not only to buy and validate travel tickets but also to access to a vouchers market. Customers may acquire discounts and offers at restaurants, boutiques, gyms and other service providers, with points earned with the purchase of travel tickets. So, the more customers travel, the more points they earn and the more discounts and deals they have access to. This solution revealed to be intuitive and useful for customers, and was very valued by PTOs and local businesses.

The proposed multiservice approach will allow to contribute to the overall improvement of the public transport service levels, image, accessibility, with the main aim to increase the use of public transport and so contributing to a sustainable mobility. It will also boost local businesses, due to increased awareness, loyalty and sales. Future work includes working on this approach, refine it, and demonstrate the value for all stakeholders involved.

References

1. European Commission: Roadmap to a Single European Transport Area – Towards a competitive and resource efficient transport system (2011)
2. Schwieterman, J., Battaglia, A.: The digitally connected traveler: measuring the growing the use of electronic devices on intercity buses, planes, & trains 2010–2013. In: TRB 2014 Annual Meeting, pp. 1–15 (2014)
3. U. S. P. E. F. F. Group: A new way to go: the transportation apps and vehicle-sharing tools that are giving more americans the freedom to drive less (2013)
4. STCP: STCP offers free Wi-Fi on their buses (2014). http://www.stcp.pt/pt/noticias/stcp-oferece-wifi-gratuito-nos-seus-autocarros/
5. Mallat, N.: Exploring consumer adoption of mobile payments – a qualitative study. J. Strateg. Inf. Syst. **16**(4), 413–432 (2007)

6. NFC Forum: NFC in Public Transport (2011)
7. Ferreira, M.C., Nóvoa, H., Dias, T.G., Falcão e Cunha, J.: A proposal for a public transport ticketing solution based on customers' mobile devices. Procedia – Soc. Behav. Sci. **111**, 232–241 (2013)
8. Ferreira, M.C., Nóvoa, M.H., Dias, T.G.: A proposal for a mobile ticketing solution for metropolitan area of oporto public transport. In: Falcão e Cunha, J., Snene, M., Nóvoa, H. (eds.) IESS 2013. LNBIP, vol. 143, pp. 263–278. Springer, Heidelberg (2013)
9. Bohm, A., Murtz, B., Sommer, C., Wermuth, M.: Location-based ticketing in public transport. In: Proceedings of the 8th International IEEE Conference on Intelligent Transportation Systems, pp. 837–840 (2005)
10. Ferris, B., Watkins, K., Borning, A.: OneBusAway: results from providing real-time arrival information for public transit. In: Proceedings of CHI, pp. 1807–1816 (2010)
11. Zimmerman, J., Tomasic, A., Garrod, C., Yoo, D., Hiruncharoenvate, C., Aziz, R., Thiruvengadam, N.R., Huang, Y., Steinfeld, A.: Field trial of tiramisu: crowd-sourcing bus arrival times to spur co-design. In: Proceedings of the Conference on Human Factors in Computing Systems (CHI), pp. 1677–1686 (2011)
12. Move-Me. http://www.move-me.mobi/
13. Falcão e Cunha, J., Galvão, T.: State of the art and future perspectives for smart support services for public transport. In: Borangiu, T., Trentesaux, D., Thomas, A. (eds.) Service Orientation in Holonic and Multi-agent Manufacturing. SCI, vol. 544, pp. 225–234. Springer, Heidelberg (2014)
14. Lüke, K., Mügge, H., Eisemann, M., Telschow, A.: Integrated solutions and services in public transport on mobile devices. In: Gesellschaft für Informatik (GI), I2 CS Conference Proceedings P-148, pp. 109–119 (2009)
15. Páez, A., Trépanier, M., Morency, C.: Geodemographic analysis and the identification of potential business partnerships enabled by transit smart cards. Transp. Res. Part A Policy Pract. **45**(7), 640–652 (2011)
16. Ferreira, M.C., Dias, T.G., Falcão e Cunha, J.: Design and evaluation of a mobile payment system for public transport: the MobiPag STCP prototype. In: MOBILITY 2014: The Fourth International Conference on Mobile Services, Resources, and Users, pp. 71–77 (2014)
17. Puhe, M., Edelmann, M., Reichenbach, M.: Integrated urban e-ticketing for public transport and touristic sites. Brussels (2014)
18. Lumsdon, L., Downward, P., Rhoden, S.: Transport for tourism: can public transport encourage a modal shift in the day visitor market? J. Sustain. Tour. **14**(2), 139–156 (2006)
19. Bhat, C.R., Misra, R.: Discretionary activity time allocation of individuals between in-home and out-of-home and between weekdays and weekends. Transportation (Amst) **26**(2), 193–209 (1999)
20. Gibbs, N.: Your Wireless Life: Results of TIME's Mobility Poll. Time, no. The Wireless Issue (2012)
21. Coelho, P.S., Henseler, J.: Creating customer loyalty through service customization. Eur. J. Mark. **46**(3/4), 331–356 (2012)

Relationship Bonds and Customer Loyalty: A Study Across Different Service Contexts

Mafalda Lima and Teresa Fernandes(✉)

Faculty of Economics, University of Porto,
R. Dr. Roberto Frias, s/n, 4200-464, Porto, Portugal
mafaldalima58@gmail.com, tfernandes@fep.up.pt

Abstract. The benefits of customer relationship strategies are well known and somewhat established nowadays. Customer loyalty emerges as the crucial glue in developing a relational approach. However, relational bonds, which relate to customer loyalty, have not yet been fully explored. Also, there is little research that takes into account the effect of service types on customer relationships and bonding. This paper develops a conceptual framework based on previous literature with a complete set of different relational bonds and examines its influence on customer loyalty across search, experience and credence services through a survey-based empirical study, with a sample of 233 consumers. The results provide guidance to managers to differentiate customer relationship strategies according to each specific service context.

Keywords: Relationships · Bonds · Customer loyalty · Services

1 Introduction

The profound effect of service quality and the mediating effect of customer satisfaction on consumer decision making are largely recognized, and have created a remarkable transfer in awareness towards customer-focused services marketing and a steady increase of research related to customer behavior in services [1, 2]. While this sector is growing and becoming more competitive, service providers are increasingly focusing on developing their competitive advantage by strategically managing customer relationships.

One of the most important determinants of customer relationships is customer loyalty [3]. Customer loyalty is strongly affected by different types of relational bonds or ties, which can act as benefits or exit barriers, and have become central concepts in the study of customer relationships. However, relational bonds have been examined in the literature mainly conceptually [4], or in a business-to-business context [5], and thus have not yet been fully explored [6]. Also, in different service contexts, different types of relationships and bonding may emerge, given differences in the nature and the value customers derive from different service types [7]. However, there is little research that takes into account the effect of service types on relational bonds, and cross-validation across different service industries (e.g. search, experience and credence services) is required [8]. Though some studies have analyzed customer relationships from context to context, in services as diverse as hairdressing, health, retail or banking (e.g. [9–11]), to date the majority of these studies are based on one service industry.

The aim of this paper is to identify a set of relational bonds and to examine its influence on customer loyalty, as well as to analyze the significance of different relational bonds across search, experience and credence services. Drawing on existing literature, we develop a conceptual framework with a complete set of different relational bonds and examine how those bonds can influence customer loyalty. We then test our hypothesis through data collected in three contexts, search, experience, and credence services. A self-administered, cross-sectional survey was conducted and a convenience sample of 233 consumers was used to perform significance, correlation and variance tests. We end up presenting the effect of different relational bonds on loyalty and concluding that relational bonds valued by customers vary significantly among the contexts studied. With this study, we aim to fill a literature gap and to provide guidance to managers to differentiate customer relationship strategies according to each specific service context.

1.1 Customer Relationships and Loyalty

Customer loyalty has been considered to be one of the main keys on achieving company success and sustainable competitive advantage [12] and one of the most important determinants of profitable long-term relationships [3]. Retaining customers has become a more attractive strategy for businesses to increase profitability than capturing new customers [13]. As loyalty increases, volumes purchased grow and customer referrals increase. Also, relationship maintenance and customer replacement costs fall as both customer and supplier learn more about each other. Finally, retained customers may pay higher prices than newly acquired customers [14].

The customer loyalty concept is a definition that has been long enriched, but an agreement in the literature has not yet been reached. Some authors may refer to customer loyalty simply as repeat purchase [15]. Nowadays this is considered a poor definition because loyalty can mean much more than just a positive buying behavior of the customer towards the company. Repeat business does not depend on customers being loyal to a company but on the company's perceived faithfulness to a specific, unique customer value [16]. Loyalty has also been described as the crucial glue in developing relationships [17].

In 1999, Oliver's work revolutionized loyalty's definition by realizing that satisfaction does not universally translate into loyalty. The author concludes that satisfaction is a "necessary step" towards loyalty but eventually there are other factors (like self determinism or bonding) that are also significant for this construct. Loyalty is thus defined as a deeply held commitment to rebuy or repatronize a preferred product/ service consistently in the future, thereby causing repetitive same-brand or same brand-set purchasing despite situational influences and marketing efforts having the potential to cause switching behavior [18].

In other seminal work, [19] suggest a combined perspective in which a favorable attitude (attitudinal loyalty) and repeat purchase (behavioral loyalty) were required to define customer loyalty. Thus, loyalty can be defined under two perspectives: behavioral and attitudinal loyalty. Loyalty as a behavioral concept believes repeat purchasing can capture the loyalty of a consumer towards the brand of interest [20]. On the other hand, researchers who endorse attitudinal loyalty state that it is a psychological process which makes an individual develop a commitment towards a brand. This way, loyalty is viewed as a positive attitude that leads to a relationship with the provider [17].

Despite the large number of studies on customer loyalty drivers, existing knowledge is still highly fragmented and the results are mixed [21]. Among other determinants, customer loyalty is strongly affected by different types of relational bonds or ties. Businesses can build customer relationships by initiating one or several types of bonds. Relational bonds can act as benefits or exit barriers [4]. Depending on their nature, these bonds can strengthen or weaken customer relationships and loyalty.

1.2 Relational Bonds or Ties

Bonds and bonding have become central concepts in the study of customer relationships [4]. Bonds are the exit barriers that tie the customer to the firm and maintain the relationship [22]. Different bonds will generate different states of mind from a customer towards a certain company and can influence loyalty towards a service provider. In this section some positive and negative effects of various bonds presented in previous literature (e.g. [4, 9]) will be explored.

Economic bonds and switching costs. Developing relationships with businesses may lead consumers to receive economic advantages. Customers who have an enduring relationship with an organization may be rewarded with financial benefits, such as special pricing considerations [23].

Switching barriers are a consequence of a customer's perception of time, money, and psychological effort required to change from one service provider to another, particularly search and learning costs that switching entails [24]. These perceptions help customers to develop capabilities required to optimally use a given product. Such capabilities are likely to be firm specific and cannot be transferred perfectly to competitors' product offerings [25]. Switching costs will most likely retain customers in the firm and make them consume their complementary products. Switching costs may be caused by various aspects such as: costs of searching for a new service provider; the loss of a friendly and comfortable relationship; having to bear learning cost; explain individual preferences; risk perceptions; or loss of special privileges [26].

Consumer switching costs give firms a degree of market power over their repeat-purchasers [26]. Thus, by exploiting this type of bond, firms can achieve a competitive advantage. Therefore, the switching costs theory predicts a direct, positive relationship between customers' switching costs and firm revenues. Shapiro and Varian [27] argue that in competitive markets where all firms in an industry have similar production costs and product quality, the profits firms earned from customers equal exactly customers' switching costs.

Social bonds. Social bonds refer to personal ties which include perceived feelings of "familiarity, personal recognition, friendship, rapport and social support" [26, p. 102].

Customers derive social bonds from long-term relationships with service firms. A considerable indirect influence of social benefits on word-of-mouth communication through commitment can also be pointed out [9].

This bond can be established, in addition to the benefits received in the delivery of the core service, as a kind of fraternization that can occur between customers and employees. It is then most likely to appear in services with a high degree of interpersonal contact between customers and employees.

Thus it is expected that the higher social bonds, the better the interpersonal relations will be between the customer and the provider which can result to higher levels of loyalty [9]. Nevertheless, managers who encourage social relationships should be aware that some customers are only willing to engage on this type of interaction to a certain point. It is crucial to realize when you're invading people's "comfort zone".

Confidence bonds. Confidence bonds are defined as "perceptions of reduced anxiety and comfort in knowing what to expect in the service encounter" [9, p. 234]. Reducing the risk in services, thus building trust, is key to provide feelings of assurance to customers [28] and also improving satisfaction. Trust creates benefits for the customer (e.g., relationship efficiency through decreased transaction costs) that in turn fosters his or her commitment and loyalty to the relationship [29].

Although this sense of confidence and trust may be inextricably tied to the quality of the core service, it is expected that this bond appears as an independent benefit of long-term relationships - particularly when customers perceive that there are comparable quality providers in the market. Thus, these bonds are perceived to be highly important in retaining relationships, and are expected to influence positively customer loyalty.

Emotional bonds. Customers develop deep emotional bonds with brands, as elaborated in the emotional attachment to brands construct [30]. Developing a relationship with a provider can indicate that there is often a comfort or feeling of security in having that bond. They feel like it's going to be good in advance or if something is wrong it will be taken care of [6].

Consumers who are emotionally attached to a brand are also likely to have a favorable attitude towards it so it's quite that the consequences of this attachment include loyalty and (possibly) a willingness to pay a price premium for the brand [31]. This feeling towards the provider appears to develop over time and only after a relationship has been established between the customer and the organization. Revenue and profit from emotionally bonded repurchase are less vulnerable to disruption. Facilitating strong emotional attachments to brands is thus an important means of realizing devoted, profitable, customer repurchasing.

1.3 The Effect of Service Type on Relational Bonds

Service companies have always spent a great deal of attention to the relations they build with their customers, as oppose to other companies [32]. This is due to the fact that these companies provide a service that needs a lot of contact from the customer in order to be provided. This type of contact gives the chance, both to the company and to the customer, to develop a strong relationship.

Services are far from homogeneous. Rather they possess different structural characteristics such as degree of customization; high versus low face-to-face contact; search, credence or experience properties; membership versus non-membership type relationship; role of the customer in service 'production' and so on [33]. In different service contexts, different types of relationship bonds may emerge, given differences in the nature and the value customers derive from the different service types [7]. The nature of the service alters consumers' motivations to enter and remain in a relationship, as benefits, costs and risks vary across different service types. However, there is little research that takes into account the effect of different service types on relational bonds [8, 34], since the majority of the studies are based on one service industry. To the authors' knowledge, the study by [35] is the only one that focuses on this effect, and it was developed within an online setting.

Following the classification originally proposed by [35–37] divide services into three types (search, experience and credence services), which may have an impact on the importance customers attach to different relational bonds. Search services are those services that the customer can obtain full information and assess the utility outcome prior to purchase. Search attributes can be verified before purchase by examining information readily available from second-hand sources without having to buy or try the product [34]. Experience services are those services that the customers can assess and measure the outcome only during or after the consumption. Products with predominantly experience attributes have to be purchased and consumed before a customer can really appraise it and (dis)confirm the claims of the product [34]. Finally, credence services are those services where is difficult to measure or asses the outcome even after the consumption [35]. As experience and credence attributes dominate in services, consumers employ different evaluation processes than those they use with products where search qualities dominate [2].

According to [35], there are more opportunities to create social, confidence and emotional bonds in experience and credence services rather than in search services, where the customer does not have to interact a lot with the service provider in order to evaluate the outcome of the transaction [33]. Also, due to customers being more aware of their expectations even before service delivery, economic bonds and switching costs are expected to play a more important role on search than experience and credence services. In the case of experience services, as customers lack insight into the prevailing characteristics of the service, they will use heuristic information that is accessible and certifiable to them [38], such as information about the service encounter and human contact, giving a more prevailing role to social bonds. Finally, for credence services, provider reputation (and, thus, confidence bonds) becomes more important than for other types of services because credence services are the hardest to evaluate. The influence of trust on service quality and customer satisfaction cannot be ignored in interpersonal-based service encounters.

2 Problem Definition and Research Methodology

Based on previous literature review, we propose the following research framework (Fig. 1). The research model shows that different relational bonds may influence the level of customer loyalty. The strength and significance of different relational bonds to customers may, however, vary across the different service types, namely search, experience and credence services, as market characteristics vary.

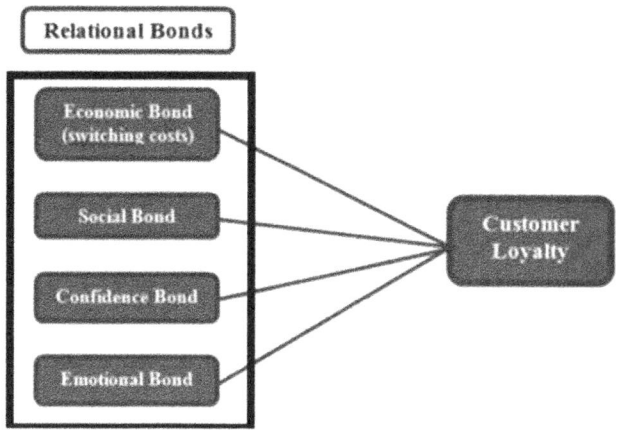

Fig. 1. Research framework.

Accordingly, attention will be focused on the following hypothesis:

H1: Relational bonds influence customer loyalty.
      H1a: Economic bonds and switching costs influence customer loyalty.
      H1b: Social bonds influence customer loyalty.
      H1c: Confidence bonds influence customer loyalty.
      H1d: Emotional bonds influence customer loyalty.
H2: The importance given by customers to each relational bond varies significantly between search, experience and credence services.

In this study, a cable TV operator will be used to symbolize search services due to its characteristics that make results easier to verify, even prior to purchase. Customers are well aware of their expectations and service attributes can be known before consumption. To represent experience services we have chosen a hairdresser because, as [39] pointed out, it's a type of service that consumers can only evaluate after some trial. Services with predominantly credence attributes will be characterized by health services since they are the most difficult to evaluate even after some trial has occurred, because consumers hardly possess any information cues or specified standards to evaluate the actual service outcome [39].

Data was collected from customers that normally use the type of services studied: search, experience and credence services. The survey instrument was administered in a self-completion format to a network of acquaintances and a sample of undergraduate and master students, due to convenience-related factors. Customers were questioned on their behaviors and expectations when choosing a cable TV operator (search service), a hairdresser (experience service) and a health service (credence service). This allowed us to examine meaningful differences across service categories, with different degrees of information asymmetry [40]. Customer loyalty was measured according to an attitudinal perspective, focusing on how strong is the customer's relationship with the service provider. An online questionnaire was produced to measure five variables: economic, social, confidence, emotional bonds (independent variables) and customer loyalty (dependent variable), and 233 answers were obtained.

The questionnaire was divided in two parts. The first one aimed at classifying the respondents: gender, age and qualifications. In the second part, each question must be answered three times in order to classify the differences between the three contexts in the same issue. There were four different items to classify each independent variable (making a total of 16 items). The measures were established scales from previous studies, adapted to the present study. Economic bonds and switching costs were measured with 4 items adapted from [23, 40]. Social bonds were measured through a four-item scale from [23], measurement of emotional and confidence bonds were based on [9, 41]. Finally, to measure the dependent variable (customer loyalty), one item from [9] was used ("I have a very strong relationship with this service provider"). All items employed a 5-point Likert scale, ranging from "totally agree" to "completely disagree" (Table 1).

3 Research Findings

The majority of the respondents (63.9 %) were female, with an average age of 25 years, and who concluded high school or had a bachelor degree (41.6 %).

Exploratory factor analysis (EFA) and reliability tests were performed on the items used to measure relational bonds. Regression Analysis was performed between relational bonds and customer loyalty, while multivariate analysis of variance (MANOVA) ascertained the impact of service type on relational bonds.

We conducted an EFA by the method of Principal Component Analysis using Varimax rotation for relational bonds. A value of Kaiser-Meyer-Olkin (KMO) equal to 0.921, and Bartlett's test with a p-value < 0.001 indicated that there was a significant correlation between the variables and the data is appropriate for a factorial analysis. The results strongly support the four factor structure for relational bonds (Table 1), with a total variance explained of 75.7 %. The scales demonstrated good reliability according to accepted standards [42]. Internal reliability tests of the identified factors showed strong Cronbach's alpha. In addition, evidence of the measures' validity is provided by the fact that all factor loadings are significant and that the scales exhibit high levels of internal consistency.

Hypothesis 1 aims to determine to what extent customer loyalty (dependent variable) is explained by relational bonds (independent variables). Thereby we proceed to Multiple Linear Regression Analysis, a statistical technique used to analyze the relationship between a single dependent variable and several independent variables [43].

Multiple regression analysis showed all bonds to be significant. Social, emotional and confidence bonds emerged as important determinants customers' loyalty. According to the literature, consumers who are emotionally attached to a brand are likely to have a favorable attitude towards it and, thus, to be more loyal [31]. Moreover, according to [9], the higher social bonds, the better the interpersonal relations will be

Table 1. Measurement scales.

Variable	Measurement scale	PCA loadings	Mean	α
I've been keeping a long relationship with service provider X because...				
Economic bonds	It provides discounts for regular customers	0.901	1.95	.817
	It offers rewards to encourage future purchasing	0.908	1.88	
Switching costs	Time and effort costs of changing to other provider are high for me	0.858	2.48	.632
	It would be inconvenient for me to change to another provider	0.834	2.75	
Social bonds	I am recognized by certain employees	0.824	2.79	.913
	I have developed a friendship with the service provider	0.857	2.34	
	I am familiar with the employee(s) that perform(s) the service	0.846	2.83	
	I enjoy visiting this service provider	0.741	2.15	
	I am emotionally attached to it	0.566	2.56	
Emotional and Confidence bonds	I know what to expect when I go in	0.620	3.52	.930
	This company's employees are perfectly honest and truthful	0.859	3.35	
	This company's employees can be trusted completely	0.856	3.23	
	This company's employees have high integrity	0.897	3.42	
	It is concerned with my needs	0.613	3.25	
	The friendliness of the staff makes me feel good	0.638	3.10	
	Although there are other alternatives, I still like going there	0.716	3.36	

between the customer and the provider which therefore would result to higher levels of loyalty. Conversely, economic bonds and switching costs were viewed as less important drivers. In fact, according to the literature, bargain hunting customers are less loyal since they constantly check for the best deals in the market, which fails to contribute to the development of strong relationships [44]. The simple correlation coefficient (R = 0.826) suggests that there is a strong positive correlation between the variables (Table 2). The adjusted coefficient of determination (adjusted R^2 = 0.681) suggests that 68.1 % of the variability of customer loyalty is explained by relational bonds considered in the model.

MANOVA ascertained the impact service type on relational bonds (Table 3). In order to determine the nature and magnitude of service type impact, a series of univariate analysis were conducted. Results showed that the type of service is relevant for each analyzed relational bond.

Table 2. H1 testing results: regression analyses between bonds and customer loyalty.

	R	R²	Adjusted R²	Durbin-Watson	
	0.826	0.682	0.681	1.707	
ANOVA	Sum Squares	df	Mean Square	F	Sig.
Regression	961,246	4	240,312	372,684	0,000
Residual	447,501	694	0,645		
Total	1408,747	698			
	B	Std. Error	Beta	T	Sig.
(Constant)	2,498	0,03		82,241	0,000
Emotional and Confidence Bonds	0,636	0,03	0,448	20,919	0,000
Social Bonds	0,962	0,03	0,677	31,661	0,000
Economic Bonds	0,196	0,03	0,138	6,445	0,000
Switching Costs	0,092	0,03	0,065	3,028	0,003

Pairwise analysis using Tukey post hoc tests shows that, customers give more importance to emotional and confidence bonds when using a hairdresser compared to a cable TV operator (mean difference = 0.787). Also, customers pay more attention to these bonds for health services than for a cable TV operator (mean difference = 0.822).

Table 3. H2 testing results: multivariate analysis of variance.

		Sum of squares	df	Mean square	F	Sig.
Emotional and Confidence bonds	Between groups	100,652	2	50,326	58,637	0,000
	Within groups	597,348	696	0,858		
	Total	698	698			
Social bonds	Between groups	258,35	2	129,175	204,494	0,000
	Within groups	439,65	696	0,632		
	Total	698	698			
Economic bonds	Between groups	70,601	2	35,301	39,161	0,000
	Within groups	627,399	696	0,901		
	Total	698	698			
Switching costs	Between groups	34,255	2	17,128	17,960	0,000
	Within groups	663,745	696	0,954		
	Total	698	698			

When comparing the hairdresser with the health service, there's a positive difference (mean = 0.034) yet not statistically significant (p > 0.005). When it comes to social bonds, again customers pay more attention to these bonds for the hairdresser than for a cable TV operator (mean difference = 1.476). The same happens when comparing the health service with the cable TV operator (mean difference = 0.908). Also, when comparing a hairdresser to a medical service, this bond is still more important for the former than the later (mean difference = 0.567).

These results were expectable, since there are more opportunities to create social and emotional bonds in experience and credence services (such as hairdressers and physicians), where there is a high degree of interpersonal contact [33], rather than in search services such as cable TV operator, where the customer does not have to interact a lot with the service provider in order to evaluate the outcome of the transaction. Services with a high degree of interaction with the customer are based mostly on the personal and customized relations between the client and the provider [45] and offer higher levels of familiarity and trust [46]. Also, in experience services, customers tend to use information about the service encounter and human contact (social bond), while credence services are mainly based on technical knowledge and reputation, rather than social features, and may not qualify for a friendship-type relationship [33, 34].

For economic bonds, it was found a positive mean difference between a cable TV operator and a hairdresser (mean difference = 0.201, yet not statistically significant. Comparing the choice between a cable TV operator and a health service, customers give more importance to economic bonds when choosing a cable TV operator (mean difference = 0.752). Economic bonds are also more important when choosing a hairdresser than a physician (mean difference = 0.551). Since credence services are the hardest to evaluate, customers are more willing to pay a premium price in order to reduce their uncertainty. For this type of service, customers may look to price for a cue and are expected to be less price sensitive [38]. Conversely, when customers are more confident of their abilities to judge the goodness of the service, they become more sensitive to price, and so discounts and other rewards may become more important.

Lastly, analyzing switching costs it was depicted that there are no significant statistical differences between the cable TV operator and the health service (mean difference = 0.143), while hairdressing was the service where the importance of switching costs was the lowest both when compared with a cable TV operator (mean difference = −0.524) and with the physician (mean difference = −0.381). This result possibly reflects the fact that, apart from the potential loss of a friendly relationship, most switching barriers are not a major consideration in hairdressing, given the abundance of alternatives [47]. Conversely, in the case of credence services such as the physician, which are intrinsically difficult for customers to evaluate, alternatives may be hard for customers to compare and match, and switching costs are considered high [48]. Surprisingly, although search services are the easiest to evaluate prior to purchase, the cable TV operator also exhibits high switching costs. One possible reason is that Cable TV operators tend to have a membership relationship with its customer base and are thus more likely to have contractual switching barriers [33].

4 Conclusion

Service companies are increasingly recognizing the fundamental interest on analyzing customer behavior. The close contact that service companies have with their customers gives them the chance to develop strong relationships and customer loyalty. The theme of customer loyalty that combines a favorable attitude (attitudinal loyalty) and repeat purchase (behavioral loyalty) has been considered to be one of the main keys on achieving company success and sustainable competitive advantage.

Loyalty can be achieved by building relational bonds with customers. Different bonds will generate different customer states of mind towards the company. Namely, economic and switching costs may retain customers; social bonds can enhance interpersonal relations between the customer and the provider; confidence bonds may reduce risk and contribute to a strong feeling of trust; and emotional bonds can increase the sense of attachment to a service provider. However, the role and relevance of relational bonds may not be the same across service contexts.

The main goal of this study was to identify a set of relational bonds and to examine its influence on customer loyalty, as well as to analyze the significance of different relational bonds across search, experience and credence services (represented by a cable TV operator, a hairdresser and a health service, respectively).

Through a Multiple Linear Regression it was shown that all four factors, Emotional and Confidence Bonds, Social Bonds, Economic Bonds and Switching Costs, had a significant positive influence on customer loyalty. Particularly, social bonds had the highest impact on loyalty. This comes in line with what was previously predicted that the higher the social bonds, the better the interpersonal relations will be between the customer and the provider which, in turn, would increase loyalty. Following, emotional and confidence bonds also had an impact on loyalty, since consumers who are emotionally attached to a provider and develop feelings of trust are likely to be loyal to the company. Lastly, economic bonds and switching costs also showed a positive influence on loyalty since switching to an alternative provider can imply a loss of economic benefits and may be perceived as time-consuming.

It was also proven that the degree of importance that each customer gives to the relational bonds analyzed varies with the type of service considered (namely, search, experience and credence services). Namely, the relevance given to relational bonds varies with differences in the nature and the value customers derive from different types of services. Emotional and confidence bonds had the most prominence on health services, social bonds had the most relevance on hairdresser's customers, and economic bonds and switching costs had a greater impact with the cable TV operator.

As a final reflection, in this investigation it became clear that managers should differentiate customer relationship strategies according to each specific service context. For example, for services high in credence and experience qualities, staff might be trained to nurture close relationships with clients, since there is an opportunity for emotional bonds or 'strong network ties' to be developed. Conversely, in the case of search services such as cable TV operators, attention should be given to economic incentives and switching barriers, such as membership relationships, since this type of services is easy to evaluate and compare and emotional, confidence and social play a minor role.

For future researches, it is important to acknowledge that this study has some limitations. First of all, since a convenience sample was used, this study shortens the possibility of generalization. It would be interesting to test the results in a sample with a broader and larger customer base, since the sample used may not be sufficient to generalize all the assumptions above. This study could be applied to other service contexts to see if it can actually be broaden to other settings or just to the ones studied here. Also, some specific characteristics of the services studied could be further analyzed. For example, for health services, customers could be inquired about specific services (e.g. a clinical visit, a specialist examination or a hospital admission); in terms of cable TV operators, it would be interesting to know if customers hold a contract agreement with the provider or not. Finally, further research could study the effect of other variables, such as low/high relational customers, on relational bonds and customer loyalty.

References

1. Palmer, A.: Principles of Services Marketing. McGraw-Hill, London (2005)
2. Zeithaml, V.A., Bitner, M.J., Gremler, D.D.: Services Marketing: Integrating Customer Focus Across the Firm. McGraw-Hill, Boston (2006)
3. Evanschitzky, H., Iyer, G.R., Plaßmann, H., Nießing, J., Meffert, H.: The relative strength of affective commitment in securing loyalty in service relationships. J. Bus. Res. **59**(12), 1207–1213 (2006)
4. Arantola, H.: Consumer bonding-a conceptual exploration. J. Rel. Mark. **1**(2), 93–107 (2002)
5. Buttle, F.A., Ahmad, R., Aldlaigan, A.: The theory and practice of customer bonding. J Bus-Bus. Mark. **9**(2), 3–27 (2002)
6. Spake, D., Beatty, S., Brockman, B., Crutchfield, T.: Consumer comfort in service relationships: measurement and importance. J. Serv. Res. **5**(4), 316–332 (2003)
7. Veloutsou, C., Saren, M., Tzokas, N.: Relationship marketing what if…? Eur. J. Mark. **36**(4), 433–449 (2002)
8. Paolo, G., Laurent, G.: Interpersonal trust in commercial relationships: antecedents and consequences of customer trust in the salesperson. Eur. J. Mark. **44**(1/2), 114–138 (2010)
9. Hennig-Thurau, T., Gwinner, K., Gremler, D.: Understanding relationship marketing outcomes: an integration of relational benefits and relationship quality. J. Serv. Res. **4**, 230–247 (2002)
10. Bloemer, J., Odekerken-Schröder, G., Kestens, L.: The impact of need for social affiliation and consumer relationship proneness on behavioral intentions: an empirical study in a hairdresser's context. J. Retail Cons. Serv. **10**(4), 231–240 (2003)
11. Odekerken-Schröder, G., Bloemer, J.: Constraints and dedication as drivers for relationship commitment: an empirical study in a health-care context. J. Rel. Mark. **3**(1), 35–52 (2004)
12. Reichheld, F.F., Teal, T.: The Loyalty Effect: The Hidden Force Behind Growth, Profits, and Lasting Value. Harvard Business Press, Boston (2001)
13. Hsu, C.: The relationship among service quality, perceived value, customer satisfaction and behavioural intentions: an empirical study of online shopping. MBA thesis, National Cheng Kung University, Tainan City, Taiwan (2007)
14. Buttle, F., Ang, L.: Customer retention management processes: a quantitative study. Eur. J. Mark. **40**(1/2), 83–99 (2006)

15. Oliver, R.L.: Satisfaction: A Behavioural Perspective on the Consumer. Irwin/McGraw-Hill, New York (1997)
16. Grönroos, C., Helle, P.: Return on relationships: conceptual understanding and measurement of mutual gains from relational business engagements. J. Bus. Ind. Mark. **27**(5), 344–359 (2012)
17. Day, G.S.: A two-dimensional concept of brand loyalty. J. Ad. Res. **9**, 29–35 (2000)
18. Oliver, R.L.: Whence consumer loyalty. J. Mark. **63**, 33–44 (1999)
19. Dick, A., Basu, K.: Customer loyalty: towards an integrated framework. J. Acad. Market. Sci. **22**(2), 99–113 (1994)
20. Ehrenberg, A.S.C.: Repeat buying—facts, theory and applications. J. Emp. Gen. Mark. Sci. **5**, 392–770 (2000)
21. Verhoef, P., Langerak, F., Donkers, B.: Understanding brand and dealer retention in the new car market: the moderating role of brand tier. J. Retail. **83**(1), 97–113 (2007)
22. Wendelin, R.: Bond audit, a method for evaluating business relationships. J. Bus. Ind. Mark. **26**(3), 211–217 (2011)
23. Gwinner, K., Gremler, D., Bitner, M.: Relational benefits in services industries: the customer's perspective. J. Acad. Mark. Sci. **26**(2), 101–114 (1998)
24. Jones, M.A., Mothersbaugh, D.L., Beatty, S.: Why customers stay: measuring the underlying dimensions of services switching costs and managing their differential strategic outcomes. J. Bus. Res. **55**(6), 441–450 (2002)
25. Brush, T., Dangol, R., O'Brien, J.: Customer capabilities, switching costs and bank performance. Strat. Manag. J. **33**(13), 1499–1515 (2012)
26. Klemperer, P.: Competition when customers have switching costs: an overview with applications to industrial organizations, microeconomics and international trade. Rev. Econ. St. **62**, 515–539 (1995)
27. Shapiro, C., Varian, H.: Information Rules: A Strategic Guide to the Network Economy. Harvard Business School Press, Boston (1999)
28. Berry, L.L.: Relationship Marketing of Services Growing Interest. Emerg. Perspect. J. Acad. Mark. Sci. **23**(Fall), 236–245 (1995)
29. Garbarino, E., Mark, S.: The different roles of satisfaction, trust, and commitment in customer relationships. J. Mark. **63**(April), 70–87 (1999)
30. Douglas, B., Hieu, G., Nguyen, P.: Antecedents of emotional attachment to brands. J. Bus. Res. **64**, 1052–1059 (2011)
31. Thompson, M., MacInnis, D., Park, C.: The ties that bind: measuring the strength of consumers' emotional attachments to brands. J. Cons. Psychol. **15**(1), 77–91 (2005)
32. Grnroos, C.: The relationship marketing process: communication, interaction, dialogue, value. J. Bus. Ind. Mark. **19**(2), 99–113 (2004)
33. Patterson, P., Smith, T.: Modeling relationship strength across service types in an Eastern culture. Int. J. Serv. Ind. Manag. **12**(2), 90–113 (2001)
34. Galetzka, M., Verhoeven, J., Pruyn, A.: Service validity and service reliability of search, experience and credence services: a scenario study. Int. J. Serv. Ind. Manag. **17**(3), 271–283 (2006)
35. Hsieh, Y., Chiu, H., Chiang, M.: Maintaining a committed online customer: a study across search-experience-credence products. J. Retail. **81**(1), 75–82 (2005)
36. Nelson, P.: Advertising as information. J. Pol. Econ. **81**, 729–754 (1974)
37. Darby, M., Karni, E.: Free competition and the optimum amount of fraud. J. Law Econ. **16**, 67–86 (1973)
38. Mitra, K., Reiss, M., Capella, L.: An examination of perceived risk, information search and behavioral intentions in search, experience and credence services. J. Serv. Mark. **13**(3), 208–228 (1999)

39. Zeithaml, V.: How consumer evaluation processes differ between goods and services. In: Donnelly, J.H., George, W.R. (eds.) Marketing of Services: AMA Special Conference, American Marketing Association, Orlando, FL (1981)
40. Sui, J., Baloglu, S.: The role of emotional commitment in RM: an empirical investigation of a loyalty model for casinos. J. Hosp. Tourism Res. **27**(4), 470–489 (2003)
41. Lin, P., Weng, J., Hisih, Y.: Relational bonds and customer's trust and commitment- a study on the moderating effects of web site usage. Serv. Ind. J. **23**(3), 103–127 (2003)
42. Nunnally, J.: Psychometric Theory. McGraw-Hill, New York (1978)
43. Hair, J., Black, W., Babin, B., Anderson, R., Tatham, R.: Multivariate Data Analysis. Prentice Hall, Englewood Cliffs (2006)
44. Kinard, B., Capella, M.: Relationship marketing: the influence of consumer involvement on perceived service benefits. J. Serv. Mark. **20**(6), 359–368 (2006)
45. Folkes, V., Patrick, V.: The positivity effect in perceptions of services: seen one, seen them all? J. Cons. Res. **30**, 135–137 (2003)
46. Ganesan-Lim, C., Russell-Bennett, R., Dagger, T.: The impact of service contact type and demographic characteristics on service quality perceptions. J. Serv. Mark. **22**(7), 550–561 (2008)
47. Patterson, P., Smith, T.: A cross-cultural study of switching barriers and propensity to stay with service providers. J. Retail. **79**(2), 107–120 (2003)
48. Patterson, P.: A contingency model of behavioural intentions in a services context. Eur. J. Mark. **38**(9/10), 1304–1315 (2004)

Exploring Opportunities to Improve Retail Store Quality Using RSQS

Marlene Amorim[✉] and Fatemeh Bashashi Saghezchi

Department of Economics Management and Industrial Engineering,
University of Aveiro, Campus Universitário de Santiago, Aveiro, Portugal
{mamorim,fatemeh}@ua.pt

Abstract. This paper presents an application of the importance-performance analysis (IPA) to identify opportunities for improving service quality in retail contexts. This work builds previous quality scales prevalent in service management literature. Data was collected for customers' quality expectations and perceptions across two different retail store formats in Portugal: supermarkets and hypermarkets. The results of the study suggested that managerial decisions regarding service in stores should be adjusted to the characteristics of each retail format. Data analysis supported the existence of differences in the IPA, between supermarkets and hypermarkets, notably for quality dimensions related to reliability and personal interaction.

Keywords: Service quality · RSQS · Importance-performance-analysis

1 Introduction

The paramount importance of service quality for customer satisfaction and loyalty, as well as its link with service providers' profitability, have been extensively documented in literature [1–4]. For this reason the development of service quality models has been a priority in the agendas of service scholars leading to intense debates about the definition and assessment of quality in service contexts [5–7].

Service quality models provide a description of the key components of service quality, as well as the relationships among them and customer satisfaction and loyalty. As such, they are tools that help managers to diagnose the performance in service delivery processes and to develop quality improvement programs [8]. Prevalent approaches acknowledge service quality as a multidimensional concept, determined by the fact that customers derive a combination of various outcomes from service delivery experiences, (e.g. direct process results, such as the availability of required items in a retail store, as well as results related to the process experience, such as store atmosphere or employee empathy, that emerge from customers' involvement in service production process). In practice, service quality measurement models typically include multiple items for capturing customers' evaluations about the various output components, organized in a set of service quality dimensions.

In the context of retail services, knowledge about customers' quality assessments for the various quality attributes is of key importance for informing adequate strategies to promote consumer loyalty [9]. To this end, and given the importance of the service retail sector in modern economies, we have witnessed the development of specific quality models and measurement scales for capturing customer appreciations about retail experiences. A key reference is the work of Dabholkar et al. [10] validated a retail service quality scale (RSQS) consisting of five dimensions: physical aspects, reliability, personal interaction, problem solving, and policy, including 28 items. Subsequent contributions [11] adapted this scale to the specificity of the reality of Spanish supermarkets, and Latin countries in general.

This study builds on the aforementioned retail quality scales to investigate the existence of differences in the relative importance of distinct quality dimensions across two retail formats: supermarkets and hypermarkets. The motivation for this work is led by the observation of the intense scenario of retail competition, which has been characterized by the development of very diversified store formats. Nowadays, customers can choose from a broad array of competing categories, including supermarkets, department stores, outlets, specialty retailers, etc., that offer various benefits to match the needs of different segments and meet different shopping situations [12]. Understanding the relative importance of various service retail attributes can provide important insights for managers seeking to implement retail differentiation strategies. Notably for the case of retailers operating multi-store portfolios that combine different store formats, which are very common in retail landscape, particularly in Europe [13].

This study reports the results of the analysis of survey data that addressed customers of Portuguese supermarkets and hypermarkets in urban areas. Data analysis involved testing for differences in customer's quality evaluations in supermarket and hypermarket settings, as well as the conduction of an importance-performance analysis to explore the weaknesses and strengths of the target retail formats in satisfying different quality dimensions. The remaining of this manuscript is structures in the following manner. We first provide the conceptual background of our study, reviewing aspects related to retail store formats and competition, followed by an overview of the conceptualization of quality in retail settings, notably the existing service quality scales for the specific setting of retail services. We follow by describing the research methodology and the objectives of the data analysis conducted. Finally, we provide a discussion of the results of the work and draw some managerial implications and directions for future research.

2 Conceptual Background

Supermarkets and hypermarkets are dominant models in European retail context, resulting from internationalization and replication strategies of leading retail chains. Hypermarkets offer relatively wider shopping surfaces and superior product variety than supermarkets. These latter, are smaller stores, having predominately an urban location, e.g. city centers and residential areas, are chosen by customers for more frequent shopping visits, for a small volume of items. In Portugal, we have observed an important growth in the number and importance of supermarkets and hypermarkets, while small stores and grocery shops have experienced some decline [14].

Retail customers distribute their shopping and spending, across different stores, including distinct store categories (e.g. shops, supermarkets, etc.) exploiting the opportunities offered [15]. Research addressing customers' choices for different shopping alternatives typically link store patronage to customers' individual characteristics and preferences as well as to store attributes such as location, breadth of assortment, price, etc., as well as to [16]. Evidence suggests that, overall, customers distribute their shopping across relatively stable store portfolios [17]. For this reason retail managers seek for knowledge about the drivers of customer retention in retail in order to promote consumer loyalty leading to profitability [9]. Several studies have put forward various store attributes that have an effect on customers' shopping satisfaction (e.g. store location, variety of item assortment) [18]. This links customer store choices to service quality dimensions, which have been acknowledge din the literature as key drivers of customer satisfaction and customer intentions to reuse and recommend a given service [5, 6, 8].

Customers are aware of differences in service attributes across store formats, as evidenced by behaviors of store switching and store combination to capture the specific benefits offered by different retail [19]. To this end, differences in retail formats can be linked to distinct customer expectations, and assessments, about the respective service process experiences, such as associating distinct levels of effort and shopping cost to the different retail store formats [20]. In this study we propose to investigate the importance of different service quality attributes (e.g. quality of the store facilities, empathy personnel, etc.) for customer satisfaction and loyalty in different store formats.

This study builds on former conceptualizations of service quality, notably on multidimensional service quality models, that rely on multiple item scales to capture customers' expectation and perceptions of quality [5, 10, 11]. Service quality plays a decisive role for retailers' differentiation and profitability. Retailers compete on quality dimensions such as facilities, convenience, etc. [21]. Examples of previous research efforts to compare distinct retail formats can be found in service literature (e.g., [22] addressed differences in customers' quality perceptions for hypermarkets and traditional retail; Goldman and Hino [23] looked at supermarkets and traditional retail). Differences in store formats bear important implications for service delivery experiences (e.g., item variety, degree of customer effort) and quality. Relevant differences include: store surface (about 4.000–10.000 m2, in hypermarkets towards the average supermarket size of 1.500–4.000 m2); assortment variety (e.g., hypermarket assortments are typically deeper); percentage of floor space assigned to different categories (groceries often being up to 40 % in supermarket outlets and 25 % in hypermarkets) [22, 23].

3 Methodology

Data collection for the study was supported by a 24-item questionnaire applied to a sample of retail customers of supermarkets and hypermarkets in Portugal, subscribing to the structure of RSQS [10, 11], that was found appropriate to measure the service quality of customer's perception in retail stores in Portugal. In order to align the RSQS measurement instrument with objectives of our study, the scale was adjusted following exploratory interviews with retail customer and managers.

In Table 1 we present a list of the 24 items used, identifying, for each item, the reference source paper where it was originally proposed, and the respective dimensions associated to each item. Items 14 and 18 were added to the list by the authors as they were mentioned to be relevant in initial exploratory interviews conducted with Portuguese retail customers. Other items (such as items 7 and 20) were subject to minor modifications (Mod.) to adjust them to the Portuguese retail context.

The target respondents addressed were retail customers which were users of the main supermarkets and hypermarkets located in this region. A total of 270 questionnaires were distributed, and from these 9 were returned with incomplete answers, for which they were discarded form the analysis. From the remaining 261, 13 of them were obtained from respondents who were customers of supermarkets which were not the main retailers operating in the country. Data analysis builds therefore on the remaining 248 complete questionnaires, from respondents who declared to use one of the main supermarkets or hypermarkets in the country. The sample included a balanced representation of customers from each gender (46.85 % male customers), age and education levels. It also included a balanced representation of customers of both retail formats (50.8 % of the respondents declared to be predominately users of supermarkets, while 49.2 % were users of the hypermarket retail format).

Data analysis involved firstly the characterization of customer service quality assessments for the two retail formats considered, using descriptive statistics. T-tests were also performed to investigate for significant differences in customer quality evaluations across supermarket and hypermarket settings.

This preliminary data exploration was followed by an importance-performance analysis (IPA) [24, 25]. Such analysis serves as a guideline for formulating effective strategies to improve the competitive strength of the target retail stores. The expectation of the clients reflects the importance of the attributes on which they base their evaluation, while their perception reflects the service quality they are offered by the retail store for those attributes. Following Vasquez et al. [11] customers' expectations and perceptions are classified into low, moderate, and high values in a way that their combination form four different zones as illustrated in Fig. 1, as follows: Competitive vulnerability (important dimensions with low perceptions); Competitive strength (high perceptions in important dimensions); Irrelevant superiority (high perceptions in dimensions which are not very important); Relative indifference (low scores in dimensions that are not very important).

The items in the first quadrant (competitive vulnerability) are those which require greater efforts from the company than those in the second quadrant (competitive strengths) to boost the customer satisfaction. For those appearing in the third quadrant (irrelevant superiority) channeling resources must be considered, assigning them to other activities of greater importance. Finally, those in the fourth quadrant (relative indifference) are attributes which do not require immediate attention. The placement of the expectation and perceptions expressed by respondents for the four service quality dimensions considered, involves the consideration of the average expectations of each of the four retail service quality dimensions, and their comparison with the average expectation of all the dimensions. The dimensions which exhibit significantly higher averages than the overall mean are placed above/right the axis lines which represented the overall mean values, whereas those with averages lower than the average values

Table 1. Retail service quality items used in the study

Items	From [10]	From [11]
Physical Aspects		
1. Modernity and attractiveness of store facilities, equipment and fixtures	x	x
2. Visual attractiveness of publicity leaflets and other materials related to the service, such as shopping bags, catalogs, etc	x	x
3. Cleanliness of the store and available support services (e.g., w c, safe-boxes, etc.)	x	x
4. Store layout and organization enabling customers to easily find the products they need	x	x
Reliability		
5. Clear indication of product prices		x
6. Appropriate and punctual information about sales promotions and discounts		x
7. Short waiting time at cash registers	Mod.	x
8. Easy location of products on promotion or discount		x
9. Employees showing great interest and motivation to resolve any difficulties or customer problems		x
10. Stock availability of products/brands desired by customers	x	x
11. Guarantees of product quality and possibility of returns		x
Personal Interaction		
12. All employees consistently showing courtesy towards customers (e.g., cashiers, replenishment staff, etc.)	x	x
13. All employees consistently willing to help customers (e.g., cashiers, replenishment staff, etc.)	x	x
14. Employees showing enough knowledge to assist and advise customers in the fresh sections (e.g., fish, fruits, etc.)	Mod.	Mod.
15. Employees having enough knowledge to assist customers in difficulties and questions	x	x
16. Employees instilling confidence in customers when assisting or advising them	x	x
Policies		
17. Offer of interesting sales promotions and discounts		x
18. Offer of free choice of alternatives for payment (e.g., in cash, via store card, credit card, etc.)	Mod.	Mod.
19. Offer of product prices which are lower than in similar establishments		x
20. Freshness and quality of products offered in the fresh sections (e.g., fish, fruit, etc.)	Mod.	x
21. Offer of products from well-known and leading brands in the market		x
22. Offer of a wide assortment of product brands and varieties		x
23. Offer of products from the retailers' own brand with high quality		x
24. Ease of access to the store and availability of parking spaces	x	

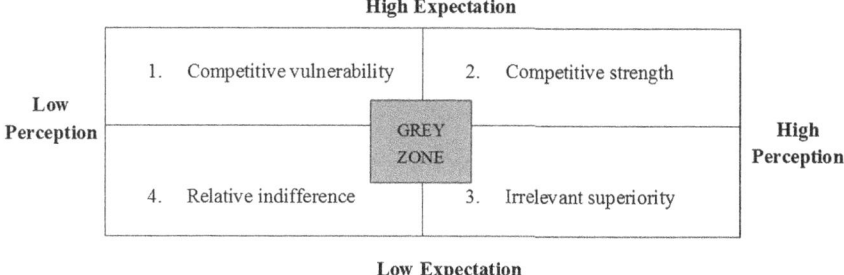

Fig. 1. Importance-performance matrix (adapted from [11])

were placed below/left the axis. A similar procedure is repeated for the perception values for all four retail quality dimensions. Following this vein IPA was conducted and differences investigated again across retail formats. The importance of the retail quality attributes was derived from customers' expectations, whereas performance was based on perceptions.

4 Analysis and Discussion

The results of the study suggested that managerial decisions regarding service in stores should be adjusted to the characteristics of each retail format. Data analysis supported the existence of differences in the IPA, between supermarkets and hypermarkets, notably for quality dimensions related to reliability (RE) and personal interaction (PI).

As a first approach descriptive analysis was conducted followed by t-tests to investigate the existence of significant differences in customer service quality evaluations across the two addressed retail formats (i.e., supermarket and hypermarket settings). The main conclusions that are drawn from the preliminary descriptive statistics of the service quality items considered were as follows.

- The most important item for respondents was freshness and quality of products offered in the fresh sections (e.g., fish, fruit, etc.), which corresponds to the dimension of policies, whereas the least important item for respondents was visual attractiveness of publicity leaflets and other materials related to the service (e.g., shopping bags, catalogs), which corresponds to the dimension of physical aspects.
- Reliability was the most important dimension for retail quality, followed by, personal interaction, policies, and physical aspects, respectively.
- Aspects related to the dimension of policies revealed the higher customer perceptions, followed by physical aspects, personal interactions, and reliability, respectively.
- Customers expressed good perceptions about the retailers' offering products from well-known and leading brands. On the other extreme, customers were not impressed about the waiting time at cash registers. The dissatisfaction about this item was stronger for the case of supermarkets as compared to hypermarkets.

- Women showed not only higher expectations but also higher perceptions than men for all the dimensions of service quality. The highest difference between the expectations of men and women was related to the dimension of personal interaction, whereas the highest difference between their perceptions was related to the policies dimension.
- The existing gaps between customers' expectations and perceptions suggested that the biggest difference between supermarkets and hypermarkets relied on the dimension of policies, whereas the smallest difference belonged to the dimension of reliability. This suggests that hypermarkets are doing better, in the eyes of the customers, in terms of policies, whereas supermarkets offer competitive service in terms of reliability.

Significant differences in expectations were found only for three items, namely for: E3 "cleanliness of the store and available support services (e.g., w c, safe-boxes, etc.)", E4 "store layout and organization enabling customers to easily find the products they need", and E23 "offer of products from the retailers' own brand with high quality". Therefore, respondent's expectations for service quality are not suggested to differ substantially across supermarket and hypermarket formats. Regarding perception, the scenario was substantially different. Results indicated significant differences for items 15 items (P1, P3, P9, P10, P11, P12, P13, P15, P16, P18, P19, P20, P21, P22, P24), with hypermarkets, generally scoring better.

The translation of the information about customers' quality assessments into the IPA, illustrated in Fig. 2 evidences that general, as seen from the figure, customers perceived higher service quality from hypermarkets comparing to supermarkets under all four dimensions. As observed, the highest perceived quality corresponds to policy dimension for both of the retail formats. On the other hand, for both retail formats,

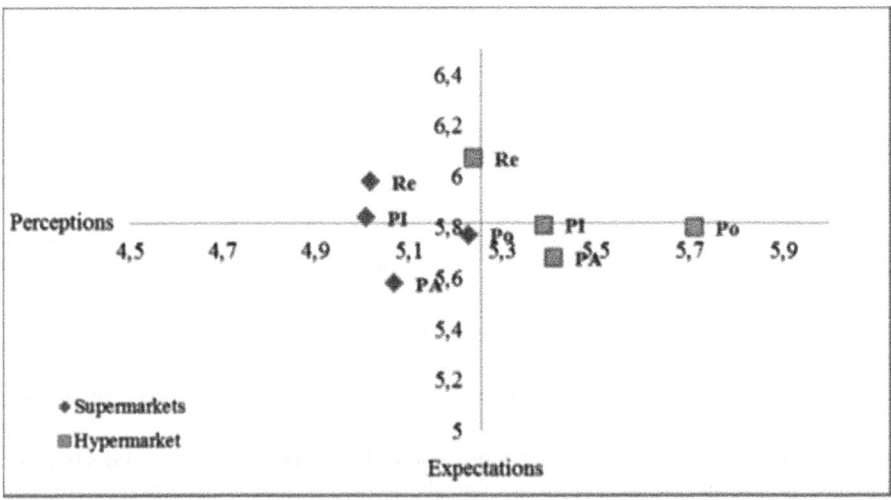

Fig. 2. IPA for service quality dimensions in retail formats (PA, physical aspects; Re, Reliability; PI, Personal Interaction; Po, Policies)

reliability and physical aspects are the most and the least important dimensions, respectively. None of the retail formats had any service quality dimension in the competitive strength zone.

Figure 2 shows the result of importance-performance analysis for both retail formats. In this graph the vertical axis represents the values for expectations (with an average value of 5.8177), and the horizontal axis represents the values for perceptions (with an average value of 5.2564). The points plotted in the graph correspond to the average values for each dimension (e.g. physical aspects, reliability, etc.), both for expectations and perceptions.

In a nutshell, Fig. 2 indicates that customers perceived higher service quality for hypermarkets for all of the service quality dimensions considered. Customers revealed high quality perceptions for the dimension of policies (PI) for both of the retail formats. This result can be explained by the numerous promotion and discounts campaigns pursued by this type of retail competitors, to which customers are very sensitive. Reliability (RE) stands out as the most important dimension calling for immediate managerial level action (i.e., competitive vulnerability), whereas physical aspects (PA) seemed to have received enough care from the addressed retail companies (i.e., irrelevant superiority). A counterintuitive result was found for the dimension of personal interaction (PI) for which customer ranked superiorly in the hypermarket formats, whereas the expected result would be to find a higher relational proximity in smaller neighborhood based supermarket stores.

After plotting these values on the graph, we also tested for "significance" of the difference between the average value for each dimension and the total mean values considered in the axis. We conducted t-tests to assess the differences between the average value for each dimension and the total mean value for expectations, as well as for perceptions. The reliability dimension proved to be very important for the clients (t-test evidenced a significant difference for the reliability dimension across the two formats, supermarkets and hypermarkets). As per perceptions, three dimensions appeared with high value (policy, personal interaction, and physical aspect) just in hypermarkets. However, for the supermarket, there is no quality dimension in the above average perception region (i.e., the right half plane) (Tables 2 and 3).

Table 2. T-test for expectations (Supermarket and Hypermarket)

Expectation	Supermarket		Hypermarket	
Dimension	T-test	Interval for μDimension- μGlobalExp.	T-test	Interval for μDimension- μGlobalExp.
Physical Aspects	(0.001)	]-0.3564, -0.0254[	(0.068)	]-0.2848, 0.0101[
Reliability	(0.011)	] 0.0394, 0.2912[	(0.001)	] 0.1089, 0.4009[
Personal Interaction	(0.708)	]-0.1140, 0.1675[	(0.960)	]-0.1863, 0.1771[
Policy	(0.469)	]-0.1746, 0.0808[	(0.859)	]-0.1750, 0.1461[

Table 3. T-test for perceptions (Supermarket and Hypermarket)

Perception	Supermarket		Hypermarket	
Dimension	T-test	Interval for μDimension- μGlobalPer.	T-test	Interval for μDimension- μGlobalPer.
Physical Aspects	(0.024)	]-0.3564, -0.0254[	(0.054)	]-0.0028, 0.3056[
Reliability	(0.003)	]-0.3944, -0.0799[	(0.834)	]-0.1950, 0.1576[
Personal Interaction	(0.017)	]-0.4397, -0.0445[	(0.173)	]-0.0586, 0.3228[
Policy	(0.778)	]-0.1782, 0.1337[	(0.000)	] 0.3018, 0.5993[

According to this analysis, although three dimensions of hypermarkets are on bounds of the second quadrant, there is not any distinctive dimension in competitive strength area. Interestingly, the result for supermarkets appear in left half (first and forth quadrants), and hypermarkets' results placed in right half (second and third quadrants). The dimensions requiring more immediate attention by the supermarket will be those concerning reliability and physical aspects as they placed in competitive vulnerability and relative indifference area, respectively. Surprisingly, physical aspect dimension in hypermarkets is improved adequately as it appeared in irrelevant superiority, and the company must consider channeling resources, allocating them to other activities of greater importance.

5 Conclusions

This paper offers a timely contribution to understand differences in service delivery quality across two retail formats, which have important differences in the service process experience offered to their customers. As the scope of this work was beyond scale validation and extension, the project work builds on formerly proposed measurement scales [11, 12] to conduct a survey about customers' quality perception for Portuguese supermarkets and hypermarkets services. Given the differences in various service delivery elements (such as store format, assortment, etc.) found between supermarkets and hypermarkets this study sets up to provide a contribution to understand the implications of such differences to customers' assessment of quality. The outcomes of the study have conceptual, as well as managerial relevance, and may prove particularly useful for assisting service differentiation for multi-format retailers. Overall, the results suggest that customers have higher perceptions about the quality of hypermarkets when compared to supermarkets. As respondents reported their perceptions about the store they visited more often, this study also suggests that customers predominantly visit the retail store which has the lowest service quality gap for the most important attributes for them (i.e., the freshness and quality of product offered in the fresh section).

The study has some limitations, notably derived from the fact it was conducted only in Portugal, therefore, implying some geographical limitations. It also reflects predominantly the views of young and educated customers which were the largest group of respondents. The concern with the length of the questionnaire motivated the choice for asking respondents to express their service quality perceptions only relatively to the retail store that they visited most often. Future development of this work will therefore need to relax each of the above-mentioned limitations. Moreover, this work, focused only on the main dimensions of the service quality. Future work may extend the study to the service quality sub-dimensions. Finally, exploring the difference between customers' shopping basket and their frequency of visits in supermarkets and hypermarkets needs further investigation.

Overall the results suggest that managerial decisions regarding service in stores should be adjusted to the characteristics of each retail format. The impacts of improvements in reliability and personal interaction differ for supermarkets and hypermarkets. The results also suggest that improvements in customers' perceptions about reliability will have relatively stronger impact on their overall satisfaction in supermarkets than the hypermarkets. On the other hand, improvements in customers' perceptions about personal interaction will result in stronger impacts for customer satisfaction in hypermarkets than the supermarkets.

References

1. Reinartz, W., Krafft, M., Hoyer, W.D.: The customer relationship management process: its measurement and impact on performance. J. Mark. Res. **41**(3), 293–305 (2004)
2. Cronin Jr., J.J., Brady, M.K., Hult, G.T.M.: Assessing the effects of quality, value, and customer satisfaction on consumer behavioral intentions in service environments. J. Retail. **76**(2), 193–218 (2000)
3. Anderson, E.W., Fornell, C., Lehmann, D.R.: Customer satisfaction, market share, and profitability: findings from Sweden. J. Mark. **58**(3), 53–66 (1994)
4. Reichheld, F.F., Sasser, W.E.: Zero defections: quality comes to services. Harvard Bus. Rev. **68**(5), 105–111 (1990)
5. Parasuraman, A., Zeithaml, V.A., Berry, L.L.: A conceptual model of service quality and its implications for future research. J. Mark. **49**(4), 1–50 (1985)
6. Cronin Jr., J.J., Taylor, S.A.: Measuring service quality: a reexamination and extension. J. Mark. **56**(3), 55–68 (1992)
7. Grönroos, C.: Toward a third phase in service quality research: challenges and future directions. Adv. serv. Mark. Manage. **2**(1), 49–64 (1993)
8. Seth, N., Deshmukh, S.G., Vrat, P.: Service quality models: a review. Int. J. Qual. Reliab. Manage. **22**(9), 913–949 (2005)
9. Knox, S.D., Denison, T.J.: Store loyalty: its impact on retail revenue: an empirical study of purchasing behaviour in the UK. J. Retail. Consum. Serv. **7**(1), 33–45 (2000)
10. Dabholkar, P.A., Thorpe, D.I., Rentz, J.O.: A measure of service quality for retail stores: scale development and validation. J. Acad. Mark. Sci. **24**(1), 3–16 (1995)
11. Vázquez, R.: Rodríguez-Del Bosque, I. A., Ma Díaz, A., Ruiz, A. V.: Service quality in supermarket retailing: identifying critical service experiences. J. Retail. Consum. Serv. **8**(1), 1–14 (2001)
12. Reynolds, K.E., Ganesh, J., Luckett, M.: Traditional malls vs. factory outlets: comparing shopper typologies and implications for retail strategy. J. Bus. Res. **55**(9), 687–696 (2002)

13. Mendes, A.B., Themido, I.H.: Multi-outlet retail site location assessment. Int. Trans. Oper. Res. **11**(1), 1–18 (2004)
14. Barros, C.P., Alves, C.A.: Hypermarket retail store efficiency in Portugal. Int. J. Retail Distrib. Manage. **31**(11), 549–560 (2003)
15. Gijsbrechts, E., Campo, K., Nisol, P.: Beyond promotion-based store switching: antecedents and patterns of systematic multiple-store shopping. Int. J. Res. Mark. **25**(1), 5–21 (2008)
16. Carpenter, J.M., Moore, M.: Consumer demographics, store attributes and retail format choice in the US grocery market. Int. J. Retail Distrib. Manage. **34**(6), 434–452 (2006)
17. Rhee, H., Bell, D.R.: The inter-store mobility of supermarket shoppers. J. Retail. **78**(4), 225–237 (2002)
18. Ailawadi, K.L., Keller, K.L.: Understanding retail branding: conceptual insights and research priorities. J. Retail. **80**(4), 331–342 (2004)
19. Uusitalo, O.: Consumer perceptions of grocery retail formats and brands. Int. J. Retail Distrib. Manage. **29**(5), 214–225 (2001)
20. Bell, D.R., Ho, T.H., Tang, C.S.: Determining where to shop: fixed and variable costs of shopping. J. Mark. Res. **35**(3), 352–369 (1998)
21. Martinelli, E., Balboni, B.: Retail service quality as a key activator of grocery store loyalty. J. Serv. Ind. **32**(14), 2233–2247 (2012)
22. Farhangmehr, M., Marques, S., Silva, J.: Consumer and retailer perceptions of hypermarkets and traditional retail stores in Portugal. J. Retail. Consum. Serv. **7**(4), 197–206 (2000)
23. Goldman, A., Hino, H.: Supermarkets vs. traditional retail stores: diagnosing the barriers to supermarkets' market share growth in an ethnic minority community. J. Retail. Consum. Serv. **12**(4), 273–284 (2005)
24. Sampson, S.E., Showalter, M.J.: The performance-importance response function: Observations and implications. J. Serv. Ind. **19**(3), 1–25 (1999)
25. Campo, K., Gijsbrechts, E.: Should retailers adjust their micro-marketing strategies to type of outlet? An application to location-based store space allocation in limited and full-service grocery stores. J. Retail. Consum. Serv. **11**(6), 369–383 (2004)

Author Index

Alcoba, Jesús   190
Amorim, Marlene   289, 340
Ayayi, Ayi   36

Bonomi, Sabrina   25, 166
Borangiu, Theodor   95, 139
Borges, José Luís   228
Brinkhoff, Peter   1

Cantino, Valter   278
Cardoso, Jorge   50
Cavallari, Maurizio   243
Clores, Ricardo   190

Dameri, Paola Renata   166
de Castro, Valeria   264
De Marco, Marco   25, 215, 243
Depaoli, Paolo   215
Devalle, Alain   278
Dias, Teresa Galvão   228, 314
Drăgoicea, Monica   95, 139

Ebron, Romano Angelico   190

Faria, José António   65
Faulkner, Stéphane   123
Felber, Heiko   301
Fernandes, Marisa   176
Fernandes, Teresa   326
Ferreira, Marta Campos   314
Fichtner, Wolf   109
Fromm, Hansjörg   109

Gandini, Silvia   278
Garrido, Eloísa Díaz   264
Giustiniano, Luca   215

Ho, Van Thai   36
Hottum, Peter   1, 253

Jochem, Patrick   109
Juntunen, Jouni   152

Juntunen, Mari   152
Jureta, Ivan   123

Kieninger, Axel   1
Kunze von Bischhoffshausen,
   Johannes   253, 301

Le Dinh, Thang   36
Lima, Mafalda   326
Lopez-Sanz, Marcos   264

Machado, Ricardo J.   80
Maciel, Rita S.P.   80
Marcos, Esperanza   264
Marzo, Francesca   243
Mejia, Grace Cella   190
Melão, Nuno   289
Militaru, Gheorghe   95, 139
Morariu, Cristina   95
Morariu, Octavian   95
Mostajo, Susan   190

Negoiță, Olivia Doina   139
Nomo, Theophile Serge   36
Nóvoa, Henriqueta   65

Paras, Rowell   190
Pedrinaci, Carlos   50
Peña, María Luz Martín   264
Proença, João F.   176
Purcărea, Anca-Alexandra   95, 139

Răileanu, Silviu   95
Reis, João   289
Reuter-Oppermann, Melanie   253
Ricciardi, Francesca   278
Ried, Sabrina   109
Rossignoli, Cecilia   25, 166

Saghezchi, Fatemeh Bashashi   340
Salgado, Carlos E.   80
Santos, Nuno   80

Sobral, Thiago 228
Sorrentino, Maddalena 215
Stryja, Carola 109

Tafuri, Domenico 204
Teixeira, Juliana 80

Vara, Juan Manuel 264
Varriale, Luisa 204

Verlaine, Bertrand 123
Voinescu, Iulia 95

Yurchyshyna, Anastasiya 12

Za, Stefano 25, 243
Zardini, Alessandro 166
Zerbetto, Alessandro 278

The manufacturer's authorised representative in the EU is Springer Nature Customer Service Centre GmbH, Europaplatz 3, 69115 Heidelberg, Germany. If you have any concerns regarding our products, please contact ProductSafety@springernature.com

Printed and bound by CPI Group (UK) Ltd, Croydon, CR0 4YY

23/03/2026

02076672-0019